Your College Experience

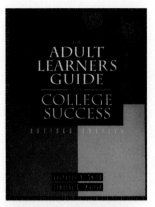

The Wadsworth College Success™ Series

The Adult Learner's Guide to College Success, Revised Edition,
by Laurence N. Smith and Timothy L. Walter (1995), ISBN: 0-534-23298-1

Orientation to College Learning, by Dianna L. Van Blerkom (1995),
ISBN: 0-534-24528-5

Learning Your Way Through College, by Robert N. Leamnson (1995),
ISBN: 0-534-24504-8

Your Transfer Planner: Strategic Tools and Guerrilla Tactics, by Carey E. Harbin
(1995), ISBN: 0-534-24372-X

I Know What It Says . . . What Does It Mean?: Critical Skills for Critical Reading,
by Daniel J. Kurland (1995), ISBN: 0-534-24486-6

College Study Skills: Becoming a Strategic Learner, by Dianna L. Van Blerkom
(1994), ISBN: 0-534-21288-3

Mastering Mathematics: How to Be a Great Math Student, Second Edition,
by Richard Manning Smith (1994), ISBN: 0-534-20838-X

Toolkit for College Success, by Daniel R. Walther (1994), ISBN: 0-534-23052-0
with *The Pocket Toolkit: Study Skills Software* (1994), ISBN: 0-534-23054-7

Integrating College Study Skills: Reasoning in Reading, Listening, and Writing,
Third Edition, by Peter Elias Sotiriou (1993), ISBN: 0-534-17892-8

Right from the Start: Managing Your Way to College Success, by Robert Holkeboer
(1993), ISBN: 0-534-19290-4

Turning Point, by Joyce D. Weinsheimer (1993), ISBN: 0-534-19422-2

Merlin: The Sorcerer's Guide to College Success, by Christopher F. Monte (1990),
ISBN: 0-534-13482-3

The Freshman Year Experience℠ Series

Success, Your Style! Left and Right Brain Techniques for Learners,
by Nancy L. Matte and Susan Green Henderson (1995), ISBN: 0-534-24468-8

Your College Experience: Strategies for Success, Concise Edition,
by A. Jerome Jewler and John N. Gardner (1993), ISBN: 0-534-19962-3

The Power to Learn: Helping Yourself to College Success, by William E. Campbell
(1993), ISBN: 0-534-19404-4

The Senior Year Experience℠ Series

Ready for the Real World, by William C. Hartel, Stephen W. Schwartz,
Steven D. Blume, and John N. Gardner (1994), ISBN: 0-534-17712-3

*For more information or to purchase any of these Wadsworth texts,
please contact your local bookseller.*

▼▼▼▼▼▼▼▼▼▼▼▼▼▼▼▼▼▼▼▼▼▼▼▼▼▼▼

Your College Experience

Strategies for Success

Second Edition

John N. Gardner
Director, University 101
Associate Vice Provost, Regional Campuses and Continuing Education
Professor, Library and Information Science
University of South Carolina, Columbia

A. Jerome Jewler
Professor, Journalism and Mass Communications
University of South Carolina, Columbia

Wadsworth Publishing Company
I⟨T⟩P™ An International Thomson Publishing Company

Belmont • Albany • Bonn • Boston • Cincinnati • Detroit • London • Madrid • Melbourne
Mexico City • New York • Paris • San Francisco • Singapore • Tokyo • Toronto • Washington

The Wadsworth College Success™ Series and the
Freshman Year Experience_{SM} Series Editor: *Angela Gantner Wrahtz*
Assistant Editor: *Lisa Timbrell*
Development Editor: *Alan Venable*
Editorial Assistant: *Kate Peltier*
Production Editor: *Jerilyn Emori*
Designers: *Ann Butler, Carolyn Deacy*
Print Buyer: *Diana Spence*
Permissions Editor: *Robert Kauser*
Art Editor: *Marty Kongsle*
Copy Editor: *Thomas Briggs*
Cover Design: *Three Communication Design*
Cover Photography: *Chicago Photographic Company, W. Woodworth/
    Superstock, Inc., Chuck Savage, The Stock Market*
Compositor: *Steven Bolinger, Wadsworth Digital Productions*
Printer: *The Banta Company*

Illustration Credits
John Nelson: Exercise, Journal, Box icons; chapter numerals and chapter opening illustrations; and
the illustrations on the following pages: 9, 73, 75, 106, 113, 115, 121, 127, 132, 159, 182, 211, 214,
267, 274, 300, 306, 313, 317, 347, 383, 384. Optional chapters: 28-9, 29-9, 29-16, 30-4, 30-6, 31-10
Mary Ross: pp. 61, 93, 112, 131, 140, 145. Optional chapters: 25-2, 26-5, 28-2, 29-8, 32-8, 32-16
Jeff Tucker: Freshman Survey graphs
Alexander Teshin Associates: All other illustrations

For more information, contact Wadsworth Publishing Company:

Wadsworth Publishing Company
10 Davis Drive
Belmont, California 94002, USA

International Thomson Publishing Europe
Berkshire House 168-173
High Holborn
London, WC1V 7AA, England

Thomas Nelson Australia
102 Dodds Street
South Melbourne 3205
Victoria, Australia

Nelson Canada
1120 Birchmount Road
Scarborough, Ontario
Canada M1K 5G4

International Thomson Editores
Campos Eliseos 385, Piso 7
Col. Polanco
11560 México D.F. México

Internationl Thomson Publishing GmbH
Königswinterer Strasse 418
53227 Bonn, Germany

International Thomson Publishing Asia
221 Henderson Road
#05-10 Henderson Building
Singapore 0315

International Thomson Publishing Japan
Hirakawacho Kyowa Building, 3F
2-2-1 Hirakawacho
Chiyoda-ku, Tokyo 102, Japan

Library of Congress Cataloging-in-Publication Data
Your college experience : strategies for success / [edited by] John N. Gardner, A. Jerome Jewler. —
  2nd ed.
     p. cm. — (The Freshman year experience series) (The Wadsworth college success series)
  Includes bibliographical references and index.
  ISBN: 0-534-30960-7
  1. College student orientation—United States.   2. Study skills.   3. Success—United States.
  I. Gardner, John N.   II. Jewler, A. Jerome.   III. Series.   IV. Series: The Wadsworth college success
  series.
  LB2343.32.G37   1994
  378.1'98—dc20   94-36748

▼▼▼▼▼▼▼▼▼▼▼▼▼▼▼▼▼▼▼▼▼▼▼▼▼▼

We thank our wonderful families and colleagues for their patience over the past several years as we watched this book take shape. We thank our students for proving to us that the basic assumptions in this book really do work. We thank faculty, staff, and administrators at colleges and universities for believing in those same basic assumptions. Most important of all, we welcome all new first-year students to their college experience and urge them, in the words of Tennyson, to be "strong in will, to strive, to seek, to find, and not to yield."

▼▼▼▼▼▼▼▼▼▼▼▼▼▼▼▼▼▼▼▼▼▼▼▼▼▼▼▼▼▼▼▼

Brief Contents

▼ ▼

Contents

▼▼▼▼▼▼▼▼▼▼▼▼▼▼▼▼▼▼▼▼▼▼▼▼▼▼▼▼▼▼

▼▼▼▼▼▼▼▼▼▼▼▼▼▼▼▼▼▼▼▼▼▼▼▼▼▼▼▼▼▼▼▼▼▼

Timely, Interactive, Comprehensive, Flexible

I am a part of all that I have met;
Yet all experience is an arch wherethro'
Gleams that untravelled world....

From "Ulysses" by Alfred, Lord Tennyson

The first edition of Your College Experience *united many voices of the student success movement in a flexible, practical program of strategies for success. Our aim for the second edition is to continue that tradition and to reflect the discoveries and insights of the movement in the past two years.*

This book supports a dynamic, holistic course. Its single most important aim is a constructive, interactive classroom experience for every student.

A FRAMEWORK FOR SUCCESS

We know what first-year college students most need to do:

► Make friendships and form groups that support their college goals

► Assess their own preparation, interests, and commitments

► Learn new ways to define and accomplish goals

► Confirm and extend basic study skills to more active, critical, creative learning

► Pass beyond "survival" thinking to an attitude for true success

► Make writing an integral part of learning

In support of those goals, college success courses continue to evolve in response to national and local changes. On a national scale we see a growing desire among instructors to help students develop academic strategies beyond the basic reading, note-taking, and test-taking skills. This edition therefore includes four new chapter topics by specialists in their fields:

► **Speaking for Success:** A practical guide to short oral presentations and ad hoc speaking

► **Problem-Solving and Success in Math and the Sciences:** An aid for problem-solving in situations outside math as well

► **Thinking in College:** A practical, exercise-based approach to training students to argue less on emotional grounds and more on evidence and careful thinking

► **Computing for College Success: Technology on Campus:** Strategies for understanding technology on campus and for improving one's personal use of it

On the local level, every campus must design the course around its own unique blend of student and institutional needs. To support that goal, we have included several other innovations:

► A chapter to help students develop survival skills for college and life

► An exciting chapter on cultural diversity with interactive exercises designed to make every new student feel welcome and respected

► A new library research chapter that supports your campus process for teaching information-retrieval skills

► A separate chapter on the value of a liberal arts education

We have also made the book more flexible by dividing it into more chapters. In the interest of brevity, several sections in the first edition have been moved to the optional, customizable portion of materials (see "Building Your Own Book," below), including the sections on returning students, nutrition and fitness, and assertiveness. At the same time, we have retained essential coverage from these units in the core book—for example, the "Tips for Returning Students" in Chapter 1. The former appendix on money management has been expanded to a full chapter, including exercises, available in customized versions.

Other organizational improvements follow the pattern of changes made in *Your College Experience,* Concise Edition. For example, discussions of academic advisors and the college catalog have been united in one chapter.

BUILDING YOUR OWN BOOK

In addition to the twenty-three full-color chapters of the new edition, instructor sample copies of this text include nine optional black-and-white chapters, available for custom adoptions. Completely new optional chapters address such topics as leadership and living away from home.

Instructors either can simply adopt the standard, full-color version or can arrange one of several customized versions. One choice is to adopt the standard full-color edition along with selected optional black-and-white chapters bound separately. Another is to select chapters from the standard chapters and the optional chapters, which then can be combined and bound as one black-and-white edition of the book. Along with customized selection of chapters, you can arrange to have materials from your own campus included in the bound volume.

For more information on the optional chapters and how to "build your own book," please consult the pages preceding the optional chapters at the back of this book.

SUPPLEMENTS AND SUPPORT

Several useful supplements accompany this volume. These include:

▶ **The Wadsworth College Success Course Guide:** A general resource for instructors that covers a range of subjects, from building support for a freshman year course to administering the course and redefining and shaping it for the future

▶ **Instructor's Manual to Accompany** *Your College Experience,* **Second Edition:** A volume dedicated to helping you teach the chapters of *Your College Experience,* incorporating advice, questions students commonly ask, additional activities and exercises, suggestions for evaluation, and more

▶ **Test Package:** A collection of test and quiz items designed to support the chapters of the main text

▶ *The Keystone* **Newsletter of the Wadsworth College Success Program:** A substantive newsletter that allows you to share ideas with colleagues around the country

▶ **Wadsworth's Film and Video Policy:** A way to enhance your course presentations. Consult your local sales representative for more details

Additional support for you and your course includes the following:

▶ **Video Series,** *Your College Experience: Strategies for Success:* Produced by the University of South Carolina and South Carolina Educational Television, twelve 5–7-minute video programs, based on the text, are designed to teach, inform, motivate, and stimulate lively group discussion. The series is highly adaptable to many educational settings. To order or to request information, call or write: SCETV Marketing, Box 11000, Columbia, SC 29211, 803-737-3441; fax 803-737-3503. The series is also available through PBS Adult Learning Satellite Service: Call weekdays 9:00 AM to 5:30 PM eastern time: 1-800-257-2578; fax 703-739-8495.

▶ **Teacher Training Seminars with Wadsworth Authors:** Held several times a year in various regions, these workshops allow you to interact with the author and develop your teaching skills in general

▶ **Additional Training and Seminar Information:** Available through the National Resource Center for the Freshman Year Experience at the University of South Carolina at 803-777-6029

▶ **Custom Publishing:** Contact Wadsworth's Customer Service Department at 1-800-245-6724 for immediate assistance and answers to your questions regarding content, quantities, binding options, and price

► **Bundling Options:** Consult your local sales representative or customer service at 1 800-245-6724 for more information on the availability of shrink-wrapped packaging of your local materials with the main text

ACKNOWLEDGING A NATIONAL EFFORT

One great reward of our work on this book is the extent to which it keeps us in touch with a vibrant national community of educators committed to their students' success in college. The book continues to be a rewarding national collaborative effort of students and educators.

In this edition we are pleased to thank our new chapter contributors: Roger A. Ballou, Marilee Birchfield, Faye A. Chadwell, Steven W. Gilbert, Kenneth C. Green, William C. Hartel, Richard B. Lawhon, Mary-Jane McCarthy, Mary Ellen O'Leary, Joan A. Rasool, Stephen W. Schwartz, Al Siebert, Constance Courtney Staley, and Robert Stephens Staley II. Thanks also to Freshman Survey feature author Linda J. Sax and to student contributors, Adam Cahill and "Meredith."

For reviewing and advising, we thank Linda Garcia-Ennenga, American River College; Eileen McDonough, Barry University; Janet K. Baxter, Belmont Abbey College; Lisa Gray-Shellberg, California State University, Dominguez Hills; Cindy Hillman, Calumet College of St. Joseph; Gaila Moore, Chabot College; Irwin Blatt, College of Staten Island; Kathy Fish, Cumberland College; Cyril Russell, Hutchinson Community College; Lisa Kerr, Loyola University (Chicago); Dorothy Clark, Montgomery County Community College; Peg Adams and Robin Wright, Northern Kentucky University; James Hipp, Northern Virginia Community College; Esther Winter, Northwest Missouri State University; Marilee McGowan, Oakton Community College; Helen Swanwick, Orange County Community College (New York); Mel Testerman, Pittsburg State University; Sharon Parsons, Prairie View A&M University; Marcia Birken and Nancy Shapiro, Rochester Institute of Technology; Shelley Kirkpatrick, Saint Francis College (Pennsylvania); Mary Conley Law, Saint Martin's College; Melissa Garrett, Slippery Rock University; Karen J. Patty-Graham, Southern Illinois University, Edwardsville; Michael Fleming, State University of New York at Farmingdale; Irene Honey, University of Colorado, Boulder; Gretchen Van der Veer, University of Maryland at College Park; Tom Ward, Ray Davis, Eileen Korpita, University of South Carolina; Christine Wolf, University of Texas, San Antonio; Andrea Reeve, University of Wyoming; Nancy Lukic, Virginia Wesleyan; Tom Mount, Yakima Valley Community College; James Chalmers, Wayne State University; Lawrencella E. Dukes, Community College of Allegheny County; Timothy J. Ebner, Midland Lutheran College; Marilyn Middlefield, Oklahoma State University, Stillwater; and Judith G. Wolfe, Frostburg State University.

Our thanks to the staff at Wadsworth Publishing Company, who continue to support our efforts with insight and enthusiasm. Special thanks to our editor, Angela Gantner Wrahtz, and to assistant editor Lisa Timbrell, editorial assistant Kate Peltier, development editor Alan Venable, production editor Jerilyn Emori, book designers Ann Butler and Carolyn Deacy, and marketing director David Leach.

Finally, we express our sorrow at the recent and premature death of Kenneth F. Long. A marvelous teacher at the University of Windsor, Ontario, Ken played a major role in the creation of this book. We will miss him as colleague and friend.

Keys to Success

John N. Gardner
University of South Carolina

I just stood in line for an hour and spent over a hundred dollars on three books. Now I'm broke and have three exams scheduled for the same week in October. First week of college and I'm already stressing out.

At least I've met a few interesting people. Wish I had the time to talk to them!

You've just taken another major step in life: You've decided to invest in a college education. Will the results be worth the investment? That depends on one thing more than any other: the goals you set as you begin. Before you read on, take a few moments now to consider what you hope to accomplish.

EXERCISE 1.1   Your Reasons for Attending College

Briefly list three reasons why you've entered college.

1. _____

2. _____

3. _____

Which one of these three is the most important? In the space below, explain why this reason is the most important:

_____

_____

_____

_____

We'll come back to this soon.

NOTE: Many of the exercises in this book are accompanied by the following icons: ✎ indicates a writing exercise; ☻ indicates an exercise involving class or small group discussion.

WHO ARE YOU, ANYWAY?

People attend college for different reasons and have different hopes and concerns about it. It helps to consider who you are and to compare what you want from college with what other students want. Which one of the following sounds *most* like you? Which ones may also apply?

► You did just fine in high school and are ready for everything college can throw at you. You're also ready for a lot more personal freedom— and for new territory to explore.

► You're not really sure what you're after. You just want to test the waters, find what's out there, try a few courses, and see what happens.

► You know exactly what you want to study and where it will take you later on. You have a career in mind, and you can already see yourself making your mark on the world.

(Less Todd/photo courtesy of Duke University)

▶ You started a few other things before you got around to college—job, marriage, kids. Your attention feels a bit divided.

▶ You know why you're in college but wonder how well you'll fit in. You feel that people on campus are going to look at you as different or make other assumptions about you that aren't true.

▶ You're wondering how you're going to raise the money you need and still keep up with a full college course load.

▶ You like attending college locally, but you wonder how you're going to deal with commuting. There are also some problems with living at home that you know you'll need to work on.

▶ You're proud to be the first in your family to get this far academically. You don't plan to stop until you graduate, no matter how hard the work is.

▶ You've just had a major life change: You've lost your job due to economic recession, your marriage of some years has ended, and/or you've seen your last child "leave the nest." That's part of why you're back in college.

▶ You tried college a long time ago but weren't motivated. Now you've screwed up your courage to finally return.

▶ Your parents expected you to go to college. Everyone else in your high school group did.

EXERCISE 1.2   Why You Decided on College

Some of the most powerful and long-lasting learning takes place in small group discussions, projects, and the like. Therefore this book will frequently suggest a small group activity such as the following:

In a small group discuss the list of reasons for attending college. Which ones seem most relevant to you personally? Would you need to write a different statement to accurately describe your own situation? What would it be?

Do any of your goals in Exercise 1.1 relate to the statement that best describes you? How? Discuss this with the group as well.

Today's Student Body

In 1900 fewer than 2 percent of Americans of traditional college age attended college. Today more than 50 percent attend, with over 3,500 colleges serving more than 14 million students.

In the mid-1960s the community college movement went into high gear, as the country became more concerned with higher education for personal and job-related knowledge. Today over 55 percent of college entrants start in two-year colleges, and more often than not these students combine stud-

Don't put off making contact until everyone seems too busy. Get to know as many people as you can before you and they slide into isolated routines. (Left, photo courtesy of University of Utah; right, David Gonzales)

ies at a local school with work or family commitments. At the same time, four-year schools are admitting increasing numbers of increasingly diverse students through special admissions programs that offset deficiencies in college preparedness. Adult students also are enrolling in college in record-breaking numbers, and by the end of the 1990s, over one-third of college students will be over 25.

These changes have taken place because for most of us college is a necessity, not an option. New technologies and the information explosion are changing the workplace so drastically that few people will be able to support themselves and their families well without at least some education beyond high school. That may not have been true for earlier generations, but it's true for yours.

While a higher percentage of high school graduates in the United States (or people with equivalent education) choose college than in any other country in the world, it's distressing that so many who start never finish. For example, 40 percent of students who start in four-year programs never earn their degrees. Of those who do earn their bachelor's degree, about one-third will take up to ten years to do so. In two-year colleges, up to half of the entering class will drop out by the end of the first year.

Dealing with New-Found Freedom

It's often not academic unreadiness that causes college students to drop out. Of those who quit, about three-fourths are in good academic standing. Clearly, a lot else besides academic talent will affect your success in college.

One problem is simply choosing the courses you will need to complete in order to graduate. It used to be simpler: A generation ago, students typically chose a standard major and followed an established curriculum. Today students often face a staggering number of course and program options, and most need an advisor to help them choose and coordinate courses.

This book won't take the place of a living, breathing advisor or counselor, but it will help you avoid some common pitfalls and support your academic goals and enjoyment of college in the broadest sense.

The New Majority

American women were at one time barred from higher education. In 1833 Oberlin College became the first to admit women, as well as African-Americans. It was only when publicly funded, land grant universities were founded under the Morrill Act of 1862 that "coeducation" became at all common. And only in the last twenty-five years have most men's colleges become schools for men and women, with fully integrated degree programs, residences, and curricula. Facing social and financial pressures, many formerly all-women's colleges have also opened their admissions to men. Women now make up the majority of college students—about 54 percent.

(Photo by Hilary Smith)

Eliminating the Negatives

A self-fulfilling prophecy is something you predict is going to happen, and by thinking that's how things will turn out, you greatly increase the chances that they will. For instance, if you decide that today just isn't going to be your day, chances are it won't be. You'll look for ways that things can go wrong—and you'll find them. Students often enter college with a good many negative self-fulfilling prophecies and other mental baggage. Here are some widespread fears and problems:

► Fear of too much freedom or not being able to manage your time

► Anxiety over adjusting to a new environment

► Fear that college will be too difficult

Commuter Power

About how many of America's 14.5 million college students would you guess are commuters? (The answer appears at the bottom of page 21.)

a. 2.83 million (20 percent)

b. 5.66 million (40 percent)

c. 8.49 million (60 percent)

d. 11.32 million (80 percent)

The fact that you commute may work to your advantage in some ways. In others you will need to work harder than the campus resident. Look over the twenty-one "persistence factors" on pages 8–12. Do you think any of these will be harder for you to achieve because you commute? Compensate with special effort. Interact fully with your campus. Use the goal-setting process described on pages 16–19 and in Exercise 1.9 to ensure that you do *get involved* in a campus activity, do *explore* campus resources, and do *find* someone on campus who knows and cares about you.

If you are living at home with your parents, negotiate home responsibilities up front. Your parents may need to understand that your college work will take more time than high school. You may not have as much time to devote to family errands and chores as before.

► Homesickness

► Lack of good study habits

► Difficulty in understanding instructors

► Fear of competition from brighter, younger, or older students

► Fear of disappointing people or not getting their support

► Problems with new living arrangements

► Worry over choosing the wrong major

► Shyness

► The expectation that you may have to cheat to survive

► Fear of being perceived by other students as a klutz

► Problems in juggling work, family, and studies

► Inability to pay for college

If some of these concerns sound familiar, take comfort: Most other entering students share the same fears. Remember also that each of the worries is attached to a negative self-fulfilling prophecy that you can exchange for a positive one. That's basically what setting goals is all about: creating and implementing positive self-fulfilling prophecies.

EXERCISE 1.3

The Good, the Bad, and the Not-So-Bad

Think about things that have happened already this term.

1. Name one thing that's been fun or easy.

   _____

2. Name one thing that was hard that you knew would be hard.

   _____

3. Name one thing that was hard that you *didn't* know would be hard.

   _____

4. Name one thing that you expect to happen and think will be hard.

   _____

Share your answers in a group. What problems do you have in common with other people in your class? What problems seem to be yours alone? How are these problems likely to be influenced (for better or worse) by self-fulfilling prophecies?

EXERCISE 1.4

Solving a Problem

What has been your biggest unresolved problem to date in college? What steps have you attempted to solve this? In a letter or memo to your instructor answer these two questions.

KEYS TO SUCCESS IN COLLEGE

Researchers have identified certain things students can do to ensure success. Ironically students are often unaware of what these "persistence factors"— or keys to success—are and how much they really matter. Here are twenty-one basic things you can do to thrive in college. This book is built on these suggestions and will show you how to implement them.

1. **Find and get to know one individual on campus who cares about your survival.** It only takes one. It might be the leader of your orientation seminar or some other instructor, an academic advisor, someone at the career or counseling center, an advisor to a student organization or group, or someone where you have an on-campus job. You may have to take the initiative to establish this relationship—but it will be well worth it.

2. **Learn what helping resources your campus offers and where they are located.** Then use them. Most campuses have academic and personal support services that are free and confidential. Successful people seek help.

3. **Understand why you are in college.** Your college years will be much more productive if you identify specific goals. This chapter introduces you to a useful goal-setting process.

4. **Set up a daily schedule and stick to it.** If you can't do it alone, find someone on campus or at home who can help—perhaps someone in your academic skills or personal counseling center. Get a day-timer or "week-at-a-glance" calendar from your bookstore. Chapter 5 will get you started at assigning sufficient time for study, work, sleep, and recreation. If you have family or work obligations, find ways to balance them with academic demands. A serious talk with family members may be in order.

5. **If you're attending classes full-time, try not to work more than 20 hours a week.** Most people begin a downhill slide beyond 20 hours. If you need more money, talk to a financial aid officer. Also, try to work on campus. Students who work on campus tend to do better in classes and are more likely to stay enrolled than those working off campus. Visit someone in your college placement office.

6. **Assess and improve your study habits.** Develop a better understanding of your own learning style. This book will help you learn how to take better notes in class, read more efficiently, and do better on tests. If your campus has an academic skills center, pay a visit.

7. **Join at least one study group.** Study with a friend regularly and form a study group in a class. Studies have shown that students who study in groups often get the highest grades.

8. **See your instructors outside class.** It's okay to go for help. Studies have shown that students who interact with instructors outside class stay in college longer.

9. **Choose teachers who involve you in the learning process.** Take classes in which you can actively participate. Unfortunately, most students choose their classes based on what will fit best in their schedule, not on the instructor. Ask upper-class students who the best instructors are. If your student government publishes course/instructor evaluations, use them to select instructors who encourage discussion.

10. **Know how to find information on your campus, including at the library.** The library isn't as formidable as it might seem, and it offers a wealth of resources.

11. **Improve your writing.** Employers want graduates who can write. Write something every day—the more you write, the better you will write. Do the journal and other writing assignments in this book.

12. **Develop critical thinking skills.** Challenge. Ask why. Look for unusual solutions to ordinary problems and ordinary solutions to unusual problems. There are few absolutely right and wrong answers in life, but some answers come closer to the "truth" than others.

13. **Find a great academic advisor or counselor.** The right advisor can be an invaluable source of support, guidance, and insight throughout your college years.

"Am I Smart Enough?"— Tips for Returning Students

If you're a returning student, read these tips for ways to reduce your anxieties about returning to school.

1. **Don't doubt your abilities.** Recent studies have shown that contrary to popular belief, learning ability does not decline with age. In fact, verbal ability actually increases as one grows older.

2. **Expect teachers to be glad to see you.** Most teachers will welcome you because your practical life experiences will enrich class discussions. Your experiences will also provide you with good material for written assignments.

3. **If school seems stressful, enroll part-time.** Adjust the number of courses you're taking to control the amount of strain, especially in the first term.

4. **Enlist the support of your spouse, partner, or family.** Seek adjustments in household routines and duties. Let family members know when you'll need extra time for exams.

An actively supportive partner is a great ally. A nonsupportive partner who interferes with study time can reduce your success in college. If your partner feels threatened and seems to undermine what you are doing, sit down and discuss the problem. Or seek counseling. Changes in relationships between partners often go hand in hand with enormous growth.

5. **Find faculty and staff support on campus.** Find out about on-campus child care and other support. If your school has special advisors for adult students, they will know the most about weekend and evening courses. Look for adult advocates in student affairs or continuing education programs. If your campus does not now offer support services at night or on weekends, ask for them. Many schools welcome petitions asking them to extend their services.

6. **Develop peer support.** Find out about classes, programs, or organizations where you can meet other adult learners. Or put

14. **Visit the career center early in your first term.** Begin your career development now. See a career counselor before you get too far along in college. Even if you have chosen your academic major, the career center may offer valuable information about careers and about yourself.

15. **Make at least one or two close friends among your peers.** College is a chance to form new and lasting ties. Choose your friends for their own merits, not for what they can do for you. In college, as in life, you become like those with whom you associate.

16. **If you're not assertive enough, take assertiveness training.** Check at your counseling center for workshops and programs on assertiveness training. It's never too late to learn how to stand up for your rights in a way that respects the rights of others.

17. **Get involved in campus activities.** Visit the campus (or student) activities office—usually found in the student union. Work for the campus newspaper or radio station. Join a club or support group. Play intramural sports. Most campus organizations welcome newcomers—

an ad in the campus paper and form your own group. Find a classmate to meet for coffee, study with, or exchange notes with if one of you has to miss a lecture.

7. **Take review courses or a course in how to study.** Most adults have let their study habits become rusty. After learning the study skills tools in this book, consider taking a longer study skills course. You may need to review basic math or languages before tackling advanced courses. Fortunately, relearning something is much easier than learning new material. Try studying on your own, or look for review courses on campus or in adult programs at local high schools.

8. **Be realistic.** Weigh your expectations about grades against your other important commitments.

(Photo courtesy of Berea College)

you're their lifeblood. Students who join even one group are more likely to stay in college, to prosper, and to graduate.

18. **Take your health seriously.** How much sleep you get, what you eat, whether you exercise, and what decisions you make about drugs, alcohol, and sex all contribute to how well or unwell you feel. Get into the habit of being good to yourself and you'll be happier and more successful.

19. **If you can't avoid stress, learn how to live with it.** There are healthy ways to deal with stress. Your counseling center can introduce you to techniques that will help you worry less and accomplish more.

20. **Show up for class.** When asked what they would do differently if they could do it all over again, most seniors say, "go to class." Instructors tend to test on what they discuss in class, as well as grade in part on the basis of class attendance and participation. Why abuse your new freedom? Being there is your responsibility. Simply attending class every day will go a long way toward helping you graduate.

21. **Try to have realistic expectations.** At first you may not make the grades you could be making or made in high school. If you were a star athlete in high school, you might not be in college. This book can help you develop more realistic goals.

Do most of these suggestions sound simple? If you follow them, they can make a difference in your life, as they already have for thousands of others.

EXERCISE 1.5   **Counting Your Ways**

Review the twenty-one "keys to success." Place a check mark next to five or six that seem more important in your own case. Place an X next to a few that seem least important. In a group, compare and discuss your choices. Together browse the table of contents of this book. Find at least one chapter that addresses each of your most important concerns.

THE VALUE OF COLLEGE

Few decisions will have as great an impact on your life as your decision to go to college. In addition to increasing your knowledge and self-understanding, college will expand your career horizons and can help you make the right career decisions. It will probably also affect your views on family matters, social issues, community service, politics, health, recreation, and consumer issues.

Education, Careers, and Income

Will your college education lead to greater income? Consider the average monthly income for individuals in 1990, shown in Table 1.1.

Table 1.1 Differences in Average Monthly Earnings by Educational Level, 1990*

EDUCATIONAL LEVEL	AVERAGE MONTHLY EARNINGS	INCREASE OVER PREVIOUS LEVEL ($)	INCREASE OVER PREVIOUS LEVEL (%)
No high school diploma	$492	—	—
High school diploma	1,077	585	119
Vocational training	1,237	160	15
Two years of college and an associate degree	1,672	435	35
Bachelor's degree	2,116	444	27
Master's degree	2,822	706	33
Doctorate degree	3,855	1,033	37

*Reprinted with permission from Hartel, William, et al., *Ready for the Real World*, Wadsworth, Inc., 1994, p. 7.

SOURCE: U.S. Department of Commerce, Bureau of Census, Current Population Reports (Washington, D.C.: Government Printing Office, 1990).

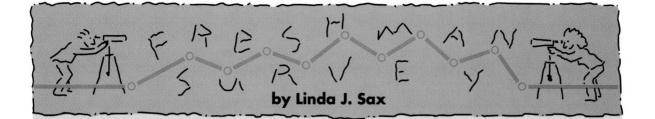

by Linda J. Sax

College, Money, and Career

In the previous decade entering students increasingly thought of college as a link to jobs and money. As the figure shows, in Fall 1993 a record 75.1 percent of first-year students indicated that making more money was a very important factor in their decision to attend college. Survey data also show that an all-time high of 82.1 percent of new students come to college "to get a better job."

More than ever before, students view college as a means to financial security and career development rather than as a chance for intellectual growth and personal development. Although some might interpret this as an indication that they have become more materialistic, the economic upheaval that has shaken the nation for the past two decades suggests that students are simply being realistic about the future.

High inflation in the late 1970s, severe recession in the 1980s, and a dramatic economic restructuring in the 1990s have had significant effects on the job market. Today's college graduates are sometimes referred to as "Generation X"—recipients of bachelor's degrees who face limited career opportunities and often must resort to jobs for which they are "overqualified."

Although the economy is expected to improve by the time you graduate from college, the 1990s is a time of significant change for American workers. Corporations across the country are hiring fewer new workers and reducing overall employment. Increased competition both at home and abroad means that American businesses—both large corporations and small firms—are making every effort to work faster, wiser, and smarter, *and with fewer people*.

How are students of the 1990s reacting to the possibility of an economically troubled future?

Reasons for Attending College, 1976–1993 (percentage of freshmen indicating "very important")

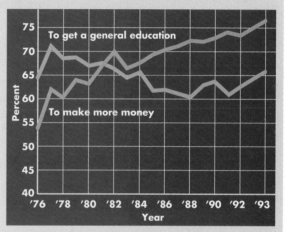

Source: Higher Education Research Institute, UCLA

One common response among undergraduates is to build a portfolio of skills, contacts, experiences, and credentials to present to potential employers. A growing number of students are making choices about college and majors based in part on what they think will protect them in the job market of the twenty-first century.

Linda J. Sax, associate director of UCLA's Higher Education Research Institute and the Cooperative Institutional Research Program (CIRP) Freshman Survey project, wrote the Freshman Survey reports that appear throughout this book. The CIRP Freshman Survey results are based on data collected by the Higher Education Research Institute each year from hundreds of thousands of college students at campuses across the country.

According to a report by the Carnegie Commission on Higher Education, as a college graduate you will have a more continuous, less erratic job history, will be promoted more often, and are much less likely to become unemployed than nongraduates. You are also likely to be happier with your work than those who didn't attend college.

Critics of higher education occasionally point out that some people with college degrees are unemployed or underemployed (particularly due to the recession of the early 1990s), but you have only to look at the employment figures of high school graduates and high school dropouts to see that the better educated you are, the better your opportunities. As the saying goes, "If you think education is expensive, try ignorance."

The Broader Benefits of a College Education

Of course college will affect you in many ways besides financially. How will you change in ways that differ from those of people who decided to go directly to work, join the military, or do something else rather than go to college? The evidence from many studies suggests:

- College has a strong positive impact on how effectively people think. You can expect to increase significantly your knowledge, intellect and tolerance, and interest in lifelong learning.

- College educates the *whole* person. It gives students the opportunity to clarify and improve their sense of possibility and self-worth, to develop a personal identity, and to improve certain skills and competencies. This self-esteem is one of the principal benefits of a college degree. You will also tend to know better how you might make a difference in the world.

- You will tend to be more adaptable, more future-oriented, more liberal in your outlook, more interested in political and public affairs, and less prone to criminal activity.

- College has an important influence on family life. You will tend to delay getting married and having children, to have fewer children, to plan your children's births, and to share child-care and household responsibilities. You will also tend to allocate more thought, time, energy, and money to child rearing. You and your peers will have a slightly lower divorce rate than non-college-educated people, and your children generally will have greater abilities and achieve more than children of non-college-educated parents.

- In addition to making more money, you will be a more efficient consumer. Chances are you will save more money, make better investments, and spend more money on home, intellectual, and cultural interests and on your children. As a consumer and citizen, you will also be more able to deal with bureaucracies, the legal system, tax laws and requirements, and advertising claims.

- In your leisure you will spend less time and money on television and movies and more time on intellectual and cultural pursuits, including continuing education, hobbies, community and civic affairs, and vacations.

- You are likely to be more concerned with wellness and preventive health care. Through diet, exercise, stress management, a positive attitude, and other factors, you will live longer and suffer fewer disabilities.

EXERCISE 1.6   Goals: Your Own and Others'

Look back at the reasons for attending college you listed in Exercise 1.1. Did your list include any long-term goals—say, something you want to achieve five or ten years from now? Compare your goals to the benefits of higher education just listed. Add a long-term goal to your list, or make other changes that now seem appropriate.

In small groups, compare your goals with the goals of others in the group. Do you share the same goals? How do you differ? Compare your findings with those of other groups in the class.

SKILLS AND RESOURCES

Whatever your goals, you'll get off to the best start if you know your own strengths and also know where to look for help when you need it. In later chapters we'll focus on specific study skills. For now, let's take an informal preliminary look at your basic study skills.

EXERCISE 1.7   Assessing Your Basic Skills

Think about your strengths and weaknesses in areas such as reading, writing, and math. Have you ever consciously thought about exactly how you approach listening in class, taking notes, writing papers, reading textbooks, and studying for tests?

For each item below, rank yourself either 1 (very strong); 2 (okay); or 3 (not strong).

_____ Taking notes in class

_____ Learning facts and concepts from textbooks

_____ Reading comprehension

_____ Computer literacy (word processing)

_____ Time management

_____ Oral presentation skills

_____ Studying for tests

_____ Writing

_____ Math and science skills

If you found yourself writing some 3's, you'll want to look for help on campus. Keep this in mind as you do the next exercise.

Most college campuses offer a multitude of support and recreational resources. The box on page 17 lists typical support services on a college campus, along with the types of services they offer. If a vital support service is not offered on your campus, ask that it be made available. Many colleges will welcome petitions to extend support services.

EXERCISE 1.8

Finding Out About Campus Resources

Your campus probably offers most or all of the programs listed in the support services box, as well as other services. Make a list of types of campus support services or resources you might be interested in. Include not only "serious" support needs but also things that will help you relax and enjoy campus life to the fullest.

1. _____
2. _____
3. _____
4. _____
5. _____

Pool your list with others in your class. Use a campus map, student handbook, or other tools to find out which are available on your campus. Divide into teams of two and assign one or more items to each team. Visit the resource in teams and report back to the class or follow your instructor's suggestions for a written report.

SETTING GOALS

College is an ideal time to begin fulfilling conscious goals. First, you will need to differentiate between short- and long-term goals. During your first semester, begin to test some of the short-term goals. It's okay if you don't yet know what you want to do with the rest of your life or what you should be majoring in. Be patient. Practice setting and achieving some short-term goals by means of the following process:*

1. **Select a goal.** State it in measurable terms. Be specific about what you want to achieve and when (not "improve my study skills" but "master the double-entry system of note-taking by the end of October").

*Adapted from *Human Potential Seminars* by James D. McHolland and Roy W. Trueblood, Evanston, Illinois, 1972. Used by permission of the authors.

Where to Go for Help—Typical College Support Services

College support services are not always located where you might think or named what you might expect. If you're not certain where to look for a particular service, there are several ways to begin. You might ask your academic advisor or counselor, consult your college catalog and phone directory, or call or visit the office of student services (called student affairs at some schools) for assistance. The majority of these services are free.

► **Academic Advisement Center**
Guidance about choosing classes
Information on degree requirements

► **Academic Skills Center**
Improve study skills and memory skills
Help on how to study for exams
Individual tutoring

► **Adult Re-Entry Center**
Programs for returning students
Supportive contacts with other adult students
Information about services such as child care

► **Career Planning and Placement**
Career materials library
Career interest assessments
Career goal counseling
Computerized guidance programs
Assistance finding a major
Full-time, part-time, co-op, internship, and campus job listings
Opportunities for graduating students to interview with employers
Help with resumes and job interview skills

► **Chaplains**
Worship services and fellowship
Personal counseling

► **Commuter and Off-Campus Services**
Listings of nearby available housing
Roommate listings
Orientation to the community

Maps, information on public transportation, babysitting lists, and so forth

► **Counseling Center**
Confidential psychological counseling on personal and interpersonal concerns ranging from roommate problems to prolonged states of depression
Programs on managing stress

► **Financial Aid and Scholarship Center**
Information about financial aid programs, scholarships, and grants

► **Health Center and Enrichment Services**
Tips on personal nutrition, weight control, exercise, and sexuality
Information on substance abuse programs, adult children of alcoholics, and general health care, often including a pharmacy

► **Housing Center**
Assistance in locating on- or off-campus housing

► **Legal Services**
Legal services for students (If your school is affiliated with a law school, check to see whether senior students in the law school are available for counseling.)

► **Math Center**
Help with math courses

► **Physical Education Center**
Free or inexpensive facilities for exercise
Recreational sports facilities and equipment for swimming, racket sports, basketball, archery, weight training, dance, and so on

► **Physically Challenged Student Services**
Support in overcoming physical barriers or learning disabilities

► **Writing Center**
Help with writing papers and reports

Tips for "Minority" Students

The "minority" population of the United States is growing so fast that the common use of the term to denote Americans of non-European ancestry is rapidly becoming outdated. For the present, however, students of non-European ancestry still often find themselves in a distinct minority on campus.

If this is your situation, you are probably aware of ways in which your background differs from those of other students, and there may be ways that you are treated or regarded differently.

Some of the twenty-one keys to success are particularly important for most students of color, especially the keys related to establishing contact with faculty and other students. Focus on those keys. Don't let yourself become isolated. Form or join study groups. Visit your instructors outside class. Take advantage of support services. Take part in co-curricular activities outside class. Join at least one organization.

Here are several more suggestions that can make a big difference in your life:

1. **Keep that "I can do it" attitude and stay in college.** A positive attitude matters. Too many minority students drop out of college when they could have gone on. Stay in college.

2. **Shoot for an A.** Grades matter. If you're not already thinking about getting a master's degree or doctorate now, you probably will in the future. Your undergraduate GPA will be an important part of your application to grad school. Some employers also review college transcripts.

3. **Attend college full-time if you can.** If you work, look for a campus job and try to work no more than 20 hours a week. Ask at your financial aid office for information about work-study programs, grants, and scholarships. Try to avoid taking out large loans so you won't be deep in debt when you have to decide whether to go on to graduate school.

4. **Take advantage of minority support services.** Your campus may have centers for minority students. Visit these places and introduce yourself to the staff. Ask for help with problems. Take advantage of mentoring programs, especially if your campus has a minority student mentoring program with minority faculty and staff.

5. **Don't be afraid to take math and science courses or to go into math- and science-based fields.** Scholarships for minority students are increasingly available to those pursuing math and science careers.

2. **Determine whether the goal is achievable.** Do you have enough time to pursue it, and more important, do you have the necessary skills, strengths, and resources? Modify the goal as needed to make it achievable.

3. **Be certain you genuinely want to achieve this goal.** Don't set out to work toward something only because you feel you should. Be sure that your goal will not have a negative impact on yourself or others and that it is consistent with your most important basic values.

6. **Practice for standardized tests.** Anyone can improve his or her performance on standardized tests such as the ACT, SAT, or GRE. Enroll in test preparation sessions offered at your college or other agencies, especially if you're heading for graduate school.

7. **Choose a career with long-term payoffs.** Careers requiring several years of education take longer to attain but will do more for you in the long run. Shoot for being a teacher, not a teacher's aide; a lawyer, not a paralegal; a doctor or registered nurse, not a doctor's or nurse's assistant. Be sure that your coursework matches your goal.

8. **Explore alternative learning activities and environments.** Find out about possible co-op opportunities, internships, and national and international exchange programs. Consider spending a semester at a historically black college. In many cases studying at another school doesn't cost any more than being at your present school.

9. **Maintain connections with your "home base."** But be aware of the changes you may be going through and the impact of those changes on family and friends. They may put pressure on you to stay the same or accuse you of "selling out" for being a successful student.

(Lane/Photo Researchers, Inc.)

10. **Be proud of your heritage and culture.** Minority groups can become empowered only by participating fully in the country's economic, scientific, and political future. In college you may hear racist remarks and witness or be the target of behaviors rooted in ignorance, bigotry, fear, and hatred. Stand tall. Be proud. Refuse to tolerate such behaviors.

    Take courses in African-American, Hispanic, and other cultural studies. Help other minority students. Make friends with students from different racial and ethnic backgrounds. Get to know minority faculty and administrators. Get involved in sensitizing others to cultural diversity.

4. **Identify why this goal is worthwhile.** Be sure that it has the potential to give you a sense of accomplishment.

5. **Anticipate and identify difficulties you might encounter.** Plan ways to overcome these problems.

6. **Devise strategies and steps for achieving the goal.** What will you need to do to begin? What comes next? What may you need to avoid? Set a timeline for the steps.

A First-Year Journal

Each chapter in this book ends with a journal assignment such as the one below. It's important to get into the habit of asking questions as you read and keeping track of your thoughts in writing. Periodically throughout this book you should be asking yourself questions like these:

1. What do I think of what I just read?

2. What did I learn?

3. How do I react to what I've learned?

4. What is there here that I can apply to my own life?

Each journal assignment poses questions to help you focus your thoughts. Use them if they stimulate your thinking. If other, related questions concern you more, write about those instead.

Your instructor may ask you to write these entries strictly for your own private reading and reflection or as a hand-in assignment. Instructors who ask to read your journal entries generally do so because they know this to be an excellent means of private communication between you and them.

Depending on your instructor's preferences, you may record your journal entries on separate

(Photo by David Gonzales)

looseleaf sheets, on typed pages, or in a journal notebook. Whatever the format, be sure to collect and keep these writings so that you can periodically review them, especially at the end of the semester and later in your college career.

EXERCISE 1.9   Setting a Short-Term Goal

Review your responses to the previous exercises in this chapter. Pick one problem that you can resolve as a short-term goal. (Ask your instructor whether this will overlap with work assigned later in the course.)

Start by discussing this goal with your group. Identify how this short-term goal relates to your long-term goal of doing well in college.

In group discussion and writing, complete the six steps for achieving a short-term goal. Establish a date (perhaps a week or month from now) when you will determine whether the goal has been achieved. At that time set at least one new goal.

Be sure your goal is:

► Something you genuinely want to achieve

► Written down in measurable terms

► Achievable

Also be certain to:

► Identify and explore potential problems

► Create a specific set of steps for achieving the goal

► Set a schedule for the steps

► Set a date for completion

In completing this exercise you are learning a goal-setting process that with practice can become a lifelong skill. Apply this process at least three times this term and you will have mastered a technique that will help you all your life.

This book will ask you to use this goal-setting process in later chapters. Look for other chances to use it. Point these out to your instructor and other members of the class.

JOURNAL

Which of the "keys to success" listed in this chapter have you already begun to incorporate into your college life? Which others can you start working on soon?

Many adult students know that their study skills are rusty and fear the competition for grades from younger students. These younger students, however, usually appreciate the insights and experiences older students bring to class. If you are a returning student, write some advice to the younger students in your class. If you are a younger student, give the adults the benefit of your knowledge about how to study effectively. Consider sharing these thoughts in class.

SUGGESTIONS FOR FURTHER READING

Astin, A. W., Kenneth C. Green, and William S. Korn. *The American Freshman: National Norms for Fall 1993.* Los Angeles: Higher Education Research Institute, University of California.

Bird, Caroline. *The Case Against College.* New York: McKay, 1975.

Boyer, E. L. *College: The Undergraduate Experience in America.* New York: Harper & Row, 1987.

Erikson, Erik. *Identity: Youth and Crisis.* New York: Norton, 1968.

Friedan, Betty. *The Feminine Mystique.* New York: Dell, 1962.

Hartel, William C., et al. *Ready for the Real World.* Belmont, Calif.: Wadsworth, 1994.

Parks, Sharon. *The Critical Years: Young Adults and the Search for Meaning, Faith and Commitment.* New York: HarperCollins, 1991.

Sheehy, Gail. *Passages: Predictable Crises of Adult Life.* New York: Dutton, 1974.

Upcraft, L., and J. N. Gardner. *The Freshman Year Experience.* San Francisco: Jossey-Bass, 1989.

ANSWER (to question in box on page 7): d—commuters account for 11.32 million of America's 14.5 million college students. That number is more than the combined populations of Norway and Israel. There are more commuter students than there are people in the greater Boston and Philadelphia areas combined. If all commuter students parked in the same parking lot, the lot would have to be larger than the city of Boston. No wonder parking is often cited by commuters as one of their major problems!

Exploring the Student-Teacher Connection

A. Jerome Jewler
University of South Carolina

She's so smart, how can I talk to her? Walks in and starts talking about her passion for geology, then asks us questions about things I've never even thought about. We have to have a conference with her during office hours to talk about how we're doing. Alone. And mine is today. I'm doing all right in the course, I think. But what in the world am I going to say to her?

In a scene from David Mamet's Oleanna, *"Carol" tries to get a clear message from her professor about how he is reacting to her work. The play probes the complexities of the college teacher–student relationship. (Ken Friedman/Photo courtesy of American Conservatory Theater of San Francisco)*

Quite often, theater can be more revealing than real life, or so it seemed as I walked along a New York City street after being blown away by a performance of David Mamet's recent play, *Oleanna*.

This brief two-character drama gives us John, a college professor who does not really believe in teaching but relishes the opportunity to lay down the law. John has never forgotten how he hated his own pompous, unfeeling college instructors. Yet somehow, in a sort of twisted form of revenge, he has become one of them.

The other character, Carol, is a student. Although earnest in her quest for education, she appears to be confused about its purpose. Her belief is that teachers ought to teach, that they owe it to students; but she seems to resent the fact that they know things she does not.

As one drama critic explains, John teaches not in order to lead, but to hear himself talk; he listens admiringly as his brain disposes of the problems and uncertainties of others. When he explains something, however, it only sounds more confusing.

He has the power; the pupil has the responsibility. "I'm not here to teach you," he explains to Carol, "I'm here to tell you what I think." He describes higher education as a game in which those who hold the power (professors) test the powerless (the students) by asking idiotic questions that only measure one's ability to "retain and spout back information." Pure nonsense, John tells Carol.

Yet when she fails to understand anything he says, Carol revolts. She reports him, alleging incompetence, sexual harassment, and a number of other violations, which threaten his career as a professor. She reprimands him for forgetting just how hard she has worked to get to college and how he is depriving her of her natural right to learning by "one low grade which keeps us out of graduate school…one capricious or inventive answer on our parts, which, perhaps, you don't find amusing." Now he understands what it is to be subject to that power, she concludes.

EXERCISE 2.1 Is the Power Struggle for Real?

Mamet's *Oleanna* makes some bold assertions about the relationship between college professor and student. Do you agree that professors hold absolute power over students, that whether a student passes or fails is sometimes subject to the whims of the professor? Do you believe that higher education is a game of memorizing and regurgitating information? Write your thoughts about this issue, and be prepared to share them in class.

THE TEACHER'S CHALLENGE

Although some teachers may be involved in power trips, the majority of us look upon teaching as a challenge to help students develop themselves as more literate individuals and as critical thinkers by presenting them with challenges of their own.

I experienced this challenge from a different perspective recently when I signed up for an undergraduate acting course, a subject not related to my discipline of mass communications, but rather to an avocation—theater— that I have pursued seriously for the last five or six years.

I called the instructor ahead of time to ask how she would feel about having a middle-aged professor in the class. I had been fortunate to have been cast in a local show under her direction and I respected her talent greatly. Her first words were, quite frankly, a surprise to me.

"Are you going to be serious about this?" she asked.

"Of course I'm going to be serious," I told her! "Matter of fact, it's going to be a real pleasure to be a student again, to have a chance to learn more about a field I find exciting, personally rewarding, and mind broadening."

Later, as I pondered her question, I found it to be quite appropriate. As teachers, we want every student to be "serious" about what takes place in our classroom. So the very next term, I gave my class a new assignment to turn in. It was this:

EXERCISE 2.2 How Serious Are You Going to Be?

Using this course or another you are currently taking, write a paper that answers this question:

Just how serious are you planning to be about this course?

Consult the syllabus to detail those portions of the course you believe you will find particularly challenging, as well as those portions you believe will be easy for you. Note any foreseeable problems that the syllabus suggests (deadlines, reading assignments, workload, and so on), and suggest how they might be solved. Also state, in detail, just what you believe you will gain from the successful completion of this course and how you might apply that knowledge in future endeavors.

What Your Instructors Expect

Note that I actually asked my students for their input—for feedback about how they saw the challenges of my course and, to some extent, how I was managing the class. I'm not the only college professor who does this. But were you ever asked to do this in high school? If you believe that high school teachers were supposed to have all the answers and that their main purpose was to transmit those answers to you, it may come as a mild shock to know that most college teachers view education as more of an exchange of ideas than as one-way communication. To new college students, it may come as a shock to hear that knowledge is no longer etched in stone, that new ideas are welcomed, that traditional ways of thinking may not be the best; to college teachers, that makes good sense. If all questions were already answered, what would be the point of further scholarship?

Fortunately or otherwise, this new attitude toward learning is hardly the only difference you'll be aware of during your first term in college.

In high school you were taught by individuals who took courses in teaching. Strangely, your college professors may never have taken such courses, but focused instead on learning in their fields. If your professor has a doctoral degree, he or she has written a dissertation, a book-length document about some question that has not been studied in such detail before.

But that just begins to tell the differences between high school and college teachers. Can you guess other differences? Generally, college teachers:

► Will supplement textbook assignments with related information from other sources

► Will give quizzes and exams covering both assigned readings and lectures

► Will insist there is more than one way to interpret information, may question conclusions of other scholars, and may accept several different opinions from students regarding some question of the day

► May never check to see if you are taking adequate notes

► May or may not take attendance—or count it in determining grades

What's more, college teachers are likely to expect much more of you than your high school teachers did. They may:

► Be more demanding in how much they ask you to read, how many quizzes they give, and how much participation they expect in class.

► Expect you to be aware of topics related to their field and the particular course as well as the material for the course itself.

► Be sympathetic to excuses you may have for missing class or assigned work, but hold firm to high standards for grading. You may be on good terms with your professor and find you have failed the course because you did not complete some part of the assigned work!

EXERCISE 2.3 — What Do College Teachers Expect of Students?

Look back over the lists of differences between high school and college teachers. Then list the qualities and behaviors you believe college teachers want in their students. Compare your response with that of several classmates. Ask one of your teachers to comment as well.

What Your Instructors Do

To understand why college teachers approach learning in this manner, it helps to know more about their lives beyond the classroom and the financial constraints they have been under in recent years. According to Jacques Barzun, American historian and educator and former provost of Columbia University, college teaching is

> *backbreaking work that would fray the nerves of an ox.... An hour of teaching is certainly the equivalent of a whole morning of office work. The pace, the concentration, the output of energy in office work are child's play, compared with handling a class, and the smaller the class, the harder the work. Tutoring a single person—as someone has said—makes you understand what a dynamo feels like when it is discharging into a non-conductor.*

Faced with the reality of shrinking budgets, colleges and universities have been demanding more of their faculty: more teaching, more committee assignments, more publications, and more service to the college and community. Yet, despite other demands on their time, effective teachers know that teaching takes time and patience, that it goes beyond the classroom, spilling over into student conferences, academic advising, and career counseling. Thus, while the average teacher may spend 9–15 hours in the classroom each week, he or she probably works another 60 or more hours between Monday and Monday.

To stay current in their fields, college teachers are constantly reading books, journals, and magazines. They update lecture notes, which takes more time than delivering the lecture. They may conduct experiments in their fields, review manuscripts for journals, or write articles and books. They may address community and professional groups, as well as consult with private corporations or government agencies. They advise students on academic courses, career paths, personal problems, or specific class assignments. In the time left, they'll work as administrators on campus, serve on committees, grade papers, and still find time to be responsible parents and providers.

EXERCISE 2.4   A New Look at What College Teachers Do

The last few paragraphs describe how college teachers spend their time and should dispel the notion that college teachers don't work very hard. What have you learned about the duties of a college teacher that you didn't know before? How much does this knowledge help you understand the actions of your current college teachers?

MAKING THE MOST OF THE LEARNING RELATIONSHIP

Just as most college teachers work faithfully to succeed at their roles as teachers, so should you feel an obligation to gain the most from your hours in class, if for no other reason than that you've probably paid dearly for the right to an education. Here are some ways to accomplish your goals and to show your teachers that you are serious about learning.

1. **Make it a point to attend class regularly and on time.** If you must miss a class, you'll need to ask another student for notes. That's okay as long as the student agrees and you don't make a habit of it. But remember, learning is easier when you are there every day. Save your cuts for emergencies; you will have them. When you know you will be absent, let your professor know in advance. Depending on the size of the class, you may choose to do so by a written note delivered to the professor's office, a phone message, or in person at the end of a class period.

2. **Sit near the front.** Studies indicate that students who do so tend to earn better grades. That should be no surprise; sitting up front forces you to focus, to listen, and to participate.

3. **Speak up!** Although you may be nervous about challenging instructors when you don't agree with them or about asking questions when you want clarification, you'll find that most of your comments will be appreciated.

4. **See a teacher outside of class when you need help.** Professors are required to keep office hours for you. If possible, make an appointment by phone or at the end of class. Doing so will make the conference more convenient for both parties.

TEACHING AND LEARNING: A TWO-WAY CHALLENGE

What other effects did that undergraduate acting course have on my teaching? At first I felt awkward and isolated sitting on a bare stage with twenty or so people who were much younger than I. But things improved rapidly. I played a scene with a woman less than half my age, and a young chap slapped me on the back when I finished and exclaimed, "That was great, man!" I became a player in the chatter that goes on during lulls in instruction. I became part of their group. In addition, I was able to watch a teacher

Most college teachers are busy people who enjoy contact with their students. That's one reason they chose to become teachers. (Photo courtesy of University of Tulsa)

who came to class prepared, who set reasonable deadlines for assignments and made it clear how failure to meet those deadlines would throw the entire class schedule out of whack, who went out of her way to be certain students were developing the acting skills appropriate for this course, and who used her knowledge of the plays and playwrights we were assigned to instill in us a new way of thinking about those works. I learned not only how you students feel sitting "out there" but also how much energy and preparation it takes to keep a class interesting day after day after day.

What's more, seeing another teacher in action, I became aware of how motivating to students teachers can be when they take the time to bring out the best in each of them. As in any group, ability levels ran the gamut, yet I never felt a single individual was slighted because he or she didn't perform as well as someone else. Like any good teacher, this one believed in the importance of establishing a comfortable, positive relationship with each student in the class. If put into words, this relationship might be summed up as follows: "As long as you make an effort to do the assigned work to the best of your ability, as long as you listen to my advice and attempt to improve your understanding of this work, and as long as you demonstrate persistence to learn throughout this class, you're worth the time it's taking me to help you."

Effective teachers constantly attempt to challenge their students. They make an effort to connect with you and to establish a relationship that will support both their goals and yours. As a professor of advertising, I'm struck by the fact that one of the new trends we're talking about is called "relationship marketing." Many relatively new companies that have enjoyed rapid growth—Ben and Jerry's, The Body Shop, Nike—have discovered the rewards of nurturing a long-term relationship with their customers, who in turn support them through loyalty to their brands.

Critical to the building of such relationships are a number of avenues for two-way communication between company and consumer. In fact, companies are learning to be good listeners. They encourage consumers to talk to them through 800 numbers, surveys and panels, seminars and trade shows.

Now change the word *company* to *teacher* and the word *consumer* to *student* and you begin to see the value of building long-term relationships to foster learning. Many of your instructors may encourage such relationships through teaching techniques that stress class participation (discussions, presentations). Some may write extensive comments on your written assignments and quizzes. Others may even ask you to write your feelings, anonymously, about the class and drop them off at the end of the hour. During a major study of teaching at Harvard University, one of the many suggestions for fostering relationships that could improve learning in the classroom was a simple feedback exercise called "The One-Minute Paper." At the end of each class, students were asked to write what they felt was the main issue of that class and what the unanswered questions were for the next class. Remarkably, as students became aware they would be asked to do this daily, they found themselves beginning to listen more deliberately for "the main issue" each day! Even though the responses were unsigned, most students wanted to let the professor know they were listening.

EXERCISE 2.5　　**The One-Minute Paper**

Whether or not your teacher asks for it, choose one of your classes and consider writing at the end of each class what you felt was the main issue of the day and what the unanswered questions are for the next class. During the next class, see if those questions are answered. If not, consider raising your hand to ask them. Try this for a week. Did this help you master the information in the class? In what way?

COMMUNICATION AND ACADEMIC FREEDOM

Although academic freedom has its origins in the Middle Ages, it continues to be a burning issue. You may have college teachers who don't give a hoot if the basketball team has a winning season, who criticize the college administration for its lenient admissions policies, or who argue that you're wasting your time watching TV sitcoms and soaps. As college instructors, we believe in the freedom to speak our thoughts, whether it be in a classroom discussion about economic policy or at a public rally on abortion or gay rights. What matters more than what we believe is our right to proclaim that belief to others without fear. Think of where education would be if we were governed by more stringent rules regarding free speech! On the other hand, no one says you must think as we do.

Colleges and universities have promoted the advancement of knowledge by granting scholars virtually unlimited freedom of inquiry, as long as human lives, rights, and privacy are not violated. Such freedom is not usually possible in other professions.

Some teachers may insult a politician you admire or speak sarcastically about the president. In college, as in life, you must tolerate opinions vastly different from your own. You need not accept such ideas, but you must learn to evaluate them for yourself, instead of basing your judgments on what others have always told you is right.

FINDING THE RIGHT TEACHER

When students were asked in a survey to rank the characteristics of good teaching, they listed clarity and organization at the top. Close in importance were those things that help "humanize" the teacher: high levels of interaction with students outside the classroom, a genuine effort to make courses interesting, frequent examples and analogies in teaching, references to contemporary issues as appropriate, and relating the course to other fields of study.

In fact, studies of teaching confirm that the best learning takes place when the teacher involves students in the learning, through class discussion, library research, oral presentations, and small discussion groups that report their findings to the rest of the class. Add enthusiasm and clear, well-organized presentations, and the fact that students appreciate teachers who assign more work and more difficult work, and you have a complete picture of the effective teacher: one who is actively involved with students, who comes to class prepared, who gives students a voice in the classroom, and who is academically demanding but highly nurturing. One teaching expert likens teaching to coaching, explaining that a good teacher challenges students and works them hard, but somehow students know that this same teacher cares about their success.

EXERCISE 2.6 Describing Your Ideal Teacher

Jot down some adjectives that describe the best teachers you have ever had. Now jot down some adjectives that describe the worst teachers you have ever had. Be prepared to explain why you chose these words to describe good teachers and poor teachers.

Best Teacher	Worst Teacher
_____	_____
_____	_____
_____	_____
_____	_____
_____	_____

Finding a Mentor

In his study of the aging process in men, Yale psychiatrist Daniel J. Levinson discovered several things about those who tended to be successful in life:

► They had developed a dream in adolescence, an idealized conception of what they wanted to become.

► They went on to find a mentor—an older successful individual—who personified that dream.

► They also cultivated friendships with a few other people who encouraged, nurtured, and supported them in their pursuit of that dream.*

A mentor is a person who, in some respect, is now what you hope to be in the future. What mentors have you had previously? What specific qualities have you tried to emulate? Do you have a mentor right now? If you do, what might you do to make more use of him or her? What are you looking for in a college mentor?

*D. J. Levinson et al., *The Seasons of a Man's Life* (New York: Ballantine Books, 1978).

(Photo by David Gonzales)

How do you find great teachers? Ask. Ask other students, especially juniors and seniors in your major. Ask your academic advisor. If you enroll in a class and your "gut feeling" tells you on the first day that there is going to be a conflict with your style of learning and this teacher's approach to the topic, consider changing sections immediately. Find out if your student government has published a guide that evaluates faculty and courses. Visit a teacher before you register for class; by asking about the class, you'll learn more about the person, too.

What if you get a bad instructor? See if you are beyond the point in the term when you can drop the course without being penalized. Arrange a meeting to see if you can work things out. Getting to know the teacher as a person may help you cope with the way the course is taught.

If things are really bad, you might consider sharing your concerns with higher levels of authority, in keeping with the prescribed chain of command (department head, dean, and so on). Keep in mind, however, that a teacher's freedom to grade is a sacrosanct right, and no one can make teachers change their grades against their will. Don't let a bad instructor sour you on the rest of college. Even a bad course will be over and done with by the end of the term.

EXERCISE 2.7 Interviewing a Teacher

Choose a teacher to interview—perhaps your favorite instructor or one you'd like to know more about. You may even wish to choose an instructor whose course is giving you problems, in hopes that you can find out how to resolve those problems in the course of the interview. Make an appointment for the interview and prepare your questions before you go, but also be ready to "go with the flow" of your conversation. Then write a paper about what you learned and what surprised you the most.

Suggested Questions

1. What was your first year of college like?
2. At what point in your life did you decide to teach? Why?
3. What steps did you take to become a teacher in your field?
4. What do you like most about teaching? Least?
5. What are some of the things that keep you busiest outside the classroom?
6. What do you expect from your students? What should they expect from you?

Dr. Eliot Engel of North Carolina State University believes teaching is very much like farming. We cultivate our crops in the fall and harvest them in the spring, he explains. We boast of the sprouts that burst into vibrant bloom and sigh over those that withered on the vine, believing like a farmer that luck had much to do with the blooms, and our own failure with the blights. Engel warns that a society blighted by a dearth of great teachers soon finds itself in danger of growing nothing but a bunch of blooming idiots. He continues:

> Great teachers know their subjects well. But they also know their students well. In fact, great teaching fundamentally consists of constructing a bridge from the subject taught to the student learning it. Both sides of that bridge must be surveyed with equal care if the subject matter of the teacher is to connect with the gray matter of the student. But great teachers transcend simply knowing their subjects and students well. They also admire both deeply.*

That's a far cry from the relationship of the professor and teacher in Mamet's *Oleanna*, discussed at the beginning of the chapter. Mamet's professor seems to instill fear in his student. He might have listened to Albert Einstein, who said, "The worst thing seems to be for schools to work with

*From a column in the *Dickens Dispatch,* the newsletter of the North Carolina Dickens Club, January 1989.

methods of fear, force and artificial authority. Such treatment destroys the healthy feelings, the integrity, and the self-confidence of pupils."

Finally, if you doubt the value of a well-taught class, one in which you know the instructor is working hard to make learning enjoyable, heed the words of Alfred North Whitehead, noted American philosopher, mathematician, and logician, writing in the *Atlantic Monthly* in 1928: "The university imparts information, but it imparts it imaginatively.... A university which fails in this respect has no reason for existence.... A university is imaginative or it is nothing—at least nothing useful."

Perhaps it is this imaginative imparting of information that distinguishes the best teachers from all the rest. What do you think?

JOURNAL

Obviously your college teachers are different from your high school teachers. How are you reacting to those differences? Describe one or more of your instructors. What do you like most about them? Least? Explain why. What further questions do you have about college teachers and how to deal with them? Which of these would you like to raise in class?

SUGGESTIONS FOR FURTHER READING

Distinguished Teachers on Effective Teaching. New Directions for Teaching and Learning, #28. San Francisco: Jossey-Bass, 1986.

Freedman, Samuel G. *Small Victories. The Real World of a Teacher, Her Students, and Their High School.* New York: Harper Perennial, 1991.

Guide to Effective Teaching. A national report on eighty-one outstanding college teachers and how they teach: lectures, computer, case studies, peer teaching, simulations, self-pacing, multimedia, field study, problem solving, and research. New Rochelle, N.Y.: Change Magazine Press, 1978.

Mamet, David. *Oleanna.* New York: Pantheon Books, 1992.

Pirsig, Robert. *Zen and the Art of Motorcycle Maintenance: An Inquiry into Values.* New York: Morrow, 1974.

CHAPTER 3

The Value of a Liberal Arts Education

William C. Hartel
Marietta College

*P*hilosophy, history, art, biology, math, anthropology. Good grief! Why can't I just get on with my major? Who needs all that other stuff?!

You may have heard a conversation something like this recently. Carlos, Ruth, Susan, and Tim are first-year students hanging out at lunch a few weeks into the term who get to talking about their courses. Ruth mentions some trouble she's having with her composition class. Carlos is surprised.

He says, "I really like my writing class so far, but writing's easy for me. It's my intro to computers that's getting me down. And biology. I'm just not interested that much in science."

Tim laughs. "How can anyone *not* be up on computers—the wave of the future?! Me, I'd take computer science any day instead of English."

"Yeah, but that's your major," said Carlos.

"Well," says Susan. "I don't have a clue what I'm going to major in. I do know it's going to be something with a job waiting at the other end. I mean, I already have *loans* to pay back!"

Ruth says, "I can't think about that now. All I want to do is get all these requirements out of the way this year so I can get on with what I really want to do! I mean, why should I have to *pay* for courses that *they* say I have to take?"

I remember as a child asking my mother why I had to do such and such and her sometime response "Because it's good for you." I have vague memories of at first not being completely satisfied with that answer, and even stronger memories later that I had a right to better explanations. It's important to ask why about a lot of things and to not accept an unconvincing "good-for-you" response.

As a first-year student you are probably asking why quite often now, either openly or under your breath. As a more and more active learner you need to find satisfying answers. One question I hope my first-year students will ask me is "Why should I seek a liberal arts education?" I always hope that in our exchange of ideas, convincing reasons will emerge.

EXERCISE 3.1   ## What Your School Means by "Liberal Arts"

Before reading further, look at your course catalog. Find the mission statement and graduation requirements for your institution, and see whether they use the phrase *liberal arts*. Does the catalog make it clear what this refers to? Be prepared for class discussion about what the liberal arts mission and requirements are on your campus.

(Photo/The Bettmann Archive)

WHAT IS A LIBERAL ARTS EDUCATION?

Roots in the Past

Just as what you are today is in large part the result of your own past experience, so our shared institutions, values, and customs are also rooted in history. Colleges and universities date back to medieval times (the European Middle Ages, ending around 1500), but the idea of a liberal education can be traced back to the ancient Greeks. Of course, there have been many changes in what that education entails and for whom it is designed, but what has not changed is the basic concept that free individuals need a certain kind of education to fully appreciate life. In his 1959 work *Liberal Education and the Democratic Ideal and Other Essays*, A. Whitney Griswold summed it up this way:

> *The proper meaning of the phrase "liberal arts" is "the arts becoming of a free man," and that from earliest times these have included the sciences. (In the Middle Ages the liberal arts were arithmetic, geometry, and astronomy, in addition to grammar, rhetoric, logic, and music.) In other words, the liberal arts are rooted in freedom, not privilege, and they are broad, not narrow, in educational scope.*

We have to remember that in ancient and medieval times—even more so than today—not all people were free. Many were slaves, serfs, or servants. In general, only the powerful few were educated according to the standards of the time, and education enabled the powerful to remain so. It helped them maintain their hold as leaders and the so-called cultured ones in their societies. This does not mean that the rest of society did not have obligations to "learn." But what they learned was how to work, serve, and survive. By the Middle Ages in Europe, the guild system was responsible, in the main, for the more organized learning for work—in essence, on-the-job training for artisans and craftsmen.

The eighteenth-century Enlightenment brought ideas of progress, change, and faith in the rationality of human beings. Along with that came new possibilities concerning education. In your own liberal education you may study figures like Rousseau and Jefferson and discover that they had ideas about opening up education ultimately for "everyone"—or at least for all white males, since the world was still generally dominated by racist and sexist concepts. By the end of the Enlightenment, however, the prevailing norm was still education for the elite. The seeds of democracy were slow to germinate and grow.

The idea of extending liberal education outside the old elite grew stronger throughout the nineteenth century, especially in western Europe and North America. By the end of the century, both women and minorities were beginning to pursue higher education. It is probably no coincidence that the more democratic a region became, the more willing it was to expand the categories of those who could qualify for a liberal arts education. By the end of the century, the United States was leading the way.

The Present

In the second half of the twentieth century, most of Europe, the United States, and Canada have witnessed what some have called an education revolution. Formal education at all levels has been opened up not only to minorities but to virtually every socioeconomic group. Perhaps your father or grandfather received higher education through what was called the G.I. Bill, a federally subsidized program for veterans of World War II, the Korean War, and the Vietnam War. Your father or mother may have been supported in higher education by the governmental financial assistance programs of the late 1960s and early 1970s; you may be getting similar assistance now. At the same time, both public and private institutions are making serious efforts to become accessible to physically challenged students, who formerly were prevented from seeking higher education. Clearly a liberal arts education is available to almost anyone who chooses it, not just an economic or social elite.

THE LIBERAL ARTS CURRICULUM

The liberal arts curriculum is grounded in the basic Western concept of balance in those fields of study that society considers necessary to produce responsible citizens. Today the fields are broadly defined as the fine arts, the humanities, and the natural and social sciences (although there is still some difference of opinion about the inclusion of the social sciences).

The *fine arts* include the study of art, music, dance, and theater. The *humanities* embrace literature, foreign languages, history, philosophy, and religious studies. Among the *natural sciences* we find mathematics, astronomy, geology, physics, biology, and chemistry, among other subjects. The *social sciences* derive mainly from the nineteenth century and include economics, political science, sociology, and psychology. However, the divisions have become somewhat blurred as methods from one area become useful in another. For example, anthropology is now sometimes grouped with the humanities and sometimes with the social sciences.

A liberal arts curriculum requires you to do some study in each general category. The scope of the requirements depends on the history, mission, and other circumstances of your college or university. The discipline you choose as your major is the centerpiece of your undergraduate education, providing in-depth study in a particular discipline. The electives and general education requirements enhance your skills and knowledge in the liberal arts.

For example, Tim looks headed for a computer science major and will most likely graduate with a bachelor of science degree. In order to fulfill his liberal arts requirements, he might range through courses in art history, the history of jazz, introduction to philosophy, American history, economics, biology, and human physiology, depending on his interests.

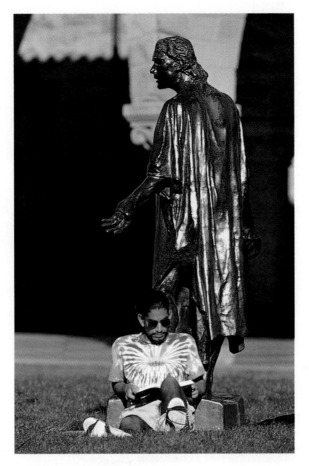

(Photo by David Gonzales)

Ruth might choose to major in journalism and satisfy her other requirements in a more calculated manner, with courses, say, in drama, literature, history, and American government that she sees benefiting her writing career.

As a rule most institutions are very flexible about general education requirements. For example, your school may let you satisfy some liberal arts or elective requirements with credits earned by a special experience such as a semester abroad. Your school may also have requirements in addition to a liberal arts distribution, such as volunteer experience—called "service learning"—that can have great personal value.

As a wise investor in your own education, try to see the "requirements" as an opportunity not only to receive that ideal education that the ancients wrote about but to explore new fields and even to change your life. You will get the most out of them if you can view them not as hurdles to "get out of the way" as painlessly and quickly as possible, but as opportunities to expand and grow.

I remember a student of mine who avoided for two semesters the "opportunity" to fulfill his arts requirement. When I suggested that he take a course in the fine arts, he looked at me with horror and said, "I have absolutely no artistic talent!" When he did take the course, not only did he discover his talent, but he became a fine arts major.

A liberal arts education is an opportunity to explore new interests, new talents, new ways of seeing and expressing oneself. (Photo courtesy of the University of Tulsa)

EXERCISE 3.2   Liberal Arts Choices

Use your course catalog for this exercise. First, list the general requirements you will have to fulfill outside your major. Then list the courses you might consider to fulfill the requirements. In a group share your choices. What courses have others in the group chosen? Compare your reasons for choosing the courses and your ideas about their value. Listen for ideas about how you might want to change your initial choices.

CHOICE AND CONSEQUENCES

Immediate Outcomes

Most students don't enter college knowing what they will major in. Among those who do enter "knowing," many later change direction. One immediate outcome of your liberal arts course selection can be to help you find the area in which you really want to focus. Think of these courses as a buffet—a chance to sample widely. If you are required, for example, to take two courses in the humanities, take those courses in different disciplines, say, literature and history. The more open you are to new possibilities in your early courses, the more likely you will find a major that truly holds your interest.

Don't necessarily expect to be satisfied with all the choices. The simple truth about freedom to explore is that some paths turn out to be more interesting than others. That's how we learn. You may find that the same subject you dismiss now will hold more meaning a few years later. You may also find some subjects in which you had a bad experience in your prior education now becoming areas in which you can thrive and excel.

EXERCISE 3.3   ## Creating a Strategy

Using your catalog as a reference if necessary, write down a short list of academic disciplines that you expect to be *most* comfortable with. Write a second list of the disciplines that you expect to be *least* comfortable with. For the second list, where do your feelings come from? Past experiences? Intuition? Things you've heard from others? Other factors?

Now select one discipline from the second list and look in your catalog at the range of courses in that field. Come up with several courses that might spur your interest more than you originally thought.

In a small group talk about the discipline you selected. Explain why you feel uncomfortable with it. Come up with a strategy that might help you overcome your discomfort and help you at least fulfill any requirement you might have in that area. Keep in mind that a worthwhile education does require taking risks.

Graduation Day

No doubt you can barely imagine graduation day yet, but before long you will actually be looking back and saying to yourself, "It went so quickly!" What will your accomplishments look like to you then? Recently one of my students summarized it this way as he was preparing to continue his education in law. Not only had he been able to major in both history and music, but along the way he'd learned a lot about the philosophy of Immanuel Kant, the physical laws of Isaac Newton, the American vision of Willa Cather, the poetic *Tao* of Lao Tzu, and the language of Japan. What the liberal arts had done for him, he told me, was to foster his love of learning. Had he discovered the meaning of life? On balance he had probably discovered more questions than answers in college—a true accomplishment in lifelong learning!

The Rest of Your Life

Spelman College president Johnnetta Cole (1993) has said that a liberal arts education "doesn't just educate you for the first job, it educates you for all jobs. Not just for the first few days after graduation, but...for living for the rest of your life." What might it do for you?

The current "experts" on the future are saying that, more and more, people will have not only many jobs but also many different careers. Those who cannot adapt to this world may be not only under- or unemployed but constantly dissatisfied with life in general. The skills and knowledge that you enhance through your liberal arts education will be crucial for your adaptation to constant change. For example, you will have a better understanding of how people and societies in the past have coped with change.

The message of the liberal arts is that you can take greater charge of your own fate. The liberal arts should free you from a narrow concept of purpose and a shallowness of spirit. It should strengthen your ability to articulate clearly in thought, speech, and writing, your resolve to act, and your willingness to confront and accept ambiguity. You will almost certainly be more imaginative, more curious, and more creative in how you combine work and leisure—in other words a more interested and interesting person. Combined with the knowledge and expertise you have gained in your major, this is probably the strongest foundation you can have for every kind of success in life.

Finally there is your involvement with your community. Suzanne W. Morse, Director of Programs at the Charles F. Kettering Foundation, writes:

> *A multitude of challenges face the nation as we approach the twenty-first century—the environment, education, the inner cities, at-risk children, and so forth.... You may be wondering how your generation will deal with the problems at hand. What choices need to be made to build a better world?*

Your liberal arts education will better equip you to participate in what Morse calls "public talk, public thinking, public judgment, and public imagination." It may also prepare you to become a leader in your community.

EXERCISE 3.4   Voices of Experience

Interview a senior or a staff or faculty member at your school, or anyone you know who is willing to share with you what they value from their liberal arts education. Share your findings with others in a group.

A liberal arts education is certainly no guarantee of a perfect or easy life. Equally certain, there are many people who have found ways to educate themselves to high levels without formal liberal arts training. Your liberal arts background will, however, provide opportunities that you cannot yet foresee. In the final analysis it is still up to you to take advantage of them. As you do, keep in mind that you are the inheritor of a long tradition in which a broad, enriching education is no longer a privilege of the few.

EXERCISE 3.5   Looking to the Future

Choose part A or part B.

A. In a small group choose one of the following scenarios. How might a liberal arts background help you in the situation? What sorts of courses in the liberal arts curriculum might be useful? Discuss the question in the group and report briefly back to the class.

1. You are a mayor with little money in your city's budget for needed repairs to city playgrounds.

2. You are a member of an environmental group that has just discovered that the leader of the group is a heavy investor in what may be the largest polluting corporation in your state.

3. You discover that a local hate group is planning to picket your children's school because a particular student was elected class president.

4. You just got fired from your position as head of a corporation and you suspect it is because you are approaching age 60.

B. It is the year 2010 and the "Thought Police" have just announced that a liberal arts education is too expensive for society to offer anymore. From now on the only education will be strictly within the disciplines. For example, if you wish to major in computer science, you will only take computer science courses and will therefore graduate in two years. Discuss this idea in a group. In a short paper or an oral presentation, assume that this is the year 2010; tell what you think of the idea and why.

JOURNAL

Do you have a clear idea of what the general education and liberal arts requirements are at your school? In what ways do they seem a difficulty? In what ways an opportunity?

SUGGESTIONS FOR FURTHER READING

Cole, Johnnetta. "On Campus with Women." *Association of American Colleges and Universities* 22, no. 4: 3.

Griswold, Alfred Whitney. *Liberal Education and the Democratic Ideal, and Other Essays.* New Haven, Conn.: Yale University Press, 1959.

Hartel, William C., Stephen W. Schwartz, Steven D. Blume, and John N. Gardner. *Ready for the Real World.* Belmont, Calif.: Wadsworth, 1994, Chapter 20.

Jacobus, Peter H. *Liberal Arts: Education and Employability.* Pennsylvania Department of Education, 1973.

Nadler, Burton Jay. *Liberal Arts Jobs: What They Are and How to Get Them,* 2nd ed. Princeton, N.J.: Peterson's Guides, 1989.

CHAPTER 4

Surviving College

Al Siebert
Counseling Psychologist

Sometimes I think I'll never make it to graduation. So much can happen between now and then—and knowing my luck, a lot of it probably will be more than I can handle.

First-year students often feel bewildered and disoriented when they start college. For students coming directly from high school, it is the biggest transition of their lives up till now. Older students who have not taken classes or studied for years have many fears and concerns. Almost all students wonder, "Will I survive? Will I make it through to graduation?"

These are legitimate concerns because you are starting a journey that many of your entering classmates will not complete. A reality of college is that surviving and succeeding take more than simply passing tests in the classroom. You must also face—and overcome—other, nonacademic tests. Some of your brightest classmates will not survive because they don't recognize the difference between surviving academic challenges and surviving life's challenges.

To attain a college degree, you must have skills for coping with life as well as good study skills. You must handle the academic program and also deal with all the challenges that will test your emotional strength, attitudes, and character.

SEVEN SURVIVAL TESTS

There are seven tests you need to pass in order to increase your chances of survival and success in college:

- ► **Test 1:** Making the transition from a teaching environment to a learning environment
- ► **Test 2:** Dealing with new-found freedom
- ► **Test 3:** Replacing feelings of discouragement with optimistic self-talk
- ► **Test 4:** Building healthy self-esteem
- ► **Test 5:** Developing empathy for roommates, fellow students, and even instructors
- ► **Test 6:** Accepting and appreciating seemingly contradictory thoughts and feelings
- ► **Test 7:** Learning how to learn from experience

The following guidelines and suggestions will help you not only to survive but to profit from these nonacademic tests.

Test 1: Making the Transition from a Teaching Environment to a Learning Environment

In high school you were taught by trained, certified teachers who were evaluated based on how much they taught you in their classes. You were in a teaching environment.

College, however, is a learning environment. How much you learn in any college course is primarily your responsibility, not the instructor's. This will be a challenge because, as you will discover, many college instructors have never taken classes on how to teach. They focused instead on their academic areas of interest. You may find yourself working harder to learn in a course taught by an instructor who is brilliant in his or her field but is not very skillful at teaching the subject.

Curiosity is the key to doing well in a learning environment. In high school you could wait passively for a teacher to tell you what to learn. In college, however, your most valuable learning comes from asking questions and searching for answers. An essential skill developed by successful college students is that of asking and answering questions. They actively seek and find useful information. They do not sit back and wait for someone to tell them what they need to know.

EXERCISE 4.1   How College Differs from High School

At your high school commencement was anyone in your graduating class honored for being the best at asking questions? Probably not. Make a list comparing all the ways college is different from high school. Include what it is like to become a new student again after being a senior.

Compare your lists with other class members. See if you agree on differences between a teaching environment and a learning environment.

High School (Teaching)   **College (Learning)**

_____   _____

_____   _____

_____   _____

_____   _____

_____   _____

Adult students: If high school seems a long way back, modify this exercise by listing and talking about other changes you face in starting college.

Test 2: Dealing with New-Found Freedom

Many students flounder in college because they cannot overcome ingrained habits. All their lives they have gone along with all the external forces organizing and controlling things for them. They probably came to college because they were told to. They go through orientation waiting to be told what to do; wait for an advisor to tell them what courses to take; wait for an instructor to tell them what to study.

For students conditioned to accept external controls over their lives, the freedom of the college environment can be overwhelming. And unless they can develop internal controls to replace the old external controls, they may party too much, study too little, have unsafe sex, drink too much or start taking drugs, and spend themselves into bankruptcy.

Students who pass the "freedom test" are those who feel personally responsible for how well they do in college. The primary control over what they do is inside them. They have an internal guidance system that they follow in the absence of external controls.

EXERCISE 4.2   Being Responsible for Your Success

For each of the following pairs of statements, which one do you believe is more true than the other?

1a. My grades in college will reflect how well I study, pass tests, and do the course work.

1b. Instructors decide what grade a student gets. How hard I study doesn't affect my grades very much.

2a. My career success will be determined by how competent I become.

2b. Real career success is determined more by fate than hard work.

3a. I expect my college roommates to be interesting and friendly.

3b. You're lucky if you get a good roommate.

This is an attitude test. There are no right or wrong answers. The real issue here is understanding that whatever you believe becomes a self-fulfilling prophecy. If you believe the "a" statements—that your actions determine your success in college—your belief will be proven true. If you believe the "b" statements and expect your fate in college to be determined by forces beyond your control, your belief will be proven true.

Write about how much you do or don't feel responsible for your success in college and in life.

Test 3: Replacing Feelings of Discouragement with Optimistic Self-Talk

Most college students feel discouraged at times. For example, in high school you may have gotten good grades with little studying, but in college you get a C– on your first test even though you studied hard. That first low grade can be a major shock. Your old habits don't work here. You feel discouraged. You think maybe you aren't college material and conclude that your situation is hopeless. The question is, what happens next?

The first step is to recognize that discouragement is a perfectly normal human emotion. The next step is to recognize the value of positive self-talk. Students who overcome discouragement replace pessimistic self-talk with optimistic statements. Research by Martin Seligman and other psychologists shows that you can learn to be optimistic about your future efforts. Optimism is an essential skill for overcoming difficult challenges in college. The best copers in college see setbacks and difficulties as temporary. They learn from the negative experience, expect to do better next time, repeat positive statements to themselves, and take action to do better.

EXERCISE 4.3   **Turning Pessimism into Optimism**

List several pessimistic statements you've heard from other students, and some that you may have said yourself.

1. _____
2. _____
3. _____
4. _____

Write down and rehearse three or four optimistic statements that you can repeat to yourself if you feel hopeless or discouraged.

1. _____
2. _____
3. _____
4. _____

Don't be misled, however, into believing that all negative thinking should be replaced by positive thoughts. A very trusting person who thinks in only positive ways runs blindly into unexpected problems that others avoid. Some negative thinking can increase your chances for success.

The best survivors in college spend less time actually "surviving" because they anticipate and avoid difficulties better than other students. To do this requires being able to think in both optimistic and pessimistic ways.

Daydreaming? Evidence suggests that those who daydream some about what they hope to become are more likely to reach their goals. (Photo by David Gonzales)

David McClelland, a famous Harvard psychologist, discovered that college students destined to have the most career success do the following:

1. Daydream about possible accomplishments.
2. Try to anticipate all the things that could keep them from succeeding.
3. Take steps to avoid potential problems and get around all the blocks and barriers.

In other words, successful students use pessimism in productive ways. Negative thinking gives their optimistic thinking a better chance of leading to successful action.

EXERCISE 4.4   **A Different Approach to Setting a Goal**

This is a slightly different approach to goal setting than the one you learned in Chapter 1. It integrates the benefits of both positive and negative thinking. Start by thinking about a goal you have in one of your courses. Ask yourself if the goal is one you believe you really can reach with good effort. Then use McClelland's three-step approach to see if you can improve your chances of reaching it. For example, if your goal is to get an A on a term paper, you should do the following:

1. Think about how good it will feel to have completed your research, to have prepared a well-organized outline for your topic, and to be in the final stages of writing the paper.

2. Consider the time period between the present and the due date. How far along are you in this project? Have you checked to see if your topic offers adequate opportunities for research? Have you set a timetable for accomplishing each portion of the project? Have you asked your instructor to comment on the appropriateness of your topic or the focus of your paper? Will you find yourself putting off the inevitable because of laziness, invitations to "take a weekend off," or other distractions?

3. Address the possible stumbling blocks you have listed above, work out ways to overcome them, and put a schedule in writing in your calendar. Stick to it.

Now choose your goal and write your three steps.

Test 4: Building Healthy Self-Esteem

To survive emotionally as a first-year college student requires healthy self-esteem. As a high school senior you had status, were invited to parties, may have held a student body office, and were recognized for achievements in school, sports, or music. Adult students have enjoyed the status gained from their jobs and community activities. But when you start college many of these external sources of esteem no longer exist. You may feel awkard and inadequate for the first time in years.

Students who relied on external sources (praise from parents, compliments from friends, job title, and so on) for feelings of esteem may be devastated because they find they lack inner self-esteem. Those students who survive "starting all over" have strong *conscious* self-esteem and self-confidence. Self-esteem is like a thick blanket of energy around you. If other students put you down, you can compare your opinion of yourself with theirs, decide that you like yours better, and shrug off the barb without feeling wounded.

Healthy self-esteem determines how much you learn after you have done poorly on a test or a paper. Students with weak self-esteem can't handle negative feedback very well. They will blame an instructor for a low grade or claim that the low grade was caused by something that kept them from doing well. Healthy self-esteem lets you examine your failings and short-comings in a way that leads to improvement. It also allows you to better accept compliments.

EXERCISE 4.5   Self-Esteem

A. Make a list of all the things you like and appreciate about yourself. Silently practice positive self-talk about yourself.

B. Get together with several friends and interview each other about what each of you likes and appreciates about yourself. Practice giving and receiving compliments.

C. In a small group discuss the following:

1. Why does a person with weak self-esteem get nervous when complimented? Why does a person who brags all the time seem to be trying to hide feelings of weak self-esteem?

2. If having strong self-esteem is so important, why do so many parents admonish and scold a child who brags or feels proud about something? If having healthy self-esteem is desirable, why do so many parents react as though it is undesirable?

Test 5: Developing Empathy for Roommates, Fellow Students, and Even Instructors

How do you react to difficult instructors or to an irritating roommate? Do you call them names? Do you give them negative labels? If so you're building still another barrier to surviving and coping.

Cutting down someone you dislike is the reaction of an emotionally fragile person. People with weak self-esteem try to build themselves up by tearing others down. Suppose you have a roommate who is negative all the time. Like many students you might label this person "a griper," "a complainer," or "a pessimist" and think, "If only they would change, things would be much better." The problem, however, is not that your roommate is negative. The problem is that you have a negative attitude about his or her negative attitude!

When someone acts or talks in a way that upsets you, take a deep breath and work to understand how things look from their point of view. The ability to understand ways of acting, thinking, and living that you disagree with is a high-level empathy skill. Empathy does not mean, however, that you agree with or approve of the other person's views or actions. It means only that you comprehend.

EXERCISE 4.6   Empathizing with a Difficult Person

Discuss the following questions in a small group: Why do you think negative thinking is seen so negatively in our culture? Why are people with positive attitudes usually so negative about people with negative attitudes? Is it ever okay to be negative? Is it phony to be always positive?

Try thinking of a negative roommate or classmate as a teacher in the school of life. This person knows how to do and say things you can't handle. The way to learn new skills from associating with a bothersome person is to stop blaming that negative person for your reactions and to ask yourself, "What advantages, benefits, and payoffs does he or she get from being negative all the time?" One big payoff, for example, is attention. Look at the person's negative behavior with curiosity and empathy and attempt to guess the payoffs that person may have in mind.

Next ask yourself, "How could I react differently so that I'm in control of my feelings?" Here are some possibilities:

1. Say, "You may be right." Then change the subject.
2. Ask him or her to also say something positive.
3. Play with this person's negative way of thinking by giving him or her a dose of their own medicine. Plan ahead, and after hearing a negative comment say, "You know, it is much worse than you realize." Then list three negative things about college, life, and the world that he or she has overlooked.
4. Learn to be active, not reactive. Before the person says anything negative, ask him or her to point out what could go wrong with your plans.

The key to coping well with any difficult person is to experiment. Play, learn, and develop response choices. Regain control. And silently thank the negative person for providing you with an opportunity to learn a valuable lesson.

Test 6: Accepting and Appreciating Seemingly Contradictory Thoughts and Feelings

Consider the following conversation between Kristin, a student, and Leslie, her RA (residential advisor).

Kristin: There's one thing that puzzles me.

Leslie: What's that?

Kristin: I know I'm social. I like being with my friends. But sometimes I'm antisocial. I don't want anyone near me. I have to get away from everyone.

Leslie: I'm glad to hear that. It means you are mentally healthy!

Kristin: You mean I'm not weird?

Leslie: No. Just the opposite. I learned in my psych class that healthy people have many contrary feelings like that.

Kristin: Whew! I've worried about being weird.

Look at the following lists of personality traits. Before reading beyond it, check off any of the traits you recognize in yourself and add any important ones not listed at the bottom.

confident	fearful
strong	gentle
mature	playful
humorous	serious
distant	friendly
trusting	cautious
happy	discontent
cooperative	rebellious
proud	self-critical
selfish	unselfish
lazy	hard-working
logical	creative
calm	emotional
loving	angry
messy	neat
positive	negative
_____	_____
_____	_____

Survivors have always fascinated me. When I was in the army I knew there was something special about the paratroopers who were combat survivors. Later, when I was in graduate school, I took advantage of the interviewing and personality research skills I had learned and studied survivors in more depth.

I was fascinated with the emotional strength and good spirits of some survivors of horrible experiences. But something puzzled me: They seemed inconsistent. They would be both confident and fearful, both angry and forgiving, both trusting and cautious, both unselfish and selfish, and so forth.

Then it came to me. Opposing traits of personality, what seem to be paradoxical qualities, enable a person to be emotionally flexible. A student with one trait but not its opposite is less flexible, and thus is more limited in responding to a given situation. How emotionally flexible are you? Look back at the two lists. See how many pairs you checked off. The more pairs of traits you recognized in yourself, the more likely it is you have excellent emotional flexibility. If you added more at the bottom, that's even better.

EXERCISE 4.7 Thinking About Your Paradoxes

A. What does being "paradoxical" mean to you? Look up the meaning of *paradox* in several dictionaries. As used here the term refers to having two completely opposite personality qualities. More broadly, a paradox is something that appears to contradict itself or be contrary to common sense, but yet is true.

B. Talk with several friends about times when you may have felt criticized or put down for not thinking or feeling right. Were there times when you were told your feelings were wrong? Have you ever felt weird because your contrary feelings confused you? Were any adults supportive when you had contradictory feelings?

C. If paradoxical qualities make you feel confused and a little weird at times, practice saying to yourself, "It is all right to feel both one way and the opposite. What's important is that I check how I feel to make certain it makes sense to me and that it supports what I value, and not what I believe others would have me feel." Be specific. You might say to yourself, "Given these circumstances, it is all right to be selfish; in other circumstances I can be more unselfish."

D. Have you known anyone who had so many contradictory thoughts and feelings that the person was draining to be around? Where, for you, is the balance point being having too few and too many contradictory traits?

Test 7: Learning How to Learn from Experience

Many years spent in the classroom conditioned you first to learn a lesson and then to take a test. In the school of life, however, the sequence is reversed: First you take the test and then you learn a lesson.

Learning from experience is the learning you do on your own. It is what you learn after you've taken the history or biology test and know you could have done better. Psychologists have studied learning for almost a hundred years and have identified the following steps as the way to learn from an incident or an "experience":

1. If it is upsetting, handle your feelings first. Cry, tell a friend, or write about your feelings in a journal.

2. Reflect on the experience. Mentally replay it as if remembering a dream. The observing part of your mind manages your learning.

3. Put it into words. Write everything that happened in a journal or tell someone.

4. Ask yourself, "What can I learn from this? What is the lesson here?"

5. Ask yourself, "Next time, what could I do differently?"

6. Imagine yourself handling the situation differently, better, and getting a desirable outcome.

7. Mentally rehearse handling the situation well just in case anything like this should ever occur again.

College students who are unable to learn from experience react to something that upsets or distresses them by assigning blame or acting the victim. You can see this when classmates who fail a test blame the instructor, dwelling on all the things the instructor and the college did to cause them to fail. Not only does this attitude prevent them from learning from experience, but they typically "clutch up" when faced with a similar situation again. In contrast, students who learn from experience and spend their time thinking about "the next time" expect to do better on the next test and usually do.

When you learn the steps for self-managed learning, you develop confidence in yourself. You anticipate either handling something well or, if you don't, you expect to learn something useful.

EXERCISE 4.8   Learning from Experience

Think about an unpleasant experience when someone put you down and you didn't handle it well. Based on the steps for learning from experience, what will you do or say the next time it happens? Mentally rehearse what you will do the next time in a similar situation. Discuss your plan with others in a small group and get their reactions.

THE FINAL EXAM: DEVELOPING A TALENT FOR SERENDIPITY

Several hundred years ago writer Horace Walpole coined the word *serendipity* to describe a special talent some people have for changing an accident or misfortune into a lucky happening.

The best sign of having mastered the tests for survival in college occurs when you convert a difficult situation into something you feel thankful you went through. One college student, for example, was raised hearing her parents tell her she would become a nurse. She wasn't enthusiastic about nursing but went along with what they said. It wasn't until she started doing clinical assignments in nursing school that she realized she just couldn't go ahead with her parents' plans.

Finally, after much anguish, sleeplessness, and an upset stomach, she told her parents she had always wanted to be a writer. Her parents were surprised but accepted her decision. She switched majors and is now a successful journalist writing about health and medicine. She discovered that her prenursing background gave her an advantage over other journalists in health care topics.

When you instruct your brain to find a creative solution, it has a tendency to do just that. If you define an adverse situation too narrowly and think of it only as "bad luck," then a serendipity solution won't be able to penetrate your thinking.

Your mind will build either barriers or bridges to your future. Your survival and success in college is determined by how well you handle your feelings, cope with pressures and adversities, and learn the lessons you won't always be taught in classes. And be reassured that students who survive and cope well with the nonacademic tests in college are not better than or different from you. Their success is due to skills that almost any student can learn and develop.

EXERCISE 4.9   # The College Survival Final Exam

A. Try looking for the hidden good in a bad situation. What if your computer crashes and you lose part of a term paper you've been writing? By asking yourself, "How can I turn this to my advantage?" or "What unusual opportunity has this created?" you will activate your brain to discover how to convert the disaster into unexpected good luck.

B. Discuss the following: When ice skater Nancy Kerrigan was clubbed in the leg a few weeks before the 1994 Winter Olympics, was that a major misfortune? Good luck? All the publicity she received led to her signing commercial contracts worth over $2 million before the Olympic competition even started. How can an incident be both bad luck and good luck?

C. What do you think about the assertion that your chances of surviving in college are improved by passing the seven nonacademic tests described in this chapter?

JOURNAL

Evaluate yourself on how well you've done on the seven tests life will give to you during your time in college. Use words (not numbers) to describe how well you have done on the tests so far.

SUGGESTIONS FOR FURTHER READING

Seligman, Martin. *Learned Optimism: How to Change Your Mind and Your Life*. New York: Knopf, 1991.

Siebert, Al. *The Survivor Personality*. Portland, Ore.: Practical Psychology Press, 1993.

Siebert, Al, and Timothy L. Walter. *Student Success: How to Succeed in College and Still Have Time for Your Friends*. New York: Harcourt Brace, 1993.

Siebert, Al, and Bernadine Gilpin. *The Adult Student's Guide to Survival and Success: Time for College,* 2nd ed. Portland, Ore.: Practical Psychology Press, 1992.

Time Management: The Foundation of Academic Success

Kenneth F. Long
University of Windsor

Mary-Jane McCarthy
Middlesex Community College

*L*et's see … it's Wednesday. Wednesday!! That big review session's at four and I need to go to work. I can't work tonight, I've got a history quiz at nine tomorrow and I need to read two chapters for it. Got to pick up Susie at daycare in two hours. Better write this all down in my calendar. Now where's that calendar??

Time management is one of the keys to success in college. Yet many students entering college are weak in this area. Perhaps it's because they did well in high school without consciously practicing time management or because in most high schools students had little control over their own time.

In certain high school courses students are not expected to take much responsibility for controlling their own use of time. College is different. Once courses are selected, you are personally responsible for allocating time to attend classes, to complete assignments, to study for tests, and so on. Generally it's even your decision whether to show up for class—on time or at all! College offers a great deal of freedom. In turn, it requires you to take personal responsibility for planning and managing your time. The central aim of this chapter is to show you how to develop and stick to a time management program.

First, let's examine your personal approaches to the use of time.

EXERCISE 5.1   Assessing Your Skills

For each set of statements below, circle the number of the one that best describes you.

1. I like my watch to be set exactly at the correct time.
2. I like my watch to be set a few minutes ahead of the correct time.
3. Most of the time, I don't wear a watch.

1. I tend to arrive at most functions at least 5 minutes early.
2. I tend to arrive at most functions exactly on time.
3. I tend to arrive at most functions a little late.

1. In the course of my daily activities I tend to walk and talk quite fast.
2. In the course of my daily activities I tend to take my time.
3. In the course of my daily activities I tend to walk and talk slowly.

1. In high school I almost always completed my daily assignments.
2. In high school I usually completed my daily assignments.
3. In high school I often failed to complete my daily assignments.

1. I like to finish assignments and reports with a little time to spare.
2. I tend to finish assignments and reports exactly on the due dates.
3. I sometimes finish assignments and reports a little late.

1. I rarely spend more than 15 minutes at a time on the telephone.
2. I sometimes spend more than 15 minutes at a time on the telephone.
3. I often spend more than 15 minutes at a time on the telephone.

1. I rarely spend more than an hour eating a meal.
2. I sometimes spend more than an hour eating a meal.
3. I usually spend more than an hour eating a meal.

1. I never watch more than 1½ hours of TV on a weeknight.
2. I sometimes watch more than 1½ hours of TV on a weeknight.
3. I usually watch more than 1½ hours of TV on a weeknight.

Now add up the numbers that you have circled: _____

The higher the total, the more you need to work on time management skills now that you are in college. If your total is over 10, you probably need to adjust your priorities and begin to take more responsibility for managing your time.

Time management involves planning, judgment, anticipation, and commitment. First, you must know what your goals are and where you will need to be at some future time. Second, you must decide where your priorities lie and how to satisfy competing interests. Third, you must make plans that anticipate future needs as well as possible changes. Finally, you must commit yourself to placing yourself in control of your time and carrying out your plans.

SETTING PRIORITIES

To manage your time in college, you must first set priorities. The decision to attend college is a commitment to being a professional student for the next few years. Any professional—businessperson, athlete, doctor, or student—attends to his or her professional responsibilities above most other things in life. Usually work comes *before* pleasure. As a student you must identify your priorities and develop a system for living each day accordingly.

What are your current priorities? Managing your time begins with an honest appraisal of what you want to do with it.

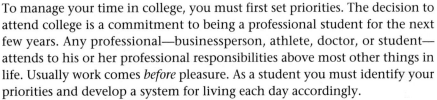

EXERCISE 5.2 Identifying Your Priorities

A. Rank the following pursuits in order of their importance to you. In the left-hand column write 1 beside the most important, 2 beside the second most important, and so on. Next, under "Estimated Hours," record the amount of time per week you believe you spend at this pursuit. Be honest, now!

Rank		Estimated Hours	Actual Hours
_____	Class attendance	_____	_____
_____	Relaxation	_____	_____
_____	Volunteer service	_____	_____
_____	Time with family	_____	_____
_____	Exercise	_____	_____
_____	Clubs/organizations	_____	_____
_____	Required reading	_____	_____
_____	Hobbies or entertainment	_____	_____
_____	Time with girlfriend/boyfriend or spouse	_____	_____
_____	Studying	_____	_____
_____	Working at a job	_____	_____
_____	Religious activities	_____	_____
_____	Shopping	_____	_____
_____	Nonrequired reading	_____	_____
_____	Sleeping	_____	_____
_____	Other: _____	_____	_____

B. Monitor the amount of time you spend at each pursuit over the course of one week, and record the total figures under "Actual Hours." Compare your estimates with the actual figures. Are there any important differences? If so, how do you explain them?

C. Discuss your rankings and your use of time with your peers and your instructor. How are your choices and habits similar to or different from theirs?

TAKING CONTROL IN THE FIRST WEEK: THE TIMETABLE AND MASTER PLAN

By the time we get to college, some of us are already better than others at setting priorities. Let's first consider a student who has some problems setting priorities. Joe is a well-intentioned, promising student who happens to be in danger of failing his first semester. He complains about having too much work and not enough time. Unfortunately, like many students, Joe wastes many hours every day. How does this happen?

First, Joe socializes at the drop of a hat. Naturally he wants to be popular, so he is available when anyone calls. He also likes to enjoy himself and often stays out fairly late, even during the week. To catch up on his sleep, he sometimes skips his 8:00 class, figuring he can make it up later. Other times Joe makes it to class even when he is still tired and manages to take notes, usually from the back of the room. In general Joe's social life makes it hard for him to keep up with his studies.

Joe is a person of good character, as shown by his other activities. He is a frequent volunteer at a children's center and never disappoints his little friends. He also writes an occasional column for the student newspaper and faithfully meets his deadlines, usually at the expense of his studies. This is when Joe complains about never having enough time.

Of course Joe has the same number of hours in each day as you or I. But rather than controlling the various attractions of college life, Joe lets them control him. Rather than deciding what his basic responsibilities are, he proceeds on a vague agenda of personal preferences.

By contrast, Carmen is a more aware, committed student. Let's see how she handles priorities. Carmen's first step each semester is to create a personal timetable and master plan (see Figure 5.1). The timetable is determined mostly by her course selections and other fixed responsibilities (shaded in the figure). Note that her timetable includes five courses, the typical load for full-time students on the semester system. (If you work long hours or have significant family responsibilities, you should take on a smaller course load.)

The classroom time for Carmen's five courses (History, College 101, Geology, Psychology, and Expository Writing) totals only 16 hours per week. That leaves her with lots of free time, right? Well, no. To that figure Carmen adds 2 hours outside of class for *every hour* in class. Thus, based on her 16 hours in class, she plans for 32 more hours of schoolwork outside of class, for a total of 48 hours. A 48-hour work week?! Who says college students have it easy? Obviously both Joe and Carmen have to schedule their time wisely and efficiently.

Carmen begins by scheduling 17 hours of study time into her normal weekday hours (see Figure 5.1). Her trick is to use the many hours tucked into the day between her widely scheduled classes. For instance, on Tuesdays and Thursdays she gets an early (but not too early) start; completing 4 of the 6 hours of study for Psychology. Now look at Monday, Wednesday, and Friday mornings, which are more complex. Carmen knows that it is best to review right after class, so on Mondays and Wednesdays she uses the hour between College 101 and Geology to review her notes from the two classes she has already attended on those mornings. Nor does she waste the time after lunch on Monday before her Geology lab at 2:00.

Since Tuesday evening is her 3-hour writing workshop, Carmen schedules time for writing right before the workshop and again the following afternoon. Although short bursts of study are sometimes ideal for review, writing requires longer, uninterrupted periods.

Now that she has accounted for 17 of the 32 study hours, Carmen should be able to find time for the additional 15 hours. When will she add these hours or, on certain weeks, put in even longer hours as her courses may require? The master plan makes it clear that Carmen will most likely be using many Thursday afternoons as well as evenings and weekends to meet her basic commitment. Oh, no, the weekends?! Sad but true. You should plan to work a good portion of many weekends. But take heart—it's worth it. Once you have met your academic (and other) commitments, the free time left over will be all yours. It will relax you totally, letting you enjoy yourself and return refreshed to your studies.

Let's review the steps Carmen followed to gain control from the first day of college:

► **Step 1:** She obtained a blank timetable form or purchased a calendar organized by day and hour, which often provides blank timetable forms as well.

Figure 5.1 Carmen's Timetable and Master Plan

	Sunday	Monday	Tuesday	Wednesday	Thursday	Friday	Saturday
6:00							
7:00							
8:00		History		History		History	
9:00		College 101	Read/ Study Psych.	College 101	Read/ Study Psych.	College 101	
10:00		Review Hist. & College 101	↓	Review Hist. & College 101	↓		
11:00		Geology	Psych.	Geology	Psych.		
12:00		LUNCH	↓	LUNCH	↓	LUNCH	
1:00		Study Geology	LUNCH	Study Geology, etc.	LUNCH	Read/ Study History,	
2:00		Geology Lab	Work on Writing	↓		College 101, etc.	
3:00		↓				↓	
4:00			↓	Work on Writing			
5:00				↓			
6:00	Library Job		Expository Writing			Library Job	
7:00			Workshop				
8:00			↓	Library Job			
9:00	↓			↓		↓	
10:00							

Total class hours: 16
Total study hours needed: 16 x 2 = 32

Total study hours allotted: 17
Additional study hours needed: 15

▶ **Step 2:** As soon as she was registered in her courses, she filled in the days and times for each course. She also made a list of buildings and room numbers, consulted a campus map, and took a tour before the first day of class. Colleges frequently organize these tours for new students.

▶ **Step 3:** She began to organize her class hours according to effective strategies for study, also including some time for nonacademic pursuits.

Although Carmen is the ideal time manager, and it might be difficult for Joe to do everything she does, let's consider how she organizes her study time to see which strategies Joe might use. Later you will have a chance to use her strategies to create a master plan for yourself.

EXERCISE 5.3   Joe's Timetable and Master Plan

Make two photocopies of Figure 5.2. Working alone or with two or three students, organize a time schedule for Joe using some of Carmen's strategies. Assume that he is carrying five academic subjects and schedule those in a sensible manner. Then create a plan that prioritizes his extracurricular activities.

EXERCISE 5.4   Your Timetable and Master Plan

Using the second copy of Figure 5.2 (photocopied in Exercise 5.3), construct your own timetable and master plan. First, fill in your scheduled commitments: classes, job, child care, and other activities. Then block out study hours according to the suggestions discussed previously. Share and discuss these with your peers and instructors. Check particularly to see if your work schedule or family responsibilities are too demanding and prevent you from putting in the necessary study hours.

If you are a commuter, you may wish to do Exercise 5.8 on pages 76–77 before creating your timetable and master plan.

ORGANIZING THE SEMESTER: THE WEEKLY ASSIGNMENT PLAN

Weekly assignment plans are the next important tool for staying in control. These add into the timetable all your assignments and tests. In the first week of classes you may receive course outlines, or *syllabi,* that explain the nature and purpose of each course and state the criteria and due dates of all assignments. Use these syllabi to structure your weekly study plans. If the instructor does not provide a syllabus, ask him or her for the specific study requirements for that week and mark them on your timetable. If the course syllabus doesn't give due dates, don't be bashful. Ask the instructor, and write the dates on your copy of the syllabus.

Figure 5.2 Timetable and Master Plan

(1) List all class meeting times. (2) Try to reserve about one hour of daytime study for each class hour. (3) Reserve time for meals, exercise, free time. (4) Try to plan a minimum of one hour additional study in evenings or on weekends for each class.

	Sunday	Monday	Tuesday	Wednesday	Thursday	Friday	Saturday
6:00							
7:00							
8:00							
9:00							
10:00							
11:00							
12:00							
1:00							
2:00							
3:00							
4:00							
5:00							
6:00							
7:00							
8:00							
9:00							
10:00							
11:00							
12:00							

EXERCISE 5.5   Semester Assignment Previews

To see the "big picture" of your workload this quarter or semester, fill in the following assignment preview sheet, listing all tests, reports, and other deadline-related activities.

Week	Course	What's Due
1	_____	_____
	_____	_____
	_____	_____
2	_____	_____
	_____	_____
	_____	_____
3	_____	_____
	_____	_____
	_____	_____
4	_____	_____
	_____	_____
	_____	_____
5	_____	_____
	_____	_____
	_____	_____
6	_____	_____
	_____	_____
	_____	_____
7	_____	_____
	_____	_____
	_____	_____
8	_____	_____
	_____	_____
	_____	_____
9	_____	_____
	_____	_____
	_____	_____

Week	Course	What's Due
10	_____	_____
	_____	_____
	_____	_____
11	_____	_____
	_____	_____
	_____	_____
12	_____	_____
	_____	_____
	_____	_____
13	_____	_____
	_____	_____
	_____	_____
14	_____	_____
	_____	_____
	_____	_____
15	_____	_____
	_____	_____
	_____	_____
16	_____	_____
	_____	_____
	_____	_____

Use photocopies of your timetable as weekly assignment plans, one sheet for each week. Carefully study all of the course outlines, and write in the due dates of all tests, papers, and special assignments. After you have recorded due dates, note on the weekly assignment sheet when you will begin to work on each major project, paper, report, or exam. Then schedule planning time during each subsequent week. You may wish to buy a large desk-size calendar for scheduling this information. The large size lets you describe your tasks in detail and view an entire week's or month's work at a glance.

Complete this early in the term. Typically the first two or three weeks will be free of due dates, but the midterm (fifth through seventh weeks) will be full. This lets you see in advance what planning is necessary to handle these demanding weeks.

Let's look at a week for Carmen when she will face preparing for three tests while also turning in two essays (see Figure 5.3). Carmen keeps her timetable where she can consult it often, but she knows that good time

Figure 5.3 Carmen's Timetable and Master Plan—Week 6

	Sunday	Monday	Tuesday	Wednesday	Thursday	Friday	Saturday
6:00							
7:00		Final Study College 101					
8:00		History		History		History ESSAY DUE	
9:00		College 101 TEST	Read/ Study Psych.	College 101	Read/ Study Psych.	College 101	
10:00		Review Hist. & College 101	for Test	Review Hist. & College 101			
11:00		geology	Psych. TEST	Geology	Psych.		
12:00		LUNCH	LUNCH	LUNCH	LUNCH	LUNCH	
1:00		Study Geology Final Review	Work on Writing Review and Proofread Essay	Study Geology, etc.		Read/ Study History, College 101, etc.	
2:00		Geology Lab					
3:00		TEST					
4:00				History Essay			
5:00				Final Draft			
6:00	Library Job	Study for	Expository Writing		Review and	Library Job	
7:00		Psych. Test	Workshop ESSAY DUE		Proofread History Essay		
8:00				Library Job			
9:00							
10:00							
11:00							
12:00							

management is flexible. She will generally stick to her routine, but when things are going well, she will slack off a bit. She also knows that certain days and weeks will be unusually demanding.

In order to manage this week, she will need to have done some planning and a lot of studying in advance. Note her early wakeup on Monday for a "final" study session. In other words Carmen has studied all the important material prior to Monday morning. (Later chapters will say more about long-term study for exams.) The same will be true for the lab test on Monday afternoon. Now look at 1:30 on Tuesday. All Carmen can do here is proofread and make minor revisions. This means that the essay itself was researched, written, and revised some days earlier—certainly not the day before, in the midst of preparing for and taking tests on Monday and Tuesday morning!

The rest of the week is not so difficult, but note that for the history essay, only the final draft and proofing stages are planned for. Once again success depends on Carmen's completing the bulk of the work for this essay well before this week. Only by crafting a detailed weekly plan for each week of the semester can Carmen—and you—see in advance how to get everything done well and on time. You don't want to find yourself scrambling to write an essay when you need to be studying for a test!

Your master plan and weekly assignment plans should be completed no later than Monday morning of the second week of classes so that you can continue to plan, anticipate, judge, and use your time effectively. Purchase some type of pocket calendar that you can use and carry with you everywhere.

Note how versatile the weekly assignment plan is: It reminds you, on a week-to-week basis, of your major assignments during the semester. The master plan serves a more global purpose: It tells you when you must be in class and encourages you to structure the hours outside of class. You should have access to both plans at all times for reference.

Guidelines for Scheduling

1. Examine your toughest weeks. Can you finish some of these assignments early in order to free up some time to study for tests?
2. Break large assignments like term papers down into smaller steps (choosing a topic, doing research, writing an outline, writing a first draft, and so on). Add deadlines in your schedule for each of these smaller portions of the project.
3. Start working on assignments days before they are due. Good student time managers frequently finish assignments before actual due dates to allow for emergencies.

ORGANIZING THE DAY: THE DAILY PLAN

With master and weekly plans in place, it will be easy for you to plan each day as a 24-hour package. Let's look at one of Carmen's daily plans. This daily plan is nothing more than a note that she has written to herself the prior evening (see Figure 5.4).

Being a good student does not necessarily mean grinding away at studies and doing little else. By planning her time carefully, Carmen is able to balance her academics with a modest amount of recreation. By working two-thirds of her class and study hours into the normal working day, she has reduced the additional studying she will need to do to about 15 hours. Thus

Figure 5.4 Carmen's Daily Plan

Thursday

7:00 — Up

Scheduling early classes and rising early will give you a jump on the day.

8:00 – 9:00 — Review science and hist. notes with Rob over breakfast

Rob is also a well-organized student — a good study partner.

9:00 – 10:00 — Read/study psych. in library, review notes from last lecture

Reading and reviewing notes will help prepare you for class.

11:00 – 12:30 — Psych. lecture

12:30 – 12:45 — Review/Recall/Recite

As you will discover, to prevent forgetting it's very important to review as soon after class as possible.

12:45 – 1:45 — Lunch

1:45 – 2:30 — Bookstore for supplies; textbook

Right after lunch is a good time for miscellaneous activity. It's hard to study on a full stomach.

2:30 – 4:00 — Read/study history

Always take a short break in the middle of a study session to maintain alertness.

4:00 – 5:30 — 25 min. jog with Alice; shower, sauna

Regular exercise is important. It actually aids studying by promoting alertness.

5:30 – 6:30 — Dinner

6:30 – 7:15 — Free time

Schedule free time. It keeps you balanced emotionally.

7:15 – 10:00 — Study for hist. quiz, prepare for College 101, write schedule for Friday

In extended study sessions schedule a variety of activities, each with a specific objective.

Time management is a lifelong skill. The better the job you have after college, the more likely that you'll be managing your own and possibly other people's time. (Photo by David Gonzales)

a few hours spent studying each evening should cover most of the required study time. Her weekends can be somewhat free, as can selected regular times during the week, for other commitments and interests.

Note that Carmen honors the age-old principle "Sound mind, sound body." Her timetable includes two commitments to exercise, and she'll work out once more on the weekend. Your schedule should also include regular exercise time of at least an hour (including shower) three times a week. Research consistently shows that regular exercise gives you more, not less, energy.

EXERCISE 5.6   Starting Your Time Management System

A. Review your "Assignment Preview" sheet from Exercise 5.5. Then begin to structure a schedule allowing you time to finish all your assignments. Be sure to try to find time during your hours on campus to study. Try to follow this schedule for a week.

B. Jot down what you found to be the main obstacles to your time management system. Working with your peers, make a list of the obstacles each of you encountered during the week. Brainstorm strategies for overcoming these obstacles and share them with the rest of the class.

C. Choose partners. Decide how you might be able to help each other overcome particular obstacles. Plan to take a few minutes before class one day each week to discuss your progress.

"Do Not Disturb"

Read how one single-parent commuter handles distractions:

I made it a point to select one area of the house for serious study. I selected a specific block of time to study. When I entered the room, I would place a red sign outside my door to signal the kids that I was not to be disturbed.

My kids didn't buy into this right away, but they soon learned that I was not going to alter this strategy. I was amazed at how soon they adjusted. Later they were a big help in keeping me on schedule.

I feel much better about working at home because I am no longer under pressure to get things done in a piecemeal fashion. My children feel better too. They feel that they have a part to play in helping me with my studies.

Reduce Distractions

Female ticks will remain dormant on a branch or leaf for weeks waiting for an unsuspecting mammal to pass directly beneath. Only the odor of butyric acid, which is emitted from the mammal's skin, will trigger the tick to fall on the animal host. The odor is a "sign stimulus" triggering the tick's behavior.

Are there any such sign stimuli in your life? For instance, just when you are preparing to study, does a host of would-be distractors suddenly descend upon you like so many ticks? When this happens, ask yourself whether you are unwittingly giving them a signal to approach.

One sign stimulus may be study location. If you study in the living room, in front of the television, or in other places associated with leisure, you may be giving the message that your study isn't serious. Study time is another signal. Studying at times associated with meals or family interaction can signal others that you want to be approached. Method of study also carries a message. Studying while lying on your bed, walking around the house, or listening to the radio can signal to others that you really aren't studying.

Use sign stimuli to *reduce* distractions. Set aside specific study times at locations not associated with socialization. Behave in a way that is consistent with academic work and that signals others not to disturb you.

EXERCISE 5.7   Study Time Without Distractions

Whether you live on campus or at home, there will be distractions that interfere with your ability to study. List the things that tend to distract you the most. Then, using the goal-setting process in Chapter 1, work in small groups to brainstorm ways to avoid distractions and send signals to distractors that you are not to be disturbed.

ON CAMPUS

Study location: _____ time: _____ to _____

Potential distractors (human and physical):

_____

_____

Actions against physical distractions:

_____

_____

Signals to human distractors:

_____

_____

AT HOME (OFF-CAMPUS OR ON-CAMPUS RESIDENCE)

Study location: _____ time: _____ to _____

Potential distractors (human and physical):

_____

_____

Actions against physical distractions:

_____

_____

Signals to human distractors:

_____

_____

How to Beat Procrastination

Procrastination may be your single greatest enemy. Getting started when it's time to start takes self-discipline and self-control. Here are some ways to beat procrastination:

1. Say to yourself, "A mature person is capable and responsible and is a self-starter. I'm that kind of person if I start now." Then start!

2. On a 3 × 5 notecard write out a list of everything you need to do. Check off things as you get them done. Use the list to focus on the things that aren't getting done. Move them to the top of your next day's list and make up your mind to do them. Working from a list will give you a feeling of accomplishment and lead you to do more.

3. Break big jobs down into smaller steps. Tackle short, easy-to-accomplish tasks first.

4. Apply the goal-setting technique described in Chapter 1 to whatever you are putting off.

5. Promise yourself a suitable reward (an apple, a phone call, a walk) whenever you finish something that was hard to undertake.

6. Take control of your study environment. Eliminate distractions—including the ones you love! Say no to friends who want your attention at *their* convenience. Agree to meet them at a specific time later. Let them be your reward for doing what you must do now. Don't make phone calls during planned study sessions. Close your door.

TIME MANAGEMENT FOR COMMUTERS

If you are a commuter you probably have less time for college than students who live on campus. Not only do you spend more time traveling, but you are also more likely to have commitments to family and work that seriously compete with your class and study time. Your greatest problems probably occur during exam time or when papers and projects are due. In addition to the time management strategies already described, you can do other things to manage your time efficiently.

Be Realistic in Your Time Management Plans

To keep your problems to a minimum, be realistic. As you fill out your daily and weekly plans, be sure to allow time for travel, family, work, or other responsibilities. If there is really not enough time to meet your commitments and carry the hoped-for number of courses, reduce your course load. Take care to record the critical exam dates and assignment due dates on your family calendar to avoid conflicts. Let your family know ahead of time the days or weeks that you will need more time of your own.

EXERCISE 5.8   Do Commuters Have Time for Success?

The following shows how typical *residential* first-year students allocate their time on a weekday.*

Activity	Hours per Day
Class time	3
Studying	3
Employment	1/4
Idle leisure	3
Social	2 1/4
Travel (between classes)	1
Eating	1 1/2
Grooming	1
Resting	6 1/2
Recreation	1 1/2
Other	1

Notice that new students who live on campus devote almost 7 hours each day to socializing, recreation, and leisure pursuits. How might a commuter use those 7 hours? The following chart lists some activities that commuters may have to carry out on a typical weekday. If you are a commuter, estimate the time you take for each. Write your response in the "hours per day" column.

Activity	Hours per Day
Class time	_____
Studying	_____
Employment	_____
Travel	
Home to college	_____
Between classes	_____
College to work	_____
Work to home	_____
Other	_____
Total travel	_____

*Data adapted from David W. Desmond and David S. Glenwick, "Time-Budgeting Practices of College Students: A Developmental Analysis of Activity Patterns," *Journal of College Student Personnel* 28, no. 4 (1987): 318–23.

Activity	Hours per Day
Home responsibilities	
Shopping	_____
Meals	_____
Housecleaning	_____
Laundry	_____
Other	_____
Total home	_____
Family responsibilities	
General time	_____
Child care	_____
Care for elderly or disabled	_____
Other	_____
Total family	_____
Civic responsibilities	
Volunteer work	_____
Other	_____
Total civic	_____
Personal	
Grooming/dressing	_____
Newspaper	_____
Rest	_____
Other	_____
Total personal	_____
Other	_____
Total time for all responsibilities	_____

Do you need to make some adjustments? What are they? Use the goal-setting process in Chapter 1 to help yourself make them.

Don't Be a "Blockhead"

As a commuter you may tend to use block scheduling, running all your classes together without any breaks or attending school only one or two days a week. You may be doing this to cut down travel costs and have more free time on other days.

(Photo by Anestis Diakopoulos/Stock Boston)

However, you may be unaware of problems associated with block scheduling. Fatigue can kill your efforts in classes held later in the day. You will probably tend to forget lecture material because you don't have enough time between classes to digest information. You may also sometimes feel compelled to miss one class in order to prepare for another. If you are on a two-day schedule (for example, all your classes on Tuesday and Thursday), you will find it difficult to finish assignments between one class meeting and the next. And if you are on a one-day schedule and fall ill on that day, the consequences of missing all your classes that week can be devastating. You will also feel stress when all your midterm or final exams fall on the same day. With back-to-back block scheduling, you may not have even a free period between several exams.

For a more effective schedule:

1. **Arrange a "double-up" schedule.** Try to schedule classes in which instructors teach the same course at different times or on different days. This will give you a chance to catch up if you miss a class. Ask your instructors if you can attend an alternate class.

2. **Split your schedule.** Try to alternate classes with free periods. This will give you time to prepare for the next class, visit the library, talk and study with other students, meet with a professor, or just recoup.

3. **Seek a flexible schedule.** Look for teachers who will allow you flexibility in completing assignments. Find out about independent study, correspondence, and televised courses.

Follow a Routine

Humans have a built-in biological clock that helps them establish a rhythm and routine. Some psychologists believe this natural rhythm is thrown out of sync when events conflict with our biological expectations.

Perhaps the best-known example of this problem is jet lag. Similarly many shift workers such as nurses and police officers are less productive and more lethargic and irritable as they adapt to new time schedules. Commuting students likewise may have time lag problems when they adjust their schedules to satisfy competing obligations or when block-scheduling requires them to vary their schedules. For instance, if you study 2 hours every night Monday through Thursday, then engage in leisure activities during these times Friday through Sunday, you are likely to have trouble getting back into studying on Monday evening. Like the victim of jet lag, you confuse your body about whether it should study, play, or vegetate during this time of day. Likewise students who sleep in on weekends often find it hard to make it to Monday morning classes.

As a commuter you face more schedule challenges than the residential student. Keep your biological clock running smoothly by establishing as much routine as possible.

EXERCISE 5.9   Commuter's Telephone Directory

Devise a commuter's telephone directory and keep it handy. Begin with phone numbers for any of the following that apply:

1. All professors _____

    _____

2. Campus security/local police _____

3. Campus lost and found _____

4. Campus health service _____

5. Dean of students _____

6. Campus counseling center _____

7. Campus legal services _____

8. Child-care centers _____

9. Emergency road service _____

10. Landlord (home and work) _____

11. Employer (home and work) _____

12. Campus tutorial center or learning center _____

13. Campus commuter student service center (if available) _____

14. Neighbor _____

15. Local taxi service _____

16. Public library _____

17. Friends and study mates (for each class) _____

_____

_____

_____

18. College FAX numbers (to FAX a paper long distance if you get stuck)_____

_____

Also place your class schedule and the number for campus security in a convenient place at home so that people can reach you in an emergency.

JOURNAL

How would you evaluate yourself as a time manager right now? Are you more like Carmen or Joe? What do you see as your greatest asset in terms of time management? What do you think will be the greatest hindrance to effectively managing your time? How do you intend to deal with this hindrance? How might you use your assets to overcome your weaknesses?

SUGGESTIONS FOR FURTHER READING

Fanning, Tony, and Robbie Fanning. *Get It All Done and Still Be Human: A Personal Time Management Workshop*. Menlo Park, Calif.: Open Chain, 1990.

Hunt, Diane, and Pam Hait. *The Tao of Time*. New York: Henry Holt, 1989.

MacKenzie, Alec. *The Time Trap: The New Version of the 20-Year Classic on Time Management*. New York:

AMACOM (Div. of American Management Association), 1990.

Sotiriou, Peter Elias. *Integrating College Study Skills: Reasoning in Reading, Listening, and Writing*, 3rd ed. Belmont, Calif.: Wadsworth, 1993. See Chapter 2, "Managing Your Time and Your Study Area."

Learning Styles

Steven Blume
Marietta College

My friend Janet always sleeps
through U.S. history. That is totally
weird because I could listen to
Dr. Moroney lecture on Grant and
Lee all day. Janet says she likes
discussion classes. Those freak me
out. I guess there's more than one
way to learn. I hope so.

One student's analytical style may thrive on the complexities of history. Another's satisfaction at mastering facts and understanding how they are related may lead her into science. (Left photo by Richard Tauber; right, Michael Kagan/Monkmeyer Press Photo)

In high school certain subjects appealed to you more than others. For one thing, some came easier than others. Perhaps you found history easier than mathematics, or biology easier than English. Part of the explanation for that has to do with what is called your *learning style*—that is, the way you acquire knowledge.

Learning style affects not only how you process material as you study but how you absorb it. Some students learn more effectively through visual means, others through listening to lectures, and still others through class discussion, hands-on experience, memorization, or various combinations of these.

Your particular learning style may make you much more comfortable and successful in some areas than in others. Consider Mark, whose favorite subject is history. Mark generally receives B's on his history exams, and he is satisfied with his performance. One of the things he likes best about history is the study of historical movements—the development of ideas as they inform historical events. When he studies for his exams, he analyzes those events, trying to determine what is responsible for the various social, political, and historical changes he has been reading about. While he recognizes the importance of names and dates, they are less significant and interesting to him than the analysis of why certain events occurred and what effects have resulted from such occurrences. For example, he studies to understand *why* the pilgrims came to America and *how* they created the Plymouth Plantation rather than to discover who the leaders of the emigration were, who the first settlers were, when they arrived in America, what crops they grew, and what treaties they signed with the Indians. What he is interested in and how he studies are integral parts of his learning style.

Mark is also taking Introductory Biology, and as is natural for him, he studied for his biology exam in the same way he studied for his history test. Unfortunately he was able to use very little of the knowledge gained from his studying and thus received an F on his biology exam. Instead of studying facts, committing important terminology to memory, and learning definitions, Mark had stressed concepts when he studied, and this *analytical learning style* turned out to be inappropriate for this course, or at least for the way his instructor taught the course.

The reverse can also be true. Another student, Anne, has a *factual learning style* that makes her comfortable with memorizing facts. Anne would do very well on that same biology test and yet find the history exam that stressed concepts and analysis of material very difficult. Just as we all have different skills, so we have different learning styles. Although no one learning style is inherently better than another, it is important to be able to work comfortably no matter what style is required in a given course. An awareness of your learning style can be helpful in emphasizing your strengths and helping you compensate for your weaknesses.

In this chapter we'll examine learning styles of students both in and out of the classroom, as well as discuss the teaching styles of professors.

AN INFORMAL MEASURE OF LEARNING STYLE

To begin to define your own learning style and to understand how it affects your responses in class, do the following exercise.

EXERCISE 6.1 **Your Learning Style: A Quick Indication**

A. List three or four of your favorite courses from high school or college:

1. _____
2. _____
3. _____
4. _____

What did these courses have in common? Did they tend to be hands-on courses? Lecture courses? Discussion courses? What were the exams like? Do you see a pattern from one course to the next? For example, did your favorite courses tend to use information-oriented tests such as multiple-choice or true-false? Or did they often include broader essay exams? Did the tests cover small units of material or facts, or did they draw on larger chunks of material?

Now list three or four of your least favorite courses from high school or college:

1. _____
2. _____
3. _____
4. _____

What did these courses and their exams have in common? How did they tend to differ from the courses you liked?

What conclusions can you draw about your preferences for learning based on these common elements in course presentation or exams? Do you prefer to make lists and memorize facts or to analyze the material, searching for concepts and considering broader implications? If you prefer the former, your learning style is more factual, like Anne's; if you prefer the latter, your learning style is more analytical, like Mark's. Can you understand why Anne prefers biology and Mark prefers history?

B. After doing part A, form a small group with two or three other members of the class. Brainstorm about what courses you are taking that seem to require factual learning styles, analytical learning styles, or a combination of both. Prepare an oral group presentation to the class about your conclusions and the reasons for them. What is the best way to prepare for an exam in these classes, and why? (Read the rest of this chapter before you give your presentation.)

If you prefer listening to lectures, taking notes, and reading your notes aloud to yourself, you have a more *auditory learning style*. You might even read your notes into a tape recorder and play them back when you study for an exam. If you prefer instructors who outline their lectures on the blackboard or who make liberal use of the board by illustrating the important points they are trying to make, you have a more *visual learning style*. You probably find that copying and recopying your notes helps you learn the material better.

Being more aware of your learning style preferences can help you exploit your strengths in preparing for classes and also help you better understand why you may be having difficulty with some of your courses and what you might do to improve.

MORE FORMAL MEASURES OF LEARNING STYLE

A number of instruments can help you determine more effectively just what your preferred learning style is and better understand other learning styles as well.

Classroom Behavior

One approach is based on the ways in which students behave in the classroom. For instance, psychologists Tony Grasha and Sheryl Riechmann have put together the *Grasha-Riechmann* instrument. This tool assesses six learning styles based on classroom behavior: (1) *competitive*, (2) *collaborative*, (3) *participant*, (4) *avoidant*, (5) *dependent*, and (6) *independent*.

To understand which classroom learning style you are most comfortable with, you need to answer certain questions. For example, do you find the study questions or review questions passed out by your instructor helpful? Do you enjoy and find helpful studying with and learning from other students in your class? Do you like it when the instructor engages the class in discussion? If so, then you probably have a more collaborative, participant, and dependent learning style and will work best with an instructor who has a correspondent teaching style. On the other hand, you may prefer an instructor who lectures in class with minimal class participation. You may feel that straightforward study of your lecture notes and textbook is the most effective means of study. If so, your learning style is more competitive, independent, and avoidant.

Personality Preferences

Another approach explores basic personality preferences that make people interested in different things and draw them to different fields and lifestyles. The *Myers-Briggs Type Indicator,* based on Carl Jung's theory of psychological types, uses four scales:

- ► **EI (Extroversion/Introversion).** This scale describes two opposite preferences depending on whether you like to focus your attention on the outer or the inner world.
- ► **SN (Sensing/Intuition).** This scale describes opposite ways you acquire information—that is, whether you find out about things through facts or through intuition.
- ► **TF (Thinking/Feeling).** This scale describes how you make decisions, whether by analysis and weighing of evidence or through your feelings.
- ► **JP (Judging/Perceiving).** This scale describes the way you relate to the outer world, whether in a planned, orderly way or in a flexible, spontaneous way.

You will often feel most comfortable around people who share your preferences, and you will probably be most comfortable in a classroom where the instructor's preferences for perceiving and processing information are most like yours. But the Myers-Briggs instrument also emphasizes our ability to cultivate in ourselves all processes on the scale.

EXERCISE 6.2   Assessing Your Learning Style

PERSONAL STYLE INVENTORY

Just as every person has differently shaped feet and toes from every other person, so we all have differently "shaped" personalities. Just as no person's foot shape is "right" or "wrong," so no person's personality shape is right or wrong. The purpose of this inventory is to give you a picture of the shape of your preferences, but that shape, while different from the shapes of other persons' personalities, has nothing to do with mental health or mental problems.

The following items are arranged in pairs (*a* and *b*), and each member of the pair represents a preference you may or may not hold. Rate your preference for each item by giving it a score of 0 to 5 (0 meaning you *really* feel negative about it or strongly about the other member of the pair, 5 meaning you *strongly* prefer it or do not prefer the other member of the pair). The scores for *a* and *b must* add up to 5 (0 and 5, 1 and 4, or 2 and 3). Do not use fractions such as 2½.

I prefer:

_____ 1a. making decisions after finding out what others think

_____ 1b. making decisions without consulting others

_____ 2a. being called imaginative or intuitive

_____ 2b. being called factual and accurate

_____ 3a. making decisions about people in organizations based on available data and systematic analysis of situations

_____ 3b. making decisions about people in organizations based on empathy, feelings, and understanding of their needs and values

_____ 4a. allowing commitments to occur if others want to make them

_____ 4b. pushing for definite commitments to ensure that they are made

_____ 5a. quiet, thoughtful time alone

_____ 5b. active, energetic time with people

_____ 6a. using methods I know well that are effective to get the job done

_____ 6b. trying to think of new methods of doing tasks when confronted with them

_____ 7a. drawing conclusions based on unemotional logic and careful step-by-step analysis

_____ 7b. drawing conclusions based on what I feel and believe about life and people from past experiences

_____ 8a. avoiding making deadlines

_____ 8b. setting a schedule and sticking to it

_____ 9a. inner thoughts and feelings others cannot see

_____ 9b. activities and occurrences in which others join

_____ 10a. the abstract or theoretical

_____ 10b. the concrete or real

_____ 11a. helping others explore their feelings

_____ 11b. helping others make logical decisions

_____ 12a. communicating little of my inner thinking and feelings

_____ 12b. communicating freely my inner thinking and feelings

_____ 13a. planning ahead based on projections

_____ 13b. planning as necessities arise, just before carrying out the plans

_____ 14a. meeting new people

_____ 14b. being alone or with one person I know well

_____ 15a. ideas

_____ 15b. facts

_____ 16a. convictions

_____ 16b. verifiable conclusions

_____ 17a. keeping appointments and notes about commitments in notebooks or in appointment books as much as possible

_____ 17b. using appointment books and notebooks as minimally as possible (although I may use them)

_____ 18a. carrying out carefully laid, detailed plans with precision

_____ 18b. designing plans and structures without necessarily carrying them out

_____ 19a. being free to do things on the spur of the moment

_____ 19b. knowing well in advance what I am expected to do

_____ 20a. experiencing emotional situations, discussions, movies

_____ 20b. using my ability to analyze situations

PERSONAL STYLE INVENTORY SCORING

Instructions: Transfer your scores for each item of each pair to the appropriate blanks. Be careful to check the *a* and *b* letters to be sure you are recording scores in the right blank spaces. Then total the scores for each dimension.

Dimension		Dimension	
I	**E**	**N**	**S**
1b. _____	1a. _____	2a. _____	2b. _____
5a. _____	5b. _____	6b. _____	6a. _____
9a. _____	9b. _____	10a. _____	10b. _____
12a. _____	12b. _____	15a. _____	15b. _____
14b. _____	14a. _____	18b. _____	18a. _____
TOTALS: I _____	E _____	N _____	S _____

Dimension		Dimension	
T	**F**	**P**	**J**
3a. _____	3b. _____	4a. _____	4b. _____
7a. _____	7b. _____	8a. _____	8b. _____
11b. _____	11a. _____	13b. _____	13a. _____
16b. _____	16a. _____	17b. _____	17a. _____
20b. _____	20a. _____	19a. _____	19b. _____
TOTALS: T _____	F _____	P _____	J _____

PERSONAL STYLE INVENTORY INTERPRETATION

Letters on the score sheet stand for:

I — *Introversion*   **E** — *Extroversion*
N — *iNtuition*   **S** — *Sensing*
T — *Thinking*   **F** — *Feeling*
P — *Perceiving*   **J** — *Judging*

If your score is: *The likely interpretation is:*

12–13	balance in the strengths of the dimensions
14–15	some strength in the dimension; some weakness in the other member of the pair
16–19	definite strength in the dimension; definite weakness in the other member of the pair
20–25	considerable strength in the dimension; considerable weakness in the other member of the pair

Your typology is those four dimensions for which you had scores of 14 or more, although the relative strengths of all the dimensions actually constitute your typology. Scores of 12 or 13 show relative balance in a pair so that either member could be part of the typology.

DIMENSIONS OF THE TYPOLOGY

The following four pairs of dimensions are present to some degree in all people. It is the extremes that are described here. The strength of a dimension is indicated by the score for that dimension and will determine how closely the strengths and weaknesses described fit the participant's personality.

Introversion–Extroversion

Persons more introverted than extroverted tend to make decisions somewhat independently of culture, people, or things around them. They are quiet, diligent at working alone, and socially reserved. They may dislike being interrupted while working and may tend to forget names and faces.

Extroverted persons are attuned to the culture, people, and things around them. The extrovert is outgoing, socially free, interested in variety and in working with people. The extrovert may become impatient with long, slow tasks and does not mind being interrupted by people.

Intuition–Sensing

The intuitive person prefers possibilities, theories, invention, and the new and becomes bored with nitty-gritty details and facts unrelated to concepts. The intuitive person thinks and discusses in spontaneous leaps of intuition that may neglect details. Problem solving comes easily for this individual, although there may be a tendency to make errors of fact.

The sensing type prefers the concrete, factual, tangible here-and-now, becoming impatient with theory and the abstract, mistrusting intuition. The sensing type thinks in detail, remembering real facts, but possibly missing a conception of the overall.

Thinking–Feeling

The thinker makes judgments based on logic, analysis, and evidence, avoiding decisions based on feelings and values. As a result, the thinker is more interested in logic, analysis, and verifiable conclusions than in empathy, values, and personal warmth. The thinker may step on others' feelings and needs without realizing it, neglecting to take into consideration the values of others.

The feeler makes judgments based on empathy, warmth, and personal values. As a consequence, feelers are more interested in people and feelings than in impersonal logic, analysis, and things, and in harmony more than in being on top or achieving impersonal goals. The feeler gets along well with people in general.

Perceiving–Judging

The perceiver is a gatherer, always wanting to know more before deciding, holding off decisions and judgments. As a consequence, the perceiver is open, flexible, adaptive, nonjudgmental, able to see and appreciate all sides of issues, always welcoming new perspectives. However, perceivers are also difficult to pin down and may become involved in many tasks that do not reach closure, so that they may become frustrated at times. Even when they finish tasks, perceivers will tend to look back at them and wonder whether they could have been done another way. The perceiver wishes to roll with life rather than change it.

The judger is decisive, firm, and sure, setting goals and sticking to them. The judger wants to make decisions and get on to the next project. When a project does not yet have closure, judgers will leave it behind and go on to new tasks.

STRENGTHS AND WEAKNESSES OF THE TYPES

Each person has strengths and weaknesses as a result of these dimensions. Committees and organizations with a preponderance of one type will have the same strengths and weaknesses.

	Possible Strengths	Possible Weaknesses
Introvert	is independent	avoids others
	works alone	is secretive
	reflects	loses opportunities to act
	works with ideas	is misunderstood by others
	avoids generalizations	dislikes being interrupted
	is careful before acting	

	Possible Strengths	Possible Weaknesses
Extrovert	interacts with others	does not work without people
	is open	needs change, variety
	acts, does	is impulsive
	is well understood	is impatient with routine
Intuitor	sees possibilities	is inattentive to detail, precision
	works out new ideas	is inattentive to the actual and practical
	works with the complicated	is impatient with the tedious
	solves novel problems	loses sight of the here-and-now
		jumps to conclusions
Senser	attends to detail	does not see possibilities
	is practical	loses the overall in details
	has memory for detail, fact	mistrusts intuition
	is patient	is frustrated with the complicated
	is systematic	prefers not to imagine future
Feeler	considers others' feelings	is not guided by logic
	understands needs, values	is not objective
	is interested in conciliation	is less organized
	demonstrates feelings	is overly accepting
	persuades, arouses	bases judgments on feelings
Thinker	is logical, analytical	does not notice people's feelings
	is objective	misunderstands others' values
	is organized	is uninterested in conciliation
	has critical ability	does not show feelings
	is just	shows less mercy
	stands firm	is uninterested in persuading
Perceiver	compromises	is indecisive
	sees all sides of issues	does not plan
	is flexible	does not control circumstances
	decides based on all data	is easily distracted from tasks
	is not judgmental	does not finish projects
Judger	decides	is stubborn
	plans	is inflexible
	orders	decides with insufficient data
	makes quick decisions	is controlled by task or plans
	remains with a task	wishes not to interrupt work

NOTE: This exercise is an abridgment of the Personal Style Inventory by Dr. R. Craig Hogan and Dr. David W. Champagne, adapted and reproduced with permission from Organization Design and Development, Inc., 2002 Renaissance Blvd., Suite 100, King of Prussia, Pa., 19406. For information on using the complete instrument, please write to the above address.

A good study group shares a common goal of success for all its members. It also asks each member to contribute according to his or her own special perspective and style. (Photo by David Gonzales)

As you reflect on your performance on the previous exercise, keep in mind that your score merely suggests your preferences; it does not stereotype or pigeonhole you. Remember, too, that no one learning style is inherently preferable to another and that everyone knows and uses a range of styles. The fact that many of us exhibit behaviors that seem to contradict our preferences shows that we each embrace a wide range of possibilities.

Using Knowledge of Your Learning Style

Discovering your own strengths empowers you to recognize what you already do well and provides you with some insights into the kinds of learning experiences in which you are likely to do your best. Discovering your weaknesses is also useful, because it is to your advantage to cultivate your less dominant learning styles. While certain disciplines and certain instructors may take approaches that favor certain styles, no course is going to be entirely sensing or entirely intuitive, entirely thinking or entirely feeling, just as you are not entirely one thing or another.

STUDY GROUPS AND LEARNING STYLE

Knowing your own learning style preference can help you to study more effectively with other students. Chapter 9 tells more about study groups and why they matter so much.

When you form a study group, seek out students with some opposite learning preferences, but be sure, too, that you have some preferences in common. The best teamwork seems to come from people who differ on one or two preferences. If you prefer intuitive fact gathering, you might benefit from the details brought forth by a sensing type.

If you are in a math class, don't always try to solve problems alone. Share your ideas in a group. Talk about the steps you went through to solve a problem, and share study techniques that worked for you. In other classes study for exams by comparing notes and reviewing the main points covered in class.

EXERCISE 6.3   Working with Other Learning Styles

A. Form a group with one or two other students whose learning style preferences are different from yours in one or two dimensions. Review the chart in Exercise 6.2 on strengths and weaknesses and make some notes about yours so that you can find the best "match" with other study group members:

Strengths: _____

_____

_____

_____

Weaknesses: _____

_____

_____

_____

   How will your strengths help others? What strengths will you look for in others that will help you?

How I can help others: _____

_____

_____

How others can help me: _____

_____

_____

   In your next session ask that each person share his or her strengths and weaknesses and talk about how the group might work for everyone's benefit.

B. Try working on an assignment with someone who has a preference that is opposite of your own on either the sensing/intuitive or thinking/feeling scale. Discuss how this worked. Did you get more out of the assignment? Did you consider more issues than you might have alone? Did you learn something about how to study? What did you discover about the other person's learning style?

DEALING WITH YOUR TEACHERS' LEARNING/TEACHING STYLES

Just as your learning style affects how you study, perform, and react to various courses and disciplines, so your instructor's teaching style affects what and how he or she teaches. Some awareness of your instructor's teaching

How to Develop Other Learning Styles

The key ingredient in developing your less dominant style is awareness. Try to develop one process at a time.

Raising Your Sensing (S) Learning Style

1. Whenever you walk, try to notice and jot down specific details of the scenery—shapes of leaves; size, color, and types of rocks; and so on.

2. Three or four times a day pay careful attention to, and then describe to a friend, what someone else is wearing.

3. Do a jigsaw puzzle.

4. Break down a physical activity into its component parts.

5. Describe in detail something you just saw, such as a picture, a room, or the like.

Raising Your Intuitive (N) Learning Style

1. Imagine a given situation or circumstance in a new light by considering, "What if...?" For example, what if the pilgrims had landed in California—how would their lifestyle have changed? What if you had gone to a bigger (smaller) school? What if X were your roommate instead of Y?

2. Pretend you saw an article ten years from now about your hometown, your lifestyle, American values, or the like. What would it say?

3. Read a novel and imagine yourself as one of the characters. What would happen to you following the novel's conclusion?

Raising Your Feeling (F) Learning Style

1. Write down a feeling statement about your class, your day, your job, or your emotions, and make sure you use a simile. For example, "I feel like a puppy that's just been scolded." Note that if you use *think* in a statement, it's not a feeling statement. Write down five feeling statements every day.

2. Write down what matters most in your relationship with someone or something else.

Raising Your Thinking (T) Learning Style

1. Have someone write down a problem that's bothering them or a problem related to the college or your environment. Then answer questions that explain who, what, where, when, and why, and provide the details that back up each response. Doing this every day for 15 or 20 minutes will teach you how to be objective.

style may also help you study and prepare for exams. The syllabus for the course, the lecture, and the discussion questions, as well as handouts, assignments, and exams, can provide some helpful hints not only about your instructor's teaching style but also about ways you can utilize the strengths of your own learning style or compensate enough to perform effectively in the class.

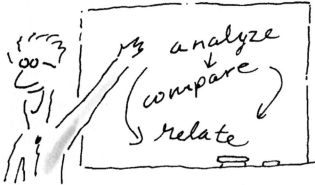

Clues to Teachers' Teaching Styles

The best clue to your instructor's teaching style is the language he or she uses. If your learning style is more visual, you can sense those clues more easily from printed material such as the syllabus or course handouts. If your learning style is more auditory, pay attention to the language your instructor uses when lecturing, asking discussion questions, or phrasing oral test questions.

For example, earlier we discussed two ways of receiving and processing information: (1) sensing, that is, factual and informational, and (2) intuitive, that is, analytical and conceptual. An instructor who uses words such as *define, diagram, label, list, outline,* and *summarize* will tend to have a more sensing teaching style. He or she will want you to be extremely specific and provide primarily factual information. Words such as these really ask for very restricted answers. (See Chapter 9, pages 136–138, for more on the meaning of each of these terms.) Whereas Anne will be very comfortable with this instructor, Mark will be less so. Recognizing his instructor's teaching style, however, would be to Mark's benefit since he would have a better idea of what to expect. He could then adjust his approach to the material in order to perform satisfactorily in class and on exams.

On the other hand, an instructor whose syllabus or lecture is sprinkled with words such as *concept, theme, idea, theory,* and *interpretation* will tend to have a much more intuitive and analytical learning style and expect similar kinds of responses from students. On exams or on assignments he or she may use terms such as *describe, compare, contrast, criticize, discuss, evaluate, explain, interpret, justify,* or *relate.* (Again see Chapter 9 for definitions.) You may notice that instead of asking you to provide factual data or information, these words ask you to act on that information—that is, to use it in relation to other pieces of information, to evaluate it, or to examine it in terms of your own experience. An instructor who uses these words has a much more intuitive teaching style and will expect more analytical, imaginative, and conceptual responses. He or she will expect you to see that information in a new context rather than simply restate the facts as they have been given to you or as they appear in the textbook.

Mark will, of course, feel far more comfortable with this instructor. Anne will have to recognize when she studies in this course that learning the facts is not enough. She will be expected to see them in other contexts, to think about their relationships to one another. While this may not be easy for her, she can certainly adapt to it if the instructor's teaching style and expectations demand it.

Exam Preparation and Learning/Teaching Style

Understanding learning styles can help you to perceive more clearly the expectations of an instructor whose teaching style is incompatible with your learning style and thus allow you to prepare more effectively for his or her exam. You saw earlier, for example, how Mark's learning style, essentially an intuitive (N) style, was suited to his history course but not to his biology exam. By contrast Anne's more sensing (S) style was suited to the biology course but not the history course. In order to perform better on that biology exam Mark would need to modify his way of studying.

Let me illustrate further with an experience of my own. When I was learning about the Myers-Briggs Type Indicator, I attended a workshop for college instructors. One of its purposes was to help them understand how different learning styles can cause them to construct exams that will be much easier for students who share the instructor's learning style preference than for students who do not.

Those of us attending the workshop were divided into two groups, sensing and intuitive. Each group was given a five-page essay about the effects of divorce on young children and asked to construct a short exam based on the reading. The sensing group was then asked to take the exam constructed by the intuitive group while the intuitive group was asked to take the exam constructed by the sensing group.

In dealing with the questions we could not believe that both groups had read and discussed the same essay. Those of us in the intuitive group had been asked to construct lists of details and respond to much factual data that we had regarded as less essential than the more analytical and conceptual themes of the essay. And those in the sensing group were quite taken aback by the very broad thematic questions my group had asked about the implications of divorce on the children and the larger questions about the children's future. (Keep in mind that all of the people at the workshop—sensing and intuitive—were successful professionals.)

Our very different ways of acquiring and processing information (part of our learning styles) had led us to emphasize very different information and to require very different responses to that information. It would have been much easier for those who favored sensing to respond to an exam constructed by other sensing people, and vice versa. That same situation has probably been true for you in classes and will continue to be true—you will be most comfortable in a course taught by an instructor with a teaching style similar to your learning style.

EXERCISE 6.4   Exams and Learning Styles

As a class, select some piece of writing such as a newspaper article or short magazine piece. Read the article. Then divide into groups in which people of similar learning styles are together. Within each group create a short test based on the reading. Reconvene as a class and compare the tests from the various groups. Did the different learning styles of the groups have any influence on the kinds of tests they created?

EXERCISE 6.5   Assessing Your Courses and Instructors

Take some time over the next few days to think about the courses you are taking now. How well does your preferred learning style fit the style reflected in the syllabus, handouts, lectures, and study questions in each of your courses?

Do any of the key sensing words mentioned previously (*define, diagram,* and so on) or some close approximation of them appear? If so, list them and place a check mark next to each of them each time the word appears. Do any of the key intuition words (*describe, compare,* and so on) or similar words appear? List them also and note their frequency. Listen carefully in class. What key words do you hear? Write these down also. Which type of word do you hear most frequently? That will begin to give you some idea of each instructor's learning/teaching style.

INSTRUCTOR/COURSE 1: _____

Sensing Words   **Intuition Words**

_____   _____

_____   _____

_____   _____

_____   _____

_____   _____

_____   _____

Instructor's preferred style: Sensing _____   Intuition _____
Other teaching style observations:

_____

_____

_____

_____

_____

INSTRUCTOR/COURSE 2: _____

Sensing Words	Intuition Words
_____	_____
_____	_____
_____	_____
_____	_____
_____	_____
_____	_____

Instructor's preferred style: Sensing _____   Intuition _____

Other teaching style observations:

_____

_____

_____

_____

_____

INSTRUCTOR/COURSE 3: _____

Sensing Words	Intuition Words
_____	_____
_____	_____
_____	_____
_____	_____
_____	_____

Instructor's preferred style: Sensing _____   Intuition _____

Other teaching style observations:

_____

_____

_____

_____

_____

INSTRUCTOR/COURSE 4: _____

Sensing Words	Intuition Words
_____	_____
_____	_____
_____	_____
_____	_____
_____	_____

Instructor's preferred style: Sensing _____ Intuition _____

Other teaching style observations:

_____

_____

_____

_____

_____

How does your learning style as measured in Exercise 6.2 fit with the learning/teaching style of each instructor? Which courses will require some adjustment on your part? Discuss these problems with other students in class. Keep these problems in mind as you complete the next three chapters, which focus on your study skills.

Are there things your instructors could be doing to help you take advantage of your strengths and learn more efficiently? In class discuss what these ideas are and how you might convey them to the appropriate instructor.

If your instructor's teaching style is compatible with your learning style, then you should be able to perform well simply by keeping up with your work. If your instructor's style is incompatible with yours, you might consider either mastering more factual material or interpreting or analyzing that material in order to be better prepared for exams or papers. In any case a greater awareness of both your learning style *and* your instructor's teaching style can be of real benefit.

A variety of additional tests can help you learn more about your learning style. These are generally available through your college guidance office. A guidance counselor will both administer the test and help you interpret the results. Ask about the following:

► The Myers-Briggs Type Indicator
► The complete Hogan/Champagne Personal Style Indicator
► The Kolb Learning Style Inventory

JOURNAL

What's your learning style? How are you trying to adapt your style to the teaching styles of some of your instructors? Outside class do you tend to associate with people who have learning styles similar to your own or with people whose learning styles are different? Thinking about this may help you uncover some clues about compatibility between you and some of the significant people in your life, in both short-term and long-term relationships.

SUGGESTIONS FOR FURTHER READING

Lawrence, Gordon. *People Types and Tiger Stripes.* Gainesville, Fla.: Center for the Application of Psychological Types, 1982.

Malone, John C., Jr. *Theories of Learning: A Historical Approach.* Belmont, Calif.: Wadsworth, 1991.

Pauk, W. *How to Study in College,* 4th ed. Boston: Houghton Mifflin, 1989.

Perry, William. *Forms of Intellectual and Ethical Development in the College Years: A Scheme.* New York: Holt, Rinehart & Winston, 1970.

CHAPTER 7

Listening and Learning in the Classroom

Kenneth F. Long
University of Windsor

Mary-Jane McCarthy
Middlesex Community College

I'm looking over my notes from psych. "Personalities affecting behaviors . . . something . . . something . . . abnormal." What does that mean? I guess I write too fast. What's this say? "Ask Sarah to go out Friday." That's not psych. These notes are useless. I'd better get them from somebody else.

Should schools abandon the lecture system? Like other skilled performers and communicators, a good lecturer can stimulate many minds, each in its own direction. (Zimbel/ Monkmeyer Press Photo)

Learn to make every minute count. That means not merely *attending* classes but making the most of the time you spend *in* your classes. Participate in the activity of the classroom, taking meaningful, efficient notes that will enhance your ability to understand and recall the material once the class is over.

Lecturing is only one mode of teaching, and for a variety of reasons including the relatively short attention span of many people, it is often not the best. However, to succeed in college, you should know what lecturing entails and how to deal with it. The lecture method is teacher-dominated (they talk, you listen), is information-laden (you take notes and study later), and allows for large amounts of material to be covered quickly. (We almost said "efficiently," but if most students aren't really listening after 15 minutes, it can hardly be called efficient, can it?)

Lectures can seduce you into taking a passive role in the classroom. Some students have a second self, a "stenographer," who tries to write down everything a teacher says. For them a full notebook creates a false sense of security. In reality indiscriminate note-taking wastes a lot of time because it leaves all of the learning for later and invites forgetting. It's not enough to say, "I'll write everything down and worry about what's important later." Improper note-taking encourages intellectual laziness in the classroom and gets in the way of active listening—and learning. Not surprisingly, poor note-taking skills often correlate with poor grades. Look at the students with good grades and you will probably find good note-taking skills, too.

This chapter provides you with a proven system for taking good notes in lectures—one that you can use to prepare for class, get the most out of class, and draw on as you review material for tests.

EXERCISE 7.1   Your Note-Taking IQ

Mark each of the following statements either T (true) or F (false).

_____ 1. If you can't tell what is really important in a lecture, you should write down everything the instructor says.

_____ 2. If an instructor moves through the material very fast, it is better to tape record the lecture and not worry so much about listening in class.

_____ 3. If the instructor puts an outline on the board or on an overhead projector, you should copy it down immediately.

_____ 4. In a class that is mainly discussion, it is best just to listen and talk rather than to take notes.

_____ 5. The best way to take notes is to use a formal outlining system with Roman numerals, letters, and numbers.

The correct answers are given on page 102. Discuss the answers with your instructor or in small groups.

NOTE-TAKING AND FORGETTING

As an undergraduate one of this chapter's authors was dismayed to find himself studying material over and over again, rereading chapters that seemed almost new, laboring over notes that were only a month old. Some years after college he learned something unforgettable about forgetting. He read about an experiment (discussed in Pauk, 1989) involving people who were tested at various intervals after reading a textbook chapter. Researchers discovered that most forgetting takes place in the first 24 hours and then tapers off (see Figure 7.1). Within two weeks almost 70 percent of the material is lost.

Because many instructors draw the bulk of their test items from the content of their lectures, remembering what is presented in the classroom is crucial to doing well on exams. A note-taking system that lessens the forgetting curve of the first 24 hours and organizes the information for later recall can greatly improve your chances for success on exams.

A SOUND APPROACH TO NOTE-TAKING IN LECTURES

Although the lecture system itself may not induce active learning and retention, there are things you can do to make it more efficient. An organized, planned approach to the lecture includes three phases: before, during, and after the lecture. The objectives will be (1) increased on-the-spot learning, (2) longer attention span, (3) better retention, and (4) better notes for later study, particularly at exam time.

Figure 7.1 Learning and Forgetting

Psychologists have studied human forgetting in many laboratory experiments. Here are the "forgetting curves" for three kinds of material: poetry, prose, and nonsense syllables. The curves are basically similar. The shallower curves for prose and poetry indicate that meaningful material is forgotten more slowly than nonmeaningful information. Poetry, which contains internal cues like rhyme and rhythm, is forgotten less quickly than prose.

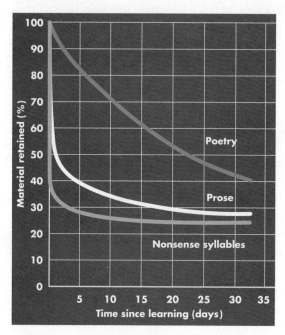

SOURCE: Used with permission from Wayne Weiten, *Psychology: Themes and Variations* (Pacific Grove, Calif.: Brooks/Cole, 1989, p. 254. Based on data from D. van Guilford, Van Nostrand, 1939).

Before the Lecture: Reading and Warming Up

If a lecture is a demanding intellectual encounter, then you need to be ready intellectually. You wouldn't go in cold to give a speech, interview for a job, plead your case in court, or compete in sports. For each of these situations you would prepare in some way and set out with attention focused. So always prepare for class, especially when you are not asked, apparently, to do anything more than listen and take notes. Active listening, learning, and remembering begin *before* the lecture.

1. Do the Assigned Reading. Many students blame lecturers for seeming disorganized or confusing, when in fact the student has not done the reading that the lecture required. Some instructors explicitly assign readings for each class session and refer frequently to readings; others will simply hand out a syllabus and assume you are keeping up. Either way, doing the assigned readings helps you to listen well, and active listening in turn promotes good reading. So keep up with your reading and most lectures will come alive—that is, the lectures will answer questions you may have had as

ANSWERS (to Exercise 7.1): All the statements are false.

You'll get more out of a lecture if you prepare ahead of time. Stay abreast of the readings. Get your own ideas flowing by reviewing notes from the previous lecture. What questions were left unanswered? Where should today's session begin? (Photo by David Gonzales)

you read. If you go into a lecture without having done the reading, the material will be unfamiliar and perhaps overwhelming.

2. Warm Up for Class. If you have read well and taken good notes, this should be quite easy. Warm up by quickly referring to the underlinings in your readings (see Chapter 8) and/or to the recall columns in your previous class notes. This gets you ready to pay attention, understand, and remember.

During the Lecture: Taking the Right Kind of Notes

Now that you're ready for class, you need to develop your listening and note-taking skills.

1. Identify the Main Ideas. Good lecturers always present certain key points in their lectures. The first principle of effective note-taking is to identify and write down the four or five most important ideas that the lecture is built around. Although some supporting details may be important as well, your note-taking focus should be on the main ideas. These may be buried in detail, statistics, anecdotes, or problems to solve, but you need to locate and record them for later study.

As you listen, keep these two frames of thinking in mind: general material (main idea) and specific information (supporting details). Every good lecturer is trying to express one or several main ideas. This is your general frame of reference. For example, in a psychology lecture on learning curves, you would likely formulate a main idea statement like the following: "There are three learning curves presented in this study." Then you would be alert for the specifics that would explain this general statement: "prose, poetry, and nonsense syllables."

Lecturers sometimes announce the purpose or offer an outline, thus providing you with the skeleton of main ideas and details. Some change their tone of voice or repeat themselves at each key idea. Some ask questions or promote discussion. These are all clues to what is important. Ask yourself, "What does my instructor want me to know at the end of today's session?"

A good lecture is an exploration. As part of the expedition, think critically about the direction of a teacher's thought. Try to predict where the lecture is heading and why. What are the major landmarks and key ideas along the way? (© 1992, Chuck Savage/photo courtesy of Beloit College)

Certainly not everything needs to be written down. Because of insecurity or inexperience, some first-year students try to write everything down—they stop being a thinker and let the stenographer take over. Don't fall into this trap. Be an *active listener,* always searching for main ideas and for the connections among them—those general assertions that must be supported by specific comments. After a week's practice, as you get to know your instructors, you will have better, and *shorter,* notes.

Unfortunately some of your instructors may teach in a manner that makes it difficult to take good notes. You can still use the same techniques, however, to organize the lectures for your own use. Even though some of your instructors may not teach as you would like them to, you are ultimately responsible for making sense of what they said.

When a lecture is disorganized, you must strive to organize what is being said into general and specific frameworks; and when this order is not apparent, you need to take notes on where the gaps in the lecture's organization lie. After the lecture you may need to consult your reading material or your classmates in order to try to fill in these gaps.

2. Leave Space for a Recall Column. In addition to helping you listen well, notes provide an important study device for tests and exams. This is the second principle of effective note-taking. In anticipation of this, treat each page of your notes as part of an exam-taking system.

On each page of notepaper draw a vertical line to divide the page into two columns (see Figure 7.2). (Looseleaf is a good choice, but write on one side only.) The column on the left, about 2½ inches wide, is called the "recall column" and remains blank while you take notes during class in the column on the right. The momentarily blank recall column, you will discover, is an incredibly powerful study device that reduces forgetting, helps you warm up for class, and promotes understanding in class. It also lets you review efficiently right after class. This recall column is essentially the place where you can sift through your note material to determine main ideas and important details.

Figure 7.2 Sample Page for Note-Taking

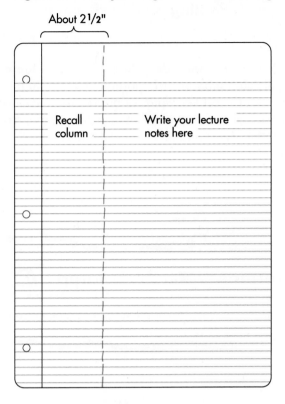

About 2½"

Recall column | Write your lecture notes here

EXERCISE 7.2

Determining Main Ideas and Major Details

Divide a piece of paper as shown in Figure 7.2. Read the following excerpt from a psychology lecture on memory, and take notes on only the right side of the paper, leaving the recall column blank. Using any system you are comfortable with, identify the main idea and supporting details. Then discuss your notes with your classmates and instructor. How many main ideas did you note? Which specific details and examples seemed important?

Today we will continue our discussion of memory and treat the idea of distributed practice—an important aspect of memory. This is the practice of learning a little bit at a time, as opposed to a lot at a time. Cramming for a test is an example of the opposite kind of practice known as massed practice. Distributed practice is what you need to develop as you study for your classes.

Further, what you learn tends to be remembered easily if you can attach it to similar knowledge. This is the third term I want to discuss today—the depth-of-processing principle. That is, information is stored in the brain on various levels. If it is stored superficially, the material cannot attach itself to rich associations. If it is stored deeply, the knowledge finds a series of associations to attach itself to. Storing material deeply allows for retention of it, while, as you would guess, storing superficially tends to lead to forgetting.

After the Lecture: Filling in the Recall Column, Reciting, and Reviewing

After class you still have some important work to do to combat forgetting.

1. Write the Main Ideas in the Recall Column. This is where the blank recall column becomes important. For 5 or 10 minutes quickly review your notes and select key words or phrases (or make up some) that will act as labels or tags for main ideas and key information covered in the notes. Highlight the main ideas, and write them in the recall column beside the material they represent.

EXERCISE 7.3   Creating a Recall Column

Create a recall column for the notes you took in Exercise 7.2.

2. Use the Recall Column to Recite Your Notes. Now cover the notes on the right and use the tags in the recall column to help you recite out loud a brief version of what you understand from the class you have just participated in. If you do not have 5 or 10 minutes after class to review your notes, find some time during the day to review what you have written. You might also want to ask your instructor to glance at your recall column to see if you have noted the main ideas.

3. Review the Previous Day's Notes Before the Next Class Session. As you sit in class the following day waiting for the lecture to begin, use the time to review quickly the notes from the previous day. This will put you in tune with the lecture that is about to begin and will also prompt you to ask questions about material from the previous lecture that may not have been clear to you. These "engagements" with the material will pay off later, when you begin to study for your exam.

Why Is This Process So Powerful? The key to this system is the fact that you are encountering the same material in three different ways: (1) active listening and writing, (2) reading and summarizing in the recall column, and finally (3) saying aloud what you understand from class. Your whole person—mind and body—is involved. All of these actions promote learning.

Recitation is a particularly effective guard against forgetting. The very act of verbalizing concepts gives your memory sufficient time to grasp them. That is, you move material from short-term memory to long-term memory, where you can call upon it as needed. Strictly speaking, we never really forget anything; we just lose control of it somewhere in our minds. Having a good memory really means having an organized method of capturing and recalling whatever our mind encounters, and recitation bolsters this practice.*

Now you may object, "I have three classes in a row and no time for recall columns or recitation between them. What can I do?" Well, recall and recite as soon after class as possible. In the case of successive classes review the most recent class first. Never delay recall and recitation longer than one day because by then you will have forgotten too much material. It will take you much longer to review, make a recall column, and recite. With practice you can fill in recall columns in 5 or 10 minutes when material is still fresh. Recitation need only take a few more minutes. Done faithfully, these two activities are great aids to understanding and remembering.

EXERCISE 7.4   Creating and Using a Recall Column

A. Suppose the information in this chapter had been presented to you as a lecture rather than a reading. Using the system described previously, your lecture notes might look like those in Figure 7.3. Now create a recall column that includes the main ideas for these chapter notes. Discuss your recall notes with your classmates and instructor.

B. Look over the sample notes. Then cover the right-hand column. Using the recall column, try reciting in your own words the main ideas from this chapter. Uncover the right-hand column when you need to refer to it. If you can phrase the main ideas from the recall column in your own words, you are well on your way to mastering this note-taking system for dealing with lectures. Share your results with your classmates and instructor. Does this system seem to work? If not, why not?

EXERCISE 7.5   Comparing Notes

Pair up with another student and compare your class notes for your study skills class. Are your notes clear? Do you agree on what is important? Take a few minutes to explain to each other your note-taking system. Agree to use a recall column during the next class. Afterward share notes again and take turns reciting what you learned to each other.

*In addition to recitation's power to combat forgetting, it also has value in preparation for the actual writing of a test or exam. (See Chapter 9.)

Figure 7.3 Sample Lecture Notes

Sept. 21 *How to take notes*	
Problems with lectures	Lecture *not* best way to teach. Problems: Short attention span (may be only 15 minutes!). Teacher dominates. Most info is forgotten. "Stenographer" role interferes with thinking, understanding, learning.
Forgetting curves	Forgetting curves critical period: over $\frac{1}{2}$ of lecture forgotten in 24 hours.
Solution: Active listening	Answer: Active listening, really understanding during lecture. Aims— (1) immediate understanding (2) longer attention (3) better retention (4) notes for study later
Before: Read Warm up	BEFORE: Always prepare. Read: Readings parallel lectures & make them meaningful. Warm up: Review last lecture notes & readings right before class.
During: main ideas	DURING: Write main ideas & some detail. No steno. What clues does prof. give about what's most important? Ask. Ask other questions. Leave blank column about $2\frac{1}{2}$" on left of page. Use only front side of paper.
After: Review Recall Recite	AFTER: Left column for key recall words, "tags." Cover right side & recite what tags mean. Review / Recall / Recite

LEARNING: A COMPLEMENTARY PROCESS

Now that you know what to do to make the lecture system work as well as possible on your end, let's examine four things your professors can do to make their lectures clearer and to help you listen actively. Ideally, where feasible, your professors will follow these practices. Whether they do these things or not, remember the things you can do to maximize your learning:

1. **They:** Always refer specifically to any reading that relates to a forthcoming lecture; pose specific questions in advance to help you read well.
   You: Always read in preparation for class.

2. **They:** Always begin with an outline and/or a statement of purpose that helps you know what is important.
   You: Always search for important ideas.

3. **They:** Plan pauses in every lecture at 10- to 15-minute intervals for questions, illustrations, and learning activities; this helps rein in wandering minds.
   You: Use active listening and note-taking activities to keep your attention level high.

4. **They:** Stop lecturing with 5 or 10 minutes left in class to let you make recall columns, recite, or discuss for better retention and understanding.
   You: Review, recall, and recite as soon after class as possible, and review again just prior to the next class.

Following the "before/during/after" system will maximize learning even when the teaching is not ideal. If you use this three-phase method for each day's classes, you will be actively learning on a daily basis and preparing for effective study later.

TAKING NOTES IN NONLECTURE COURSES

Of course you must be flexible in how you apply the system. When you encounter other, nonlecture styles (question-answer sessions, group discussions, workshops, seminars, and so on), always be ready to adapt your note-taking methods. In fact, group discussion is becoming a popular way to structure college learning, often replacing the traditional lecture format. In these discussion groups you must still keep in mind the two basic types of information—general and specific.

Assume, for example, that you are taking notes in a problem-solving roundtable of four classmates. You would begin your notes by asking yourself, "What is the problem?" As the roundtable progresses you would list the views or solutions offered. These would be the main ideas. The major details would include the pros and cons of each view.

The important thing to remember when taking notes in nonlecture classes is that you need to record the information presented by your classmates as well as that of the instructor. You must be sure to consider all reasonable ideas, even those that may be different from your own.

Suppose you are taking notes on a class discussion concerning a controversial subject such as euthanasia (mercy killing). You would begin your notes by stating the aspect of the issue being addressed. For example, the class might be focusing on whether mercy killing is moral or whether mercy killing should be limited in a particular way. Your notes would then be divided into arguments "for" and arguments "against." The details would include the reasons given to support each argument. It is important that you record *all* reasonable arguments, even if you do not agree with them, because your instructor may ask you to defend your own opinion in light of the others.

EXERCISE 7.6

Applying an Active Listening and Learning System

Examine the study schedule on page 69 in Chapter 5, and then answer the following questions:

1. Where do you see evidence of plans to use the recall column?

   _____

   _____

   _____

2. What problems will the student have in performing review/recall/recite as soon after class as possible?

   _____

   _____

   _____

3. How can these problems be solved?

   _____

   _____

   _____

Share your answers with other students in a small group.

JOURNAL

Compare and contrast your present style of lecture note-taking with the approach suggested in this chapter. Consider a course in which you are experiencing difficulty taking what you consider satisfactory notes. List what you consider to be the "problems" you are encountering. How might the approach offered in this chapter help? Which particular strategies do you need to implement immediately?

SUGGESTIONS FOR FURTHER READING

Pauk, Walter. *How to Study in College,* 4th ed. Boston: Houghton Mifflin, 1989. See Chapter 5, "Forgetting and Remembering."

Sotiriou, Peter Elias. *Integrating College Study Skills: Reasoning in Reading, Listening, and Writing,* 3rd ed. Belmont, Calif.: Wadsworth, 1993. See Part 3, "Taking Lecture and Study Notes."

A Sound Approach to Textbooks

CHAPTER

8

Kenneth F. Long
University of Windsor

Mary-Jane McCarthy
Middlesex Community College

I've read this paragraph five times and I still don't understand it. How am I supposed to be ready to discuss this chapter tomorrow when I can't even get through the first page? There's gotta be a better way. Can't someone just drill a hole in my head and pour it in?

What typically happens when you start to read those four chapters assigned for class two days away? At 7:00 P.M. you intend to start reading, but first you visit the bathroom (5 minutes), make a quick call to a friend (6 minutes), go get an apple (4 minutes), and then sit down to read, but only after clearing your desk, sharpening pencils, and arranging some notes (5 minutes). It is almost 7:30 and you haven't read a word yet! Then you start and quickly tune out. You continue to read, but your mind is wandering. Each time you catch yourself drifting off, you have to flip back a page or two to find where to start reading again.

This situation reflects two common problems students encounter when reading: procrastination and short attention span. The result is not only unfinished work but a feeling that reading for study is something they *cannot* do. When this happens over and over, it's no wonder students come to dislike reading. No one likes repeatedly having to do what they don't do well.

Reading a textbook is tough work, and you almost certainly need to improve at it. Studies have shown that if you are a typical first-year student, your attention span for college material is only about 5 minutes. That's not long enough! You need to be able to focus on your reading for at least 15 minutes at a stretch for immediate academic survival—and even more as you progress.

Where to begin? Perhaps we should start by considering how reading for study differs from reading for pleasure. Reading a newspaper or favorite magazine for news or entertainment is generally easy because it's relaxing, and relaxing because it's easy. In your own mind, and in the writer's, what you actually learn from the newspaper or magazine is often of secondary importance. Similarly most novels are frankly devoted to providing pleasure and entertainment, appealing not only to the intellect but to the imagination and emotions. Certain themes are ever popular—power, sex, and adventure. In short the best-selling novel is written with you, the reader, in mind, and its ultimate message is "Relax, enjoy."

The well-written textbook is also crafted with you in mind, but its appeal is almost purely to the intellect, and its message is "Wake up!" This is why it's so demanding, and also why your professor has assigned it. If you are going to learn from your academic reading, you must assume a great deal of responsibility, just as you must take responsibility as an active listener in the classroom.

Don't despair. You can learn how to take advantage of procrastination, dramatically lengthen your attention span, and hence improve your reading skill. If you apply a system like the one suggested for dealing with lectures in Chapter 7, it can become (and must become) a very manageable task.

It's a lot like jogging. At first you may not be able to run a mile. However, with planning and perseverance, a mile soon becomes only a warmup, and running, which was once boring and frustrating, becomes enjoyable and exhilarating. This chapter tells you how to get the most out of your textbooks—and how to enjoy doing so.

EXERCISE 8.1   What's Your Current Reading Attention Span?

Select a textbook from one of your courses. Begin reading a portion of it, timing yourself with a clock or stopwatch. Determine your attention span (the number of minutes you read before your mind begins to wander) and the number of words read. Don't prepare to read by skimming or using other techniques; just read. Try this activity three separate times for the same chapter. Report your scores here:

Attention span (minutes): 1. _____ 2. _____ 3. _____

Total number of words: 1. _____ 2. _____ 3. _____

We'll be referring back to these figures shortly.

A PLAN FOR READING TEXTBOOKS

The following planned approach to reading will increase your reading speed, promote understanding, and facilitate study for tests and exams. This system is based on two basic principles, each embodied in specific activities: (1) planning before reading and (2) marking, reviewing, and reciting.

Planning and Reading

Planning to read is an undemanding but important activity that can fit nicely into your procrastination time. The purpose is to create "advance organizers" in your mind by quickly surveying the pages to be read and looking for headings or key words or sentences that suggest what the reading is about. Sometimes chapters conclude with lists of main points, summary paragraphs, or questions. These are particularly useful in creating advance organizers, so read them as part of your planning. Creating advance organizers is similar to getting an overview of a trip by glancing at a map before you leave to get a general idea of your ultimate destination and to highlight route markers along the way.

If your instructor specifically mentions connections between readings and classroom instruction, reconsider these clues before you read. Use any or all of this to warm up your mind and create a general plan for reading. Ask yourself questions like "Why am I reading this?" and "What do I want to know?"

EXERCISE 8.2   Creating Advance Organizers

Quickly survey the rest of this chapter by reading each heading and phrase in bold print. Then answer these questions:

1. How many pages does this chapter have? _____

2. What are the five major topics or skills covered?

     a. _____

     b. _____

     c. _____

     d. _____

     e. _____

1. Measure the Reading Assignment. Measure the assignment and divide it up according to your own attention span and reading speed. Recall that a first-year student's attention span for reading textbooks is typically as short as 5 minutes, at a rate of far less than one page per minute. So let's say you can read about one or two pages in 5 minutes. You can either accept the reality of your current rate and plan accordingly, or you can deny it and take your chances. If you choose the latter course, most likely your mind will soon be wandering, and more time will be wasted. Accept your current attention span as measured in Exercise 8.1. Measure the assignment, warm up with some planning activities, and then read.

2. Read a Specific Amount in a Short Period, and Know What You Have Read. Try to read a page or two in 5 minutes, increasing the rate as you become more comfortable with the system. An effective warmup alone will lengthen your attention span and boost your reading speed. Practice will increase them even further. Some students report a doubling of capacity very quickly. Surprisingly, faster reading speed can also aid concentration and comprehension. Soon you should be able to divide a fifteen-page textbook reading assignment into four intense sessions of 10 minutes each.

EXERCISE 8.3   **Planned Reading**

A. Take up the same textbook you used in Exercise 8.1. Read the next portion of the chapter, timing yourself with a clock or stopwatch. This time, before you read, survey the chapter for advance organizers. Again, read until your attention begins to wander, and then record the results below.

    Attention span (minutes): _____

    Total number of words: _____

How do these scores compare with the scores in Exercise 8.1? How much improvement was there?

B. Now read another portion of the same text. Before reading, measure out the number of pages you should be able to read attentively and increase the amount slightly. Repeat this process one more time.

    Were you able to sustain attention for the measured pages? Discuss the results of this exercise with your classmates and instructor.

Marking, Reviewing, and Reciting

The more actively you participate in the reading process, the more readily you will comprehend and retain the material. Therefore during your intense reading sessions use the following procedures.

1. Use Your Pencil as You Read. During the actual reading underline, circle, or draw arrows to important material and/or write notes in the margin. This is a part of active reading. Use your markings to point out key ideas and connections. Doing this will force you to concentrate as you seek out important ideas and supporting details. See how main ideas and supporting details inform what you read.

    Don't be afraid to mark up your textbooks. Sure, they cost a lot, but it's a foolish economy to keep them clean and neat for resale. If you read a chapter one week without marking it, you'll find you've all but forgotten it a few weeks later. At test time you'll have to reread that unmarked text as though it were brand-new. The only alternative to marking is taking notes, but that is quite time-consuming. Read well, mark well, and transform your text on a regular basis into a study device that facilitates review.

Write as you read. Taking notes on your reading helps you focus on the key ideas and summarize as you go. You take in and digest the material rather than skim it. (Tom Jorgenson/ photo courtesy of The University of Iowa)

The sample pages in Figure 8.1 discuss some ideas about improving memory. See how the reader marked the pages with underlinings and marginalia. Note that the underlining is selective and that much material is passed over. This shows that the reader consciously searched for what was important—the main ideas of the excerpt and the key supporting details. Note also that the marginalia state connections between important ideas. What the reader has done here is analogous to what you did in Chapter 7 when you divided your lecture note page into columns and used the recall columns to recite. Here the marginalia serve as the recall column while the underlined text provides supporting detail. The reader has created a means to review the text quickly and efficiently before an examination. When your reading results in pages like these, that will be proof that you have read well the first time.

EXERCISE 8.4   The Well-Marked Page

Photocopy Figure 8.2, which shows the next two pages of the book reproduced (and marked) in Figure 8.1. Then read and mark the two pages using your own underlinings and marginalia.

Compare your underlinings with those of your classmates. Are you picking out the main ideas? Are you noting connections? Should you be underlining less or more for effective later review? Pointed, serious discussion with willing, equally serious partners is a great way to practice using a well-marked-up textbook. It lightens the workload, too.

Figure 8.1 Sample Marked Pages

IMPROVEMENT, LOSS, AND DISTORTION OF MEMORY

How improve memory?

How can we improve memory?
Why do we sometimes forget?
Why do we sometimes think we remember some-
thing, when in fact we are wrong?

At one point while I was doing the research for
this book, I went to find an article that I remembered reading, which I thought would very nicely
illustrate a particular point I wanted to make. I was
pretty sure I remembered the name of the author, the name of
the journal, and the date of the article within a year.
So I was certain it would not take me long to find
the article.

About four hours later I finally located it. I was
right about the author, but I was wrong about the
journal and the year. Worst of all, I discovered that
the results the article reported were quite different
from what I remembered. (The way I *remembered*
the results made a lot more sense than the *actual*
results!)

Why does my memory—and probably yours as
well—make mistakes like this? And is there any
way to improve memory?

IMPROVING MEMORY BY IMPROVING LEARNING

"I'm sorry. I don't remember your name. I just don't
have a good memory for names." "I went to class
regularly and did all the reading, but I couldn't
remember all those facts when it came time for the
test."

When people cannot remember names or facts,
the reason is generally that they did not learn them
very well in the first place. To improve your ability

to remember something, be very careful about how
you learn it.

Distribution of Practice

Distribution — over time

You want to memorize a part for a play. Should you
sit down and study your lines in one long marathon
session until you know them? Or should you spread
your study sessions over several days? Research
indicates that **distributed practice**—that is, a little
at a time over many days—is generally better than
massed practice, the same number of repetitions
over a short time. One reason is that it is hard to
maintain full attention when you repeat the same
thing over and over at one sitting. Another is that
studying something at different times links it to a
wider variety of associations.

Depth of Processing

Depth — associations

Once again, how well you will remember something depends on how well you understood it when

"Alas! poor Yorick. I knew him, Horatio." Hamlet delivers some two
dozen soliloquies (solo speeches) of hundreds of words each. (In
comparison, the Gettysburg Address is 266 words.) Actors generally
use distribution of practice to learn their parts, memorizing a little
daily over weeks. They also associate their lines with emotional
motivations, physical movements, cues from other actors, and their
own memories to help them remember.

IMPROVEMENT, LOSS, AND DISTORTION OF MEMORY   295

SOURCE: Pages reproduced with permission from James W. Kalat, *Introduction to Psychology,* 2nd
ed. (Belmont, Calif.: Wadsworth, 1990).

Figure 8.1 (*continued*)

you learned it and how much you thought about it at the time. According to the **depth-of-processing principle** (Craik & Lockhart, 1972), information may be stored at various levels, either superficially or deeply, depending on the number and type of associations formed with it.

[margin note: Repetitions –shallow]

At the most superficial level, a person merely focuses on the words and how they sound. If you try to memorize a list by simply repeating it over and over, you may recognize it when you see or hear it again, but you may have trouble recalling it (Greene, 1987). Actors and public speakers who have to memorize lengthy passages soon discover that mere repetition is an inefficient method.

[margin note: Associations]

A more efficient way to memorize is to deal actively with the material and to form associations with it. For example, you read a list of 20 words. At a slightly deeper level of processing than mere repetition, you might count the number of letters in each word, think of a rhyming word, or note whether the word contains the letter *e*. Such activities require a more active involvement on your part and establish more connections among the words on the list and other items in your experience. At a still deeper level of processing, you might consider the meaning of each word and try to think of a synonym for it. According to this theory (and according to many experimental results), the deeper the level of processing, the more you will remember. *(How can you use this principle to develop good study habits?)*

[margin note: Deeper associations → meaning]

The depth-of-processing principle resembles what happens when a librarian files a new book in the library. Simply to place the book somewhere on the shelves without recording its location would be a very low level of processing, and the librarian's chances of ever finding it again would be slight. So the librarian fills out file cards for the book and puts them into the card catalog. To fill out just a title card for the book would be an intermediate level of processing. To fill out several cards—one for title, one for author, and one or more for subject matter—would be a deeper level of processing. Someone who came to the library later looking for that book would have an excellent chance of finding it. Similarly, when you are trying to memorize something, the more "cards" you fill out (that is, the more ways you link it to other information), the greater your chances of finding the memory when you want it.

[margin note: Association like multiple listings]

You can improve your memorization of a list by attending to two types of processing that are largely independent of each other (Einstein & Hunt, 1980; McDaniel, Einstein, & Lollis, 1988). First, you can go through the list thinking about how much you like or dislike each item or trying to recall the

[margin note: Remembering lists: two types of processing ① Each item]

last time you had a personal experience with it. That will enhance your processing of *individual items.* Second, you can go through the list and look for relationships among the items. That will enhance your processing of the *organization* of the list. You might notice, for example, that the list you are trying to memorize consists of five animals, six foods, four methods of transportation, and five objects made of wood. Even sorting items into such simple categories as "words that apply to me" and "words that do not apply to me" will enhance your sense of how the list is organized and therefore your ability to recall it (Klein & Kihlstrom, 1986).

*[margin note: ② Relation- ships *organ- ization]*

Concept Check

4. Here are two arrangements of the same words:
a. Be a room age to the attend hall will over party across be there 18 you after wild in the class must.
b. There will be a wild party in the room across the hall after class; you must be over age 18 to attend. Why is it easier to remember b than a—because of processing of individual items or because of processing of organization? (Check your answer on page 312.)

Self-Monitoring of Reading Comprehension

What is the difference between good readers (those who remember what they read) and poor readers (those who do not)? One difference is that good readers process what they read more deeply. But how do readers know when they have processed deeply enough? How do they know whether they need to slow down and read more carefully?

Good readers monitor their own reading comprehension; that is, they keep track of whether or not they understand what they are reading. Occasionally in reading, you come across a sentence that is complicated, confusing, or just badly written. Here is an example from the student newspaper at North Carolina State University:

[margin note: Keep track of under- standing]

He said Harris told him she and Brothers told French that grades had been changed.

What do you do when you come across a sentence like that? If you are monitoring your own understanding, you notice that you are confused. Good readers generally stop and reread the confusing sentence or, if necessary, the whole paragraph. As a result, they improve their understanding and their ability to remember the material. When poor readers come to something they do not understand, they generally just keep on reading. Either they do not notice their lack of understanding or they do not care.

296   CHAPTER 8: MEMORY

Figure 8.2 Sample Unmarked Pages

The same is true for whole sections of a book. A student who is studying a textbook should read quickly when he or she understands a section well but should slow down when the text is more complicated. To do so, the student has to monitor his or her own understanding. Above-average students can generally identify which sections they understand best; they single out the sections they need to reread. Below-average students have more trouble picking out which sections they understand well and which ones they understand poorly (Maki & Berry, 1984).

Actually, most people—including bright college students who get good grades—could improve their comprehension through better self-monitoring (Glenberg, Sanocki, Epstein, & Morris, 1987; Zabrucky, Moore, & Schultz, 1987). Many educators recommend that a reader pause at regular intervals to check his or her understanding. The Concept Checks in this text are intended to encourage you to pause and check your understanding from time to time.

A self-monitoring system you can use with any text is the SQ3R method: Survey, Question, Read, Recite, and Review.

- *Survey.* Read the outline of a new chapter and skim through the chapter itself to get a feeling for what the chapter covers. (Skimming a mystery novel would ruin the suspense. Textbooks, however, are not meant to create suspense.)

- *Question.* Write a list of what you expect to learn from the chapter. You might include the review questions in the chapter, questions from the Study Guide, or questions of your own.

- *Read.* Study the text carefully, take brief notes, and stop to think about key points. (The more you stop and think, the more retrieval cues you form.)

- *Recite.* Reciting does not mean simply repeating without thinking. It means producing correct answers. Use what you have read to answer the questions you listed.

- *Review.* Read the chapter summary, skim through the chapter again, and look over your notes.

A similar system is the SPAR method: Survey, Process meaningfully, Ask questions, and Review and test yourself. Both SQ3R and SPAR rest on the principle that readers should pause periodically to check their understanding. Start with an overview of what a passage is about, read it, and then see whether you can answer questions about the passage or explain it to others. If not, go back and reread.

Encoding Specificity

A new book titled *Brain Mechanisms in Mental Retardation* arrives in the library. The librarian places it on the appropriate shelf and fills out three cards for the card catalog: one for the author, one for the title, and one for the subject, *mental retardation.* I happen to read a section in this book on the physiological basis of learning. Three years later I want to find the book again, but I cannot remember the author or title. I go to the card catalog and look under the subject headings *physiology* and *learning.* But the book I want is not listed. Why not? Simply because the librarian filed the book under a different heading. Unless I use the same subject heading the librarian used, I cannot find the book. (Had the librarian filled out several subject cards instead of just one, I would have had a better chance of finding it.)

A similar principle applies to human memory. (Note that I say *similar.* Your brain does not actually store each memory in a separate place, as a librarian stores books.) When you store a memory, you attach to it certain retrieval cues, like file cards. These retrieval cues are the associations you use both when you store a memory and when you try to recall it. Depending on your depth of processing, you may set up many retrieval cues or only one or two. No matter how many cues you set up, however, it helps if you use those same cues when you try to find the memory again.

The **encoding specificity principle** states that your memory will be more reliable if you use the same cue when you try to retrieve a memory as you used when you stored it (Tulving & Thomson, 1973). Although cues that were not present when you stored the memory may help somewhat to evoke the memory (Newman et al., 1982), they are less effective than cues that were present at the time of storage.

Here is an example of encoding specificity (modified from Thieman, 1984). First, read the list of paired associates in Table 8.3. Then turn to Table 8.5 on page 301. For each of the words on the list there, try to recall a related word on the list you just read. *Do this now.*

The answers are on page 313, answer C. Most people find this task difficult and make only a few of the correct pairings. Because they initially coded the word *cardinal* as a type of clergyman, for example, the retrieval cue *bird* does not remind them of the word *cardinal.* The cue *bird* is effective only if

SOURCE: Pages reproduced with permission from James W. Kalat, *Introduction to Psychology,* 2nd ed. (Belmont, Calif.: Wadsworth, 1990).

Figure 8.2 (*continued*)

cardinal is somehow associated with that cue at the time of storage. In short, you can improve your memory by storing information in terms of retrieval cues and by using the same retrieval cues when you try to recall the information.

Encoding Specificity: Context-Dependent and State-Dependent Memory

Almost anything that happens during an experience may serve as a retrieval cue for that memory. The environment at the time is likely to be associated with the experience and thus to become a retrieval cue. It may then be easier to remember the event in the same environment than in some other environment—an instance of **context-dependent memory**. For example, Duncan Godden and Alan Baddeley (1975) found that divers who learn a word list while 4.5 meters underwater remember the list much better when they are tested at the same depth underwater than when they are tested on the beach.

One's physiological condition at the time can also serve as a potent retrieval cue. A **state-dependent memory** is a memory that is easier to recall if a person is in the same physiological state he or she was in when the event occurred. Someone who has an experience while under the influence of alcohol, nicotine, or some other drug will remember that event more easily when under the influence of the same drug again (Lowe, 1986; Warburton, Wesnes, Shergold, & James, 1986).

All sorts of influence may lead to state-dependent memories. For example, the physiological condition of your body is different at different times of day. Other things being equal, your memory is slightly better when you try to recall an event at the same time of day at which it occurred (Infurna, 1981). (You may have noticed that when you wake up in the morning you sometimes start to think about the same thing you were thinking about the morning before.)

A person's mood may also contribute to state-dependent memory, although the evidence for mood-dependent memory is weak. Evidence is stronger for a related phenomenon: When someone is happy, he or she is more likely to think of happy events and words associated with happiness; a person who is sad is more likely to think of unhappy events and words associated with sadness (Blaney, 1986).

When you are trying to recall an event that happened first thing in the morning or when you were sick or when you were in some other distinct physiological state, trying to reconstruct how you felt at the time may strengthen your memory by opening up your access to state-dependent memories.

Mnemonic Devices

When you know that you will have to remember certain information at a future time—such as tasks you must tend to on Thursday or items you need to buy at the grocery store—what can you do to make sure you will remember?

One strategy is to repeat the list over and over again. That is the way Ebbinghaus memorized his lists of nonsense syllables. It may work fairly well for you, though you will probably forget at least part of the list.

A better strategy is to write out the list. Unless you lose the list, you need not worry about forgetting any of the items. Even if you do lose the list, you are likely to remember more items than if you had never written it out (Intons-Peterson & Fournier, 1986). (This is one reason it pays to take notes during a lecture.)

But what if you have no pencil and paper handy? Someone says, "Quick, we need supplies for the party. Go to the store and bring back ginger ale, ice, cups, instant coffee, napkins, hot dogs, paper plates, and nacho chips." One way to remember is to take the initials of those items—GICINHPN—and rearrange them into the word PINCHING. Now you just have to remember PINCHING and each letter will remind you of one item you need to get.

Any memory aid that is based on encoding each item in some special way is known as a **mnemonic device**; the word *mnemonic* ("nee-MAHN-ik") comes

How to Read Fifteen Pages of Textbook in Less Than an Hour

It takes practice—but it can be done!

Pages 1–3	Read and mark	10 minutes
	Review and recite	2 minutes
Pages 4–7	Read and mark	10 minutes
	Review and recite	2 minutes
Pages 8–12	Read and mark	10 minutes
	Review and recite	2 minutes
Pages 13–15	Read and mark	10 minutes
	Review and recite	2 minutes

Review and recite for all fifteen pages. Answer aloud the questions "What did I learn? How does it relate to the course?"   8 minutes

Total   56 minutes

Done. Take a break—you've earned it!

2. Review and Recite. At the end of each 10 minutes of reading, use the markings to review and recite what you have learned. The same recitation technique that works for lecture notes will also work for reading. It will keep your concentration level high through a long assignment. Review and recitation for three or four pages should take only 2 or 3 minutes. For the fifteen-page assignment you should spend about 40 minutes actually reading (and marking) and about 8 minutes reviewing, for a total of 48 minutes.

Add 8 minutes for final review and recitation of the total assignment, reconnecting it to the purpose you established in your original warmup. Finish by answering aloud the questions "What did I learn, and how does it fit into the course?" You now have completed 56 minutes of highly concentrated reading—a demanding, rigorous, and rewarding intellectual exercise.

Not even most professors read textbook-type material at a high level of understanding for much longer than an hour at a time. It's simply too fatiguing. All good readers punctuate bouts of reading with little pauses, or "breathers" for the mind. By planning these pauses and using them for review, you continually reinforce what you are learning, and you avoid becoming lost and feeling defeated. You develop and maintain a "can do" attitude about reading and about the course itself. Certainly you will be tired at the end of a reading session, so take a break, or study something else.

EXERCISE 8.5   Reviewing and Reciting

Using the sample markings in Figure 8.1 as well as your own markings in Figure 8.2, practice the review and recite process. The four pages should take about 5 minutes—10 minutes if you choose to work with a partner.

MAINTAINING FLEXIBILITY

With effort you can improve your reading dramatically, but remember to be flexible. How you read should depend on the material. Assess the relative importance of assigned readings, and adjust your reading style accordingly. Some material may echo what you've read elsewhere and therefore warrant only quick review. In such cases skip quickly from idea to idea. Connect the whole to another important idea by asking yourself, "Why am I reading this? Where does this fit in?" When textbook reading is virtually identical to lecture material, you can save time by concentrating mainly on one or the other.

Remember that reading serious material with sound understanding and good recall is not something that one becomes adept at overnight. A planned approach, regularly applied, is the surest way to success. So always keep in mind the following rules for textbook reading:

1. Plan to read in your prime study time.
2. Use warmup time to prepare to read.
3. Set a specific number of pages to read within a specific amount of time.
4. Organize your work into short tasks for high concentration.
5. Underline, review, and recite for each section of reading.
6. Review and recite again for the whole reading.
7. Reward yourself.

EXERCISE 8.6   Play It Again, Sam

Did you use a pen or pencil to mark this chapter as you read it? If not, read it again, making notes in the margins and underlining as you go. Share your underlinings and notes with your peers and instructor.

MASTERING THE PRÉCIS

In this chapter we have been looking at techniques for increasing comprehension and recall of important material in your textbooks. Another technique for doing this is writing the précis.

A *précis* ("pray-see") is a written summary of the main ideas in a longer document. Being able to write an accurate précis is a skill that will be valuable to you not only in college and graduate school but also in many lines of work, including business, research, administration, teaching, and journalism.

A précis is particularly useful when you are expected to read a variety of materials on a subject and compare their main points. In college you will be writing such summaries mainly for study purposes. Later you may be writing them to condense and convey information efficiently to a business team leader, a client, or the general public.

A précis must be short. Generally it will include only the main ideas of the document and transitional phrases that show how the main ideas are related. The following describes the process of writing a précis as it might apply to an academic article.

1. **Read the article.** Underline and mark main ideas as you go. Work hard on reading well. Weak reading will result in an inaccurate précis.

2. **Analyze the article.** What is its purpose? Does it set out to *define* a particular concept, *compare* two points of view, or *prove* a certain idea? (See the "key task words" list in Chapter 9, beginning on page 136, for a summary of terms that describe the purpose of most writings.) Mark connections between main ideas. What is the overall main point (thesis) of the article? How well do the various secondary ideas support the main point? Does the article accomplish its purpose? If the writer of the article holds some apparent attitude or bias, what is it?

3. **Select and condense.** Review the material you have underlined and mentally begin to put these ideas into your own words. You may want to number these underlinings now to reflect the order you think you will want to write them in the précis. What other main or connecting ideas does the article contain, apart from those you underlined? Jot some notes on those connections.

4. **Draft.** Begin your draft by writing one statement that states the author's purpose in writing the article and/or the author's main point. Continue with additional sentences that summarize the author's ideas in support of the main point and any other brief statements that will allow you to evaluate how well the author has achieved the purpose of the article.

5. **Rewrite.** Read over the draft. Supply missing transitions and connecting words (*so, but, therefore, because, although,* and so on). Look back over the article to see whether you have left out any main ideas. Make other revisions for completeness, clarity, and brevity. Rewrite the précis so that it will be easy to read the next time you look at it. Head it with the author's name, the title, source, and date of the article, and any other information you will need to locate the original material.

EXERCISE 8.7   Writing a Précis

Using the underlining and margin notes you have made for this chapter, write a précis of this chapter (or some other material) following the directions in the preceding section. Exchange your précis with that of another student and discuss how effectively each précis summarizes the information.

JOURNAL

What do you think of the planned approach to textbook reading in this chapter? Which aspect of the approach is most appealing to you? Which aspect is least appealing? With which aspect were you most successful as you worked through the exercises? Which aspects will you have to work the hardest at? What problems do you foresee in using the entire plan? How might you overcome these problems?

SUGGESTIONS FOR FURTHER READING

Gross, Ronald. "Improving Your Learning, Reading, and Memory Skills." Chapter 6 in *Peak Learning.* Los Angeles: Jeremy R. Tarcher, 1991.

Phillips, Anne Dye, and Peter Elias Sotiriou. *Steps to Reading Proficiency,* 3rd ed. Belmont, Calif.: Wadsworth, 1992.

Smith, Richard Manning. *Mastering Mathematics: How to Be a Great Math Student,* 2nd ed. Belmont, Calif.: Wadsworth, 1994.

Sotiriou, Peter Elias. *Integrating College Study Skills: Reasoning in Reading, Listening, and Writing,* 3rd ed. Belmont, Calif.: Wadsworth, 1993. See Chapters 3–8.

CHAPTER 9

Making the Grade

Kenneth F. Long
University of Windsor

Debora A. Ritter
University of South Carolina

Mary-Jane McCarthy
Middlesex Community College

Three tests in the next two days! I am never going to live through this week. I mean, I did everything they said about how to read and how to take notes. I even studied all the homework I got back. I should be ready, but I'm freaking out. My nails are gone, I can't sleep. Help!

This chapter focuses on preparing for tests and exams. While grades do not necessarily reflect what you really know, they are the common method by which learning is evaluated.

There are two basic types of tests: the essay and the objective. The objective test may take a number of forms such as multiple-choice, true-false, matching, or identification. Each type is quite different in terms of preparation, planning, and execution. By focusing on these differences we can get a good grasp of the study strategies that can apply to all types of exams.

You will benefit most from this chapter if you have already read the preceding chapters on time management, note-taking in the classroom, and textbook reading.

WHAT YOU SHOULD KNOW AND DO BEFOREHAND

The days and hours immediately prior to a test are critical. How much time do you need to prepare? The answer varies, but it is always important to set aside enough time to study for the test and to know how to get the most out of that time. Good communication with your instructor, purposeful notes, well-reviewed texts, exam information, and refined time management all support your best efforts.

EXERCISE 9.1 Test-Taking Inventory

Place a check mark in front of the sentence in each pair that best describes you.

_____ 1a. I always study for essay tests by developing questions and outlines.

_____ 1b. I rarely study for essay tests by developing questions and outlines.

_____ 2a. I always begin studying for an exam at least a week in advance.

_____ 2b. I rarely begin studying for an exam a week in advance.

_____ 3a. I usually study for an exam with at least one other person.

_____ 3b. I rarely study for an exam with another person.

_____ 4a. I usually know what to expect on a test before I go into the exam.

_____ 4b. I rarely know what to expect on a test before I go into the exam.

_____ 5a. I usually finish an exam early or on time.

_____ 5b. I sometimes do not have enough time to finish an exam.

_____ 6a. I usually know that I have done well on an exam when I finish.

_____ 6b. I rarely know whether I have done well on an exam when I finish.

_____ 7a. I usually perform better on essay tests than on objective tests.

_____ 7b. I usually perform better on objective tests than on essay tests.

Now write a brief paragraph about yourself as a test-taker based on your answers to the inventory and your feelings about test-taking in general.

Find Out About the Test

In order to use the right test-taking strategies, find out several days in advance what type of test it will be and what kinds of questions will appear on it. It is at least inefficient, and possibly disastrous in terms of grades, to study for an essay exam when the format is multiple-choice or a mix of styles.

Find out how long the exam will last and how it will be graded. If you don't know, ask your instructor. This information affects your study strategy and your work on the exam itself. For example, suppose a one-hour test will include a short-essay question worth 25 out of a possible 100 points. Knowing that, you should plan to devote about one-quarter of your preparation time to the short essay and to spend about 15 minutes on it during the exam. If you enter the exam without such a plan and find you can answer the short-essay question better than you can the other questions, you may be tempted to spend 25 or 30 minutes on it. The result may be that you "earn" the 25 points several times over but leave too little time for the rest of the test and end up with a lower grade than you deserved based on your knowledge and ability.

Also obtain copies of old test questions if they are available and if your instructor allows it. Some teachers will provide you with sample questions that will help you focus on the central ideas.

Study Throughout the Course

Students who don't study strategically and manage time well throughout the course cannot make the best use of the critical time just prior to an exam. They usually have to complete other assignments and fulfill various other commitments when they should be preparing for a test. The result is overload, panic, and underachievement. Clear, focused study time results only when you see well in advance what other responsibilities will converge with test preparation.

Similarly, if you have not taken an organized approach to classroom learning and to textbook study, you are certain to be discouraged by pages and pages of unsummarized notes and many chapters of unmarked text, all bearing somehow on the test. What can be done? In the case of the textbook, your only recourse is the lengthy process of rereading and marking. And the unsummarized lecture notes, some several months old, will have to be reread, reunderstood, and rememorized.

Fortunately, by employing active daily study skills from the first week of classes, you can take the test under very different conditions. With good time management you can postpone or rearrange "extra" commitments, leaving ample free time for study. You can reduce classroom notes regularly to recall columns and review and recite them in preparation for classes. You can reduce, review, and recite textbook readings in similar fashion.

The result will be a lean body of concepts and information. Regular recitation at the end of study sessions and again as a warmup for class will have secured much of the material in long-term memory. While other students may be dealing with the material as though it were still all brand-new, for you it will be quite familiar. Now you can practice recalling information and refamiliarizing yourself with detail.

Develop a Study Group

Calculus professor Philip Uri Treisman is a prominent figure in the development of collaborative learning strategies to help African-American and Hispanic students succeed academically. In the 1970s he began to question why Chinese students at UC–Berkeley outperformed African-American students in freshman calculus. He discovered that one very important factor was the Chinese students' reliance on study groups. When Treisman proceeded to organize African-American students into groups, they too succeeded at calculus.

Research has indicated that studying in groups can raise your chances of success in other subjects as well, because as you share notes and ideas about your courses with other students, you gain:

- ► Clarification of classroom notes
- ► Different views regarding instructors' goals and objectives
- ► Partners to quiz on the facts, concepts, and so on
- ► The enthusiasm of others to help sustain your own attention to and enthusiasm for the task

Study groups work as follows: The group meets a week or so before the exam and before each of you has studied alone. During that time the group members share notes and ideas. Together you devise a list of potential questions for review. Then each of you spends time studying alone, developing answers, outlines, and mind maps. The group then meets again shortly before the test to share answers and prep one another for the exam.

EXERCISE 9.2   Forming a Study Group

Use the goal-setting process from Chapter 1 to form a study group for at least one of your courses this semester. As you do this, think about your strengths and weaknesses in a learning or studying situation. For instance, do you excel at memorizing facts but find it difficult to comprehend theories? Do you learn best by repeatedly reading the information or by applying the knowledge to a real situation? Do you prefer to learn by processing information in your head or by participating in a "hands-on" demonstration? Make some notes about your learning and studying strengths and weaknesses here.

Strengths: _____

_____

_____

Weaknesses: _____

_____

_____

In a study group how will your strengths help others? What strengths will you look for in others that will help you?

How you can help others: _____

_____

_____

How others can help you: _____

_____

_____

In your first study group session, suggest that each person share his or her strengths and weaknesses and talk about how abilities might be shared for everyone's maximum benefit.

THE ESSAY EXAM

An essay exam requires focused, detailed study on selected topics that you think are likely to appear on the exam. As you prepare for an essay exam, you will want to concentrate mainly on key ideas, the evidence supporting these ideas, and their relationship to other key ideas. Essay exam questions generally focus on such broad questions rather than on details. The grade is generally based in part on how well organized your answer is.

The Basic System for Studying for Essay Exams

First select several pages of notes covering a body of information that you regard as a likely essay topic. Lay your pages of notes on the desk in front of you with each page covering two-thirds of the one before so that only recall columns show. (This is why we recommended in Chapter 7 that you write on only one side of the piece of paper.) Let the recall columns prompt you through a paraphrased recitation of the material at hand. When you get stuck, consult the supporting details to "boost" the recall column and then continue to recite. Work through the text chapters in similar fashion by using your markings to prompt recitation. When you can recite, you can feel confident you know the material. At this point you have little reason for anxiety.

This method of study trains your mind to respond to the test situation. The words in the test questions act like the words in the recall columns to prompt your thought processes and your written answer. This is exactly what you have been practicing all along in looking for and marking important material and reciting. So the essay exam situation is really nothing new. Moreover this system adapts easily to virtually any kind of study that requires review of material.

At this point you can refine the process by organizing the information you have studied into potential questions for the exam. Familiarize yourself with the common task words used in essay questions (see pages 136–138) and determine which would best organize the material you have learned. As you work through the material, create outlines of the answers using the information in your recall columns. Solid understanding is necessary in order to formulate questions, so composing and answering questions increases concentration.

EXERCISE 9.3   Essay Exam Strategies

Working with a partner, use the information already presented in this section to develop and then answer two essay questions dealing with different material in this section or in a previous chapter. Share your questions and responses with your classmates and instructor.

Improving on the System: Super Recall Columns and Mind Maps

You can refine the basic system even further, especially for an exam covering large amounts of material. Let's say you have selected 100 pages of notes and supporting text. Divide these materials into ten more or less equal logical units or questions. As you work through each unit, continue to reduce each ten-page unit to one page, which will take the form of what is called a *super recall column* or *mind map*.

The best way to conceive a super recall column is to imagine that you were allowed to bring one page of notes into the exam with you. What would you put on that page? You would probably want it to contain recall information that surveys the course—a "super" recall column. A mind map is essentially a super recall column with pictorial elements added. Its words and visual patterns provide you with highly charged cues to "jog" your memory. The task of making the super recall column or mind map is itself a form of concentrated study. Practicing responses to the cues in the mind map is like responding to the word cues in the questions on the exam. You may even see exactly the same words on the exam that you have used in your mind maps. Even if they aren't the same, your study method represents an accurate rehearsal of the kind of thinking you'll have to do in the exam.

Figure 9.1 shows what a mind map might look like for Chapter 7, "Listening and Learning in the Classroom." Note the use of lists, arrows, and circles, all powerful aids to memory. When something can be visualized, it is easier to remember, and mind maps are highly visual. Visualizing the mind map during the test will help to release the flow of words you will need to answer the question, as will your previous recitation of the material.

Figure 9.1 Sample Mind Map on Listening and Learning in the Classroom

Family Emergency?
Your Instructor
Needs to Know

Emergencies do happen. Even though your instructor may have warned you that there is no excuse for missing a quiz or turning in a paper beyond the deadline, he or she may see things in a different light if it's a true emergency. Here are some things you can do to mitigate the consequences of missing class:

1. *For a recurring medical condition that you know may keep you home unexpectedly on some days:* Let the instructor know about it early in the term. Schedule a meeting during office hours and make it clear you are not asking for relief from required work, but for some allowance for turning in work late if you are unable to attend on an important day.

2. *For an emergency:* If possible, phone in and leave word. Many faculty have answering machines and will get your message even if they're not in the office when you call. Leave a number where you can be reached. If you don't know where you'll be, leave the number of a friend or relative who could relay the message to you.

3. *For a situation when you know in advance you can't make a class:* Tell the instructor as soon as you know. Even if the excuse seems unimportant to everyone but you, it's always worth asking; do it early so there's more of a

possibility that arrangements can be made for you to turn in work early or make up work when you return.

At some colleges your academic advisor or counselor or the student services office can distribute a memo to all of your instructors to inform them of the emergency, especially if you will be missing classes for a week or more.

Even if you missed an important quiz or deadline for dubious reasons, let your instructor know anyway. It's better to make a fool of yourself by admitting you overslept or even forgot a paper was due or left the essay at home than to get a zero. Instructors forget or leave things at home, too, and may give you the benefit of the doubt.

Remember: It's better to tell the truth, no matter how ridiculous it makes you seem. Sometimes you'll strike out, but you never know. If you are polite and reasonable in your approach, you may be surprised how willing your instructor is to help you in your dilemma.

Super recall columns and mind maps are particularly useful in the last hour, right before the start of the exam. Whereas notes and texts are too unwieldy to be of much use at this point, mind maps allow for quick, effective review.

Consistent daily study and the right exam strategy are the surest means to real learning and strong performance. Note that the strategies recommended here are not those of memorization. Too often memorization reflects only shallow understanding, although it can be useful in remembering

If you've set realistic goals and used good study techniques, chances are you'll make high marks. Remember, though, that grades aren't the only measure of academic accomplishment. (Photo by David Gonzales)

lists of items (see the box on pages 140–141). The mechanics of our in-depth system require you to apply yourself repeatedly and attentively to the material, focusing always on *understanding* the significant points in large amounts of written material. How else could you make recall columns or mind maps?

EXERCISE 9.4   The Power of the Mind Map

Working with your partner, review the mind map in Figure 9.1. Create a mind map for each of the essay questions you developed in Exercise 9.3. Use them to prompt a recitation of the material needed to answer each question. Put the mind maps away for a day. The next day, try to re-create the mind maps from memory. You should find your retention of the material has increased. Share these maps with your classmates and instructor, and see how theirs differ.

Three Principles for Taking Essay Exams

Following all of the previous suggestions won't be enough if you don't then perform well on the exam itself. Here are three principles for taking essay exams and ways to implement them.

1. Use Exam Time Well. Quickly survey the entire exam and note the questions that are easiest for you. To build confidence and start the recall process, answer these questions first. But be careful. Knowing certain material very well may tempt you to write brilliantly for 30 minutes on a question worth only 10 points, leaving little time for a harder question worth 30 points. This is how to get a C when you are quite capable of achieving a B or an A. Avoid this costly error by knowing ahead of time the basic exam structure, the point allotments, and the types of questions. Then govern yourself during the exam according to a plan for choosing questions and allocating the right amount of time for each. Also be sure to wear a watch to the exam. If you forget to do so, ask the instructor to periodically call out or write the time or the time remaining on the board.

2. Write Focused, Organized Answers. Many well-prepared students write fine answers to questions that have not been asked. This problem stems either from not reading a question carefully or from hastily writing down everything you know on a topic in the hope that somehow the question will be answered. This is like shooting at a target with a shotgun, never completely missing, perhaps, but rarely hitting the bull's-eye. Instructors agree that shotgun answers are frustrating to read because of their lack of focus and organization. A simple seven-point strategy will help you stay focused and organized:

1. Read the entire question carefully.
2. Take the time to read it again and underline key words. This forces you to read the question accurately. The underlined words will stimulate recall of relevant information.
3. Brainstorm. Write down all the ideas you can think of in response to what the question asks. Then read over your notes, underline the most important points, and use them in your answer. If you do this extra writing on the exam paper, be sure to cross it out if you do not want it counted for credit.
4. Use the underlined words in the question and in your written brainstorming to construct a brief outline. This ensures good organization.
5. Begin your answer by rewriting the question or problem. This reinforces your focus.
6. Write the rest of the answer according to your outline. For each major idea try to write at least one paragraph and give at least one supporting example. If new ideas come to mind as you write, add them at the end.
7. Make sure each answer begins with an introduction and ends with a conclusion.

Here is a sample question from a psychology test, selectively underlined to focus the question.

Modern educational psychology has discovered a great deal about <u>how students learn</u>, and this has led to the development of several powerful <u>study techniques</u>. <u>Identify three such techniques and explain how and why they work</u>.

Figure 9.2 shows how an outline for answering the question might be written during the actual exam. Commentary is provided on the right. While writing the essay our hypothetical test-taker remembers an additional important idea—visualization and mind maps—and adds that at the end of the essay.

Figure 9.2 Sample Essay Exam Outline

Introduction

Brief statement of topic or question and the approach.

Modern educational psychology has a lot to offer the student who wants to learn how to study more efficiently.

A simple direct restatement begins the answer with a focus on *how*.

Define efficiency.
Describe forgetting as the problem.

The answer will build on two key concepts: efficiency and the problem of forgetting.

4 Advance organizers (conclusion)
3 Recitation
1 Recall columns
2 Super recall columns
5 Multiple-choice strategies (conclusion)

The techniques are first listed without numbers, in the order remembered. Then the techniques are numbered in the order that seems most logical for presenting them in the written answer. The first three techniques will appear in the body of the answer. The last two will be mentioned in a concluding paragraph, just to show that there are more than three.

Conclusion

Brief summary—final thoughts and perspectives.

3. Know the Key Task Words in Essay Questions. Essay questions often use certain task words such as *discuss* or *define*. Help yourself to focus more quickly and avoid misinterpretation by becoming familiar with them now. Don't feel you must memorize the exact definitions of these terms, and don't "lock up" on the exam if you can't define them precisely. A general familiarity will do. Perhaps your instructor will tell you which of these terms (what kinds of tasks) will appear on the test. Why not ask? Here are some of the most frequently used terms and their meanings.

Be sure you're answering the question that was asked. Before you start writing an essay, analyze the question and make notes that will collect your ideas and organize your response. (Photo by David Gonzales)

Key Task Words

Analyze: to divide something into its parts in order to understand it better, then to see how the parts work together to produce the overall pattern. Analyzing a problem may require you to identify a number of smaller problems that are related to the overall problem.

Compare: to look at the characteristics or qualities of several things and identify their similarities. Instructions to compare things often are intended to imply that you may also contrast them.

Contrast: to identify the differences between things.

Criticize/Critique: to analyze and judge something. Criticism can be either positive or negative, as the case warrants. A criticism should generally contain your own judgments (supported by evidence) in addition to whatever authorities you might invoke.

Define: to give the meaning of a word or expression. Definitions should generally be clear and concise and conform with other people's understanding of the terms. Giving an example of something sometimes helps to clarify a definition, but giving an example is not in itself a definition.

Describe: to give a general verbal sketch or account of something, in narrative or other form.

Diagram: to show the parts of something and their relationships in pictorial form, such as a chart. You are usually expected to label the diagram, and you may be asked to explain it in words as well.

Discuss: to examine or analyze something in a broad and detailed way. Discussion often includes identifying the important questions related to an issue and attempting to answer these questions. Where there are several sides to an issue, a discussion involves presenting this variety of sides. A good discussion explores as much of the relevant evidence and information on a topic as it can.

Enumerate: to respond in the form of a concise list or outline rather than in great detail.

Evaluate: to judge the worth or truthfulness of something. Evaluation is similar to criticism, but the word *evaluate* places more stress on the idea of making some ultimate judgment about how well something meets a certain standard or fulfills some specific purpose. Evaluation involves discussing strengths and weaknesses.

Explain: to clarify or interpret something. Explanations generally focus on *why* or *how* something has come about. Explanations often require you to discuss evidence that may seem contradictory and to tell how apparent differences in evidence can be reconciled.

Illustrate: on an essay examination, to give one or more examples of something. Examples help to relate abstract ideas to concrete experience. Examples may show how something works in practice. Providing a good example is a way of showing you know your course material in detail. Sometimes the instruction to illustrate may be asking you to literally draw a diagram or picture. If you're uncertain of the intention, ask the instructor.

Interpret: to explain the meaning of something. For instance, in science you may be asked to interpret the evidence of an experiment, that is, to explain what the evidence shows and what conclusions can be drawn from it. In a literature course you may be asked to interpret a poem, that is, to explain what a specific passage or the poem as a whole means beyond the literal meaning of the words.

Justify: to argue in support of some decision or conclusion, to show sufficient evidence or reason in favor of something. Whenever possible, try to support your argument with both logical reasoning and concrete examples.

Label: to point to and name specific parts of a figure or illustration.

List: to present information in a series of short, discrete points. See also *enumerate.*

Narrate: to tell a story, that is, a series of events in the order in which they occurred. Generally, when you are asked to narrate events, you are also asked to interpret or explain something about the events you are narrating.

Outline: to present a series of main points in appropriate order, omitting lesser details. Also, to present some information in the form of a series of short headings in which each major idea is followed by headings for smaller points or examples that fall under it. An outline shows the correct order and grouping of ideas.

Prove: to give a convincing logical argument and evidence in support of the truth of some statement. Note, however, that academic disciplines differ in their methods of inquiry and therefore also differ in what they require in statements of proof.

Relate: to show the relationship between things. This can mean showing how they influence each other or how a change in one thing seems to depend on or accompany a change in the other. In showing how things relate, it's often a good idea to provide an example.

Review: to summarize and comment on the main parts of a problem or a series of statements or events in order. A review question usually also asks you to evaluate or criticize some aspect of the material.

Summarize: to give information in brief form, omitting examples and details. A summary should be short yet cover all of the most important points.

Trace: to narrate a course of events. Where possible, you should show connections from one event to the next. Tracing a sequence of events often points to gaps in the sequence that you may need to fill in by logical suppositions about what might link one event to the next.

EXERCISE 9.5   **Keying on Task Words**

Essay questions may require quite different responses depending on their key task words. Write brief answers to the following. Focus on what each task word is asking you to do, and tailor your responses accordingly.

1. Define the purposes of this course, chapter, or book (pick one).

_____

_____

_____

_____

2. Evaluate the purposes of this course, chapter, or book.

_____

_____

_____

_____

3. Justify the purposes of this course, chapter, or book.

_____

_____

_____

_____

Discuss your responses with your classmates and your instructor.

Summary Time Management Plan for Essay Exams

1. Study your notes using the recall column throughout the semester.
2. Set aside time for study in your weekly planner a week or two before the exam.

3. Find out from the instructor the basic exam structure, the point allotments, and the types of questions.

4. Allot an appropriate percentage of study time for each potential exam section.

5. Set aside time just before the exam to review notes and jog memory.

6. Use exam time well. Quickly preview the entire exam to determine the value of each section, and then allot time accordingly. Answer the questions you are sure of first. Try to allow time for a quick review at the end. And wear a watch!

THE MULTIPLE-CHOICE EXAM

Studying for multiple-choice exams is different from studying for essay exams. However, preparing for multiple-choice exams still requires purposeful notes, well-reviewed texts, and active daily learning. Whereas an essay exam requires focused, detailed study on selected topics (excluding a lot of material altogether), the multiple-choice exam requires a light review of nearly everything covered. Thus you should plan to review the material several times before the exam. Use your notes and text markings, aided by regular recitation, to quickly review large amounts of material.

Take advantage of the many cues that multiple-choice questions contain. With careful reading you will find that the right answer is frequently apparent. Two suggestions will be helpful here. First, question those choices that use absolute words such as *always, never,* and *only.* These choices are often incorrect. Second, read carefully for terms like *not, except,* and *but,* which may come before the choices. Look at the following sample multiple-choice question on writing an essay exam:

> *1. In answering an essay question it is wise to do all of the following except:*
> *a. review your notes before the exam*
> *b. write out study maps to synthesize the material*
> *c. always memorize specific details at the expense of main ideas*
> *d. both a and b*

Do you see how choice *d* would seem to be acceptable if you had not read the "except"? Also, did you notice the use of the qualifier "always" in choice *c?*

Some questions will be puzzlers. Skip over these questions as you first work quickly through the exam, but mark them so that you can find them easily later. When you have finished answering all of the obvious questions, return to the puzzlers. You will discover that you now know the answers to some of them. Why? Because a multiple-choice exam is a review of interrelated material, and information given in question 46 may contain or suggest the answer to question 10. This technique lets the nature of the exam work in your favor.

For the few puzzlers that remain, try another strategy. Since you can't find the right answer, try eliminating those that are clearly wrong. Usually at least one of the choices is far-fetched, another unlikely, and a third a "maybe." Eliminate as many choices as you can so as to increase the odds in your favor, and then make the best guess possible. You can often reduce your choices to two, so that your odds for correctly answering the question are 1 out of 2 rather than 1 out of 4 or 5.

Hard to Remember?
Tips on Memory

Thirty days hath September, April, June, and November....
Doe a deer, a female deer. Ray, a drop of golden sun....
A pint's a pound, the world around.

Out of desperation and amusement, the human mind has discovered ingenious ways to remember vital information. Here are some methods that may be useful to you when you're nailing down the causes of the Civil War, trying to remember the steps in a physics problem, or absorbing a mathematical formula for tomorrow's quiz.

1. **Use mnemonics.** Create rhymes, jingles, sayings, or nonsense phrases that repeat or codify information. "Homes" is a mnemonic word for remembering the five Great Lakes: Huron, Ontario, Michigan, Erie, and Superior. "Spring forward, fall back" tells many Americans how to set their clocks.

"Every Good Boy Does Fine" is a mnemonic sentence: The first letter of each word is the letter of a line of the music staff, bottom to top. Setting a rhyme to music is one of the most powerful ways to make words memorable.

2. **Associate.** Relate the idea to something you already know. Make the association as personal as possible. If you're reading a chapter on laws regarding free speech, pretend your right to speak out on a subject that's important to you may be affected by those laws. In remembering the spelling difference between *through* and *threw*, think of walking through something "rough," and that "threw" comes from "throw."

3. **Peg.** Visualize in order a number of locations or objects in your home. To remember a list of things, associate each item in the list with

Following these strategies can often mean a difference of 5 or 6 percentage points, which in turn can be the difference between a B and a C. Light, quick review of material (several times if necessary) and good exam room strategy make multiple-choice exams that much easier.

A word of caution: Make sure you know the scoring system. If, for example, there is a built-in factor to penalize you for guessing (number right minus a percentage of number wrong), it is not wise to guess. When in doubt, ask the instructor what the scoring procedure will be.

THE TRUE-FALSE EXAM

You will find that true-false questions are often used in examinations. True-false questions contain only two choices, rather than the four or five you often find in a multiple-choice question, so your chances for selecting a correct answer are better. Like the multiple-choice question the true-false question tests your understanding of detail more than your mastery of general concepts.

one of the locations or objects. For example, let's memorize three classic appeals of advertising (appetite, fear, and sexual attraction):

► *Appetite:* The first peg is the corner countertop. Visualize some creature devouring your favorite chocolate cake.

► *Fear:* The second peg is the coat rack. Visualize a menacing coat rack running after you.

► *Sexual attraction:* The third peg is a sofa. Use your imagination.

4. **Visualize.** Make yourself see the things that you've associated with important concepts. Concentrate on the images so they'll become firmly planted in your memory.

5. **Overlearn.** Even after you "know" the material, go over it again to make sure you'll retain it for a long time.

6. **Use flashcards.** Use index cards. Write the word or information to be learned on one side and the definition or explanation on the other. Review the cards often; carry them with you. Prepare them well in advance of the day of the test and spend more time on the hard ones.

7. **Categorize.** Even if the information seems to lack an inherent organization, try to impose one. Most information can be organized in some way, even if only by the look or sound of the words.

8. **Draw a mind map.** (See the previous discussion in this chapter.) Some speakers claim they can prepare an hour-long talk simply by arranging the main topics on a single sheet of paper and connecting the points in logical fashion by arrows, dots, and so forth. Large points are written in large boxes or circles, smaller points in smaller ones. Subgroups are placed under major headings. Drawing relationships on paper—even faces, objects, or stick figures—can help you visualize them later.

Here are some hints for answering the true-false question:

1. Be sure that every part of the question is correct. For the question to be true, every detail within it must also be true.

2. Check to see how qualifiers are used. As with multiple-choice questions, true-false questions containing words like *always, never,* and *only* are usually false. Conversely less definite terms like *often* and *frequently* suggest that the statement may be true. Note how the use of *always* makes the following statement false, while the use of *often* makes it true:

_____ 1. *True-false questions always test specific information.*

_____ 2. *True-false questions often test specific information.*

The first statement is suspect, because if you can think of even one example to counter the claim, the statement is automatically false. By contrast the second statement allows for a few exceptions and is thus more likely to be true.

3. As with the multiple-choice question, read through the entire exam to see if information in one question will help you answer a question whose answer you are unsure of.

THE MATCHING EXAM

Matching questions are still used on objective exams, particularly those that use a combination of objective questions: multiple-choice, true-false, and matching. Unlike these other two types of objective questions, the matching question is the hardest to answer by guessing. With the matching question, you need to know your stuff. Often matching questions test your knowledge of definitions as well as names and events. In one column you will find the term, in the other the description of it.

Before answering the matching-question part of the exam, review all of the terms and descriptions. See if a pattern emerges—perhaps terms on one side and definitions on the other, people in one column and descriptions of them in the other, or a combination of both. Match up those terms you are sure of first. As you answer each question, cross out both the term and its description. This will enable you to see more clearly which choices remain.

Here is an example of part of a matching test on this chapter:

_____ 1. *essay question*   a. *often the most difficult objective question to answer*

_____ 2. *multiple-choice question*   b. *requires knowledge of general concepts*

_____ 3. *true-false question*   c. *only provides two choices*

_____ 4. *matching question*   d. *usually presents four or five choices per question*

Do you see how this set of matching questions asks you to match up a term with a description of it? Now go back to these four questions and answer them, crossing out each correct match that you determine.

EXERCISE 9.6   Designing an Exam Plan

A. Use the following guidelines to design an exam plan for one of your courses:

1. Find out what the characteristics of the exam are: What material will be covered? What type of questions will it contain? How long will it be? How many questions will there be? What is the grading system?

2. Based on these characteristics, determine what type of studying is necessary.

3. Establish how much time and how many study sessions you will need to complete your studying.

4. Create a study schedule starting one week before the test. Indicate the length of each study session, the material to be covered, and the study techniques to be used. Arrange with family or roommates to assure quiet time for your study needs.

Share your responses with other students and with your instructor. See how their responses are similar to or different from yours.

B. Create a study group of three or four others in the class. Review the material in this chapter. Create a hypothetical exam containing both essay and objective questions. Share it with the class, modifying it as needed. Then, after studying the material individually, come together as a group to share the answers.

EXERCISE 9.7   An Essay Exam

Treat the following as an essay exam question. Use techniques (such as mind maps or outlines) and information from this section and previous chapters to organize and write your answer:

> How soon is a student likely to forget lecture material even when full notes are taken? How much is likely to be forgotten? How can this problem be alleviated? Based on your own experience and your reading here, what is your opinion of recitation as a study technique?

Share your response with your classmates and instructor.

ACADEMIC HONESTY

Higher education evolved in America with a strong commitment to the "search for truth," uncovering new knowledge and solving problems to benefit society. The commitment to truth was accompanied by the concept of academic freedom, which is the freedom of faculty and students to pursue whatever inquiry they feel is important and to speak about it in classrooms without fear of censorship.

Honesty and integrity are crucial to the search for truth and academic freedom. Imagine where our society would be if researchers reported fraudulent results that were then used to develop new machines or medical treatments. The integrity of knowledge is a cornerstone of higher education, and activities that compromise that integrity damage everyone.

Most colleges and universities have academic integrity policies or honor codes that define clearly enough cheating, lying, plagiarism, and other forms of dishonest conduct, but it is often difficult to know how those rules apply to specific situations. For example, is it really lying to tell an instructor you missed class because you were "not feeling well" (whatever "well" means) or because you were experiencing that conveniently vague and all-encompassing malady "car trouble"? Some people would argue that car trouble includes anything from a flat tire to difficulty finding a parking spot!

Types of Misconduct

Institutions vary widely in how specifically they define broad terms like *lying* or *cheating*. For instance, one university's code of student academic integrity defines cheating as "intentionally using or attempting to use unauthorized materials, information, notes, study aids or other devices... [including] unauthorized communication of information during an academic exercise." This would apply to all of these:

- ► Looking over a classmate's shoulder for an answer
- ► Using a calculator when it is not authorized
- ► Procuring or discussing an exam without permission
- ► Copying lab notes
- ► Duplicating computer files

EXERCISE 9.8   ## Finding Out About Your School's Academic Code

Investigate the academic integrity standards for your school. Where did you find them? What specific behaviors do they prohibit? What procedures are followed when a student is suspected of violating the standards? Record three or four of the code's key rules here:

1. _____

2. _____

3. _____

4. _____

Use this information as the basis for a discussion on how your school would view each of the activities in the five-item list preceding the exercise. Ask some of your instructors for their opinions.

Plagiarism is especially intolerable in the academic culture. *Plagiarism* means taking another person's ideas or work and presenting them as your own. Just as taking someone else's property constitutes physical theft, taking credit for someone else's ideas constitutes "intellectual theft."

Rules for referencing (or "citing") another's ideas apply more strictly to the papers you write than to your responses on a test. On tests you do not have to credit specific individuals for their ideas. On written reports and papers, however, you *must* give credit any time you use (1) another person's actual words, (2) another person's ideas or theories—even if you don't quote them directly—and (3) any other information *not* considered common knowledge. Check with your instructors about how to cite material they've

Does Cheating Hurt Anyone?

What About the Individual?

► **Cheating sabotages academic growth.** Cheating confuses and weakens the process by which students demonstrate understanding of course content. Because the grade and the instructor's comments apply to someone else's work, cheating prevents accurate feedback, thus hindering academic growth.

► **Cheating sabotages personal growth.** Educational accomplishments inspire pride and confidence. What confidence in their ability will individuals have whose work is not their own?

► **Cheating may have long-term effects.** Taking the "easy way" in college may become a habit that can spill over into graduate school, jobs, and relationships. And consider this: Would you want a doctor, lawyer, or accountant who had cheated on exams handling your affairs?

What About the Community?

► **Cheating jeopardizes the basic fairness of the grading process.** Widespread cheating causes honest students to become cynical and resentful. This is especially true when grades are curved and the cheating directly affects other students.

► **Widespread cheating devalues the college's degree.** Alumni, potential students, graduate schools, and employers learn to distrust degrees from schools where cheating is widespread.

covered in classroom lectures. Usually you do not need to provide a reference for this, but it is always better to ask first.

Students are sometimes confused about how to represent material from written sources accurately and honestly. Read the following excerpt, which is part of a critique by Mark Twain of the famous author James Fenimore

Cooper and his novel *The Deerslayer*. Then read the examples of student writing that follow, which illustrate the difference between plagiarism and correct referencing of work.

> *Cooper's gift in the way of invention was not a rich endowment but such as it was he liked to work it, he was pleased with the effects, and indeed he did some quite sweet things with it. In his little box of stage properties he kept six or eight cunning devices, tricks, artifices for his savages and woodsmen to deceive and circumvent each other with, and he was never so happy as when he was working these innocent things and seeing them go. A favorite one was to make a moccasined person tread in the tracks of the moccasined enemy, and thus hide his own trail. Cooper wore out barrels and barrels of moccasins in working that trick. Another stage-property that he pulled out of his box pretty frequently was his broken twig. He prized his broken twig above all the rest of his effects, and worked it the hardest. It is a restful chapter in any book of his when somebody doesn't step on a dry twig and alarm all the reds and whites for two hundred yards around. Every time a Cooper person is in peril and absolute silence is worth four dollars a minute, he is sure to step on a dry twig. There may be a hundred handier things to step on but that wouldn't satisfy Cooper. Cooper requires him to turn out and find a dry twig, and if he can't do it, go and borrow one. In fact, the Leatherstocking Series ought to have been called the Broken Twig Series.**

Example 1

INCORRECT: *Although Cooper was not richly endowed in the area of invention, he did try some sweet things whose effects were quite pleasing.*

This version is unacceptable because you may not simply change the order of another writer's words in an attempt not to plagiarize. The main idea must be preserved and rephrased in your *own* words and must include a reference to the source from which you borrowed it.

CORRECT: *Twain notes that Cooper used but a few creative effects, and these appeared over and over again throughout the book.[1]*

In this version the phrasing is original, and the superscript number at the end of the passage leads the reader to the footnote or endnote where you provide the author's name, publication title, year of publication, and other information. This also allows the reader an opportunity to find more information on the topic.

Example 2

INCORRECT: *Twain supports my view of Cooper's brilliant creativity: "Cooper's gift in the way of invention was ... a rich endowment ... and indeed he did some quite sweet things with it."[2]*

An ellipsis (...) is used when intervening words from the original quoted sentence or passage are omitted. However, as in this example, using the ellipsis to omit words and thereby change the meaning of the passage is misrepresentation, and thus unethical.

---

*Anne Ficklen, ed., *The Hidden Mark Twain: A Collection of Little-Known Mark Twain* (New York: Crown Books, 1984).

CORRECT: Twain offers only partial support for my view of Cooper's brilliant creativity: "Cooper's gift in the way of invention was not a rich endowment but...indeed he did some quite sweet things with it."[2]

In this example the use of a direct quote accurately expresses the original author's meaning. Remember that quotes that run more than five lines should be set off in a separate paragraph, with indentations on both margins and without quotation marks.

EXERCISE 9.9   Paraphrasing and Referencing

In the space below try correctly paraphrasing and referencing the last part of Twain's passage. Convey his opinion of Cooper's use of the "broken twig effect":

_____

_____

_____

_____

_____

_____

_____

Share your version with a classmate and discuss your use of paraphrasing.

Many schools prohibit other activities besides lying, cheating, and plagiarism. For instance, the University of Delaware prohibits fabrication (intentionally inventing information or results); the University of North Carolina outlaws multiple submission (earning credit more than once for the same piece of academic work without permission); Eastern Illinois University rules out tendering of information (giving your work or exam answer to another student to copy during the actual exam or before the exam is given to another section); and the University of South Carolina prohibits bribery (trading something of value in exchange for any kind of academic advantage). Most schools also outlaw helping or attempting to help another student commit a dishonest act.

Some outlawed behaviors do not seem to fall within any clear category. Understanding the mission and values of higher education will help you make better decisions about those behaviors that "fall through the cracks."

EXERCISE 9.10 Identifying Problem Behaviors

Review the behaviors listed below. Put a Y for yes by any you think constitute cheating, an N for no by those you think are legitimate shortcuts, and a question mark (?) by those that could be either, depending on the situation.

_____ 1. Taking an exam in place of another student or having someone take an exam in your place

_____ 2. Rewriting passages (so they sound better) of a paper you're typing for a friend

_____ 3. Having someone write a paper to submit as your own work

_____ 4. Discussing your outline/ideas for a paper with a friend in your class who is writing on the same subject

_____ 5. Allowing another student to copy from you during an exam

_____ 6. Changing your lab results to reflect what you know they should have been, rather than what you got

_____ 7. Turning in the same paper to two different classes

_____ 8. Studying from old exams

_____ 9. Getting questions or answers from someone who has already taken the same exam

_____ 10. Borrowing an idea for a paper without footnoting the source

_____ 11. Working on homework with other students

_____ 12. Including a few items, which you didn't really use, on a bibliography

_____ 13. Changing a few answers on a graded exam and resubmitting it for a higher grade

_____ 14. Reading just the abstracts of articles, rather than the entire article, when doing research for a paper

_____ 15. Asking someone to proofread your draft of a paper

Discuss your answers with other students in small groups. Of the behaviors that everyone agrees are cheating, which are the most serious? How do they relate to the mission and values of higher education?

For those behaviors you disagreed about, where does the disagreement lie? Discuss the different values that might determine one's opinions. Are any of these values related to prior personal or cultural experiences?

NOTE: Adapted, with permission, from Melora A. Sundt, based on materials from: E. Nuss. "Academic Integrity: Comparing Faculty and Student Attitudes." _Improving College and University Teaching_, 3, no. 32 (1984).

Reducing the Likelihood of Problems

In order to avoid becoming intentionally or unintentionally involved in academic misconduct, consider the reasons it *could* happen.

Ignorance is one reason. In a survey at the University of South Carolina, 20 percent of students thought that buying a term paper wasn't cheating. Forty percent thought using a test file (a collection of actual tests from previous terms, usually kept by an organization such as a fraternity or sorority) was fair behavior. Sixty percent thought it was all right to get answers from someone who had taken an exam earlier in the same or in a prior semester.

This may not be so unusual in light of the fact that in some countries students are encouraged to review past exams as practice exercises. In other countries it is also acceptable to share answers and information for homework and other types of assignments with friends. These behaviors are not only acceptable, they are considered acts of generosity and courtesy.

Instructors also may vary in their acceptance of such behaviors. Since there is no universal code that dictates such behaviors, you should ask your instructors for clarification. When a student is caught violating the academic code of a particular school or teacher, pleading ignorance of the rules is a weak defense.

A second reason some people cheat is that they overestimate the importance of grades, apart from actual learning, and fall into thinking they must "succeed" at any cost. In part this may reflect our society's competitive atmosphere, but it also may be the result of pressure from parents, peers, or teachers. The desire for "success at any cost" is often accompanied by a strong fear of failure that is hard to confront and deal with.

A third common cause of cheating is a student's own lack of preparation or inability to manage time and activities. The problem is made worse if he or she is unwilling to ask an instructor to extend a deadline so that a project can be done well.

Other factors make cheating seem more or less acceptable, such as knowledge that peers are cheating, ads for term papers for sale, and the conspicuous existence of test files. Teachers and administrators bear some responsibility if they do not (1) explain their standards, (2) provide an environment conducive to honesty, and (3) respond with swift and severe discipline to incidents of dishonesty. However, final responsibility always lies with you.

If you are discouraged or depressed by this discussion, take heart. There's a lot you can do to avoid cheating in the first place or stop once you have started:

1. Know the Rules. Learn the academic code for your school. If a teacher does not clarify his or her standards and expectations, ask exactly what the rules are.

2. Set Clear Boundaries. Work with a partner or study group to prepare for a test, but refrain from discussing past exams with others unless it is specifically permitted. Tell friends exactly what is acceptable or unacceptable if you lend them a term paper. Refuse to "help" others who ask you to help them cheat. In test settings keep your answers covered and your eyes down, and put all extraneous materials away. Help friends to resist temptation. Make sure your typist understands that he or she may not make any changes in your work.

3. Improve Self-Management. The most effective method to assure academic integrity is to be well prepared for all quizzes, exams, projects, and papers. This may mean *un*learning some bad habits (such as procrastination) and building better time management and study skills. Keep your own long-term goals in mind and firmly resist pressures to socialize when you know you must study.

4. Seek Help. You may want to seek help on campus. Find out what is available for assistance with "methods"—study skills, time management, and test-taking—and take advantage of it. If your methods are in good shape but the content of the course is too difficult, consult with your instructor. Ask for assistance to ensure you cite others correctly in your work.

5. Withdraw from the Course. Consider cutting your losses before it's too late. Your school has a policy about dropping courses, and you may choose this route and plan to retake the course later. Some students may choose to withdraw from all their classes and take some time off before returning to school. This may be an option if you find yourself in over your head, or if some unplanned event (a long illness, a family crisis) has caused you to fall behind with little hope of catching up. Again, see what your school's policy is about withdrawing for a period of time.

6. Reexamine Goals. You need to stick to your own realistic goals instead of giving in to pressure from family or friends to achieve impossibly high standards. What grades do you *need,* and what grades do you have the potential to earn? You may also feel pressure to enter a particular career or profession. If this isn't what you want, your frustration is likely to appear in your lack of preparation and your grades. It may be time to sit down with your parents and tell them you need to choose your own career.

JOURNAL

This chapter suggests some strategies that can help you perform well and honestly on exams. What ideas are you already following? What new ideas can you apply?

Consider the person who believes in getting ahead at any cost versus the person who believes that honest work is the true path to success. How might each of these people define "success"? Are there any public figures you would associate with these definitions? Suppose there were no rules about academic honesty at your college. What would be the pros and cons of cheating for good grades, as opposed to working for them?

SUGGESTIONS FOR FURTHER READING

Buzan, Tony. *Use Both Sides of Your Brain.* New York: Dutton, 1974.

Cahn, S. M. *Saints and Scamps: Ethics in Academia.* Totowa, N.J.: Rowman & Littlefield, 1986.

Hesburgh, T. *The Hesburgh Papers: Higher Values in Higher Education.* Kansas City, Mo.: Andrews & McMeel, 1979.

McKowen, Clark. *Get Your A out of College: Mastering the Hidden Rules of the Game.* Los Altos, Calif.: Crisp Publications, 1979.

Morrill, R. L. *Teaching Values in College.* San Francisco: Jossey-Bass, 1980.

Thriving in the Information Environment: Your Campus Library

Marilee Birchfield
University of South Carolina

Faye A. Chadwell
University of South Carolina

I've heard about people who've been lost for years in the New York City Public Library. They just go in and never come out. They fall asleep and die, or else they get slimed like those guys did in Ghostbusters.... Actually I kind of like the long, tall rows of books. They seem to absorb all human sound, like snow. I don't mind libraries. I just never seem to know what I'm looking for or how to find it.

The Information Age is no longer encroaching on us—we are of and in it. What makes this age exciting and potentially empowering for millions of people is not that information has just been invented or that people are just beginning to look for it. Rather, it's the amount and diversity of information that is available through innumerable sources, the ease and speed with which you can obtain this information, and the incredible possibilities for applying it to everyday situations.

Just imagine:

▶ By means of fiber optics, AT&T transmits information from Chicago to the East Coast at 6.6 gigabits per second—equivalent to the information contained in 1,000 books. At this rate the entire book holdings of the Library of Congress, totaling 23 million volumes, could be dispatched in 24 hours. On the computers of yesterday, this process would have taken 2,000 years (Wriston, 1992).

▶ One CD-ROM (Compact Disc Read-Only-Memory) can store as much as 1,000 standard floppy disks used by regular personal computers (Tehranian, 1990).

▶ The Internet, or the information superhighway, allows users to send electronic mail messages across the world, connect to hundreds of databases and library catalogs worldwide, participate in on-line discussion groups on topics of personal or professional interest, and review news and weather updates. As of 1993, an estimated 5,000 individual networks connecting 2 million computers and 15 million people comprised the Net, as it is known by its travelers (Gaffin, 1994).

The growth of computer technology has had a tremendous impact on campus. Nowhere is this more evident than in the library, a central information resource. Most campus libraries now are using computerized library catalogs or networks rather than the traditional card catalog. Many libraries also provide access to resources like Internet, on-line computer databases, and CD-ROMs, in addition to the library's typical printed sources. Overall the changes brought on by the Information Age make the library an excellent place for experiencing the transformation from print technology to computer technology.

Unfortunately students often share several common misconceptions and even fears about their campus library, particularly those students who are intimidated by computers. Your concerns about using the library are certainly warranted, especially when you consider that a lack of good information-gathering skills may adversely affect you not only in the classroom but in other areas. Consequences of not maximizing your use of the library and its computer technology include poor time management and hurried completion of assignments, low grades, and narrow and uninformed or weakly developed viewpoints. Poor performance in class can lead to inadequate preparation for your first job, unfulfilled career and personal goals, and a mediocre return on your investment in college. This chapter will help you to strengthen your information-gathering skills and will make library resources more accessible (the chapter ends with a glossary of common library terms).

EXERCISE 10.1 Some Possible Misconceptions

Look over the following list of common concerns and misconceptions about libraries and librarians:

➤ I should automatically know how to use the library.

➤ The library is too big, and I never find what I need.

➤ Librarians speak a language that only they understand.

➤ Librarians look too busy to help me.

➤ I don't know how to use the library's materials; its computers just make it more complicated.

➤ My friends will consider me a bookworm or intellectual—just like the librarians.

➤ Librarians in the past haven't helped me.

➤ I hate doing research and writing papers.

➤ Doing research usually requires having to talk to someone and ask for help, which can be tough.

Think about your own experiences using libraries—both the rewarding and the challenging or frustrating ones. What are some of your concerns or feelings? Discuss them with others in a group. Of the items listed above, are there any that you would not consider misconceptions?

EXERCISE 10.2 Power and Information

Consider the following situations:

➤ Pat's local newspaper publishes an ad for what appears to be a terrific job with a company for which he would really like to work. Pat interviews with the company and takes the offered position. Within six months, to his surprise and dismay, the company closes its door, leaving him without a job. As it turns out, according to the same local newspaper, the company had been in financial trouble for some time.

➤ Laura has been dating Chris for several months. Chris tells her that he has been sexually active in the past year with another person, but that there is no need to use a condom when they decide to have sex since his sexual activity was limited to just one person. Laura wants to believe Chris; however, having read a free pamphlet from the college health center, she knows that having unprotected sex with Chris is risky because every one of his previous partners, and each of their partners, may not have always practiced safer sex.

Discuss the following in a group:

1. Do the two scenarios reflect the idea that "Power resides with the information holder"? In each case, what is the information problem and how might it be handled?

2. Have you ever been in a position of power because you were able to withhold information? Have you ever been in the opposite situation in which information was withheld from you or only grudgingly offered? Create at least one other brief scenario in which problems arise because of a person not having adequate information-gathering skills.

STARTING AT THE BEGINNING

The first step is to familiarize yourself with your library system *before* you have to use it. Is there more than one library on campus? If so, is one geared toward helping undergraduates? Does your library offer tours? (Your class may be able to schedule one.) Does your library offer a self-guided tour describing library services? Try taking a tour to discover what some of the services and various departments offer you. Maybe your library offers an orientation via a computer system.

Does your library have handouts describing various services and different library departments and their hours? Get these handouts. Note the different library departments that might interest you—for example, government documents, reserve, interlibrary loan, or a special collection devoted to one subject area.

Selecting and Surveying a Topic

Usually before you go to the library, you will have selected a topic of interest or your instructor will have provided an assignment for you to complete. (In the exercise at the end of this chapter, you will be asked to select a topic.) This is not always an easy task. If you find it difficult, focus on selecting something in which you are genuinely interested. Browse through recent newspapers and news magazines for ideas. Also, talk to your instructor or your peers about possible ideas. Some libraries have books listing possible research topics, or you may consult a librarian.

If you already have a general topic but have not focused on one specific area, don't panic. Defining and refining your topic is a natural process and one of the objectives of doing research. During your first visit in the library, your goal should be to survey the topic and obtain ideas on how you might want to develop it. When you don't have a clear sense of what you are looking for, give yourself time to reflect before trying to find information.

When surveying the topic, you might ask, "Does there seem to be enough information? Is there too much?" If there is not enough information, you may want to try a broader approach. If there is too much information, you may want to zero in on one aspect of a more general topic. For instance, instead of looking for information on crime, you might want to focus on a particular crime, like carjacking, and examine how the police are responding to it. Often the amount of time you have to spend on an assignment and its requirements in terms of length and expected coverage will help you determine how much information you need.

Defining Your Need for Information

You can begin to gather information by asking yourself several questions even before you physically or electronically enter the library. The following questions will give you ideas on how to think about your topic before actually searching for information. Carefully thinking through your topic will

Libraries everywhere have been computerizing their catalogs. In many cases, however, not all resources are listed yet in the computer. Ask a librarian about sources that may not show up on the screen. (Photo by David Gonzales)

not only help you focus but also help you communicate your needs to a librarian. Sometimes these questions may be difficult to answer when you are starting out. Don't worry. Try talking through your topic with a friend or consulting a librarian or your instructor.

1. What Do You Already Know About Your Topic? Consider names, events, dates, places, terms, and relationships to other topics. Clarifying your topic in this way may give you leads on how to look for more information. And have confidence: You will know something about your topic.

2. Who Would Be Writing About Your Topic? For example, what scholars, researchers, professionals in specific fields, or other groups of people might be interested? Asking this question helps you to see your topic more fully and identify new aspects of it. This basic question will also help you relate your topic to a major way libraries and information resources are organized—by discipline, or field of study. Disciplines are broadly classified as the *arts* (performing and fine arts such as music, painting, and architecture), *humanities* (religion, philosophy, literature), *social sciences* (psychology, sociology, communications, education, anthropology, law, political science, criminology, economics), and *natural sciences* (biology, chemistry, mathematics, engineering, physics, computer science).

3. What Do You Want to Know About This Topic? Asking these questions further focuses your research or your assignment. Sometimes your first question may be too general and not easily answered. For instance, your original question may be "Is the increasing amount of violence on television ruining society?" There isn't one answer to this question. It isn't a factual question; it is a research question that leads you to additional questions you might need answered in order to answer the original question. For example: Are there measures of the amount and type of violence portrayed on television, and have these measures changed over time? Is there research linking viewing to actual behavior or changes in attitude toward violence? Does violence on television affect different populations differently—children, teenagers, adults, males, females? Are particular types of television broadcasting becoming more violent—children's shows, news, primetime dramas, commercials? What arguments can be made for government regulation versus personal responsibility in determining what is viewed?

Additional Research Tips

Writing the "Write" Way

1. Come prepared with the necessary supplies: paper, notecards, pen or pencil, computer disks for downloading, your college ID, and cash for photocopying.

2. Find an efficient system of note-taking suitable for you.

3. Be wary of plagiarizing. Plagiarism is using someone else's work without giving that person credit. Be clear in your notes if you are taking down information verbatim (direct quotes) or if you are paraphrasing.

4. Write down all the appropriate information about sources to avoid unnecessary and frus-trating backtracking when it comes time to write up your bibliography or cite your sources.

Avoiding Frustration

1. If the necessary sources are not on the shelf, ask for help. They may be misshelved, checked out, or available in another library through interlibrary loan, a service that finds the material in another library and then borrows it for you.

2. Be sure to give yourself enough time to gather necessary relevant sources and to do the assignment or write the paper to the best of your ability.

4. What Is the Vocabulary of Your Topic? What words describe it? Are there specialized terms? Some words are what you might call context-sensitive. For example, the word *dating* means one thing to a sociologist and another to an archaeologist. Also, if you are using a specialized database or index focusing on, say, biology, you probably would not use the term *biology* as a vocabulary term because the whole database or index covers biology. For more in-depth discussion of what vocabulary to use, see the section "Looking for Books on a Subject."

5. What Do You Want to Do with This Information? Are you writing a research paper, giving a speech, preparing for a debate or an interview, looking for a single fact or statistic, satisfying your curiosity about the nature of something, persuading someone to believe your ideas or someone else's, explaining a phenomenon, informing others, or telling a story? While these examples are not comprehensive, they will help you determine how much information you need and where to look.

6. What Are the Characteristics of the Information You Need to Find? Characteristics or qualities of information don't necessarily fall into discrete categories, but can occur in combinations or along a continuum. Characteristics include the following:

- ► **Introductory:** provides general information on a topic and is written for an audience without prior or special knowledge in an area

- ► **In-depth:** provides specialized and detailed information on a topic and is written for an audience with prior or special knowledge in an area

- ► **Biographical:** is about someone but by another person

Before you talk with the librarian, think about what information you're really looking for rather than the specific book or section of the library where you assume the information will be. The librarian my know of other places worth looking, other sources you haven't considered. (Photo by Hilary Smith)

► **Autobiographical:** is about someone and by that same person

► **Current:** is an event or idea that just occurred

► **Contemporary:** is a perspective at the time an event occurred

► **Retrospective:** means written by someone reflecting on a topic

► **Summative:** is a summary or overview of a topic

► **Argumentative or persuasive:** expresses a strong point of view

► **Analytical:** breaks an idea down into its components

In summary, answering these questions will help you to clarify the information you want and to articulate your needs to a librarian. In fact, you may find that these questions are similar to those a librarian will ask you.

Tips on Talking to Librarians

"A problem without a solution is usually a problem that is put the wrong way."

1. Recognize that librarians are usually more than willing to help you. Asking them for help may be scary or seem undignified, but go ahead and ask. Librarians can save you time and effort.

2. Don't feel you have to know everything about a topic, every aspect of using the library, or any specialized language or jargon. When a librarian uses a term you do not know, ask for clarification just as you would if a lawyer, mechanic, or teacher used an unfamiliar term. Also use the glossary at the end of the chapter.

3. Accept responsibility for your work. Librarians will expect you to know what your assignment is; to bring relevant assignment sheets, class notes, textbooks, and so on; to make decisions about the usefulness of sources; to ask questions; and to discuss clearly what steps you have already taken.

4. Be aware that not all librarians are alike. Often different librarians have different communication styles and areas of expertise. If you are not satisfied after talking to one librarian, seek another if possible.

5. Ask as many questions as you find necessary. Librarians do not have a quota for the number of questions you may ask.

6. Word your requests carefully to a librarian just as you would to describe symptoms to a doctor. For various reasons students may often not ask for what they want. For example, one student may ask where the science books are when actually he is looking for information on rain forests. Another student may need to locate research on memory studies in psychology journals, but she asks instead where the psychology journals are. Ask for what you want and be descriptive. You may think you're saving the librarian and yourself time, but more often than not, shortcuts waste time. In most cases the librarian will interview you to determine how to meet your needs. The librarian's questions will be similar to those listed in the section "Defining Your Need for Information."

7. Don't worry if your topic is of a controversial or personal nature. Librarians have a professional responsibility to treat your request confidentially.

FINDING YOUR WAY IN THE LIBRARY

"Cheshire-Puss," she began rather timidly.
"Would you tell me, please, which way I ought
to go from here?"

"That depends a good deal on where you want
to get to," said the cat.

"I don't much care where—" said Alice.

"Then it doesn't matter which way you go,"
said the cat.

Lewis Carroll, *Alice in Wonderland*

Sometimes just exploring is fun, but unlike Alice, usually you will care where you get to so it will matter which way you go. Knowing the general pathways to information is an important step in learning to find and use information wisely. Typical information sources include almanacs, bibliographies, catalogs, dictionaries, directories, encyclopedias, and indexes. The following sections emphasize the most frequently used sources: encyclopedias, catalogs, and indexes.

General Encyclopedias

The word *encyclopedia* comes from the Greek meaning "instruction in the circle of knowledge." Encyclopedias, especially general ones that attempt to cover the world of information, are often good starting places because they can (1) give you some background on a subject, (2) provide you with an overview on a broad topic and suggest possible ways to narrow it, (3) recommend other reading to you, and (4) give clues on how to search the topic in other sources by giving you terminology, key personalities, or events. A major disadvantage of encyclopedias, however, is that they become outdated. It generally takes seven years for an encyclopedia to be published,

and not all of the articles are updated when a new edition is issued. If your topic is current, an encyclopedia may not help much.

Following are some sample titles that may be available in your library. Encyclopedias are not all equal, and which is best will depend on your topic. (Use the checklist in Exercise 10.3, part A, to evaluate an encyclopedia.) When looking for information you may want to compare several encyclopedias or ask a librarian to recommend one. See a reference librarian if at least one of these is not in your library.

Encyclopedia Americana

World Book Encyclopedia

Collier's Encyclopedia

Compton's Encyclopedia

Encyclopaedia Britannica

Grolier's (on compact disc; need a computer to search)

Information Finder (on compact disc)

Subject Encyclopedias

Subject encyclopedias are constructed the same way as general encyclopedias, but they are more specialized. They concentrate on a narrower field of knowledge and cover it in greater depth. (Use the checklist in Exercise 10.3, part B, to evaluate an encyclopedia.)

In its quiet way, having explored the "stacks" of the library may become one of your fondest memories of college. But you'll get the most out of your exploration if you've prepared well beforehand by exploring catalogs and indexes. (Photo courtesy of University of Connecticut)

The subject encyclopedias listed here are grouped by general areas. This is not a comprehensive list. If you cannot find a title that fits your area of interest, ask a librarian to suggest one.

Arts

The New Grove Dictionary of Music and Musicians

Encyclopedia of World Art

McGraw-Hill Encyclopedia of World Drama

Humanities

Encyclopedia of Philosophy

Encyclopedia of Bioethics

Encyclopedia of Religion

Handbook of American Popular Culture

History

Encyclopedia of American Social History

The African American Encyclopedia

Dictionary of American History

Social Sciences

International Encyclopedia of the Social Sciences

Encyclopedia of Educational Research

International Encyclopedia of Communications

Encyclopedia of American Economic History

Encyclopedia of American Foreign Policy

Encyclopedia of Psychology

Encyclopedia of Sociology

Guide to American Law

Natural Sciences

McGraw-Hill Encyclopedia of Science and Technology

Encyclopedia of Computer Science

Catalogs

A catalog is a list of books and periodicals (magazines, newspapers, or journals) owned by the library. The catalog may also list other materials like films, videos, audiotapes, manuscripts, and government documents. Your library's catalog may be the traditional card catalog; it may be computerized ("on-line" as librarians say); it could be a combination of cards and computers; or it could even be available on microfiche or in another format. Nowa-

Library of Congress Subject Headings

If you have trouble finding the right subject headings, you may want to consult an official list, such as that found in the set of volumes entitled the *Library of Congress Subject Heading* or *LCSH*. If your term is not a preferred subject heading, *LCSH* will refer you to appropriate terms. For instance, if you look up the term *College life*, *LCSH* will tell you to use *College students*. *LCSH* will also offer related terms and even subheadings or subject divisions once you have located the preferred subject heading. Below is one *LCSH* entry:

College students *(May Subd Geog)*

    UF   College life

           Counterculture

           Undergraduates

           Universities and colleges—Students

           University students

    BT   Students

    NT   College freshmen

           College seniors

           Graduate students

           Junior college students

           Minority college students

           Talented students

           Teachers college students

           Vocational school students

           Wages—College students

           Women college students

—Attitudes

—Library orientation

—Sexual behavior

—Social conditions

    UF   College students' socioeconomic status

This entry tells you that *College students* is the authorized term. The comment *(May Subd Geog)* tells you that the term *College students* may be subdivided geographically. That is, you may be able to locate information on college students in your state—for example, *College students—North Carolina*. The *UF* means "used for." The term *College students* is used for the terms listed after *UF*. You may have *University students* as a term, but in this case *LCSH* is telling you that the authorized term *College students* is used for *University students*. *BT* means "broader term." If you do not find enough information using the term *College students*, you may want to use the authorized term *Students*. *NT* means "narrower term." If you are finding too much information using *College students*, you may want to use one of the authorized terms following *NT* to help focus your search. *RT* (not shown in this example) means "related term" or a synonymous term. If the term *College students* is not exactly the term you want to use, one of the terms following *RT* might provide more useful information. The boldfaced terms following dashes (—*Attitudes* and so on) are examples of subject divisions. Subject divisions help you focus your search if your first topic is too broad.

days, you also may be able to gain electronic access or "log on" to your catalog without even going to the library. Whatever the format, it is important to familiarize yourself with the library's catalog and the particulars of looking for a book or other materials by its author, title, or subject.

Looking for Books on a Subject. You generally will begin to look for information by using books. Often finding books on a subject is difficult or tricky for several reasons:

► You may not know the subject well.

► The terminology or vocabulary may be unfamiliar.

► Your term may not exactly match the catalog's. For example, the catalog may list *modern history* as *history, modern,* or it may list *light bulbs* under the heading *electric lamps, incandescent.*

► Your term may be so new that a subject heading has not been created for it. For example, before the AIDS epidemic the disease's now familiar acronym was not used as a subject heading.

► Your topic is so narrow you need to rely on a broader heading instead to gather additional information. For example, you may find some information under *hate crimes,* but to find more you might need to look under *racism* or *bigotry.*

Most of the materials in libraries are located using what are called "subject headings," "descriptors," or "index terms." Indexers, catalogers, and researchers select the terms in order to organize information; however, sometimes these professionals select terms that you or your instructor may not have thought to use. Your job is to match your own language with that used in catalogs or indexes. For example, a library source may describe cars using the subject heading or descriptor *cars, automobiles,* or *motor vehicles.* Often, when you look up a term, you will be referred to the preferred subject heading or term.

Keyword Searching. Most computerized sources also provide searching by "keyword." Here, the computer searches the entire record of an item for the words or phrases you entered. The word you entered might appear somewhere in the title, might be a subject term, or might be in another part of the description of the item. When you search by keyword, you can specify how to combine the terms you want it to search, how to position a word in relation to other words, and where to look for a word in the record (for example, only in the title).

There are advantages and disadvantages to searching either by subject heading or by keyword. What's most important is that you think about the vocabulary of your topic beforehand and use both subject headings and keywords for the best results.

Indexes

Indexes identify articles in periodicals, which may be published daily, weekly, monthly, bimonthly, or quarterly. The most common periodicals you will use are newspapers, magazines, and journals. Because articles are published more frequently and more quickly than books, they often contain more current information. When you look in an index, you do not actually find the article itself. You find a citation listing the author(s), title of the article, title of the magazine or journal, date of the issue, and volume and page numbers. Some indexes, called abstracts, also provide a short summary of the article's content, which can tell you if the article is relevant.

Using an index to locate articles saves time. You could browse through journals for information, but for more thorough coverage, use an index. Some indexes also list materials published in books, usually in collections of essays. Your library may also have a computerized version of a particular index. If you want to use a computerized version or an index on CD-ROM, ask a librarian what your library offers.

Some indexes may include both magazines and journals, so be wary if you plan to focus on one type of periodical. Magazines provide important information, but generally they do not cover topics in depth. Some well-known magazines are *Time, Newsweek, Ebony, U.S. News & World Report,* and *Science.* Scholars usually do not write magazine articles. If they do, they write the article to address a broader audience who may not understand technical terms. To distinguish between magazines and journals you can (1) look for titles containing the word *journal,* (2) look at the length of the article, because journal articles are usually longer, (3) look for titles that use technical or specialized vocabulary, a good indication of a journal article, or (4) ask a librarian for help.

Different kinds of indexes cover various types of publications. In addition to newspaper, magazine, and journal (or specialized subject) indexes, there are indexes to types of material. For example, the *Speech Index* identifies speeches published in books; *Granger's Index to Poetry* indexes poems published in collections of poetry; *Book Review Index* lists reviews of books published in periodicals.

Magazine Indexes. Magazine indexes list articles in magazines on a wide variety of topics. Some frequently used magazine indexes include the following:

Readers' Guide to Periodical Literature   *Academic Index* (computerized)
Infotrac (computerized)   *Periodical Abstracts* (computerized)
Magazine Index (computerized)

Subject or Specialized Indexes. Specialized subject indexes list articles in journals that cover a narrow subject field. Instructors may specifically request that you look for journal articles rather than magazine articles. Below is a useful, but not comprehensive list of subject indexes. Ask a librarian to suggest other indexes.

Humanities

Humanities Index

Philosopher's Index

Music Index

Religion Index One

Art Index

MLA International Bibliography (literature, linguistics)

Natural Sciences

General Sciences Index

Applied Science and Technology Index (engineering)

Life Sciences Collection (biology, botany, zoology)

Cumulative Index to Nursing & Allied Health Literature

Index Medicus (medicine)

ACM Guide to Computing Literature

Social Sciences

Social Sciences Index

Education Index

ERIC (computerized; education)

Psychological Abstracts

PsycLit (computerized version of *Psychological Abstracts*)

PAIS International (government, social issues, political science)

Sociological Abstracts

Business Periodicals Index

ABI-Inform (computerized; business)

Finding Periodicals in Your Library

Once you have chosen your articles of interest, you will have to locate the actual magazines, newspapers, or journals. Usually you will consult the library's catalog to see if the library has the title you need. Some libraries keep a separate list of their journals and magazines. However, the library's catalog may not indicate which specific issues of a periodical the library actually contains. Ask a librarian for help.

Periodicals may be shelved by call number with the books, or they may be organized alphabetically. If they are shelved by call number, you will have to look in the catalog, or possibly another list, to discover what the correct call number is. Most libraries will have the back issues of these periodicals bound into hardcover volumes by year. The more current issues are usually not bound until a volume is complete. Some periodicals are available on microform. Newspapers are almost always kept on microfilm, except for the most recent issues.

EVALUATING SOURCES

Successfully gathering information involves more than just locating enough sources. It also involves evaluating articles, books, and other materials once you have found them. Particularly in the Information Age, as the volume of available information increases daily, you should not settle for the first available sources. These sources may not be as relevant as others; they may be dated; or they may be inaccurate. To evaluate a source you might ask these questions:

1. **Is the source relevant to your information needs?** You can begin by looking at the title of the book or article, its length, the type of source you need, and the type that is available or that you have at hand.

2. **Is the information in the source accurate?** If your topic is controversial, if you are relying on just a few sources, or if you are using a questionable fact, you might want to find some reviews or additional commentary to check how accurate the information is. Compare other sources to see what they say.

3. **Does the author or the source show bias?** Consider why material was written or for whom it was written. When might you need to seek a different opinion?

4. **Is the author credible or reliable?** What are the author's credentials? If you have trouble answering this question, see a reference librarian.

5. **Is the information timely?** That is, is it the most up-to-date information you could locate? You might consider this question when using statistics or when you are in a fast-paced field constantly undergoing change (for example, computer science, medicine, economics).

Use the questions throughout this chapter and the procedures suggested by the exercises for future research projects you undertake during college and after.

EXERCISE 10.3 Finding Information in the Library

Answer the questions below.

A. General Encyclopedias

Choose one general encyclopedia from the list in the text to complete the following questions.

1. Where are the general encyclopedias located in your library?

_____

2. Is there an index, and if so, why is this aid important?

_____

_____

Choose a topic. If you have trouble, think about subjects you have discussed in class or covered in your textbook. Come up with your own topic or choose your major or a career interest.

3. What is your topic? What is the vocabulary of the topic? What words might you use to look for information in this encyclopedia?

_____

_____

_____

4. Did you find information on your topic in the encyclopedia? If not, why do you think you didn't find information?

_____ Topic is too current; encyclopedia is too old.

_____ Topic is too specific; need to look in the index and see if information is contained in an article on a broader subject.

_____ Encyclopedia doesn't use the same language as I do; need to think of other terms to look for in the index.

_____ Topic is too specialized for a general encyclopedia.

List some other reasons:

_____

_____

5. When you did find information, did the index or article list other related terms or topics to look under for more information? How might these be useful?

_____

_____

6. Are there additional sources or references listed at the end of the article? How could these be useful?

_____

_____

7. What are some reasons for using a general encyclopedia? When in the research process might a general encyclopedia be useful?

_____

_____

_____

B. Subject Encyclopedias

Using the same topic as before, choose a subject encyclopedia from the list in the text to complete the following questions. In trying to decide which subject encyclopedia to use, think back to the process of determining your information need, especially the question, Who would be interested in the topic?

1. Where is this encyclopedia located in your library? (You may have to look up the encyclopedia by its title in your catalog to find its location. If you have trouble, ask a librarian.)

_____

2. Is there an index to the encyclopedia? _____

3. Did you find information on your topic in the subject encyclopedia? If not, why do you think you didn't find information?

_____ Topic is too current; encyclopedia is too old.

_____ Topic is too specific; need to look in the index and see if information is contained in an article on a broader subject.

_____ Encyclopedia doesn't use the same language as I do.

_____ Topic is not covered adequately by any of the subject encyclopedias.

List some other reasons:

_____

_____

4. What are some of the similarities and differences you found between general and subject encyclopedias?

_____

_____

_____

C. Library Catalogs: Looking for Books on a Topic

1. Refer back to the section "Catalogs." What type of catalog is yours? If your catalog is computerized, does it have a special name? What is it? Does your library catalog provide access to libraries at other locations? List one or two. If your catalog is half card and half on-line, what date divides the two parts?

_____

_____

2. Using your same topic of interest, consult the *Library of Congress Subject Heading* list. Ask your librarian if you do not see this set of volumes. Is your term an appropriate subject heading or does *LCSH* tell you to use another term instead? If so, what is the appropriate search term?

_____

3. List any related terms, broader terms, or narrower terms, and explain why you think these could be helpful.

_____

_____

Now locate the titles of books on your topic using the subject heading you found in *LCSH*. Pick one specific book.

4. List the author, title, date of publication, publisher, call number, and location for the book.

_____

_____

_____

5. How could you find other books by this book's author?

_____

6. Does your library contain other books by this author? If so, list a title.

_____

7. Besides subject searching, what are other ways to locate books using the catalog? (For instance, what if you knew the title or the author? What if you are using a computerized catalog?)

_____

_____

8. What can you do if your library does not have a copy of the book you need?

_____

D. Magazine Indexes: Looking for Articles in Magazines

Choose one of the magazine indexes listed in the text to complete the following questions.

1. What index did you choose?

_____

2. How is it arranged? If you are using a computerized index, describe instead some of the ways you can search.

_____

_____

Look under your topic.

3. What can you do if your exact topic or term is not listed in the index or if using your term yields no results in the computerized index?

_____

4. Find a citation. If you don't understand how to read a citation, where can you find an explanation? Does the computerized version have help screens?

_____

5. List the author, title, complete magazine title, volume, date, and page numbers.

_____

_____

_____

6. Is the magazine title abbreviated? If so, where do you find the complete title?

_____

7. To what in the citation should you pay attention to determine relevancy?

_____

E. Specialized Subject Indexes: Looking for Articles in Journals

Choose one subject index to complete the following questions.

1. What index did you choose? What discipline(s) does this index cover? Check the preface of the print index or available help screens on the computer. Look under a topic of your choice.

_____

_____

2. Are there related terms or subject headings? If you are using a computerized index, does it have a list of preferred subject terms, also known as a thesaurus? (Hint: The thesaurus may be available in print format or on the computer.)

_____

3. Find a citation. If you don't understand how to read a citation, where can you find an explanation? Does the computerized version have help screens?

_____

4. List the author, title, complete magazine title, volume, date, page numbers.

_____

_____

_____

5. If journal title is abbreviated, where did you find the complete title?

_____

F. Finding Periodicals in Your Library

Select either the magazine or journal citation that you have already written down above.

1. What is the journal or magazine title?

_____

2. Does your library have this journal or magazine? Does it have the volume you need? How did you find this out?

_____

_____

3. How are the journals and magazines shelved in your library—in one place (perhaps alphabetically by title) or arranged by call numbers like the books? Are any kept on microfilm? If your library does have the journal or magazine listed in your citation, find the volume with your article and photocopy the first page of the article.

_____

_____

LIBRARY LANGUAGE

Abstract: a summary of an article or book.

Almanac: a compilation of useful but skeletal information and statistics on countries, people, events, and subjects. Often filled with fascinating bits of information over a wide range of subjects.

Annotation: a description of an article or book. An annotated bibliography is especially useful to locate because it includes a brief summary that can help you determine if something is relevant. You may have an assignment to annotate a source. That means you would write a description of the reading.

Bibliography: a list of materials (books, articles, videos, and so on) on one subject or by one author. Bibliographies can be helpful because they gather and identify materials on a common theme. Be wary of outdated bibliographies, however.

Biography: something about a person.

Bound periodical: issues of magazines or journals arranged together under one hard cover.

Call number: a unique combination of letters and numbers used to identify items in a library. Materials are arranged on the shelves in call number order. A call number is given to an item on the basis of subject so that materials on a similar subject will be shelved together. Dewey Decimal, Library of Congress, and Superintendent of Documents are three of the major types of call numbers a library might use.

Catalog: a listing of what a library contains.

Check out: to borrow library materials for use outside of the library.

Circulate: to lend library materials for use outside of the library.

Circulation: the library department that checks out and reshelves materials, as well as usually handling overdue fines.

Citation: the written information that identifies a book or article. A citation is the information you will need to locate the item or to include as a reference in your paper. It usually includes information such as author, title, pages, and date.

Database: an organized collection of records having a standardized format and content. For example, a cookbook is a database of recipes. Computerized indexes and catalogs are two of the most common types of databases in libraries.

Dictionary: something that gives the spelling, pronunciation, meaning, and definition of words or concepts. Language dictionaries are the most common type, but there also subject dictionaries that define words and concepts in a given area, such as literature or science.

Directory: something that gives contact information (address, phone, titles of officers) and perhaps a brief description. Helpful for locating other people, experts, organizations, agencies, businesses, and so on.

Gopher: a computer program that uses simple menus to allow searchers to reach a large variety of information resources and services on the Internet.

Index: (1) in a book, an alphabetical list of names and subjects in the book along with the corresponding page number(s); (2) as a type of reference source, a systematic guide to the contents of a discrete set of materials. For example, periodical indexes allow you to search for articles published in particular magazines or journals. These indexes cover a specific time period and may be searched by subject and often by author.

Interlibrary loan (ILL): the service, and often library department, that gets materials from other libraries.

Microform: general term used for printed materials that have been reduced in size and are read using special machines. Microforms include microfilm (on a roll) and microfiche (small sheets).

Noncirculating: materials that can be used only within the library and cannot be checked out.

Periodical: a magazine, journal, or newspaper that is published at regular time periods, or periodically. A periodical is a type of serial.

Record: used most often in the context of computerized sources, refers to all the information given about a particular item. A record typically includes the citation information, an abstract, and other information such as language.

Reference: (1) another term for citation; (2) a service, and usually a department, provided by the library to help people find the information they need.

Reserve: a service, and most often a department in a library, whereby heavily used items are placed by instructors to allow access by a greater number of students. Materials on reserve can be checked out for a much shorter period of time so that they will be available for more people to use.

Serial: a publication that comes out in parts. Serials include newspapers, journals, magazines, annual reports, and yearbooks.

JOURNAL

Have your feelings or concerns about using the library changed as a result of this chapter? How? What do you need to do at this point to improve your general library skills? What else might you do now to learn more about the libraries and other information resources on your campus that might be useful to you?

SUGGESTIONS FOR FURTHER READING

Gaffin, Adam. Preface to *The Big Dummy's Guide to the Internet*. Cambridge: MIT Press, 1994. (This source is also available on the Internet; ask for help.)

Lubar, Steven D. *InfoCulture: The Smithsonian Book of Information Age Inventions*. Boston: Houghton Mifflin, 1993.

Roszak, Theodore. *The Cult of Information: The Folklore of Computers and the True Art of Thinking*. New York: Pantheon, 1986.

Tehranian, Majid. *Technologies of Power: Information Machines and Democratic Prospects*. Norwood, N.J.: Ablex, 1990, p. 155.

Wriston, Walter B. *The Twilight of Sovereignty: How the Information Revolution Is Transforming Our World*. New York: Scribner, 1992, p. 21.

Wurman, Richard Saul. *Information Anxiety Is Produced by the Ever-Widening Gap...* New York: Doubleday, 1989.

Writing for Success

Carolyn Matalene
University of South Carolina

I don't understand why writing is so important. I'm a talker. I get writer's block when I'm even in the same room with a blank sheet of paper. What do I have to say, anyway? Why can't I just tape record my ideas and hand that in instead of term papers?!

Unfortunately many college students (and even some of their professors) feel uneasy about writing. Some students are so fearful of having to write that they will actually refuse to sign up for courses that require papers.

Yet not being asked to write means being short-changed as a student, because writing is at the center of what a college education is all about. Being educated means being skillful with language—able to control language instead of being controlled by it, confident that you can speak or write effectively instead of feeling terrified. When successful people explain how they rose to the top, they often emphasize their skills as communicators: "I could write better than anyone else, and the boss liked that," or "I was the only person who could explain things simply." Again and again the essence of success lies in being an effective speaker and writer, being able to explain issues clearly and to convince others.

This chapter presents a gradual program for easing you into the role of writer. If you follow along, do the exercises, and incorporate some of the suggestions into your regular study practices, you will not only *feel* better about writing, you'll *be* better at it too. You'll get better grades and know why you are getting them.

GETTING INVOLVED—PRIVATE WRITING

Some students believe that they can "get an education" the way they get a new car or a new job. They think that if they "learn" what's in the book and become repositories of information, then they will become educated. The truth is, you can't "get educated" because education isn't an event that happens or a commodity that you purchase. Rather, it is a process that you take part in for the rest of your life by becoming a learner. Being a *rememberer,* or a passive knower, may get you through some of your exams, but you won't really succeed unless you become a *learner.* A learner does more than remember. A learner synthesizes and evaluates, questions and considers, sees relationships, and draws conclusions. A learner develops an interior voice and exhibits purpose and control.

So one of the most effective ways of becoming a learner is to become a writer. Because writing is a process uniquely suited to learning, the more you use writing as a way of studying, the more you will learn. Start with some *private writing.* Private writing means writing that you undertake as a way of learning, writing that you practice as a technique for studying, writing that only *you* see because it is not intended to communicate knowledge or information to anyone but yourself.

Private writing works as a medium for you to communicate with yourself as a learner, asking your own questions about what you read and hear, questioning your own answers, and eventually becoming fluent in the language of a discipline. Of course you will also have to produce *public writing:* the essays, exams, research papers, and critical analyses for your courses. In public writing you must go through the process of revision and editing; your writing must be finished and polished. By contrast, private writing can remain unfinished, exploratory, inconclusive—a way of remembering facts and terms even if their meaning is not yet clear to you.

In order to become an active participant in any field of learning, you have to master the language of that field. In any course you take, you need to write as well as read, speak as well as listen. Some students start out thinking that reading is enough. And certainly readers can be active learners if

Like most complex undertakings, strong writing begins with exploring one's own awareness. That begins with private writing.

they engage with the text, ask questions, make connections and comparisons, evaluate—if, in a word, they think. In order to really learn something, either in class or from a textbook, you need to combine listening and reading with a faithful system of taking and reviewing notes.

I would like to suggest another, complementary strategy to the steps suggested in the earlier chapters. For each of your courses, use one section of your course notebook for *reading notes*. Take your sociology text, for example, and read a portion, perhaps a chapter. Don't underline or highlight every sentence. Instead read thoughtfully and then close the book. Now, in your reading notebook, write a brief summary in your own words of what you read: What is the chapter really about? Next, write some of your own reactions, comments, and thoughts: What does this chapter make you think of? What can you relate it to? What examples from your own experience can you think of that would prove the major points? Or what examples can you think of that would disprove those points? What questions do you have? What seems strange? What seems unclear or hard to understand? If you could ask your instructor some questions about this material, what would they be?

As you write, you will have more ideas. By writing, you increase your chances of remembering the material because you are involved in it. You are also becoming literate in the field you are reading about; you are making the language of the subject your own. You are engaged. And that is the essence of what any teacher wants from any student—not agreement, but engagement with the subject.

EXERCISE 11.1 Engaging with the Subject

Write your thoughts about the chapter so far. What is it about? What do you think of what you have read? What questions does it raise for you?

Now write about a reading assignment you have recently completed in one of your courses. Start with a summary, then write about why you think you were asked to read it. Finally write your own personal response to the material.

RESPONDING—PROCEDURES OF THOUGHT

When you write in response to what you read or observe, you learn a lot more. Research shows that students who engage in extended writing about a topic are capable of more complex thoughts and are better able to see relationships among concepts. When you write in response to a text or a topic, your mind inevitably performs the mental procedures that all humans use to analyze experience and to learn systematically. You try different ways of looking; you practice *procedural* knowledge.

There are a number of common *procedures of thought* you can use as you respond to reading by writing. The first and most important is simply to read for the main idea: What is the main, central, or most important idea presented in this section or chapter? Once you have answered that question, you can choose from a number of analytical strategies to organize your thoughts and your writing.

Comparison and Contrast

One way to respond to a text is to draw comparisons: "What this chapter seems to be saying is *like* what we studied last week in this way" or "This chapter is *different* from what we have studied so far in these ways." Spend some time in your notebook comparing and contrasting, writing about similarities and differences. You can compare concepts or events or terms or people. Comparison is perhaps the most powerful learning tool at your disposal. Some learning specialists think that comparing is the basis of all learning, that new understanding results from matching—or comparing—the unfamiliar with the familiar, or new information with information we already have. (We can't avoid comparing, it seems, a new friend with an old one, this teacher with that one, tonight's dinner with last night's, and so on.) Another good reason for thinking in terms of comparison is that comparison questions frequently turn up on exams: Compare the economic development of Chile with that of Argentina; compare Wordsworth's theory of poetry with Pope's; compare treatments for dyslexia. Try writing some comparisons of your own *before* the exam.

EXERCISE 11.2 Comparing

Select a course you are now taking. Do some private writing (or perhaps write a note to a close friend) comparing it to a related course you took in high school. How is it similar? How is it different?

Cause and Effect

In some courses—especially history—thinking in terms of cause and effect is important: This caused the uprising; these were the major causes of World War I; these were the major effects of Roosevelt's domestic policies. Focusing on cause and effect is also a common and powerful way to structure our experience, one that we rely on again and again as we try to solve problems, effect change, and achieve new understanding. Human beings are human partly because they are always asking questions: What would happen if we mixed nitrogen and glycerine? What will be the effects of a tax cut? A competency test? A lower speed limit?

EXERCISE 11.3 Cause and Effect

What "caused" you to decide to go to college, or to this college in particular? What have the "effects" been so far? Write privately about this cause/effect relationship.

Narration

Another important thought procedure for writing in any historically oriented course is getting the order of events straight: This is what happened; this is the story of … Writing that presents a sequence of events is called a narrative, and of all the different ways of structuring writing, the narrative seems to be our favorite. Being able to tell yourself the story of an event or a discovery or a work of literature is an effective way to remember it.

EXERCISE 11.4 Narration

In private writing summarize what happened in one of your classes today. Narrate exactly what happened, in the order it happened. Make it sound like a story. What points was the teacher making? How did you and other members of the class respond? How did this particular class session fit into the course as a whole?

Theories and Opinions

In a course that involves learning the theories of "major thinkers," it is important that you do some writing in which you explain what the thinker thought—in your own words: This is what Freud thought about infantile sexuality; this is what Marx thought about surplus value. Feel free to write down what *you* think: "This is my interpretation of Nietzsche's phrase 'God is dead'" or "This is my opinion of Mary Daly's feminist philosophy." You will also discover that sometimes your teacher will disagree with the author of a textbook. Write about that: "Samuelson says this, but my instructor disagrees and says this instead. But I think they both are wrong because ..." Now you are getting practice in keeping straight who thinks what or which ideas belong to whom. And that, of course, is what academic discourse is all about.

You don't have to be serious all the time either. You might write about what would happen if Freud went to Jung for treatment or what Matthew Arnold would say about the poetry of Sylvia Plath or how Mozart would react to the Beatles, or Handel to En Vogue. Or you could write a letter to your mother telling her how complicated or strange or interesting or unusual your philosophy course is and how you feel about that.

EXERCISE 11.5 Theory or Opinion

Choose a theory you have heard about recently in one of your classes or read about in your general reading. Or choose an opinion you heard someone express recently on the radio or television or in person. In private writing or a note to a close friend, try to clarify your understanding of what that person meant. In what respects do you agree or disagree? Why?

Explanation and Argumentation

The final thought procedures are explanation and argumentation. As you learn your way into a discipline, you will be asked to act like a member of that discipline—to think like a psychologist or journalist or biologist. Each discipline has its own terminology and its own ways of explaining. Try practicing them in your private writing by role-playing an expert in the discipline you are studying: "A psychologist would explain *x* this way" or "An economist would say this happens because …"

Academics don't just explain things. They also argue whether this explanation is better than that one, this solution better than that. The more you progress in your major, the more you will be asked to explain *and* argue.

EXERCISE 11.6 Explanation and Argumentation

Explain why a subject you are studying is really important and should be studied by every student. Or explain why you have changed the way you think about a particular group of people or a political idea or an event in the past. Or argue for a better solution to a campus problem. (And send your letter to your campus newspaper!)

Engaging with Your Studies

As you write privately about your studies, you will be engaging with ideas more deeply and more personally. The difference between success and failure in college is *engagement*. Successful students don't end their studies in the classroom or with their homework assignments. They carry what they are learning into their private lives, their social lives, their family lives. They integrate what they are learning with who they are. You can too—by putting pen to paper.

GETTING CONTROL—FROM PRIVATE TO PUBLIC WRITING

Now that you've acquired some specific analytical skills and practiced using them in your private writing, you're ready to apply them to your public writing—essays, reports, exams, and so on. The transition from private writing to public writing terrifies many students, but the more you practice private writing, the less you will need to worry about exams and papers. You will gain confidence as a writer because you will be developing a composing process that works for you.

The further you go with college, the more central writing becomes, both to understanding and to communicating with others. (Photo by David Gonzales)

Writing to Study for Exams

In addition to the strategies discussed in Chapter 9, you can prepare for a test or exam by writing. You might start your review by jotting down individual words—all of the special words or terms that were used in a given course, such as *Manifest Destiny* or *Mutual Assured Destruction* or *epanalepsis* and *anadiplosis*. Then you can write a paragraph about each one, defining the term, explaining it, giving some examples, and so on. By doing this you are preparing yourself for that favorite exam mode of so many instructors, the "ident." Professors are fond of asking you to "briefly but adequately identify any ten of the following." If you are studying for a literature course, you might write down all of your (or the instructor's) favorite lines or phrases from the works you have read: "Call me Ishmael." "Do I dare to eat a peach?" "Let me not to the marriage of true minds admit impediments." (If you can't remember any such lines, refer back to your books.)

After you have warmed up on some terms or lines, try writing a summary of the entire course for an imaginary ignorant person. Explain what this course is really about, why it matters, what the essence is, and why everyone should take it. Next, try to "psych" the instructor. What questions are obviously and inevitably going to be on the exam? What questions did the instructor say would appear on the test? Write them down. Then write the answers.

Writing to Organize

Write the answers? "That's going too far. I'll do that in the exam but not now," most students say. You may think that writing the answer to an anticipated tough essay exam question represents a rather grim way to study. It might also seem that your creativity and spontaneity would suffer if you wrote the answer down ahead of time and that your answer would sound boring. Fair enough. But at least get in the habit of *outlining* the answers to some of the exam questions you have imagined. Then you will be ready to outline the answers during the exam before you start to write. While few writers will admit to actually enjoying making an outline, outlines are extremely useful. Call it planning instead of outlining if you like, but whatever the word, the key issue is *organization*. And organizing, or building a structure, is the essential transformation that must occur between the writing you do *for your own learning* and the writing you do *to show that you have learned*.

Writing to Communicate

The composing process refers to the stages a writer goes through in order to achieve results that are worth being read. Private writing can just flow as a stream of consciousness, wandering out of the main channel, stopping and starting. In private writing the focus is on the first stage of the composing process, *invention*. During the invention stage (some call it prewriting) writers concentrate on thinking, on questioning and connecting and generating and gathering and analyzing and evaluating. The drafting is fast and free, with little concern for grammar, syntax, sentence structure, and so on. When you engage in public writing, however, the drafting must yield more structured discourse; somewhere along the way, either on paper or in your head, planning must take place.

Moving from private to public writing requires you to focus on structure. If you have been studying all along—and studying, you should realize by now, means reading *and* writing—then you have been practicing invention all along. When exam time comes or when the paper assignment is given, you have available an abundance of content that you must now shape into the proper *form*. A successful piece of public writing will be based on a plan, an organizational principle, a structure so clear that a reader could outline it if need be.

Establishing Structure. The obvious technique for success in public writing—but one that many students never figure out—is to look for the tipoffs to an appropriate overall structure in the question or the assignment itself as explained in Chapter 9. Are you being asked to *compare* two things? To *explain* the effects of something? To *summarize* a theory? To *relate* what happened? To *interpret* a text or an event? Remember to focus on the structure words in the question or the assignment and do what they tell you to do.

The next step is to write a plan (an outline) that corresponds to the task. In an essay exam you will need to write the plan quickly, but you must take the time to do it. The plan will help you focus on the question asked instead of drifting and also help you budget your remaining time. For a term paper or a critical analysis, you might spend a major portion of your time on the

Stop, Read, and Listen!

How well informed are you about what's happening in the world?

1. Do you listen to National Public Radio? When you're getting dressed in the morning, do you tune in to "Morning Edition"? When you're exercising after class, do you listen to "All Things Considered" on your headset? Do you listen to your campus station? What other good local or national radio information programs do you listen to regularly?

2. Do you read your campus newspaper? Do you read the local paper every day? On Sunday do you set aside some time to read a good national paper, such as *The New York Times, The Washington Post,* or the *Los Angeles Times?*

3. Do you read a magazine or two every week? Along with *Time* or *Newsweek,* do you read *Rolling Stone, The New Yorker, Sports Illustrated, Harper's, Vogue, Vanity Fair, Esquire,* or *The Atlantic Monthly?* Do you read any of the many specialized magazines on computers, sports, cars, boats, and so on? Do you go to the open periodical room in your library and let yourself do some random reading every now and then?

4. Do you ever read some good current nonfiction? Have you ever tapped the wealth of living writers helping us make sense of our world—among them John McPhee, Joan Didion, Jane Kramer, Tracy Kidder, Garry Wills, Mark Singer, Lewis Thomas, Roger Angell, Alice Walker, Tom Wolfe, Michael Herr, Annie Dillard, Paul Theroux, Russell Baker, and Frances Fitzgerald?

The more you know about what's going on, the more you'll have to say, both in and outside class. The more you read, listen, and inform yourself in general, the better you'll write.

plan. Figuring out what you are going to say and how you are going to say it—that is, establishing your structure—is hard work, but it's essential.

Some writers, however, cannot or will not or do not plan before they write. They just plunge into writing—the same way you do in private writing. Their writing "grows from the top." The problem with this approach is that, if an idea or plan or project fails, it's much easier to discard a plan—a page with some words and arrows and circles on it—than to throw away an entire draft of hard-won sentences. Writers who do not plan, who write by drafting (and some excellent writers do proceed this way), insist they don't really throw away sentences; it only looks that way for a while. Eventually everything gets used, but maybe in a different place.

Whether you plan before you write or plan while you write doesn't matter in the long run if you are accomplishing effective writing. What does matter is that the writing you hand in goes through the transformation from private to public and has a clear structure.

What Is Structure? Maybe you are not quite sure about what the word *structure* really means when applied to writing. Don't be alarmed; you're not alone, because structure is hard to explain. When applied to writing, structure means the conceptual "skeleton" that holds the writing together. In carefully structured discourse each sentence relates to the main idea of the paragraph, each paragraph relates to the idea of that section, and each section relates to the plan of the whole. Think of structure as a hierarchical or pyramidal diagram, like the flowchart of a corporation or the chain of command in the military. Readers expect writing to be structured hierarchically. They also expect—and insist upon—writing that moves up and down the different levels on the pyramid, from abstract to concrete, from general to specific, from assertion to proof. Readers find such writing both readable and convincing. When writing remains on the same level, readers lose interest.

In fact levels of generality is what the outline is all about. An outline is a diagram that shows hierarchical structure; the main points (I, II, III, and so on) are general or abstract. They are supported or proved by less general or more specific statements (A, B, C, and so on). These in turn are supported by even more specific information (1, 2, 3, and so on). Even further down the abstraction ladder are the specifics or the details (a, b, c, and so on) that make writing believable and colorful and memorable. Try to keep an outline structure in your mind's eye as you write. Remember that good writing does not stay at the same level of generality or abstraction all of the time. Hearing only about the decisions of the generals during a battle won't tell us everything about what happened; we need information from the front as well as from headquarters. This is a metaphoric way of saying that good writing offers us information from a variety of levels; good writing "moves" between the abstract and the concrete, between the general and the specific, between assertions and proof.

Making Connections. Sometimes writers do a good job of including the concrete information necessary to support their assertions, but don't do a good job of showing their readers how the information and the assertions connect. In our culture readers want to know exactly how the pieces of information in the text they are reading fit together. They want not only good organization but also signs telling them what the organizing principle is, how the writer is proceeding, why this piece of data leads to this conclusion. Ours is a "writer responsible" culture—that is, we expect the writer to do all of the work, to spell everything out, to take us by the hand and say, in effect, "Here is where we are going, and this is how we are going to get there."

Readers like to know what's coming: "In this paper, I will analyze x in terms of y and z," or "First, I will present findings, then I will explain their relevance." They also like signpost words along the way: *therefore, thus, however, because, in conclusion,* and the like.

EXERCISE 11.7 Being Specific

Make up a generalization about the students at your school, such as "The problem with students here is apathy," "The students here are high achievers," or "Students today are too materialistic." Now provide a number of specifics to prove or support your statement. What does it take to convince your classmates that your generalization is accurate?

Before you hand in your next piece of academic writing, read it one more time to see if you have provided your reader with enough signposts, enough instructions for reading your text. (And if they seem scarce, think about adding some.)

Drafting. Drafting (that is, writing it down) may be the stage in the composing process that holds the greatest terror. Those of us who plan before we write do so not because we are virtuous but because planning makes us feel braver as we face a blank page or an empty screen. Panic, it seems, is part of the process for most writers. As with the fear you feel at the top of the ski run or on the high dive or at center stage, you have to learn to deal with it. Many would-be writers intensify their own panic by trying to do two tasks at once, two tasks that can only be achieved separately. They try to get it down and get it right at the same time. Thus, for every thought the right brain sends out, the left brain pounces on it and says, "That's stupid! You dummy! Nobody would want to read that!" The writer writes a word, crosses it out, writes a sentence, and then crumples the page. It's called writer's block. The internal editor functions as a nagging and judgmental critic.

That editor must be told to be quiet for awhile. Speak to your negative critic firmly: "Shut up! I don't have to listen to you. I will call on you later. Right now I need to take some risks, and I am too inspired to worry about your misplaced concerns."

As John McPhee, a talented professional writer, says, "You've got to put bad words down. And then massage them." What he means is his first draft, and your first draft, will probably be terrible, but only after you have something on paper can you work out the kinks. Perfectionism applied too early in the process prevents many intelligent people with interesting things to say from ever becoming capable or competent writers. In fact an important reason for engaging in private writing is that writing for yourself, quickly and furiously, will make you feel more confident about drafting. You will not be embarrassed to express outlandish ideas on paper; you will be comfortable with sloppy phrasing. Messy prose can always be tidied up, revised, and edited. Blank pages can't be turned into anything.

Revising and Editing. After you have completed the first sloppy draft, it's time to unleash your internal editor. Try to read what you have written as a reader rather than as the writer. Of course, if you are writing within the time constraints of an examination, you must speed up the entire composing process. You can't revise your answer; there isn't time. (That's why the plan matters so much.) The best you can do is to proofread carefully, add a few words, correct the obvious errors, and turn it in. But essay exams are only one kind of public writing—a special, hurried kind that *requires* you to turn in first drafts. Many college students don't seem to understand this and turn in first drafts as final versions for all of their writing assignments. Not surprisingly, they tend to get C's—or worse.

If you want to get A's on your papers, you have to hand in final versions, not first drafts. That means putting your rough first draft through the process of revision, making it clearer, better organized, more tightly focused, more interesting, and livelier. You have to make your writing work for a reader who is in fact an expert—your professor. Some professors will offer to read a draft of your paper and make suggestions before the final version is due. *Always* take them up on this. Their criticisms and suggestions are the blueprints for your A.

Revising (getting the big plan right) and *editing* (tinkering with the words and sentences to make them say what you want them to say) are essential elements of the writing process. Professional writers invest extraordinary amounts of time and energy in revising and editing. So, as an amateur, you should certainly invest some. Actually, revising can be rewarding; turning an ordinary paper into a highly respectable one feels good—though it usually feels best after you are done. And editing—searching for just the right word and changing weak sentences into powerful ones—offers pleasures too.

Some writers give their first drafts to someone else to read. The truth is, everybody needs an editor. Professional writers have professional editors. Finding a good editor for your own writing, though, can be tricky. Your roommate, your girl- or boyfriend, or your mom may like you so much that they are too kind. You need an editor who reads well and who has the courage to say to you—in a kindly way and only when asked—"No, I can't follow your argument. No, it doesn't make sense." You want an editor who doesn't gush or flatter but who can be an honest critic, someone who wants you to succeed but who knows clarity from chaos, good writing from bad.

Most of us, after finishing a first draft and even a final draft, have little ability to accurately judge our own writing. We tend to over- or underestimate its worth. We give the piece an F if we are pessimists or an A if we are optimists, and lifelong optimists may turn into gloomy pessimists late at night. Writing, after all, is one of the most complex mental tasks we try. Not surprisingly, we aren't always good at judging our own creations. The editor who didn't experience the sweat you invested in your draft may be a better judge of its worth than you are.

When you think your draft is as good as you can make it in the time available, summon up the English teacher editor from your subconscious. Let this purist worry about punctuation and spelling. If you are writing on a word processor—and you certainly should be—run the spelling check to catch the typos.

There is no use in pretending that revising and editing your own work is fun or easy or simple. Almost all writers find it worrisome, hard, and complicated—but, alas, necessary. Use the following checklist to get started. Remember, always start with the big issues; there is no point in polishing a paper that doesn't have anything interesting or insightful to say.

Revision and Editing Checklist

1. Does this draft fulfill the assignment? Is its central purpose clear?

2. Does the paper meet the needs of your audience? This is a tricky question when you are writing an academic paper. You are trying to write like an expert for an expert. Sometimes students go wrong by assuming that their reader knows it all already; if you aren't sure about how much explaining to do, talk with your instructor about just what kind of audience you should be writing for—*before* you turn in your paper.

3. Do you give your reader adequate organizational signposts? Do the paragraphs follow logically?

4. How does the paper sound? Do the sentences make sense? One of the best ways to catch problems is to read your paper out loud.

5. How does the paper look? Run a spell-check and a grammar-check one more time.

When at last you hand in your great work, you probably will feel it still isn't perfect. That's okay—nothing is. The ultimate point is not the *product* anyway, but the *process:* What has this piece of writing done for you as a learner? How have you changed because you wrote it?

Writing, private or public, is finally not about grade points. Writing is really about you, about the richness of your life lived in language, about the fullness of your participation in your community and in your culture, about the effectiveness of your efforts to achieve change. The person attuned to the infinite creativity of language leads a richer life. So can you.

WRITING WITH FRIENDS

The writing discussed in this chapter has been writing done alone, by yourself, because colleges don't grant credits or degrees to groups. You're on your own writing your term paper or taking the final exam. Yet, when you have earned your degree and are at last on the job, you will most likely be working with others, contributing to group projects, and writing collaboratively.

Probably some of your teachers will assign group projects during your college years, and then you will have the chance to work as a team and to write with others to produce a single document. If you have taken this chapter seriously, you can lead the team and help them produce a text that looks good, meets the needs of its audience, and fulfills its purpose.

JOURNAL

Write about yourself as a writer. How do you proceed when you are given a writing assignment? How well does your method work? What are your strengths and weaknesses as a writer? What sorts of comments do instructors make on your papers about your writing?

Write another journal entry about some writing you did in collaboration with someone else, as a team project or a group assignment. How was writing with a friend different from writing alone? How well did it work?

SUGGESTIONS FOR FURTHER READING

Burk, Carol, and Molly Best Tinsley. *The Creative Process.* New York: St. Martin's Press, 1993.

Goldberg, Natalie. *Living the Writer's Life.* New York: Bantam New Age, 1990.

Gordon, Karen Elizabeth. *The Transitive Vampire: A Handbook of Grammar for the Innocent, the Eager, and the Doomed.* New York: Times Books, 1984.

Masiello, Lea. *Write at the Start: A Guide to Using Writing in Freshman Seminars.* Columbia, S.C.: National Resource Center for the Freshman Year Experience, University of South Carolina, 1993.

Williams, Joseph M. *Style: Ten Lessons in Clarity and Grace,* 3rd ed. Glenview, Ill.: Scott, Foresman, 1989.

Woolever, Kristin R. *About Writing: A Rhetoric for Advanced Writers.* Belmont, Calif.: Wadsworth, 1991.

Zinsser, William. *On Writing Well: An Informal Guide to Writing Nonfiction,* 4th ed. New York: Harper & Row, 1990.

———. *Writing to Learn: How to Write and Think Clearly.* New York: Harper & Row, 1988.

Speaking for Success

Constance Courtney Staley
University of Colorado–Colorado Springs

Robert Stephens Staley II
University of Colorado–Colorado Springs

*A*re you kidding? Go talk to
the instructor? I can't even get up
enough nerve to raise my hand
when he asks a question that I
know I can answer. I don't want
to sound stupid. I don't know how
I'm going to make that little speech
next week.

The human brain is a wonderful organ.
It starts to work as soon as you are born
and doesn't stop until you get up to deliver
a speech.

George Jessel

Most of us think we communicate fairly well—after all, we've been at it all our lives, right? But some types of communication situations are downright threatening to many of us—giving speeches, for example. Having all those people staring at us suddenly can be unnerving even to those of us (like teachers) who communicate for a living.

When you get your first assignment to prepare an oral presentation for class, you may have mixed feelings about it. It may be just the chance you've been waiting for to demonstrate your enthusiasm and competence to classmates and friends. Or you may well feel anxious about standing up in front of a group of people you don't even know.

The *Book of Lists* reports that speaking in front of others is the number one fear of Americans. It's more frightening for most of us than death, sickness, deep water, financial problems, insects, or high places. Imagine how Hollywood could use this information if it only knew what really terrifies us most. Picture a movie about some poor unsuspecting fellow rounding a corner, confronting an audience of hundreds of people waiting for him to give a speech. Isn't it sad to realize that what humans fear most is each other?

In this chapter we'll present new ways of looking at this common fear and some practical antidotes for you to try. We'll also tell you ways to turn speech assignments into opportunities for success.

EXERCISE 12.1   Introducing Yourself

To try your hand at speaking in front of the class, prepare a 3-minute presentation introducing yourself to your classmates. Bring or wear a "prop" that characterizes or caricatures you. For example, if you like to ski, wear your goggles; if you flip burgers on the weekends, wear your apron and carry a spatula. You can talk about your hometown, your high school days, your family, your reasons for going to college, or some other topic your instructor suggests.

When it comes to holding forth in public, a few of us seem blessed with a wonderful sense of freedom. Most are more hesitant. Fortunately, your anxiety can help release the energy it takes to speak well to a group. (© 1992 Chuck Savage/photo courtesy of Beloit College)

BASICS OF PUBLIC SPEAKING

Speaking in front of others may be our most prevalent fear, but it doesn't have to be. Here are some essentials you may not have considered:

- ► **Once you begin speaking, your anxiety is likely to decrease.** Anxiety is highest right before or during the first 2 minutes of a presentation. If you can make it past that challenge, you're on your way to channeling your nervous energy.

- ► **Your listeners will generally be unaware of your anxiety.** Although your heart *sounds* as if it were pounding audibly or your knees *feel* as if they were knocking visibly, rarely is this the case. *You* are the one concentrating on the give-away clues to your anxiety—not your listeners. Chances are that they are rooting for your success, not your demise as a speaker.

- ► **Having some anxiety is beneficial.** Anxiety indicates that your presentation is important to you. Think of your nervousness as *energy,* and harness it to propel you before and during your talk. The more opportunities you accept to speak, the more this principle will become second nature.

- ► **Practice is the best preventative.** The best way to reduce your fears is to prepare and rehearse *thoroughly.* World-famous violinist Isaac Stern is rumored to have once said, "I practice 8 hours a day for 40 years, and they call me a genius?!" The same principle applies to public speaking.

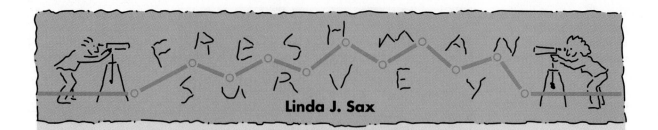

Linda J. Sax

Public Speaking

The graph shows the percentage of first-year students who rate themselves as "above average" or "top 10 percent" in four areas of ability: academics, leadership, writing, and public speaking. Contrast the level of confidence in academics and leadership with the much lower level in public speaking! If you feel anxious about speaking in public, take comfort in the fact that the person sitting next to you probably feels the same.

Self-Rated Abilities, 1993

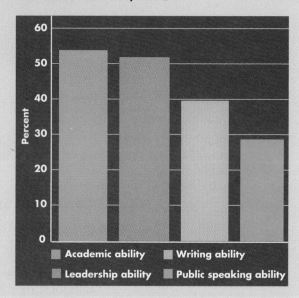

SOURCE: Higher Education Research Institute, UCLA

SIX STEPS TO SUCCESS

If you're assigned a speaking task in class, how should you proceed? Successful speaking involves six fundamental steps:

- ▶ **Step 1:** Clarifying your objective.
- ▶ **Step 2:** Analyzing your audience.
- ▶ **Step 3:** Collecting and organizing your information.
- ▶ **Step 4:** Choosing your visual aids.
- ▶ **Step 5:** Preparing your notes.
- ▶ **Step 6:** Practicing your delivery.

Step 1: Clarifying Your Objective

You need to identify what you are trying to accomplish. To *persuade* your listeners that your campus needs additional student parking? To *inform* your listeners about student government's accomplishments? *What* do you want your listeners to know, believe, or do when you are finished?

Step 2: Analyzing Your Audience

You need to understand the people you'll be talking to. Ask yourself:

1. What do they already know about my topic?
2. What do they want or need to know?
3. What are their attitudes toward me, my ideas, and my topic?

In other words, consider the audience members in terms of their *knowledge, interest,* and *attitudes*.

Knowledge. During your preliminary analysis discover how much your audience knows about your topic. If you're going to give a presentation on the health risks of fast food, you'll want to know how much your listeners already know about fast food so you don't risk boring them or wasting their time.

Interest. This may be even more important than knowing your listeners' prior knowledge. How much interest do your classmates have in nutrition? Would they be more interested in some other aspect of college life? Whenever possible, make your information match their needs and interests.

Attitudes. Recognize that your listeners will respond with both head and heart (and in this case, stomachs) to your message. How are they likely to feel about the ideas you are presenting? What attitudes have they themselves cultivated about fast food?

EXERCISE 12.2   Profiling an Audience

Profile your classmates in terms of their knowledge, interest, and attitudes on a controversial subject the class decides on together. Compare your profile with those your classmates have developed and see if you can reach consensus on what the class is really like.

Figure 12.1 The GUIDE Checklist

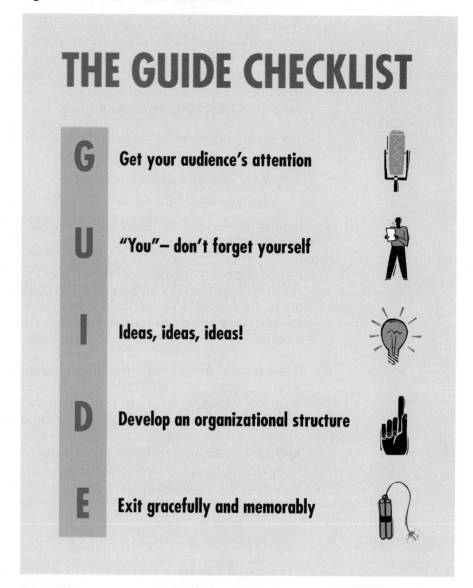

THE GUIDE CHECKLIST

G Get your audience's attention

U "You"– don't forget yourself

I Ideas, ideas, ideas!

D Develop an organizational structure

E Exit gracefully and memorably

Step 3: Collecting and Organizing Your Information

Now comes the critical part of the process: "building" your presentation by selecting and arranging "blocks" of information.

The most useful analogy for this step is to think of yourself as a GUIDE. After all, you are not communicating in a vacuum. Instead you are *guiding* your listeners through the ideas they already have to the new knowledge, attitudes, and beliefs you would like them to have.

Imagine you've been selected as a guide for next year's prospective freshman class and their parents visiting campus. Picture yourself in front of the administration building with a group of people assembled around you. You want to get their attention and keep it in order to achieve your *objective:* raising their interest in your school. You would not want to make a quick turn and leave them all wandering down the wrong pathway. Are you beginning to see how the analogy works? Let's be even more specific by discussing the GUIDE checklist in Figure 12.1.

[G] Get Your Audience's Attention. In order to guide your audience, you must get their attention right away. There are many ways to do so. For example, you can relate the topic to your listeners:

> *"Let me tell you about what to expect during your college years here—at the best school in the state."*

Or you can state the significance of the topic:

> *"Deciding on which college to attend is one of the most important decisions you'll ever make."*

Or you can arouse their curiosity:

> *"Do you know the three most important factors students and their families consider when choosing a college?"*

Or you can begin with a compelling quotation or paraphrase:

> *"Alexander Pope once said, 'A little learning is a dangerous thing; Drink deep or taste not the Pierian spring.' That's what a college education is all about."*

You can also tell a joke, startle the audience, question them, tell a story, or ask a rhetorical question. Regardless of which method you select, remember that a well-designed introduction must do more than simply get the audience's attention. You must also develop rapport with your audience, motivate them to continue listening, and preview what you are going to say in the rest of your speech.

EXERCISE 12.3   Writing an Opening

Assume you've been assigned to give a speech at another college or university on the value of your first-year seminar class. Write an introductory paragraph using one of the methods outlined above.

[U] "You"—Don't Forget Yourself. In all this talk of objectives, audience analysis, and "guides," we must not exclude the most important source of your presentation—YOU. You might think that speaking in front of others means assuming a role, being someone other than who you really are. True, you have rehearsed your presentation and are not just saying whatever comes into your mind, but that doesn't mean that you shouldn't insert yourself and your personality into your message. Even in a formal business or professional presentation, you will be most successful if you develop a comfortable style that's easy to listen to. The presentation represents you and your thinking. Capitalize on this idea. Be yourself, don't play a role. Let your wit and personality shine through.

[I] Ideas, Ideas, Ideas! This brings us to the "meat" of your presentation. One effective way to generate ideas is brainstorming. Create a list of all the possible points you might want to make. Then write them out as conclusions you want your listeners to accept. For example, let's imagine that in your campus tour for prospective new students and their parents you want to make the following points:

1. Tuition is reasonable.
2. The faculty is composed of good teachers.
3. The school is committed to student success.
4. College can prepare you to get a good job.
5. Student life is a blast.
6. The library has adequate resources.
7. The campus is attractive.
8. The campus is safe.
9. Faculty members conduct prestigious research.
10. Our college is the best choice.

For the typical presentation, five main points are the most that listeners can process. After considering your list for some time, you decide that the following five points are critical:

1. Tuition is reasonable.
2. The faculty is composed of good teachers.
3. The school is committed to student success.
4. The campus is attractive.
5. The campus is safe.

Try to generate more ideas than you think you'll need so that you can select the best ones. Then, from the many ideas you come up with, decide what is relevant and critical to your objective.

As you formulate your main ideas, keep these guidelines in mind:

Main points should be parallel, if possible. Each main point should be a full sentence with a construction similar to the others. A nonparallel structure might look like this:

1. Tuition. *(a one-word main point)*
2. Student life is a blast. *(a full-sentence main point)*

Main points should each include a separate, single idea. Don't crowd main points with multiple messages, as in the following:

1. Tuition is reasonable and the campus is safe.
2. Faculty are good teachers and researchers.

Main points should cover relatively equal amounts of time in your presentation. If you find enough material to devote 3 minutes to point 1 above, but only 10 seconds to point 2, you'd better rethink your approach.

Ideas rarely stand on their own merit. To ensure that your main ideas work, use a variety of supporting materials. The three most widely used forms of supporting materials are *examples, statistics,* and *testimony.* Let's look at how a single main point can be developed through these three types of supporting materials.

Examples

Main point: Faculty members conduct prestigious research.

Supporting example: Professor Curie, of the biology department, recently won a Nobel Prize for medicine.

Examples include *stories* and *illustrations, hypothetical events,* and *specific cases.* They can be powerful, compelling ways to dramatize and clarify main ideas, but make sure they're relevant, representative, and reasonable.

Statistics

Main point: Faculty members conduct prestigious research.

Supporting statistics: Seventy percent of faculty members at this school have published books.

Obviously, statistics are widely used as evidence in speeches. Of course, numbers can be manipulated, and unscrupulous speakers sometimes lie with statistics. If you use statistics, make sure they are clear, concise, and comprehensible to your listeners.

Testimony

Main point: Faculty members conduct prestigious research.

Supporting testimony: According to the editor of the *Chronicle of Higher Education,* our college has the most highly rated faculty among colleges of its size.

Testimony includes quoting outside experts, paraphrasing reliable sources, and generally demonstrating the quality of individuals who agree with your main points. When you use testimony, make sure that it is accurate, qualified, and unbiased.

Finally, since your audience members are each unique individuals, you are most likely to add interest, clarity, and credibility to your presentation by varying the types of support you provide.

[D] **Develop an Organizational Structure.** Now that you've decided on the main points you want to make in your presentation, you must decide how to arrange your ideas. Don't mix and match; select a format and stick with it. You'll be able to choose from a variety of structural formats, depending on the nature and objective of your presentation. For example, you may decide to use a *chronological* approach by discussing the history of the college from its early years to the present. Or you might wish to use a *problem-solution* format. You would describe a problem (such as choosing a school), present the pros and cons of several solutions (or other schools), and finally identify your school as the best solution.

Begin with your most important ideas. A case of nerves can sometimes cause you to say things you never intended to say as you try to "warm up" your listeners. Instead of "warming them up," stacking your presentation with unimportant information at the beginning can cause your listeners to "cool down" and lose interest.

Actually writing out an outline might be one of the most useful ways to spend your preparation time. Many experts suggest listing each main point and subpoint separately on a 3 × 5 or 4 × 6 notecard. This allows you to work on a large surface (such as the floor) arranging, rearranging, adding, and deleting cards until you find the most effective format. Then simply number the cards, pick them up, and use them to prepare your final outline (see Figure 12.2).

Figure 12.2 Arranging a Presentation Outline

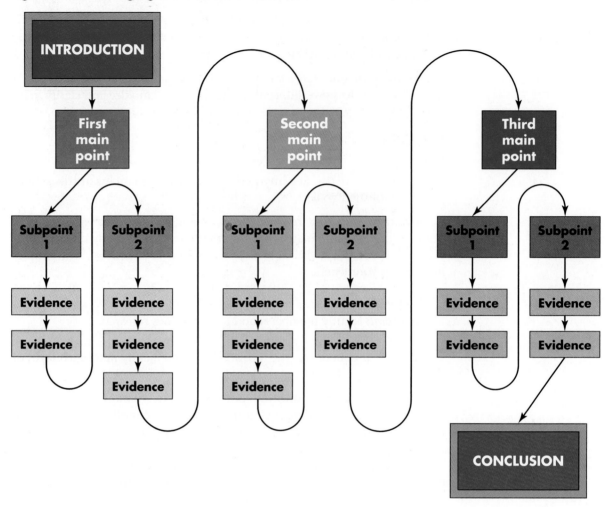

As you organize your presentation, remember that your overall purpose is to **GUIDE** your listeners. That means you must not neglect connectors between your main points. Returning to our original analogy, if you were a campus guide, you would find ways not to lose your followers between the new art gallery at one end of the campus and the football stadium at the other. As a speaker you can accomplish the same thing through the use of *transitions*. For example:

> *Now that we've looked at* the library...
>
> *The first half of my presentation* has identified our recreational facilities. *Now let's look* at the academic hubs on campus.
>
> *So much for* the academic buildings on campus. *What about* the campus social scene?
>
> *The first factor* to consider is... *The second important factor* is...
>
> *The most important point* I'll make today is...

Transitions make the difference between keeping your listeners "with" you and losing them at an important juncture.

Rehearse your talk with a friend. Ask for feedback about your words, your posture, your gestures, and anything else that contributes to the total effect of your presentation. Practicing erect and out loud will help you much more than memorizing with your head bowed. (Photo by Hilary Smith)

[E] Exit Gracefully and Memorably. Someone once commented that "a speech is like a love affair. Any fool can start it, but to end it requires considerable skill." Most of the suggestions for introductions also apply to conclusions; that is, you can effectively conclude your speech by relating the topic to your listeners, stating the significance of the topic, ending with a quotation or paraphrase, telling an anecdote, making a startling statement, asking a question, telling a story, referring back to your introduction, or issuing a challenge.

Whatever else you do, go out with style, impact, and dignity. Don't leave your listeners asking, "So that's it?" Subtly signal that the end is in sight (without the overused "So in conclusion"), summarize your major points, and then conclude.

Step 4: Choosing Visual Aids

One way to increase the chances that your listeners will understand and remember your message is to use visual aids. When visual aids are added to presentations, listeners can absorb 35 percent more information—and over time they can recall 55 percent more. Of course, you'll need to decide how your speech can be best represented. Should you prepare a chart? Show a videotape clip? Write on the blackboard? Distribute handouts? You can also make excellent overhead transparencies on the computer using large and legible typefaces. As you select and use your visual aids, consider these rules of thumb:

1. Make visuals clear and easy to follow—use readable lettering and don't crowd information.
2. Introduce each visual before displaying and explaining it.

3. Allow your listeners enough time to process visuals. Don't whip them up and then pull them down immediately, before they can be read.

4. Proofread carefully—misspelled words hurt your credibility as a speaker.

5. Maintain eye contact with your listeners while you discuss visuals. Don't make the mistake of turning around and talking to your visual aids.

Step 5: Preparing Your Notes

Prepare notes for your presentation. In your role as an effective guide, what you're doing now is creating a clear map for you to follow as you speak.

If you are like most speakers, you will find having an entire text before you to be an irresistible temptation and end up reading much more of your presentation than you had planned. One way to keep this from happening is to avoid writing out every word of your presentation. A second temptation to avoid is memorizing your presentation and eliminating notes altogether. Your memory may fail you. And even if it doesn't, your presentation could sound "canned." A better strategy is to memorize only the introduction and conclusion so that you can maintain eye contact, and therefore build rapport with your listeners as you speak.

What *should* you do to prepare notes for your presentation? The best notes are a minimal outline from which you can speak extemporaneously. You will rehearse thoroughly in advance, but since you are speaking from brief notes, each time you give your presentation, your choice of words will be slightly different, causing you to sound prepared but natural in your delivery. You may wish to use 3 × 5 or 4 × 6 notecards since they are small and unobtrusive. (Make sure you number them just in case you accidently drop the stack on your way to the front of the room.)

After you have become more experienced, experiment with other methods of preparing notes. Eventually you may want to let your visuals serve that purpose. You can always write notes to yourself lightly in pencil on charts you're displaying. A handout listing key points may also serve as your basic outline. As you become even more proficient, you may find you no longer need notes. The ability to deliver an entire talk without referring to any notes at all can be quite impressive.

Step 6: Practicing Your Delivery

As you rehearse, form an image of success rather than failure. Practice your presentation aloud several times beforehand—harnessing that energy-producing anxiety we've been talking about.

Begin a few days before your target date, and continue until you're about to go "on stage." The point is not to memorize your speech, but to become so familiar with it that you can almost hear a tape recording of yourself during your actual delivery. Make sure you rehearse aloud; *thinking* through your speech and *talking* through your speech have very different results. Practice before an "audience"—your roommate, a friend, your dog, even the mirror. Talking to something or someone helps simulate the distraction listeners cause. If possible, practice in the room you'll actually speak in so that you're used to your surroundings. Finally consider audiotaping or videotaping yourself, to pinpoint your own mistakes and to reinforce your strengths. If you ask your "audience" to critique you, you'll have some idea of what those changes should be. Beginning this process early leaves enough time to make changes if something isn't working. As the old saying goes, "The more

Think of a speech as a guided tour, with things you want your audience to see and experience along the way. Let them know where the tour is going and what you hope they'll get out of it. Choose a path of ideas that stimulates interest along the way and leads to a satisfying destination. (Photo by David Gonzales)

you sweat *beforehand,* the less you will have to sweat *during* your presentation." The bottom line is that your speaking success is largely up to you.

Of course, when you rehearse, you must make certain you're rehearsing the *right* behaviors. Spending hours practicing your golf swing does no good if your technique is wrong in the first place. With public speaking the same truism applies to practicing your delivery.

LISTENING TO YOUR VOICE AND BODY LANGUAGE

Many speakers seem to need to occupy their hands when speaking. They often jingle coins in their pockets or fidget with a pen. Other distracting hand placements include what have been called the lectern clench and the "fig leaf" position.

Instead, allow your hands to hang comfortably at your sides so you can occasionally use natural, spontaneous gestures. Avoid overgesturing or undergesturing. Some females, for example, use smaller and less frequent gestures than do their male counterparts. Although we don't recommend that you take on a "John Wayne" style, it may be helpful for you to risk more dynamic gestures than usual. On the other hand, if you are normally a hyperactive gesturer, tone down your natural tendencies so that your audience isn't lost in the thrashing. Whatever you do, vary your gestures. One gesture used repeatedly can be annoying to listeners. Robotlike gestures are even more distracting than no gestures at all.

Don't lean over the lectern, if there is one. Plan to move comfortably about the room, without pacing nervously. Some experts suggest changing positions between major points, in order to punctuate your presentation. The unconscious message is "I've finished with that point; let's shift topics." Face your audience as much as possible, and don't be afraid to move toward them while you're speaking. That communicates your interest in their needs.

Eye contact is even more important. Some speakers look only at people who wield power (such as the instructor); others watch only those who seem interested; still others fake eye contact by gazing at the back wall. Instead, make contact with as many listeners as you can by looking at individuals as directly and engagingly as possible. This also helps you read their reactions and establish speaker command.

A smile helps to warm up your listeners, although you should avoid smiling excessively or inappropriately. Smiling through a presentation on "World Hunger" would send your listeners a mixed message. In general, an active face is better than a deadpan expression. Ask for feedback from your practice audience about your facial expressions.

As you practice, also pay attention to the pitch of your voice, your rate of speech, and your volume. Project confidence and enthusiasm by varying your pitch within your natural range. Speak at a rate that mirrors normal conversation—not too fast and not too slow. Consider varying your volume for the same reasons you vary pitch and rate—to engage your listeners and to produce special effects.

Pronunciation and word choice are important, too. A poorly articulated word (such as "gonna" for "going to"), a mispronounced word (such as "nucular" for "nuclear"), or even a misused word can quickly erode credibility. One famous speaker always began a speech by thanking the person who introduced him for the "fulsome" introduction—until he learned that *fulsome* means "offensive, insincere." Check meanings and pronunciations in the dictionary if you're not sure, and use a thesaurus for word variety. Fillers such as "uhm," "uh," "like," and "you know," are distracting, too. If your practice audience hears you overusing these fillers, then, uh, like, cut them out, you know?

Finally, consider your appearance. Convey a look of competence, preparedness, and success. As Lawrence J. Peter, author of *The Peter Principle,* says, "Competence, like truth, beauty, and a contact lens, is in the eye of the beholder."

EXERCISE 12.4 Thoughts on Delivery

Think about your teachers this semester or in the past; your rabbi, pastor or priest, television speakers; and so on. What aspects of their deliveries impressed or bothered you?

SPEAKING ON THE SPOT

Most of the speaking you will do in college and after will be impromptu minispeeches given on the spot with little or no preparation. When your instructor asks your opinion on last night's reading, when a classmate stops you in the hall to find out your position on an issue, or when your best friend asks you to defend your views, you give impromptu speeches. Of course, because this kind of speaking is what you do most, it also shapes your image as a successful communicator. For this reason you need to think about how you *can* prepare for impromptu speaking.

EXERCISE 12.5   Speaking on the Spot

A. To practice becoming a dynamic speaker, come to class prepared to give a 1-minute speech on your worst pet peeve—something that *really* annoys you. Your instructor will give you a rolled newspaper. Use it to accentuate your main points and emphasize your feelings by hitting the lectern or desk with the newspaper. *OR:*

B. For this exercise your instructor will bring a shopping bag filled with common objects to class. Each class member will have an opportunity to draw out an item and give the class a 1-minute sales pitch. The catch, however, is that you must find a new use for the item. (For example, if you draw an egg slicer, you could sell it as a "pocket guitar.") *OR:*

C. Select two students to go to the front of the classroom for a "speak down." Your instructor will assign a controversial impromptu topic (for example, "the worst thing about the opposite sex"), and both students will begin speaking on the subject at the same time, each trying to capture the audience's attention and steal attention from the other speaker. After 2 minutes the instructor will call time, and class members will vote on which speaker they listened to most and discuss why.

When you must speak on the spot, it helps to use a framework that allows you to sound organized and competent. There are many ways to arrange your thoughts, but one of the most popular ways is called the PREP formula (Wydro, 1981). Short for *preparation,* this plan requires you to give the following:

[P]   **Point of view:** Provide an overview—a clear, direct statement or generalization.

[R]   **Reasons:** Give the reasons you hold this point of view, broadly stated.

[E]   **Evidence or examples:** Present specific facts or data supporting your point of view.

[P]   **Point of view restated:** To make sure you are understood clearly, end with a restatement of your position.

Let's look at an example of how you might use the PREP formula to answer a question in class:

Professor Snodgrass: Do you think the world's governments are working together effectively to ensure a healthy environment?

You: [P] After listening to yesterday's lecture, yes, I do.

[R] I was surprised at the efforts the United Nations General Assembly has focused on the environment.

[E] For example, the industrialized nations have set stringent goals on air pollution and greenhouse gases for the year 2010.

[P] So yes, the world's governments seem to be concerned and working to improve the situation.

Using a device like the PREP formula, you sound logical, organized, and competent—whether you're communicating with other students in a discussion group, talking to an instructor during office hours, or answering a question in class.

EXERCISE 12.6 Using PREP

Bring five notecards to class with each one listing a question on which your classmates would have an opinion (for example, "Should the first-year seminar be a required course at all universities?" or "Should students have a say in the hiring and firing of college faculty?"). Your instructor will place one card face down on each student's desk. One at a time, each student will turn over his or her card and answer whatever question is written there using the PREP formula. You may not turn your card over until the person before you begins to speak.

"YES, BUT..."

What if you plan, organize, prepare, and rehearse, but calamity strikes anyway? What if your mind goes completely blank, you drop your notecards, or say something totally embarrassing?

Losing your train of thought is easily remedied: Always bring notes to get back on track. Slips of the tongue can be embarrassing, but they are frequently amusing as well. Years ago, the Reverend Spooner of Oxford University would often unknowingly transpose the first letters of words in sequence: "You have hissed my mystery lesson; you have tasted the whole worm," meaning "You have missed my history lesson; you have wasted the whole term." If you commit a spoonerism or make a similar mistake, smile and pat yourself on the back for providing a lighthearted moment for your listeners.

For the most part, we're sure you'll find that things will go smoothly and your preparation will pay off. If you make a mistake, the most important factor is not *that* the mistake occurred, but rather that you as the speaker *handled* and *minimized* the problem. Don't forget, your audience has been in your position and probably empathizes with you. Accentuate the positive; rely on your wit; use the opportunity to emphasize that you're not perfect. Your recovery is what they are most likely to recognize; your success is what they are most likely to remember.

JOURNAL

What are your feelings about speaking in public? Can you identify your most successful speaking experiences? What did you do to make them successful? Can you identify speaking experiences that were less successful? How will you ensure speaking for success in the future?

SUGGESTIONS FOR FURTHER READING

Lucas, Stephen E. *The Art of Public Speaking,* 3rd ed. New York: Random House, 1989.

Meuse, Leonard F., Jr. *Mastering the Business and Technical Presentation.* Boston: CBI Publishing, 1980.

Stone, Janet, and Jane Bachner. *Speaking Up: A Book for Every Woman Who Wants to Speak Effectively.* New York: McGraw-Hill, 1977.

Wydro, Kenneth. *Thinking on Your Feet: The Art of Thinking and Speaking Under Pressure.* Englewood Cliffs, N.J.: Prentice-Hall, 1981, pp. 64–69.

CHAPTER 13

Problem-Solving and Success in Math and the Sciences

Mary Ellen O'Leary
University of South Carolina

*D*id someone say "word problems"? Ouch! I've never liked those things! First, they're hokey. Second, they're confusing and they always depend on some new twist. Sometimes I can't even get started on the solution. Trying to make the biggest box possible by cutting the corners out of a rectangle and turning up the flaps—who has a "problem" like that anyway?

Consider these real-life problems:

In your history class you will have four equally weighted tests and it takes a 90 average to get an A. Your scores on the first three tests were 87, 92, and 94. What must you score on the fourth test to get an A for the course?

What will you wear to go out tonight since it's been two weeks since you've done any laundry?

If you need to finish your paper for psychology, study for the Spanish quiz, put in 4 hours at your job, and work out a dozen bugs in your computer program that's due tomorrow, how many people do you have to be?

Would you be able to solve them? How would you go about it?

In the past you may have encountered "problem-solving" as a kind of enrichment activity in math and other courses, added on after basic techniques and computational skills were mastered. Problems were neatly organized by type, and often only one "correct" solution was allowed for each. In a calculus class the solution likely had to display the use of differential or integral calculus, while in algebra the solution involved an equation or system of equations. Each of the natural sciences also had its own techniques and prescribed formats for solving problems. The problems themselves were often contrived and artificial, and the answers tended to "come out even"—the computations were "clean" and nothing like real life.

Today problem-solving is the central focus of science, mathematics, and engineering courses. Modern technology allows students to undertake "messy" computations that would be difficult or impossible to perform by hand. Textbooks can now include more authentic problems with data from the real world. Students are encouraged to tackle a problem in a variety of ways, to experiment with methods of solution, or to start out with a trial-and-error approach. In this chapter you'll learn how to apply a simple four-step strategy to problems across the natural sciences.

THE FOUR-STEP APPROACH TO PROBLEM-SOLVING

One important milestone in our understanding of the universal nature of problem-solving was the publication of *How to Solve It* in 1945. Although this classic work was written by the distinguished mathematician G. Polya, it really is a book on how to think straight in any field. Polya endorses a method that emphasizes experimentation, discovery, and invention in training students to find things out for themselves. His approach involves inductive reasoning, in which the problem solver starts with particular facts and circumstances and works toward a general conclusion. Polya shows that solutions are found through questioning and guided discovery. He explains that the basic processes of problem-solving are the same whether the problem comes up in an academic setting or in everyday life.

How to Solve It describes the four stages of all successful problem-solving. Perhaps we want to plan the menu and quantities needed for a group outing, determine the surface area of a kidney-shaped swimming pool, or assess the effectiveness of a new medication for Alzheimer's disease. Whatever kind of problem we are tackling, we need to do four things:

► **Step 1:** Understand the problem.
► **Step 2:** Devise a plan.

Almost any problem can be solved more quickly and more pleasingly when people work together. Start by talking about ways that the problem could be defined. Listen for different perspectives that suggest different ways of resolving it. (Photo courtesy of Earlham College)

▶ **Step 3:** Carry out the plan.
▶ **Step 4:** Look back.

Polya's steps seem simple and obvious, but they embody powerful notions. As a problem solver you must first take time to fully understand the problem. Read the problem at least two times, and then reread the last sentence. It often tells you what you are trying to find. Then ask yourself, What information is given? Is it enough to solve the problem? Is there some unnecessary information that can be ignored? Ferreting out the "givens" and the "to find" is a large part of Polya's first step. Often students overlook obvious information that is important for the solution. When a student has missed an important fact, some instructors will ask a mock question like "What color is my white horse?!" You can use this question on yourself when you feel you may be overlooking something essential.

It is the second step—"Devise a plan"—that is hardest for most problem solvers. Looking back at similar problems that you have solved in the past is a time-honored approach, but other strategies will be given below.

The third step may be routine or challenging. Whether it requires simple calculations, sophisticated computer technology, or just basic logic, it should be done carefully. Check and verify the accuracy of each stage as you work out your solution.

In the satisfying glow that comes with solving a challenging problem, the fourth step is often neglected. Real growth in problem-solving is achieved by looking back, reflecting on the problem and the method that led to success. Can you think of other problems that you could solve with the same approach? If you solved the problem for a particular value of a variable, can you generalize your result for other values? Can you extend your solution to a closely related but more complicated problem?

Polya's four steps carry you successfully through a wide variety of problems—from mathematical ones like the test score needed to get an A average in history, which has a single correct answer, to ones from everyday life like the laundry dilemma, which may have several appropriate solutions.

SOME PROBLEM-SOLVING STRATEGIES

Here are nine practical strategies that will help you implement Polya's approach to problem-solving. The first four—*draw a picture, experiment and act out, find a pattern,* and *make a table*—may be especially useful in understanding a problem. The rest of the strategies—*guess and check, solve a simpler problem, use logic, work backwards,* and *use mathematical methods*—may apply more to devising a solution.

1. Draw a Picture

Often drawing a picture can help you better understand the problem and devise a plan. Imagine how hard it would be to tell someone how to drive from a house in Seattle to a house in Miami without a map that showed how various highways are connected. A map or picture can show how things are related to each other, and therefore how to go from one point or step to another.

Make your map or diagram big enough to label clearly. You may lay out or label yours differently from the next person, or you may introduce a coordinate system that is oriented in an unusual way. Don't worry. An individualized approach is fine—as long as it is consistent with the facts of the problem.

EXERCISE 13.1   **The Horse Race**

Note: Read through Exercises 13.1–13.9 as you read the chapter, but wait until you are in a group in class before you actually try to solve them. In the group share ideas about how to solve the problems. Make sure that each person fully understands the problem. Then work together in devising a plan, carrying out the solution, and looking back on the problem.

In a make-believe horse race between five famous horses, Citation finished one length ahead of Seattle Slew, Spectacular Bid finished ahead of Citation but behind Secretariat, and Man-O-War finished four lengths ahead of Seattle Slew and one length behind Spectacular Bid. What was the finish place of each horse?

2. Experiment, Act Out, and Manipulate

Do anything you can to bring the problem to life: Move pennies around, cut corners out of a piece of cardboard and turn up the flaps, make a three-dimensional model, and so on.

EXERCISE 13.2   The Intelligent Pinsetter

The bowling pins shown below have been arranged incorrectly, with the triangle pointing away from the bowler. Can you make the triangle point toward the bowler by repositioning just three pins?

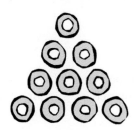

3. Find a Pattern

The better you become at recognizing patterns, the better problem solver you will be.

EXERCISE 13.3 Looking for Patterns

Fill in the following missing entries:

1. 21, 32, 43, 54, _____, _____, _____

2. A1, B2, D4, Z26, J10, C _____, _____ 7, N _____, M13, E _____, _____ 16

3. 1, 1, 2, 3, 5, 8, 13, _____, _____

4. A, E, F, H, I, K, L, M, N, _____

5. 77, 49, 36, 18, _____

4. Make a Table

Many types of problems can be better understood if the information is laid out in some kind of rectangular chart, grid, or table.

EXERCISE 13.4 Which Is Whose?

Ina, Jill, Louis, and Miguel each have a different favorite color among red, blue, green, and orange. No person's name contains the same number of letters as her or his favorite color. Louis and the boy who likes blue live in different parts of town. Red is the favorite color of one of the girls. What is each person's favorite color?

5. Guess and Check

Once discouraged in favor of algebraic or other formal mathematical methods, the guess-and-check technique now is recognized as integral to the way people really solve problems in everyday life.

EXERCISE 13.5   Circle Madness

Place the numbers 1 through 7 in the circles below so that the sum of the numbers along each line is 10.

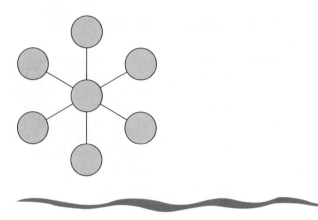

6. Solve a Simpler Problem

Often you can split the problem into smaller subproblems.

EXERCISE 13.6   How Many?

How many squares are there in the checkerboard figure below?

7. Use Logic

The basic principles of reasoning are at the heart of most problem solutions.

EXERCISE 13.7 Three Men and a Wall

Three men are wearing blindfolds and standing in a line perpendicular to a wall. From a bin containing three tan hats and two black hats, three hats are selected and placed on their heads. Then the blindfolds are removed. Each man is asked to determine what color hat he is wearing. The man farthest from the wall, who sees the two men and their hats in front of him, says, "I do not know which color hat I am wearing." The man second from the wall, who hears the reply and sees the man and the hat ahead of him, says the same thing. The third man, who sees only the wall but has heard the two replies, says, "I know which color hat I am wearing."

Which color is he wearing, and how does he know?

8. Work Backward

Try beginning at the end.

EXERCISE 13.8 The Shopper

You enter a store and spend half your money and then $20 more. Then you enter a second store and spend half your remaining money and then $20 more. Now you have no money left. How much money did you have when you went into the first store?

9. Use Algebra, Calculus, or Other Mathematical Tools

The strategies listed above will lead to complete solutions for some of the problems you encounter in your course work. At the very least they will help you get started on problems that will eventually require algebra, calculus, or some other specific mathematical method.

EXERCISE 13.9 The Squirrel

A squirrel runs spirally up a cylindrical post, making one circuit for each vertical rise of 4 feet. How many feet does the squirrel travel if the post is 16 feet tall and 3 feet in circumference? (*Hint:* You may not need as much mathematics to solve this as you think at first.)

EXERCISE 13.10 Applying Polya's Method

Think of several problems in your own everyday life. In a small group explore which of these might lend itself to Polya's problem-solving steps. Then choose one of these everyday problems and write an outline of how your solution could follow the four-step process outlined here.

SUCCEEDING IN COLLEGE-LEVEL MATH AND SCIENCE COURSES

Polya's process for problem-solving can be applied to any situation or discipline. At the same time, certain problem-solving skills are developed in very specific ways in mathematics and science classes. As you choose courses to meet general education requirements or as electives, don't avoid mathematics and science. Even outside an increasingly complex and technical workplace, you need scientific literacy in order to vote intelligently and to understand ethical and environmental concerns. You need "numeracy"—quantitative insights, estimation skills, a basic understanding of probability—to evaluate the statistical claims in advertisements and news reports; not all such claims represent valid applications of scientific and mathematical principles.

A New World of Math and Science

As you move from high school mathematics and science courses to college-level work, you will encounter familiar concepts but at more advanced levels. Here are other differences you may notice:

▶ The pace will be faster and the material more compressed. The topics covered in 180 days in high school may be presented in forty-two class meetings in college. It is likely that a new textbook section will be covered each day.

▶ Your instructor may consider your doing the assignments as essential to the course but actually collect your work only rarely or not at all. It will be your responsibility to keep up with the material regardless of whether your work is monitored.

▶ Theory—mathematical or scientific—may be the central focus. Lectures may be devoted to deriving formulas or to proving theorems. Smaller amounts of class time may be allowed for examples and problems.

▶ The classes may be larger—perhaps much larger—and the format quite different from anything you have experienced before. Classes may be organized in lecture sections, accompanied by recitations (problem sessions, often led by teaching assistants, where the lecture class is broken into smaller groups).

▶ Expectations may be different. There may be a greater emphasis on understanding concepts and applying principles than on developing manipulative skills and memorizing facts.

A Chance to Put Aside Some Myths

It is important to consider how science and math can be different at the college level, especially if your confidence is low in these areas. In high school you may have yielded to a myth like "Girls can't do math" or "Minorities don't succeed in science" or "Physics is for an elite few." With such negative attitudes you may not have performed to the true level of your real abilities. You may have been in classes where "the brains" dazzled everyone with their quick answers and perfect test scores. You may have felt inadequate by comparison and decided that you were not a math person or that science wasn't your thing.

"Congratulations! Yours Is the First Generation..."

A widely used precalculus textbook contains a startling statement that goes something like this: "Congratulations! Yours is the first generation not to suffer through long, tedious problems involving the computational uses of base-ten logarithms." An encouraging thought indeed. But turn the page and the text continues, "So now we are going to show you what you missed," and proceeds to give several pages of long, tedious computational log problems requiring "characteristics," "mantissas," "antilogs," and "interpolation"!

If these terms are foreign to you, be thankful that you are a student in this era of supercalculators and computers. This technology frees you to pursue interesting problems, look for underlying principles, and focus on the big picture in your mathematics and science course work. Thus the textbook exercises on logarithms seem like an April Fool's joke—they should have disappeared along with the slide rule.

Today logarithms are studied as a profoundly important family of functions, but logs are no longer needed to simplify arithmetic operations. Your calculator handles those operations immediately, with as many as thirteen decimal places of accuracy. But that is only the beginning of the power at your fingertips. You can produce an instant picture of a function with your graphing calculator and analyze its properties. With symbolic algebra capability on a computer or calculator, you can apply powerful mathematical methods with ease. Programming techniques allow you to customize solutions to an unlimited array of problems.

The pace of technological improvement has been breathtaking, as capability and cost have moved in opposite directions. One can only speculate on the wonders to come as multimedia approaches are tapped in education, as the communications superhighway is opened to all

citizens, and as palm-top computers become as essential as textbooks for college students. The promises of tomorrow are intriguing, but the technology of today has already significantly enhanced the study of mathematics and science. Your generation does have cause for celebration—not just because you are the first to escape tedious exercises with logarithms, but, more significantly, because you can apply the power of technology to delve deeply into real problems.

Later in the chapter we will look further at stereotyping in math and science fields. Here just consider that it's time to abandon such unfortunate and unfounded attitudes. As you embark on your college career, previous failures and frustrations can be put behind you. You are in a different setting with instructors who have little or no knowledge of past performance. This is your opportunity to begin with a more determined and confident approach.

EXERCISE 13.11 Replacing Myths

As you think back on your high school experience, describe yourself as a math/science student. Have you been influenced by a particular negative myth? Explain. Now write a short paragraph describing the positive attitude that can replace the myth in your mind.

Strategies for Success in Math and Science Courses

Here are some simple but important strategies for handling any math or science course.

1. Make Full Use of Placement Tests and Advisors. Most colleges will help you begin where you have the greatest likelihood of success.

2. Wherever Possible, Choose Your Instructors with Care. Follow the advice of those you trust who have gone before you. Remember, though, that your learning style may differ from your friend's. Also, there is much to be gained from taking a course with a demanding instructor who evokes your best efforts, even though other students may advise against it.

3. After the First Meeting in a New Class, Reflect and Plan. Write out specific goals for that course, along with a game plan for achieving them. Your goals will probably start with a desired letter grade but should also include a statement of what you hope to gain from the course. Reflect on why you are taking the class and write a paragraph for yourself on why success in this particular course is important to you and to your future. Your game plan expresses in detail your commitment to succeed. Here are some commonsense suggestions that you can incorporate in your plan to help you achieve your goals.

1. **Sit front and center.** Look alive and interested—it will help you to *feel* alive and interested.
2. **Attend every class.** Getting the notes from a friend is not the same as being there yourself. Don't get behind. In mathematics, and sometimes in science and engineering, concepts "stack up" vertically. Missing any portion undermines the whole structure.

3. **Expect to spend the time.** Unlike in high school, in college you master the material on your own outside of class. Although it's generally accepted that you need to devote 2 hours out of class for every hour in class, for some courses you will need to devote more than 2 hours, particularly when the material is dense and complicated.

4. **Be neat and organized.** Diagrams drawn with rulers, correctly labeled functions and expressions, clearly presented and legible solutions—all convey a positive impact, much like a word-processed and laser-printed term paper.

5. **Use all available resources.** Get to know the instructor and stop in during office hours. One-to-one help is even more valuable if you come prepared for the meeting—that is, if you have already worked hard on the problems and have marked questions in your notebook. Use the Math Lab if your school has one and attend review sessions when they are offered. Take advantage of technology—calculators and computers—as allowed and available.

6. **Keep track of how you are doing.** Record your scores in a specific place in your notes. Hang onto all tests, quizzes, and solution sheets, and use them to study for the final exam. Be serious about the final. Cumulative 2- or 3-hour exams that cover the entire content of the course require advance planning and intense, focused effort.

4. Think About the Bigger Picture. In addition to the practical strategies just described, try to reflect on the nature of the learning in the particular discipline that the course belongs to.

For example, physics may require mastery of dozens of formulas but contain only a few basic concepts. What are these essential ideas? In biology, in what ways are organisms or systems all more or less alike? In what ways different? How much does the discipline rely on quantitative methods? What are some of the applications? What is the role of the discipline in the economic and environmental challenges facing society?

EXERCISE 13.12 Planning for Success

Choose part A or part B.

A. *If you are currently taking math or science courses:* List each science and/or each math course that you are taking. For each course write a statement of your goals for the class including what you expect/hope to learn and your plan for achieving those goals.

From the courses you have listed, choose the one that you expect to find most challenging. Then review Exercise 9.2 on forming study groups. Write out a plan for organizing a study group in that course. Are there people in that class that you already know? Are there people you know who are in the same course but in other sections? Can you ask the instructor for help in setting up a group? Plan how you can best handle the logistics: time, place, and commitments to meet regularly.

B. *If you are not taking math or science courses now but plan to do so in the future:* Consult your course catalog. List a science and/or math course that you plan to take. Write a statement of your goals for the course including what you expect or hope to learn and your plan for achieving those goals.

Ask at least three people who have taught or taken the course what the course is like. Find out more about the purpose and requirements of the course. Find out which instructors are most likely to be right for you. Plan to do your best to take the course with one of them.

MAJORING IN MATH OR SCIENCE OR ENGINEERING

Perhaps the choice seems obvious for you. As a child you had a fascination with nature and an overflowing curiosity about how the universe works. You asked questions about clouds, you wondered how airplanes got off the ground, and you took a seed pod apart to study all the intricate detail inside. You pondered the geometric patterns in snowflakes and you learned how to build a homemade battery.

The science that you studied in prior schooling answered many of your questions and raised others. Now, as a new college student, you are considering a major in the natural sciences, engineering, or mathematics.

Or perhaps the choice was not so certain. Sometimes well-intentioned parents direct a son or daughter to a field like engineering or computer science *only* because they foresee a good job with a secure future. Students themselves may base the major decision on a romanticized view of the life of, say, a marine biologist or aeronautical engineer. Television has imprinted appealing images on all of us, and students may envision themselves swimming with dolphins or gazing from a spaceship back toward Earth.

The truth is, choosing a major should not *begin* with an analysis of the job market or with the question "What can I do with it?" Instead you should search for a field that you enjoy *for its own sake.* Parental advice and employment prospects will ultimately influence your choice, of course. But the process should begin with an awareness of your talents and interests, and the choice should comprise a "good fit" with the discipline itself.

Leaving Options Open

Whatever forces influence your choice of major, leave your options open as much as possible. As you start out, explore different disciplines and possible majors by taking as wide a variety of courses as you can. And even if your school requires an early declaration of major, this is not an irrevocable decision. Admittedly a tightly packed curriculum—like that of engineering or pharmacology—will make exploring more difficult. But wherever possible you should choose courses that will apply in more than one program, and devote your first terms in college to discovering what you enjoy and where you are motivated to excel.

How to Do Your Math— or Chemistry, Biology, Electromagnetics, or Statistics—Homework

No matter what the science or math course, the following five-step process can help ensure that you successfully complete homework assignments.

1. **Take 10 minutes to review.** Don't let your notes get cold. As soon as possible after class, skim through them. Put a question mark next to anything you don't understand at first reading. Put stars next to topics that warrant special emphasis. Try to place the material in context. What has been going on in the course for the last few weeks? How does today's class fit in?

2. **Warm up.** When you are ready to sit down and do the assignment, look through your notes again. But this time, use pencil and paper to *rework all the example problems.* Compare your solutions to the ones in your notes. Now read through the related material in the text. Go back to the examples, one at a time. Cover the solution, and *attempt to do each problem on your own.* Look at the author's work only after a serious personal effort.

3. **Do the assigned problems.** Now you can start on the homework itself. As you read each problem, ask, What is the given? What needs to be found? Of the given information, what is essential and what is extraneous? Read the problem several times and state it in your own words. The last sentence may provide a starting point; it usually spells out what you are trying to find.

4. **Persevere.** When you hit a problem you cannot readily solve, move on after a reasonable effort. After you've worked on the entire assignment, come back to those that stumped you. Try once more, and then take a break or work on another subject. You may have to mull over a particularly difficult problem for several days. Think about the problem at odd moments. Inspiration may come when you are waiting for a stoplight or just before you fall asleep.

5. **Wrap up.** When you complete an assignment, look back and reflect on the experience. Talk to yourself about what you learned from this particular problem set. Generalize about how the problems differed, which strategies were successful, and what form the answers took. Think about variations and extensions of the problems where appropriate.

You may be thinking, "The 10-minute review and the warm up are well and good, but who has time to do all that extra work? I'm lucky to get the assigned problems done." In reality the approach does work and it actually saves time. Try it for a few weeks. The frustration that comes when you tackle your homework problems cold will disappear. The hours you devote to assignments will be more productive, and you will become more comfortable and confident in the subject area.

EXERCISE 13.13 Exploring Your Options

Consider the major you are in or are planning to pursue. Explore your college catalog. Find at least two other mathematical or science-related majors that you might consider. What makes your current major better for you than the others? Discuss your choice with a group of students in other majors. Explain why your present choice is number one and why the other possibilities also make sense. Plan to explore (and possibly enroll in) at least one course related to each of those majors.

Fighting Common Misconceptions and Deterrents

Perhaps you are drawn to a major in a scientific field or to a particular career involving mathematics or science, but something is holding you back. Behind your lack of confidence lies a myth or deterrent that you can recognize and overcome.

Science Belongs to the "Elite." You may accept this common notion that science, mathematics, and engineering belong to an elite few, to exceptional individuals with special aptitudes whose genius was apparent to all at a very early age.

Scientists Are Nerds. Your mental picture of a scientist might be a person with hair slicked down and parted in the middle who wears heavy dark-rimmed glasses and a plastic pocket protector filled with pens. You think of someone who virtually lives in his laboratory and has no social life. Because of movie stereotypes and the scarcity of role models, you may not picture a woman or a member of a racial or ethnic minority when you think of "scientist" or "mathematician" or "engineer."

   In the past scientists may have come from a select and rather narrow band of the population. That is much less so today. Today we recognize that women and minorities can "do science"—indeed that they *must* do it if we are to stay competitive in a global economy.

Science Majors Are Preparing for a Narrow Line of Work. Perhaps you find science fascinating but believe that all scientists work in isolation and fear that you will not find a career that suits your personality.

   In truth there are all kinds of jobs available to those with an undergraduate or a graduate degree in a scientific field. Some involve a great deal of interaction with people; others are based in pure research. The possibilities for the kinds of work that you can do with a science background, and the kinds of ways that scientists now go about solving problems, are much broader and less compartmentalized than formerly.

Born in the U.S.A.

The question "Why do men do better than women on SAT mathematics tests?" has led some people to jump to the conclusion that there might be a possible physiological basis for this difference.

An equally interesting fact is that the number of successful women in science and mathematics who were born outside the United States is very much higher than the number of successful American-born women. A typical example is a woman physicist who emigrated from Europe to New York as a high school student and found she was considered peculiar because in America "girls were not supposed to be smart." She had not encountered this pressure in Europe.

The top women who have had successful careers in America in my own field of nuclear physics have nearly all been born outside the United States. In many countries, like France and Italy, the number of women in science is incomparably greater than in the United States. In my recent contacts with Soviet Jewish immigrants to Israel and the United States, I have been impressed by the large number of women mathematicians, physicists, and engineers. One of these women was the only woman with a tenured position in a leading American university mathematics department for several years. Recently they hired another woman as a full professor—she was born in China.*

Does this professor's information cast doubt on the idea that men are somehow more suited physiologically to mathematics than are women?

Mathilde Krim (Ph.D., genetics), founding co-chair of the American Foundation for AIDS Research. Nationality? Swiss. What explains the relative strength of European and Asian-born women in mathematics and the sciences? (Bettman Newsphoto)

Why do you suppose men do better than women in math on the SAT? How could you test your explanation?

*Adapted, with permission, from Harry J. Lipkin, "Women in Math and Science," *UME Trends* (American Mathematical Society, October 1990).

Careers in medicine are the goal for many life science majors, and many possible careers exist within the health care field. But that is only one large professional area open to people with science degrees. Your campus career center can outline the opportunities, and your advisor may be able to tell you about the various kinds of careers that recent graduates have entered.

Remember, the kind of work you end up doing is the result of a complex web of personal circumstances. The choice of undergraduate major is only one factor.

Science Is Just Too Hard. People often believe that the more math involved in a subject, the more difficult it is. The quantitative skills required for most of the sciences and for engineering present a hurdle for many students. The compression of the material—the sheer volume of information and the rapid pace of coverage—in many science courses is a challenge. The technical vocabulary and the required level of precision add to the perception of difficulty. A significant challenge to science majors is the difficult schedule. With the extra hours required for laboratory courses, students in scientific fields have very full programs.

Of course the work will be challenging, but that is a major reason why it will also be rewarding. If you are fascinated with how the universe works, or appreciate the creative process of formulating a hypothesis and designing a test for its validity, or enjoy pursuing a complicated problem to a successful conclusion, you can be successful in a scientific major and find great personal satisfaction in your chosen field.

PLANNING FOR SUCCESS

Communication and Support

Some students believe that if they go through all the right motions, make good progress and systematically check off all requirements, they will become scientists, mathematicians, or engineers. But there are less tangible elements that play perhaps an even more important role. You need to find a "home" within your chosen discipline. The personal connections and out-of-class interactions that you have with faculty and fellow students will add depth to your developing insight into the true nature of your chosen field. Through outside discussions and topics investigated simply for curiosity's sake, you will reinforce and extend the knowledge you are gaining in the classroom. A growing sense of identification with the field will help you persevere and excel in a scientific major, even in the face of mathematical hurdles, demanding class and lab schedules, and compressed course curricula.

The Key Role of Study Groups

One important study at Harvard investigated the factors affecting perseverance in science of undergraduate women who had started college as science majors. Similar research has looked at the forces affecting retention rates in scientific fields for other categories of students. These studies have yielded a common and somewhat surprising result: the crucial role played by study groups. Evidence is mounting that, from kindergarten through college, students learn best when they struggle together, when they learn from and teach each other.

Of course the study group promotes higher achievement in a particular course, but it serves other functions as well. It becomes one of the social circles of the college experience—a group of friends in which the common thread is interest in science or mathematics or engineering. The study group promotes personal identification and a sense of belonging within the discipline. It provides support and encouragement when things aren't going well. It often acts as a reality check, giving you a better sense of how much time is actually required to succeed in certain courses as well as a context within which to assess your progress.

Take a leadership role in organizing a study group if necessary. Start with a group of three to five students in one course, and progress to a second course after your first group is well established and meeting regularly. Some of the most effective groups include students from a particular major who work together through several terms and various courses.

The Wide Range of Opportunities

As your undergraduate years progress, you will want to expand your contact with other students, faculty members, and other professionals in your field, both at your school and in outside employment. In a co-op position or summer internship, you can experience the professional life of an engineer or scientist and make contacts that will be invaluable when you are looking for a permanent job. Through on-campus opportunities—as a research assistant in a faculty member's lab, for instance—you can receive formal or informal mentoring, gain specialized technical knowledge, and experience significant personal growth. All these factors enhance your course learning and nurture your development as a scientist.

EXERCISE 13.14 Creating a Major Plan

If you are considering a major in a math- or science-related discipline, write out a plan of courses that could carry you to graduation. Study your school's catalog and consult with your advisor to be sure that your list meets all requirements. If your class will also be reading Chapter 17 on choosing a major, talk with your instructor about how to coordinate this exercise with your work in that chapter.

JOURNAL

Find a "hero" in science or mathematics. The person may or may not be living today. Read a few articles about the work and personal qualities of your hero or heroine. Explore why you find this person inspiring.

SUGGESTIONS FOR FURTHER READING

Adams, James L. *Conceptual Blockbusting: A Guide to Better Ideas,* 3rd ed. Reading, Mass.: Addison-Wesley, 1986.

Polya, G. *How to Solve It: A New Aspect of Mathematical Method,* 2nd ed. Princeton, N.J.: Princeton University Press, 1955.

Paulos, John Allen. *Innumeracy: Mathematical Illiteracy and Its Consequences.* New York: Hill & Wang, 1988.

Rosser, Sue. *Female Friendly Science.* Elmsford, N.Y.: Pergamon Press, 1990.

Smith, Richard Manning. *Mastering Mathematics: How to Be a Great Math Student.* Belmont, Calif.: Wadsworth, 1991.

Tobias, Sheila. *Succeed with Math: Every Student's Guide to Conquering Math Anxiety.* New York: College Entrance Examination Board, 1987.

Computing for College Success: Technology on Campus

Steven W. Gilbert
American Association for Higher Education

Kenneth C. Green
University of Southern California

People keep telling me that it's getting easier to use computers. I'm glad to hear that. How about if I just put off learning how until they're so easy to use that I don't even know I'm using one?

If you've already had some experience using computers, this chapter will help you explore more ways that you can use them in college and benefit from information technology. If computers are new to you, that's okay too—this chapter will get you started. If you're already completely at home with computers or maybe even a techno-wizard, the chapter may reveal some unique aspects of computing on your campus.

GETTING ORIENTED

"The ATM Just Ate My Card"

Suppose you walk up to a cash machine and go through the usual steps to get some money. You are in a hurry because the movie is going to start in half an hour. Twenty dollars comes out, the right amount, but your card does not come back. You try pushing every combination of buttons possible. No card. No message. No more money. Which of the following best describes your reaction?

▶ **You love computers and are always in control.** You get your notebook computer out of your backpack, and plug into a nearby public phone with a data port. You work out a hack to get into the ATM system, find the software glitch affecting the machine, fix it, and get out. (Of course you don't alter your bank balance or anyone else's!) You return to the machine and enter a new code number, and out pops your card. You go to the movie.

▶ **You are comfortable with computers but like movies more.** You're angry; you yell at the machine. You write down the exact time and location of this event and then go to the movie. The next day you call the bank to explain what happened. You ask to have your old card canceled and a new one issued with a different PIN number. You are irritated at the inconvenience of it all but need the easy convenience of quick access to cash and related services through ATM machines. You don't expect this to happen again any time soon.

▶ **You're terrified of computers.** You know you should not have used the ATM! You've never trusted machines. You must have punched the wrong button. Perhaps you broke the machine and will have to pay the bank to have it fixed. You shouldn't have kept that card anyway—you'll never use one again. In fact you wish you didn't even have to use a bank. In any case you're much too upset to sit through a movie.

"Where's the Information?"

You've just finished a long day—classes, campus activities, maybe a few hours at your part-time job. Thinking about the work ahead for the evening, tomorrow, and the rest of the week, you remember a major assignment, due tomorrow, to develop a bibliography for a term paper. You need to get materials from the library. What do you do?

▶ **You visit the library.** You plan to spend several hours in the library, primarily looking through the old card catalog in search of materials for your paper.

▶ **You use the library's on-line catalog.** You find an open computer terminal in the library and do a topic search in the catalog, generating some hundred titles that might be relevant to your paper.

► **You navigate the Internet.** From your home, dorm room, or campus computer lab, you "surf" the Internet, searching for relevant materials from your own institution as well as other sources—other college and university libraries, government archives, text and image databases. You browse some materials on-line, checking to see if they are relevant to your topic. You download some of the material into your word processor, edit it a bit ("merge and purge"), and print the final document.

Your reactions to the two situations are a good reflection of your attitude toward and experience with computers.

Nowhere to Hide

As recently as five years ago students planning nontechnical majors could, with some effort, avoid computers and information technology. No longer. Regardless of your major or career plans, computers and information technology will be important tools and resources during your college years—and beyond. Indeed, even if your major or career seems to have little to do with technology, you're probably better off starting to master computers now than letting them master you.

By the time you graduate from college, there will be new ways to use information technology that are difficult to imagine today. For example, the much discussed "information superhighway" is a national initiative by which electronic access to books, newspapers and magazines, scientific and commercial data, movies, interactive entertainment, and more may begin to enter our homes, schools, and offices by the late 1990s. This could have tremendous benefits for students at every level of education.

What we offer here is just an introduction to some of the most obvious and accessible applications of information technology in the mid- and late 1990s. This will give you a good start if you have had little or no prior experience with computers and information technology. As you become more confident with and knowledgeable about the tools available today, you will also be better prepared to take advantage of future options and new technologies.

What You Need to Know

If you had a class on computing in high school, you probably learned something about *bits, bytes, RAM, ROM,* and other technical terms that help explain how a computer works. That's part of the traditional way of learning about computers, emphasizing the *technical aspects* rather than the *applications* (how it works rather than what you can do with it). However, for most people using a computer has become like driving a car: You don't really need to know what's under the hood. Rather, you need a general sense of how the car works—and how to make it work well for you. You will also need to know what to do if the computer "breaks" or won't do what you need it to do.

In many ways computers are still very young, "immature" technologies that are evolving very quickly. Information technology is still not standardized enough to let us give you specific instructions that will work for most combinations of computers, software, printers, and telecommunication setups. Instead we'll try to point you in the right direction, describing the skills you need to acquire and identifying where you might find help and training on your campus.

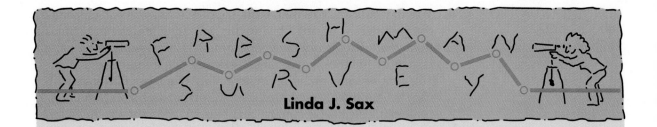

Linda J. Sax

Computers on the Rise

Students today are coming to college with much more computer experience than their counterparts did only eight years ago. Although women are less likely than men to use computers, the gender gap has become somewhat smaller over time.

How do you think the rise in computer usage has affected student performance? Study habits? Class assignments? Instructors' expectations? How do you think computers will change the college classroom in the twenty-first century?

Freshman Use of Computers, 1985 and 1993 (percentage using a personal computer "frequently" in high school)

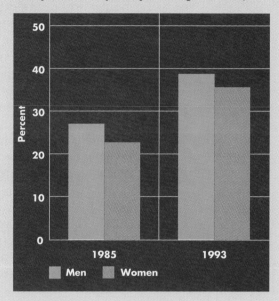

SOURCE: Higher Education Research Institute, UCLA

One reassurance and a caution: In "normal use" it is almost impossible for you to damage (or hurt) a computer—unless, of course, you spill a drink on the keyboard or hit the machine when you are angry because it "ate" or "destroyed" some of your work. And while you cannot really break a computer, you should understand that a computer can do major damage to your work; for example, it can quickly (and completely) erase the term paper you labored on late at night and through several weekends.

Computers (and People) at Your Service

Computers were created by engineers and scientists to serve people—to help them work more quickly, efficiently, and productively. If you have an experience with computers (or computer "experts") where this doesn't seem to be true, then something is wrong with the situation, not with you. Don't be reluctant to ask questions or to ask for help. Approach technology with the assumption that you are going to use it as necessary for your purposes—

Ask for help. Good helpers will know what to do but will show you how rather than doing it themselves. They will also know how to explain things to you in a way that you can understand. If they don't, ask questions. If questions don't get through, look for a different helper. (Photo courtesy of West Virginia University)

whether those purposes lead you to need information technology rarely or almost constantly.

Don't be intimidated by machines—or by "computer experts." Do the "experts" leave you the impression that you aren't up to their standards or that you'll never "master" the technology? *They are wrong!* The problem is their attitude, not your ability to understand and use the technology.

It's always best if you can find another student or a computer technology staff person who knows how to do most of the things you need to do with a computer *and* who is able and willing to explain things to you while treating you like a competent person. Best of all is someone who will let you do the work instead of taking over and turning you into an observer.

A COMPUTING STRATEGY

What Are Your Options?

You need a *computing strategy* or plan, similar to the plan or strategy your college or any business has developed for computing. And you have essentially the same three choices. You may have already chosen one of them, perhaps unconsciously, based on your prior experience. But note that your first year of college is a great time to make *conscious* choices and to change. Think a little about which of the following is the strategy you really *want* to be using and try it on for size for a while. If it doesn't fit well, try another.

▶ **Option 1: Extended Avoidance.** Try to avoid computers completely. Eventually you will encounter some situation in which it will simply be too costly (in terms of time or other issues, not necessarily just money) or painful to proceed without computing skills. For most students a long term paper provides that occasion: It's just too difficult, time consuming, and expensive to produce a good paper of more than a few pages without word processing. Writing instructors will tell you that good writing is really good *re*writing; word processing makes it easier to change, correct, modify, and amend your work. Additionally, once you become comfortable with word processing software, you'll probably find it easier to learn other computer applications.

▶ **Option 2: The "Everybody's Doing It" Strategy.** Pay attention to what your peers are doing with computers and information technology. Look around you at other students who have career goals similar to yours and are majoring in the same field. Are 20 percent or 25 percent (or more) of them using computers for term papers and other class work? If so perhaps you should begin to do the same. Making sure that a significant number of others have already begun before you jump in is a safe way of ensuring that you won't be stuck with something too complex or difficult to use. Also having the same computer tools as many of your peers means that you are likely to have several people you can ask for help when you're having trouble.

▶ **Option 3: Leader of the Pack.** Become a "technology expert." Your career goals or your personal interest in technology may prompt you to be among the first of your friends and peers to exploit the power of information technology. You might decide that you definitely need great information technology skills as you compete for jobs or academic opportunities. When asked "Why should we hire you?" you can answer, in part, "Because of my excellent technology skills." Indeed you might also enjoy being one of the people that other students (and even some faculty) turn to for help with their computer questions.

Each strategy clearly leads to different decisions and activities. Each approach depends both on you (your skills, talents, and interests in computers) and on your campus computing resources. At schools where computing has long been woven into the campus fabric, "extended avoidance" probably means using a computer only once every few weeks, probably for major writing projects. In contrast, at the shrinking number of schools where computing is still an "extra," you might be able to get through an entire year using a computer only for an occasional long paper. Your strategy will also depend on your major, the kinds of assignments you receive in various classes, and your prior experience with computers and computing.

What If You Really Hate Computers?

If you really hate computers (or feel intimidated by computer people), you could try to pick a major, specific classes, and even a way of life to help you avoid today's technology. However, these choices are getting more and more limited—and could have unfortunate consequences. Face the facts—technology skills will play a significant role in the twenty-first-century job market.

So meet this issue head on. You might begin with one of the more recent books about computers intended for people who are not interested in technology and would rather avoid it. They assume you don't have a natural enthusiasm for playing with machines or learning new technical terms. You might also look into workshops for beginners where you will learn with others who might share your fears.

Or you could make a pact with a friend who shares your fears about computers. Agree that you will help each other. Attend the same training class, review the class activities and exercises, work together after your classes, and push (and pull) each other along. Or approach someone who is just a few months ahead of you—someone who didn't really want to begin at all but has managed to take a few steps and still remembers how painful the first steps were. He or she may be happy to help a kindred soul and less likely to make you feel stupid.

A growing number of colleges provide computer instruction and give computer-based assignments in first-year courses, especially writing classes. Often "lab sessions" for these classes take you into a computer classroom to learn the basics: how to use a computer and to develop word processing skills. Sometimes these classes also teach you how to use the computer to explore the library card catalog and other kinds of on-line information resources. Many residence halls or libraries have computer labs staffed with troubleshooters who can help you with your learning.

If possible, develop your basic word processing skills several weeks before your first paper is due. Use the preparation of that paper as a practical objective to focus your efforts and distract you from your fears and discomfort. Look forward to the reward of a professional-looking paper.

EXERCISE 14.1   Choosing a Strategy

In a small group, talk about your reactions to the material presented at the start of this chapter (the ATM experience and the bibliography assignment) and the options described above. Ask what options others might choose and why. Compare your situations, your prior experience, and your concerns. Move to another group if no one in yours seems to favor your strategy. Try to find at least one other person in your class whose choice or experience is fairly similar to yours. Then talk about what you want to do.

EXERCISE 14.2   Rating Your Computer Skills

Rate your current computer skills from 1 (low) to 5 (high) for each of the following:

_____ 1. "Keyboarding" or typing

_____ 2. Word processing

_____ 3. Electronic mail

_____ 4. Computerized library search/card catalog search

_____ 5. Spreadsheets/budgeting software

_____ 6. Programming

Where do your answers cluster? Mostly 3s, 4s, or 5s suggest you have some advanced skills. Mostly 1s or 2s suggest you're just getting started and should think carefully about ways to acquire skills that will help you in and after college.

GETTING STARTED

Keyboarding

Alas, cheap and highly efficient systems for converting speech to print are not yet available and are not expected in the next few years. And machines that recognize your handwriting and convert your written notes into computer text are still very primitive. Consequently keyboarding still remains the "core skill" for using a computer. If you can type you're in good shape for working with a computer. If you can't type you need to learn. Find a keyboarding course that fits into your schedule, or learn on your own with an inexpensive "typing tutor" software package. (To find the right one, look at ads in a computer magazine or ask someone in a computer store or your campus bookstore for suggestions.)

Accessing Computers

Does your college sell computers through the bookstore? Will you have to pay a "lab fee" for computer time and access for some of your classes? Will you be charged printing fees? The answers to these questions may depend on your major or your courses.

Different campuses have different policies and procedures for providing access to computing resources for students. A small number of schools require (or strongly encourage) all students to own computers. These institutions have committed themselves to bringing information technology into nearly every aspect of academic life—from wiring residence halls into a campus network to including the cost of a computer as part of total college costs.

Many campuses encourage computer use in other ways: selling computers in the bookstore, providing campus labs for student use, and offering various support services such as training classes and "computer consultants" to help solve specific problems.

EXERCISE 14.3 Campus Strategies and Access

A. As a class find out what steps your school has taken to make information technology available to students and faculty. What seems to be its overall plan, if any? Be sure to check for any booklets and guides, intended for students and faculty, that describe services and resources.

B. Place a check mark next to each of the following that is available on your campus.

_____ 1. "Intro to Computers" classes

_____ 2. A computer support center for assistance

_____ 3. A call-in phone number for computer assistance

_____ 4. Computers for sale in the bookstore

Finding the Right Kind of Help

Even as you become comfortable doing routine computing tasks, you'll still have occasional problems or questions. Most often you'll want to ask questions like "Now that I'm doing X, how can I get the computer to do Y?" Some questions may have to do with the kinds of information sources and services available through your computer and telecommunications options. Here are some sources of help:

▶ **FAQs.** When you're getting started using computers, most of the help you will need will be what insiders call "frequently asked questions," or FAQs. Your campus may have a source of FAQs and answers "on-line." ("On-line" means that you can communicate with the source of answers via the computer itself. See the section "On-Line Services and the Internet" later in the chapter.)

▶ **Support for academic computing.** Many campuses have a group or department responsible for *academic computing*—the use of computing and information technology for instruction and research. This unit often includes a "user support service" that can help you. Academic computing is usually not the same as the department of computer science or whatever academic department is responsible for teaching computer courses for credit, but if you have trouble finding the right place, someone in the computer science department can probably tell you where it is.

▶ **A few good souls.** Find a few people with whom you feel comfortable asking questions about computing. First, identify one or two who can answer questions that you think may be "dumb." They should be people who know enough about computing and who are especially likely to treat you nicely no matter how idiotic the question may sound. Second, identify one or two others you want to reserve for questions that you think are more sophisticated. Here you need someone who has some expertise—and may not have such a great "bedside manner." Any of these "help" people might be students; if so, be sure that they know what they are talking about and are not overconfident. Also try to find at least one librarian who is able and willing to answer questions about computer-related information resources in the library and through your campus network (if you have one) and the Internet (if you have access to it).

▶ **A few good notes.** Don't be reluctant to make notes about the steps necessary to perform a task that is likely to be important to you. Computers are still so new that the sequence of steps required to do some of the things you will want and need to do may not make much sense. Don't be surprised or upset when this happens. Don't assume that something is wrong with you or that you will automatically be able to remember the magic words and motions next time. Write down the steps on these pages or in a special notebook. Keep handouts or "cheat sheets" where the information will be handy when you need it again.

EXERCISE 14.4 Help at Hand

1. Locate the user support services part of the academic computing office (it may have some other name). Fill in the following:

   Office name: _____

   Location: _____

   User support phone: _____

   User support hours: _____

2. Ask academic computing or others whether there is a list of FAQs and answers and how to get it.

3. Names, addresses, phone numbers, and hours of availability of people who are good for "dumb" questions:

   _____

   _____

   _____

   _____

4. Names, addresses, phone numbers, and hours of availability of people who are good for advanced questions:

   _____

   _____

   _____

   _____

Preventing Disaster

Whether you're using your own computer or another computer, take precautions to avoid the most serious catastrophes.

1. **Don't do anything silly to a computer.** Don't spill things on it. Don't drop it. Don't hit it. However, yelling and screaming are okay and often fairly common and acceptable behaviors.

2. **Learn how to start, stop, and restart the computer you are using.** Two common problems are (1) a computer gets "hung up" so that no matter what you do, absolutely nothing changes on the screen, and (2) you get "lost" in an application program and suddenly don't know what you're doing and can't figure out how to move back to doing something that was making sense. In both cases the last (and very desperate) option is to turn the computer off and then restart it. Usually you will lose whatever work you had done since the last time you saved or filed your work. But at least you will be back in operation.

3. **Learn how to make "backups."** Be sure you understand the different ways to make backup copies and know where you can save and store copies of your computer work (your computer *files*). Learn what *diskettes, hard disks, internal memory,* and *network server shared storage* are and whether each is available to you. Learn how to use them. Always think about how serious a problem it would be for you to re-create (from notes and memory) your current work. If it's no big deal, then don't worry about it. However, for your most important projects, you should probably:

a. *Save* the document at least every 5 or 10 minutes while you work on it. Give the file or document a name that you can easily recognize and remember. Use numbers to help identify the version number of the document. (Is it your first draft or your fourth rewrite?)

b. *Make a backup copy.* Desktop computers such as an IBM-compatible (sometimes called a Windows computer) or a Macintosh allow you to copy documents *(files)* from the computer to a diskette (and vice versa). Be sure you save your work on the document frequently and also at the end of a work session. If what you're working on is extremely important, keep the diskette in a different room or building than the computer.

c. *Print a "hard" (paper) copy* of your draft version at the end of every work session. If you think you wouldn't be able to produce a copy of your work to date on short order, then print a copy of the most up-to-date version at the end of each work session and keep it in a safe place.

EXERCISE 14.5   Preventing Disaster

For any of the following information that you don't already know, ask someone and record enough notes here to remind yourself what to do.

1. To start your computer:

_____

_____

_____

_____

2. To turn off and restart your computer (be sure that this procedure is considered safe by your "expert"):

_____

_____

_____

_____

3. To file or save a document on the computer:

_____

_____

_____

_____

While you're at it, check to see if there's a way to set the computer to file or save automatically every 15 minutes; if so, do so.

4. To file or save a document from the computer onto a diskette and to "format" or "initialize" a diskette (only format or initialize a diskette if you must and if you are ready to have any existing data on the disk erased—forever):

_____

_____

_____

_____

5. To print a document from the computer onto paper:

_____

_____

_____

_____

APPLICATIONS

The kinds of software used for college work are generally the same as or similar to those used in the business and professional world. Word processing is the most widely used, and we'll talk about it in the next section. We'll also talk in detail about electronic mail and the Internet, two forms of telecommunication software that let you communicate from your desktop computer with other computers, large and small, across the campus or across the country.

Spreadsheets

A spreadsheet program divides the computer screen into "cells" arranged in rows and columns. In each cell you can type a number, a short bit of text, or a formula that performs some calculation on the contents of other cells. Spreadsheets are most widely used for budgeting and financial analysis. They are also useful wherever there is a need to experiment and calculate with numerical data. One great advantage of a spreadsheet over old-fashioned pencil-and-paper methods is that, once you have typed in the data, the computer does all the calculations, such as finding the total of a column of numbers. Spreadsheets are better than calculators in that the spreadsheet stores the data so that it never has to be retyped. One way to learn about spreadsheets is to use one to work out your personal budget.

Computer graphics aren't only for art and video commericals. They are also revolutionizing how computers help us see, share, and analyze complex information. (Photo courtesy of University of Utah)

Databases

A database can be used to manage, sort, summarize, and print out large amounts of systematic alphabetic or numerical data. Businesses use databases to keep records of things like inventory, customers, and transactions. The electronic catalog in your campus library is a database. Researchers use databases to record and manipulate research data, such as survey results. One way to get started with a database is to use it in place of an old-fashioned personal address book.

Graphics and Presentation Software

Graphics and presentation software lets you capture, create, and display words and visual images, maps, and other graphic data on the computer monitor, on projection screens, and in printed form. Computer graphics are everywhere you look today in art and advertising. They also have many uses on campus. For example, medical schools are now creating and using graphics software to teach human anatomy and medical diagnosis.

Personal Productivity Software

Personal productivity software includes personal information managers (PIMS) such as electronic phone books, calendars, and other tools that help you manage information about your activities and contacts. Sometimes these come as bonus products when you buy computers.

EXERCISE 14.6   Knowing What Can Be Done

Review the software descriptions you've just read. If you're already familiar enough with an application to know how it might be useful to you, just place a check mark by it. For the rest consult someone else or a magazine or other source for some fairly simple explanations and write them down. Exchange your explanations with others in your class until each of you understands these terms. Add more of your favorite new applications, if any (or ones you are curious about), and do the same thing.

WRITING PAPERS WITH WORD PROCESSING

For most first-year students word processing is by far the most important application of information technology. As your instructors may have said already, there is no longer any excuse for spelling errors in written work. Learning to use word processing with a spelling checker is essential. It is equally important to learn the limitations of most word processing software: It cannot help you pick the right word, cannot supply the ideas, and cannot do the research for you. But if you learn to use a reasonably powerful word processor, your papers will look better and require less effort to write and revise. Some word processing packages can even take care of the placement and numbering of footnotes for you.

Word processing involves some risks and costs. If you are careless you can lose the results of your work just at the wrong time. You will have to invest some time to learn the more advanced features of your system. The package may be expensive to buy and update. It may be addictive: You can find yourself exploring too many features that you don't really need yet and getting too fancy with choosing fonts (sizes and styles of alphabets) and changing the appearance of your documents instead of working on the content and intellectual structure. Finally, access to a good word processing program may increase your tendency to procrastinate. If you can produce a nice-looking paper in a few hours and can make changes right up until you are ready to print, you may be inclined to put off starting, and the quality of your writing may suffer.

When you use a spelling checker, keep in mind that such programs don't end the need for your own intelligent proofreading. For example, spelling checkers won't pick up errors such as typing "there" for "their" or "too" for "to." Thus you will need to continue to proof your own work.

The main advantage of word processing over other forms of writing is that you can revise with much less effort. With practice you can find your own most effective techniques and "rhythm" of writing—but this will work only if you also learn how to plan your time to let yourself do more than one draft before the final version. "Sleeping on it" is one of the best things you can do between drafts.

EXERCISE 14.7   Word Processing—Beginning and Advanced

A. *For those not already using word processing:* Learn by doing a real task. Pick an assignment in one of your courses in which you must produce a paper, preferably not too long and due somewhere between one and five weeks from now. If your campus offers some sort of noncredit or nominal credit workshops to introduce word processing, sign up and go. If you can find a tutorial disk or video, try it.

Use the computer to write, save, revise, and print your paper. Remember that famous computer advice "If all else fails, try reading the manual." If the manual is impenetrable, buy another, easier book about your particular software package. Learn the basics of how to make your report look nice, but don't try to get too fancy this time. Keep your design simple.

B. *For those already using word processing:* Mark each of the following either T (true) or F (false).

_____ 1. When I use the computer to prepare a paper, I routinely use a spell-checking program.

_____ 2. I never turn in work with spelling errors that I have done on a computer.

_____ 3. I know how to use advanced features of my word processing program such as headers, footers, and footnotes, and I actually use them fairly often.

_____ 4. I always save my work regularly and never lose long or important pieces of my work.

_____ 5. From session to session I back up my work on disk.

_____ 6. I rarely waste much time getting fancy with fonts, paragraph formats, and other superficial stuff.

_____ 7. When I write a paper I always go through a stage in which I focus hard on deciding what I want to say and how I plan to organize my thoughts (perhaps more than once).

_____ 8. I don't procrastinate. Whenever possible I start writing a paper early and let myself sleep on it between drafts. I always plan time to revise.

_____ 9. I always proofread work before I turn it in or share it with others.

Do your answers suggest any need for improvement? Discuss this in a group.

ON-LINE SERVICES AND THE INTERNET

At its simplest level the *Internet* is many thousands of computers connected by telephone lines used to exchange messages and find or offer other forms of information. There is no recognized governing body, just widespread agreement among users on some standard ways of packaging and sending information.

The number of people using the Internet and the amount and variety of information available through it are growing rapidly. Some estimates suggest that one million people were connected to the Internet each month during 1994. And the number is increasing each month.

Most colleges and universities now have computer networks of their own and access to the Internet. The personal computer that you now own or may soon own can be hooked up to the Internet through a direct connection to your campus network or through a *modem,* a small device that lets your computer communicate with other computers via telephone lines. If your institution has a Campus Wide Information System (CWIS), you may find information available through a microcomputer about course offerings, campus policies and regulations governing students and faculty, phone numbers, faculty ratings, institutional publications, and the campus events calendar.

Consider learning more about Internet, just as you are learning about how to use your college libraries. It is a *major* resource for finding information in a variety of forms for you to use as background information or for research required for term papers. Others turn to the Internet for fun or for personal reasons. Once on the Internet, watch out for the day that you get sucked into "surfing the Internet" and look up from your computer five hours later having missed a meal!

EXERCISE 14.8   Learning to Use the Internet

A. Go to your list of "help" people and ask if it's possible to use the Internet from your campus system. Find out whether you are charged for using it. Learn how to get started.

Note: There is a difference between using a microcomputer or terminal that is connected directly to the Internet via a campus network and connecting to the Internet via a modem and telephone line. Be sure that you get the instructions that best match your situation.

B. Learn how to connect to your college library catalog (if available) and search for a book. See if you can figure out if the library has a copy of the book available to borrow right now. Find out whether other libraries have interlibrary loan agreements with yours and catalogs accessible through the Internet. From them you can request a book that your library doesn't have, at little or no cost and with little effort.

Electronic Mail—Some Basics

Like many business networks your campus network may have a system of electronic mail ("e-mail") that lets you send and receive messages via computer. These messages may be local—on your campus to other students and to faculty—and they may also be sent out on the Internet, to people at other campuses and to off-campus organizations and firms.

Perhaps the main advantage of e-mail is that it is "asynchronous"—you and the other person do *not* have to be using it at the same time. Each computer has a brief *address* (a sort of "mailbox") on the system. You can send a message that will travel instantly to someone else and will then wait until he or she sits down at the computer, reads it, and sends an answer back.

More and more faculty members are using e-mail to communicate with their students. It may be easier for you to get a faculty member to answer a question via e-mail than to wait in line after a class to try to schedule time during office hours. Indeed you might well view e-mail as just another way to communicate with your teachers.

Composing, Editing, and Sending E-mail. Most people compose e-mail by typing directly; generally e-mail involves very little editing or rewriting. Spelling, capitalization, and grammar errors are usually considered okay—and even add a touch of personality—to informal e-mail communications, but if you have too many errors they become distracting to the reader.

When sending longer or more formal e-mail messages—for example, a comment to one of your instructors—it is a good idea to compose and edit the message using your usual word processing package and then "upload" it to the e-mail system. (*Uploading* means launching a file of electronic information onto a network or into a larger system; *downloading* means taking a file down out of the system for your own use.)

On many computer systems uploading and downloading are among the more difficult and mysterious processes. When you find out how to upload, make some notes and put them and any available written instructions where you will be able to find them the next time you need to upload or download.

Computer Etiquette: Replying, Pausing, and Flaming. One nice feature of most e-mail systems is that you don't have to look up someone's e-mail address every time. Usually there is an easy way to reply to an incoming message. Unfortunately people often use the "reply" feature too quickly or without thinking carefully. Thus be sure that you understand how your "reply" option works in general and that each time you use it you know where your reply will *really* go.

One common mistake occurs when you reply to a message that got to you from a "LISTSERV"—a kind of on-line information service that relays messages provided by one person to all others on the service. When you respond to a message forwarded from a LISTSERV, it is easy to think you are replying to the original author. However, the local e-mail system may send your message to the address that sent it to you—which may be someone other than the author and may even be a list of hundreds of people. It's usually easy to find out how your "reply" feature works and easy to check that your outgoing reply is going where you intend, to one or two or three people, rather than to ten or fifty or hundreds.

Flaming refers to sending highly emotional, highly critical messages via e-mail. Sometimes this is exactly what you want and need to do, but most "flames" result from someone having an immediate strong emotional reaction to a message just received, writing an almost stream-of-consciousness response, and sending it without thinking about the consequences. The problem is that with most e-mail systems, once you have sent a message you cannot "unsend" it. Unfortunately an apology offered afterwards rarely undoes the harm or takes away the hurt.

The real solution to the "reply" problem and to the risk of inadvertent "flaming" is to pause and take a deep breath before you send any e-mail message. Take a few seconds to review what you have written and to ask yourself if what you intended to say will be clear from what you have typed. If you're aren't sure, fix it! Remember that e-mail makes it very difficult for the reader to know when you are joking or when you are extremely serious. Even typing a sideways smile—":)"—doesn't always work to convey humor. AND IF YOU TYPE ANYTHING IN ALL CAPS, IT HAS THE EFFECT OF MAKING IT SEEM LIKE YOU ARE YELLING AT THE RECIPIENT! Use these techniques sparingly.

Try to avoid flaming. Especially if you are communicating via e-mail as part of your course work, make sure that your e-mail message is something you will be proud to have others read. Also, when you communicate with your instructors, don't waste their time with unnecessary questions or comments. People are already beginning to worry about junk e-mail just like conventional junk mail.

One last reminder about e-mail: It is usually easy to "forward" e-mail—to send a copy of a message you receive to someone else or to a list of e-mail addresses. Technically this process can usually be done without permission from the original author and without the author knowing that the item has been sent to others. The ease and speed with which a message or document can spread out through the Internet is truly amazing. This has two consequences for you.

► The possibility always exists that an e-mail message that you send to one person will be seen by others. Pause and think about that before you send.

► It not only reflects common courtesy but may be a legal requirement that you get permission from the author (or copyright holder) before forwarding a message or document. Pause before sending and consider the likely wishes of the author or publisher.

Be careful to avoid publicizing what was intended as a private message. If you have any doubt about the author's wishes (or any doubt about maintaining a friendship), check with the author before sending a copy to someone else.

EXERCISE 14.9   Learning to Use E-mail

A. Is e-mail available to students on your campus? If so, learn how to use it. Find out if and how you will be charged for using e-mail. If possible, get an account and an e-mail address. Write your e-mail address here:

_____

Write your password, if any, somewhere else where you won't lose it.

B. Exchange e-mail addresses with another student enrolled in this course, and also with the faculty member teaching this course. Write in the e-mail addresses below:

Teacher name _____   E-mail address _____

Student name _____   E-mail address _____

Student name _____   E-mail address _____

Send some messages to each other. Learn how to use the "reply" and "forward" features and practice them together.

1. Learn how to use your e-mail system in conjunction with your word processing package. (If the process is too difficult, save it for special occasions that involve very long messages.)

2. Try exchanging messages with someone else on your campus and with someone at another campus who also has an e-mail account.

C. Find out if any faculty members on your campus are using e-mail. Find out if any of your own teachers are using e-mail and make a point of asking an intelligent question via e-mail and making use of the answer.

D. Send an e-mail message to the publishers of this book. Tell them how you like the book and how you think it could be improved for future first-year students. Address your message over the Internet to the editor: alan_venable@ wadsworth.com

E. Use e-mail to speak out on an issue that is important to you. Send a letter, via e-mail, to any of the following:

NBC's *Dateline* news program, in response to a story: dateline@nbc.news.com

The White House: president@whitehouse.gov

ETHICAL AND LEGAL ISSUES

Your campus may have materials or courses explaining local policy and relevant law. In any event, you are responsible as an individual for knowing enough to avoid breaking the law. With the ongoing development of so many new technologies, the environment in which you work as a student has become much more complex. You are likely to face many of the same dilemmas now facing faculty and businesspeople. Old laws don't quite address all the new situations, at least not in obvious ways. You are likely to be tempted to do things with computers that would seem clearly wrong in other situations.

The best advice is, first, don't "disconnect" your ethical principles just because you're working with computers. Second, learn enough of the relevant law to be comfortable; at least learn whom you can go to on campus for reliable advice about what is and is not permitted. The library or the computing center are good places to start.

EXERCISE 14.10 Computer Ethics

Find out if your college or university has adopted a policy or guidelines for ethical and legal use of computers and telecommunications. (Ask people in the academic computing office, the computer science department, or the library.) If it has, get a copy. Be sure you understand the policy. Are there any aspects of the policy that seem unclear or difficult to follow? Be prepared to discuss your thoughts in class.

JOURNAL

Have you been writing your journal assignments on a computer? What barriers, if any, stand in the way of your taking full advantage of the new information technology? What might you do to break through?

SUGGESTIONS FOR FURTHER READING

Things change so fast in this field that it is almost impossible to recommend books that won't be outdated by the time you read this. If you need to read something to help you get started or to use as a reference, ask your computer resource people what to read. Try skimming some computer magazines, especially if you're trying to make a decision about buying a computer. If your campus computing organization has some pamphlets, "cheat sheets," or training materials such as videocassettes, those may be very useful to you. Consider taking (even noncredit) workshops offered by your campus computing organization or your library.

CHAPTER 15

Thinking in College

Richard B. Lawhon
University of South Carolina

I learned an important lesson today. Instead of losing my temper and calling my opponents names in order to win an argument, I controlled my emotions and spoke in a firm and even voice. I tossed in a few references to things I had read that supported my side of the issue. I listed my arguments in a logical manner, to the point of numbering each argument as I went along. Even though I felt like yelling, I pretended I was as cool as a cucumber. You know what? Everybody listened to me and said I had done my homework on that issue. I guess I had.

A person's style of thinking doesn't change overnight in college. It continues to become more systematic and thorough, more focused, more patient and less controlled by emotion. (Photo by David Gonzales)

More than anything else college is a time for thinking—new thoughts about new ideas, and old ideas seen in a new way. This will not be like the thinking you have done in the past, nor will it be a revolutionary new kind of thinking. Instead the next four years should produce more of a dramatic evolution in the thinking skills you already have. It's a question of concentrating better, of being systematic and thorough, of developing thoughts that bring insight and understanding—acts that ultimately produce wisdom. Such thinking is often referred to as *critical thinking*. This chapter outlines a method that will lead to better critical thinking.

ORDERS, ARGUMENTS, AND EXPLANATIONS

For most of us the trouble started around the sixth grade. You may have missed it, though, because so much other stuff was going on. Your body changed, your voice changed, and, almost overnight childhood was behind you. How were you supposed to know that the way you were *thinking* had changed forever too? How had it changed? Well, let's *think* about it.

Your Early Thought Processes

During the first ten or eleven years of your life, you were mostly given orders: "No, you can't go outside and play." "Eat your vegetables." "Clean up your room." Even gestures of affection were ordered: "Give Uncle Joe a kiss."

(Ugh! Remember the stale cigar smoke that always hung on him?) "Hold your sister's hand when you cross the street." (You made a face and jerked your hand away the instant you reached the other side.)

Many times you didn't want to do what you were told, but you did it anyway, because you had no choice. In fact you quickly learned that to hesitate too long before doing what your parents (or teachers or preachers or almost any other adults) told you to do resulted in trouble: "If I have to call you to the dinner table one more time, no more TV for a week!" You grumbled—more and more each year—but basically you did what you were told.

Then, around the sixth grade, you began to ask "Why?" in a voice that sounded different to adults. Just growing a few years older had accomplished what tears and tantrums could not. Instead of simple orders (frequently backed up by threats), adults began to offer you arguments. Increasingly they would give you reasons for doing what they wanted you to do. You may remember as a small child being told things like the following: "Eat your spinach; it will make you grow big and strong like your brother." But reasons like that were largely ineffective—probably because looking like your brother did not appeal to you at that age—or, if it did, you wouldn't have admitted it. What worked better were promises: "If you eat all your spinach you can have ice cream for dessert." And more and more often, especially by the time you reached the age of 11 or 12, those were the kinds of promises you heard.

Thus, orders were gradually replaced by *arguments*, which basically are requests accompanied by statements of (apparent) fact called *reasons*. In this context such words as *appeals, rationalizations, negotiations, enticements, promises,* and *discussions* mean essentially the same thing as arguments. The point is that, as you grew older, people tried to persuade you to do something instead of ordering you to do it. Whether you really had any choice in the matter is not important; people wanted you to go along with their requests without resisting or delaying unnecessarily—and they didn't want you to ask too many questions or to be too stubborn about it. So they turned their orders into arguments by offering you one or more facts that you were supposed to accept as reasons for doing what you were told.

A *fact* is simply a statement you can prove to people's general satisfaction. Some "facts" were basically incentives or promises (future truths): "If you clean your room, you'll get your allowance. If you don't you won't." Other facts were more immediate: "Get back on the curb—the bus is coming!"

Since children learn mainly by imitation, you began to say things to your parents that sounded pretty much like the arguments they were making to you: "If you let me sleep over at Kathy's house tonight, I'll clean out the garage next Saturday" or "Please let me watch the Grammy Awards tonight; I promise I'll do my homework first, and I won't watch any TV for the next two days." Sometimes you got what you wanted; sometimes you didn't.

Without realizing it you were mentally cataloging the types of "facts" or incentives that made your arguments work and the ones that didn't. Early on you learned to offer more or greater incentives as the situation required: "Sit with me at lunch, Sarah, and I'll share my Grandmother's cookies with you—and I'll show you what David wrote in my notebook."

Emotions in Arguments

In retrospect your early arguments clearly had a lot to do with emotions. Sometimes you appealed to another person's loyalty or friendship to believe you.

As you became more skilled, you probably learned how to use apparent but elusive facts to make your argument sound convincing. For example, when your friends kidded you for missing the easy shots in gym, you said, "I'm tired…my elbow hurts…I have more important things to think about… buzz off!" Somehow it was easier to give some "facts" that no one else could really challenge than to say that you felt hurt that they were down on you. And you probably got away with it and were believed because in most casual conversation people tend not to question apparent facts or worry much about them.

Also it was often easier to substitute apparent facts for feelings that you didn't want to express too openly. For instance, if you were lonely or afraid, instead of saying so and asking for your friends' companionship, you might have said, "Hey, there's a cool movie at Plaza Six tonight. Anyone want to go?"

When you and they couldn't think of facts to use in your arguments, you simply raised your voice or in some other way substituted some emotion for the missing facts. Of course it's normal for people to be passionate about things they believe in—their music, their political issues, their sports teams. In fact emotions *with facts to support them* do help arguments to succeed. Thus you developed a technique of making emotional statements instead of factual statements when you either didn't have the facts you needed or thought the emotional "reasons" would be more effective. (Of course, while you were learning to conceal or use emotions in your arguments to others, they were learning to do the same thing to you; and so you had to learn to resist their similar appeals.)

The relative ease with which you used emotions successfully in place of facts served your purposes especially well *outside* the classroom. However, the further you went in school, the more you may have noticed teachers making statements to you that sounded different from the kinds of arguments you had been using outside class. In your arguments, especially with older people, you gradually learned that to be effective arguments had to convince them without upsetting them or causing them to respond to you with their own largely emotional arguments. You needed facts and sometimes had to dig for them.

It was like that with your friends as well. It was easy to make them accept arguments they wanted to go along with in the first place. When you got into notions that they weren't so ready to agree with, you had to start coming up with some facts. For example, was Winona Ryder really a better actor than Madonna? Well, what films had they made? Any Oscar nominations? What had those critics Siskel and Ebert said about their films?

Explanations in Arguments

This shift toward arguments that relied less on emotions was a shift toward explanation. As you moved into your teens, you noticed that teachers and other adults became more willing to take time to explain things to you in a fair amount of detail, and that emotion, if it was present at all, was almost always accompanied by facts.

Perhaps your ninth-grade science teacher detailed the movements of the Earth, sun, and moon as part of an explanation of what gravity is and why scientists believe the moon controls the tides. It was still an argument (an appeal to believe or do something, supported by reasons), but it was different enough from most everyday arguments that it deserved a different name: An *explanation* is an argument that relies on facts and a process of reasoning that tries to show how one idea follows from another, and it is largely separate from emotional appeals. Explanations probably worked better with you (as they do in most college settings) because they did not seem to order anyone around or to rely much on emotional appeal. Instead of provoking counterarguments from you, explanations sounded more satisfying, less combative, and therefore more acceptable.

Your thinking moved more and more in this direction toward the end of high school. For instance, when a teacher asked you to serve on a student activities committee, you explained that you were trying to win a spot on the track team, that you had to work two afternoons a week to earn spending money, and that you probably wouldn't be able to come to meetings very often. Since you were offering an entirely satisfactory explanation for turning down the teacher's request (neither exaggerating anything nor hurting the teacher's feelings), you probably succeeded in getting out of a job you didn't want to do.

When people understand the need to communicate with respect, as equals, explanations almost always get better results than other kinds of arguments. Certainly you have learned that teachers will insist on explanations, and you may have found that employers and other people in charge also treat you better when you use explanations to answer their questions or when you try to get them to do something for you.

EXERCISE 15.1   Arguments and Explanations

Read the sample student essay on pages 252–253. Be prepared to discuss the following questions in class:

1. Which paragraphs (if any) seem to you to be explanations? Which ones seem to be more emotional kinds of arguments?

2. What main point is the author trying to make you accept in each paragraph? Which paragraphs succeed best at getting you to think about and possibly accept the argument they are making? What makes these paragraphs more successful?

3. Are there any statements in the essay that the author seems to be presenting as "facts" (statements that can apparently be proved) that you think may actually be false?

Let's Stop Naming People

by Dale Morgan

Ever since Adam and Eve named their first sons Cain and Abel, parents have been naming children. But does naming children do the children or their parents any good? Perhaps back in the days when people lived hundreds of years and had huge numbers of children, names were necessary. (Adam lived nine hundred and thirty years and we don't know how many children Eve had, but it was certainly a lot.[1]) But are names still needed? My own two children never answer when I call them. So what's the point?

At one time or another, it's obvious that we will reject the name our parents gave us. If they named you Rebecca, you'd rather be Tiffany. If you were named Salvador you'd rather be Brandon. Perhaps they named you after Uncle Ezra, your least favorite relative. It might be better if your folks had waited and let you name yourself. My daughter Catherine, for example, now wants to be called Arnel. Common sense tells us that one generation misunderstands the next one.

Consider what parents hope for when they name their children versus what happens later on. Several friends of mine have harbored secret hopes that their son or daughter would be famous someday, bringing fame to both the family surname and the given name they chose. Most parents are secretly desperate to see their child become famous and to share their child's glory, but how empty is the dream! Consider the mother of "Norma Jean Baker," whose daughter ruined everything by becoming "Marilyn Monroe"! The famous American novelist James Baldwin demonstrated how futile it often is to think that one's name will become famous. Even after having written several successful books, he was reduced to calling the next one *Nobody Knows My Name*.[2] It is sad that no one knew his name, considering how famous he was, but the fact remains that names are no help in achieving fame. Of course, there may be people who have delighted their parents by bringing fame to the family name, but no one *I* know has done that.

There are other reasons to stop using names. In an article entitled "Racial and Ethnic Diversity on Campus," Joan Rasool points out that many immigrant generations have had to change their names in order to get jobs or education in mainstream American culture.[3] This is even true for strong-willed characters like Irish-American Marion Michael Morrison, later known as John Wayne, and Jewish-American Issur Danielovich Demsky, better known to late-night-movie fans as dimple-chinned Kirk Douglas. Numerous Germans of non-Jewish backgrounds also changed their names around the world wars because of anti-German hysteria, as dancer Fred (Austerlitz) Astaire would have agreed.[4] If people didn't use names in the first place, discrimination might end sooner.

Giving names to children is unnecessary, as argued by William Shakespeare through the voice of Juliet in *Romeo and*

Juliet. In the famous balcony scene, when Juliet is shocked to learn that Romeo is Romeo Montague, the son of an enemy household, she reassures him, saying

> *What's in a name? that which we call a rose*
> *By any other name would smell as sweet;*
> *So Romeo would, were he not Romeo call'd,*
> *Retain that dear perfection which he owes*
> *Without that title. Romeo, doff thy name,*
> *And for that name which is no part of thee*
> *Take all myself.*[5]

If Shakespeare, the greatest English poet, could do without names, why can't we?

You might object that, if people don't name their children, it may be difficult to keep track of who is who in school or to know how to find a child's parents if a child is arrested or run over in the street. That makes you a control freak like the Norman King William, who conquered Britain in 1066. Once in power in Britain, he created the *Domesday Book,* in which each of his subjects was required to be listed more or less by family. This was done so that the Norman overlords could collect taxes and make the Anglo-Saxons labor for the state. Of course, in spite of his position, William the Conqueror was basically a warmongering maniac who had plans of conquering Italy as soon as Britain was pacified.

But time has proven that the name-giving method of keeping track of people isn't very practical. Open the phone book and look for your friend John Smith. Can you find him? According to one authority, as far back as 1969 there were 2,238,400 Americans named "Smith"![6] Imagine how many of them were also called "John"!

If society needs to keep track of people, there is a better way to do it: at birth, instead of having parents give their child a name, let the government give the child a social security number and let everyone call him or her by that number. This is just as good as using names. Let the first three digits of the number be the child's first name—little "035" for example. This method will solve many of the problems described above. In addition, the number will be useful in sports because people will all have number-names that can be used on their jerseys.

1. *The Holy Bible,* Revised Standard Edition. Cleveland, OH: Meridian Books, 1962. Genesis 5.
2. Baldwin, James. *Nobody Knows My Name: More Notes of a Native Son.* New York: Dell, 1961.
3. Rasool, Joan. "Racial and Ethnic Diversity on Campus." In John N. Gardner and A. Jerome Jewler (eds), *Your College Experience: Strategies for Success.* Belmont, CA: Wadsworth, 1995.
4. Thomson, David. *A Biographical Dictionary of Film,* 2nd ed. New York: William Morrow, 1981.
5. Shakespeare, William. *Romeo and Juliet,* Act II, Scene II, lines 43-48. In Hardin Craig and David Bevington (eds), *The Complete Works of Shakespeare,* rev. ed. Glenview, IL: Scott, Foresman, 1973.
6. Smith, Elsdon C. *American Surnames.* Philadelphia: Chilton, 1969, p. 301.

Working Toward Explanation

Even though you may agree that learning how to explain things is more effective in the long run, in your daily life you may still find yourself depending more on types of arguments that contain more emotion than fact. For most people emotional arguments are much easier to make than explanations, and when listeners are sympathetic or careless in their thinking, emotional arguments also may be more convincing. However, in college and in the work you do after college, you will find that people question you much more closely, so your facts have to be more impressive. You will also find yourself in situations in which you need to judge how much solid fact lies behind the arguments that others use on you.

Thus you need to develop your ability to distinguish between an emotional argument and an explanation. You also need to learn more about how to change one into the other when you argue. In some situations you may need to take an argument about which you have become very emotional and turn it into something that sounds more like simple explanation. That is not dishonest, and it doesn't mean making up facts on the spot. As you have probably learned already, you can't often make something up and get away with it when others are paying attention. During the next few years your college work will get tougher, and you will have to demonstrate even more clearly that you know what you are talking about. At the same time, your success in communicating will often depend as much (or more) on *how* you say things (orally or in writing) as on *what* you say. Even if you are presenting clearly verifiable facts, your classmates and your instructor will resist your message more if you express yourself poorly.

In college and in later life you will be rewarded for your skill in gathering facts *and* presenting them in an impressive manner. The more skilled you become at understanding and making explanations, the better off you'll be.

EXERCISE 15.2   Emotion in Arguments

Consciously or unconsciously, people tend to draw arguments off track in various ways. For example, someone may attack you instead of arguing over your ideas:

> "You're saying we should all plant gardens? You're an idiot."

> "Don't bother listening; he (she) is just a communist (Republican, Democrat, racist, environmental fanatic, redneck, feminist, fundamentalist)."

Or someone may appeal to your sense of guilt or pity instead of actually explaining why something is the way it is:

> "You've upset me so you must be wrong."

> "People all over the world are killing each other. Obviously the U.S. has to stop it."

1. Examine the essay on pages 252–253. Find at least one place where the argument is drawn off track by some emotional appeal.

2. In your own recent experience have you heard an argument or explanation get drawn off track by some emotional ploy? What did the person say? How did you respond? How might you have responded more effectively?

FOUR KEYS TO CAREFUL THINKING

Four key resources can help you distinguish between weak and stronger arguments and help you make more effective explanations: (1) common sense, (2) experience, (3) experts, and (4) references. The better you are at using more than one (or even all four) of these resources together, the better you will be at thinking and communicating in college and beyond. None of these resources is new to you, but you can improve your skill with each.

Common Sense

Common sense refers to the idea that certain facts and bits of wisdom are supposed to be obvious to everyone. By this standard, common sense is automatically good, and so it's often tempting to support an argument by calling it "common sense."

One problem with basing explanations on claims of common sense is that people do not necessarily agree on what is and isn't common sense. Common sense tells you not to touch fire. But what about the mystics who walk on glowing coals or the performer who "swallows" flaming sticks? How does "common sense" apply to their behavior? For most urban Americans it is common sense to lock one's doors at night so no one can get in. For Quakers it has long been common sense *not* to lock the door at night so that if someone really needs something he or she can come in and get it. Especially between cultures, much of common sense collapses. For instance, it's common sense in this country to wash a cup after you have put your lips to it. In India it is common sense not to touch your lips to the cup.

Another problem is that common sense doesn't appear to withstand temptations very well. It's common sense not to shoot a gun off in the air, but that's how many people "celebrate" a happy event. People know it's common sense not to drink and drive but still wake up (or not) in heaps of twisted metal.

For complex questions, common sense often lines up on both sides of the argument: It's common sense that building more prisons doesn't address the root causes of crime. It's also common sense that letting prisons get more crowded doesn't enhance whatever benefits the penal system might offer to inmates.

The greatest danger in depending too much on common sense is that it is far more likely to be a *common* belief than a *sensible* belief. That is, ideas and beliefs that have been passed on for several generations may seem unassailable. For example, for years people in Western cultures—including physicians—viewed a suntan as a "healthy glow" and derided people with pale complexions as unhealthy. Today overwhelming evidence suggests that any sustained exposure of unprotected skin to the sun (especially the amount of exposure needed to tan) can lead to skin disorders, including cancer.

In the course of daily thought, people depend on common sense more often than you can afford to do in college thinking. Perhaps the greatest use of common sense is as an aid in helping you speak out when other people are prepared to act on some impulse or belief that to you seems obviously wrong. Ronald Siegel is a behavioral scientist who studies and teaches about hallucinations. To test a group of his students one evening, he had one of his assistants launch a pair of "UFOs" outside the classroom window. The UFOs were actually plastic bags beneath which candles were suspended so that the bags rose like hot air balloons and created a peculiar effect of light and shadow. On seeing them and hearing a few other people wondering aloud what they might be, Siegel writes, most of his students easily strayed from the commonsense possibility that the "hallucinations professor" might be staging the event: "Everyone was excited. Most were convinced that they had seen unidentified flying objects. A few students believed the crafts were guided by intelligence. One person said the shadows could have been life forms, perhaps extraterrestrial midgets" (Siegel, 1992).

In general, though, the more you improve your skill with other resources, the less you'll have to rely on doubtful common sense.

EXERCISE 15.3   Using Common Sense

A. Why do you suppose that each of the following statements was once (or in some circles might still be) "common sense"?

1. Men should be doctors, women nurses.

2. People need to wear sturdy leather shoes.

3. Women shouldn't run long distances.

4. People should eat three meals a day and not munch in between.

5. The salad should come before the main course.

B. Does the essay on pages 252–253 contain any appeals to common sense? Where? How successful are they?

Experience

Why do older people sometimes say that "Education is wasted on the young"? One reason is that the more experience you have, the better prepared you may be to think about certain kinds of questions.

When you have seen things with your own eyes and heard them with your own ears, those things mean more to you and you tend to remember them better. It's no surprise, then, to realize that you trust the things you know from experience more than you trust information obtained in any other way. It's also easy to see why experience is the first and most frequent thing we call upon to help us decide how to react to arguments and explanations.

Simply living teaches you something every day—and even more if you've actually been paying attention. Going beyond that, taking advantage of opportunities to meet new people or explore new places makes your experience that much more effective in detecting faults in arguments and errors of fact. Visiting other countries or another region of the United States, or even just staying a few days in another community in your own area, can give you fresh perspectives on many issues, especially on what is "common sense" or "human nature."

Two problems often emerge when students first try to apply their experience to college thinking. Some students simply don't realize that their experience is a valid part of argument and explanation. Scholars often write or speak in a style that seems to exclude experience—for example, in academic journals and books, authors avoid writing that "I" did some piece of research or gathered some fact. Even though scholars communicate in this odd way, experience is still an important resource in their gathering of facts and understanding. Don't hesitate to use your own.

A second problem contrasts with the first. Some students rely so heavily on their own experience that they fail to see its limitations. To a great extent college is an opportunity to read and hear about the experience of others. Even people growing up next door to each other can have vastly different experiences and insights. People from different parts of the country, different backgrounds, or different areas of interest have even more to gain from comparing what they know. In most instances an explanation that is consistent with the real experience of a variety of people is likely to be more compelling in the long run.

One of the best things about experience is that it sets you up to be surprised when something new and unexpected happens. Take advantage of exciting moments when someone shocks you with an experience totally different from your own, or when some event or fact defies your understanding. These moments are opportunities to take your thoughts in new directions.

EXERCISE 15.4 Using Experience

A. Think of at least one unexpected and surprising thing that's happened since you started college. Describe the event briefly in writing and then in a group discuss it. Why were you surprised? How did the event seem different from your previous experience? Was the surprise pleasant or unpleasant? Have you let this new experience change your thinking in any way? How? Or why not?

B. Arguments sometimes get off track in other ways than those mentioned in Exercise 15.2. For example, someone might claim that since no one can disprove his or her argument, it must be accepted as true. (This type of argument is actually an appeal to ignorance. The person who makes it is suggesting that, since no one present can disprove the argument, no evidence exists *anywhere* to disprove it. When someone makes such an absurd claim, try not to make up your mind until you can consult other resources, such as experts or references.) Or someone might make a hasty, sweeping generalization based on little experience or a small or doubtful fact.

A "talking head" becomes an "expert" when you treat it as such. Make use of your right not just to listen to teachers in the lecture hall but to pose honest questions and seek out your instructors' expertise in class and during office hours. (Photo courtesy of Berea College)

Look at the essay on pages 252–253 for examples of either type of problem. Where does the author rely on his or her own experience? How could the author use experience more effectively? What might the experience of you and others in the class add to the discussion, either for or against the author's main points?

Experts

An *expert* is someone who has demonstrated considerable knowledge (facts) about a subject. It doesn't matter if that person's knowledge comes from education, training, or experience. An expert is often also someone who knows how to go about analyzing a certain type of problem and help other people when they get into trouble trying to figure something out.

For the purposes of this discussion, let's distinguish between experts and "authorities." Experts may not always be in positions of authority, although it is not unusual to find them there (as doctors, lawyers, professors, scientists, and so on). Unfortunately you can easily find authorities who are not experts at anything. An old saying asserts that "Bosses may not always be right, but they *are* always the bosses." You have probably learned to respect people who are in charge of teams, governments, companies, and classrooms. And generally you should. However, you should not always assume that the people running the show know more than others who are involved—including you.

An expert is a potential resource, not just as a "talking head" who lectures from the front of a classroom or on television. Experts become truly valuable only once you have found the courage and developed the skills to talk with them and ask good questions.

Genuine experts usually welcome intelligent questions about their areas of expertise. Colleges stake their reputations on the idea that their faculty are experts in their fields. Take advantage of this. Don't just listen and accept what you are told. Ask for illustrations or examples; look for consistency among responses. Don't be taken in or put off by big words or technical language; experts should be able to explain themselves in words that others can understand. If something an expert says seems to contradict something you think you read or heard somewhere else, ask about it. Be polite, but be persistent enough to clear up your confusion.

EXERCISE 15.5 Using Experts

A. Arguments can get off track when people appeal to you by saying that some "authority" or popular personage (for example, a movie star) agrees with them. Sometimes the authorities are truly expert. Other times the so-called authorities don't really know a lot about the subject, or their name is mentioned without any related facts or statements from them that would bear on the argument.

Does the essay on pages 252–253 contain any such "empty references" to authority? Is there any place in the article where the writer mentions an authority but should say more about exactly what mentioning that authority really adds to the argument?

B. Think about an interesting course you are taking now. In a group discuss the following questions: What broad questions is the instructor in that course trying to answer? How does he or she break the large question down into smaller questions that can be answered through some kind of research? Come up with at least one question you might want to ask the instructor in his or her area of expertise.

C. Find an expert in your class. What sorts of questions can he or she answer? Find at least three more experts in the class. What are they experts in? Think of at least one question you might ask each of them about some argument. Ask the questions.

References

"You can look it up!" is a sometimes encouraging, sometimes annoying cry one overhears now and then in college. You may have said it yourself when you were exasperated with a person's refusal to accept your word for something or request for facts that you thought the person should find out or confirm for him- or herself. Sometimes people say it as a way of emphasizing their confidence in their facts—or, more likely, their opinions. As a careful thinker you should take them up on the challenge. Treat *every* "fact" intended to persuade you as something to be checked out. The ultimate place for "checking out" anything is, of course, the library, which supplies *reference* information in a wide variety of media including print forms such as books, journals, and microfilm; audiovisual forms such as film and tapes; and digital (computerized) forms such as disks and databases.

Few common questions of fact cannot be settled by spending time in the library on your campus. But make up your mind from the beginning never to depend on just one reference. By itself a single book on any subject can

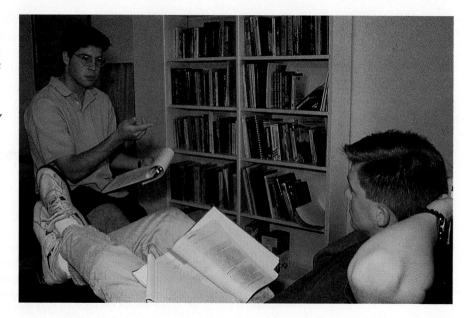

Think of references as the most dependable record of other people's experience and thought. The more you can enrich your arguments with the facts and insights of other people's experience, the more persuasive your arguments will be. (Photo by Hilary Smith)

certainly enlighten you, but look at several references before you make up your mind about something. In comparing several references begin by looking at the titles and skimming the tables of contents; do you see apparent disagreements between different authors? If not, look a bit further. At the college level you should be examining a much greater variety of ideas and opinions than you did in high school.

Different subject areas in the library house references from different disciplines, but often there is overlap among the questions they are trying to answer. Suppose you're interested in the general question of human motivation—why people do what they do, or even why they do anything at all. If you look under psychology you will certainly find theories based on research into people's attitudes and motivation. If you look under biology you will find other facts about human motivation and perhaps completely different theories having to do with facts of body chemistry. Under philosophy, economics, history, or religion you would find still other sets of relevant theories and realms of fact.

As you can imagine, theories produced by different disciplines are frequently somewhat at odds with one another, and your job as a student may be to evaluate the validity or usefulness of each, or to reconcile the differences, if you can. Thus the problem is not just to compare one reference with another, but to understand how certain lines of thought develop and to continue finding further references that help you get closer to the answer you are seeking. In that process you'll learn more *facts* than you ever thought you could. You'll also see how authors support their arguments and thus pick up—at times almost subconsciously—additional ideas you can use to develop your own explanations.

When you can't find more than one book or article about a topic, compare different types of references. Watch a videotape or a film; look at periodicals; even check newspapers. People sometimes change their views when they present their ideas in a medium other than books. Books are generally considered more reliable than other types of references because they are more comprehensive and usually written from a longer-term perspective than articles or other media. However, don't assume that length always indicates greater quality or accuracy.

EXERCISE 15.6 Using References

A. In the essay on pages 252–253, look at the information gathered from references, as indicated by the footnotes. Which references in the article seem particularly helpful? How do they help the author's argument? Are there any references that are not so helpful? Why are they not?

A USEFUL SUMMARY

Although we've covered a lot of ideas very quickly in the previous pages, in the end they boil down to a fairly simple approach:

1. Consider anything you read or hear as a statement that *you* yourself can decide whether to believe.
2. Evaluate what other people say or write as orders, arguments, or explanations.
   a. *Orders* are not always justified or even made to seem reasonable.
   b. *Arguments* contain apparent or real facts to persuade you to do something or to believe something. Emotions may be masquerading as facts in an argument. People frequently respond to arguments with arguments of their own.
   c. *Explanations* rely more on verifiable facts and less on emotions and usually do not provoke so much emotional argument in response.
3. To decide whether to believe an argument or an explanation, use the following four resources—preferably in the order listed here:
   a. *References:* Always use more than one.
   b. *Experts:* Consider a person who appears to be well informed about a subject to be an expert *only* if you can question that person. When possible try to consult at least two experts.
   c. *Experience:* If you have first-hand knowledge of something because you were "there" and "did it," consider your experience. If your experience contradicts a reference, an expert, or the experience of others, consult other references or other experts before you make up your mind.
   d. *Common sense:* Avoid relying on common sense alone. If at all possible, use either a reference or an expert along with common sense.

At first, using this approach will seem mechanical, and it will even appear to slow you down. That's because you've had several years to develop other thinking methods that you depend on now. Surely a higher level of thinking skill will take time to develop. But if you give this method of thinking serious effort and help those around you to do the same, you will make rapid progress. College instructors will reward you more quickly and more handsomely for higher-level thinking skills than for anything else you do in class. Beyond that you will find that you enjoy your studies more and find college to be more exciting and satisfying overall.

EXERCISE 15.7 Improving Arguments and Explanations

A. Individually or in a group, as your instructor advises, choose one paragraph from the essay on pages 252–253 that you think you could rewrite (and possibly expand) so that it gave stronger support to the argument it is making. Come up with several ideas about how you could rewrite it to be more effective. What additional facts, if any, might be available and useful? Revise the paragraph.

B. Read over a paper you have written recently. What basic argument or point was the paper making? What kinds of support did you use (common sense, experience, experts, references)? Discuss in a group how you might improve the force of your argument in another draft.

C. Join a group with at least three other students. Together choose one of the following topics. Decide as a group whether you are going to argue for or against the statement, or in favor of some more moderate position. Create a plan for how you would make your argument. Be sure your plan specifies how and where your argument would rely on common sense, experience, experts, and references. Describe your plan to the rest of the class.

Schools should require faculty and students to wear uniforms.

Most public elementary and secondary schools should be abolished.

Body piercing should be encouraged.

College should be free.

More drugs should be outlawed (for example, alcohol and caffeine).

More drugs should be legalized.

JOURNAL

Describe your thinking, arguing, or explaining skills at this point. Do you have any difficulties convincing other people, either in speaking or in writing? How much do you rely on common sense and your own experience? What ideas in this chapter might help you improve your ability to answer the questions that matter to you most?

SUGGESTIONS FOR FURTHER READING

de Bono, Edward. *Practical Thinking.* London: Penguin Books, 1991.

Perry, W. *Forms in Intellectual and Ethical Development in the College Years: A Scheme.* New York: Holt, Rinehart & Winston, 1970.

Siegel, Ronald K. *Fire in the Brain: Clinical Tales of Hallucination.* New York: Dutton, 1992, p. 94.

Van Oech, R. *A Whack on the Side of the Head: How You Can Be More Creative.* New York: Warner Books, 1990.

CHAPTER 16

Finding Answers:
Your College Catalog
and Academic
Advisor
or Counselor

A. Jerome Jewler
University of South Carolina

John N. Gardner
University of South Carolina

Mary Stuart Hunter
University of South Carolina

I don't know how to choose my courses. Do I need computer science? Have I taken all the math I need? Someone said to look in the catalog to find out the requirements. Maybe I can just get my advisor to explain it to me. I wish I knew what I was doing.

College catalogs and bulletins were probably an excellent resource for you when you were choosing which college to attend. Now that the decision has been made, you may be inclined to leave your institution's catalog on a shelf to gather dust or even toss it in the trash, thinking it's no longer needed. Don't. College is complex and expensive, and the college catalog is a sort of user's manual for your institution. Learn what's in your catalog—it should be a valuable resource throughout your college years.

EXERCISE 16.1   Finding Your Catalog and Starting a File

A. If you haven't already received your catalog, check with your advisor or counselor. If your advisor does not have a copy for you, contact the admissions office, the registration office, the departmental office of your academic major, or your campus bookstore. Make sure you have the catalog that is dated the year you matriculated, or entered a program of study, at your institution, *not* the year you applied for admission and were accepted.

B. Start a file for your catalog and other documents such as your grade reports, advisement forms, fee payment receipts, schedule change forms, and other proof of financial and academic dealings with your institution. Plan to keep all these things until your diploma is in your hands.

C. If it is likely that you may transfer to another college to complete an associate or bachelor's degree, also obtain a copy of the catalog for that school. It will be useful when you meet with your advisor to plan your courses.

HOW TO READ YOUR COLLEGE CATALOG

Does the previous exercise sound obsessive? It isn't. The reason that you should keep not only your catalog but all those forms and receipts is that when you apply for graduation, your department may conduct what is called a *degree audit, senior audit,* or *graduation check.* This process will compare your transcript with the academic requirements for the certificate or degree you are seeking. Any discrepancy between what you present as your academic record and the requirements in the catalog must be reconciled. Should the school's records be incomplete or inaccurate, your own file might make a difference in your favor.

What's in the Catalog?

First and foremost, the catalog is the official publication of your institution and contains valuable information about it: regulations, requirements, procedures, and opportunities for your development as a student. Although the catalog doesn't contain *everything* students need to know, it does provide an excellent summary of critical information available in greater detail elsewhere on your campus. The style of catalogs varies, but most provide you with the following information.

Publication Date. Most college catalogs are published annually or every two years; a few are published twice a year. The publication date is generally shown on the cover. It is important for you to know which catalog was in effect when you matriculated (that is, enrolled for the first time) rather than when you applied for admission, because you are subject to the rules and regulations that were in effect when you matriculated.

Colleges and universities are constantly changing admissions standards, degree requirements, academic calendars, and so on. But the catalog in use at the time of your matriculation will generally stand as your individual "contract" with the institution. This constancy is to your benefit. Imagine the chaos if you had to adjust to a new set of degree requirements with each newly published catalog! The catalog in effect at your matriculation is the one that defines the requirements for your degree, unless it states a time limit to complete the degree under those requirements.

EXERCISE 16.2   Finding Some Key Dates

Look through your college catalog. Find and record the following important dates:

Publication date of the catalog: _____

	This Term	Next Term
First day of classes	_____	_____
Last day to add a class	_____	_____
Last day (if any) to drop a class without penalty	_____	_____
Midpoint in the term	_____	_____
Last day of classes	_____	_____
Final exam period (first day)	_____	_____
Final exam period (last day)	_____	_____
Official last day of term	_____	_____
Holidays (no classes held):		
_____	_____	_____
_____	_____	_____
_____	_____	_____
_____	_____	_____
_____	_____	_____

NOTE: If not in your catalog, this information should be available in the master schedule of classes for the current term.

General Information. The introductory information in the catalog usually stresses an institution's unique characteristics, mission, and educational philosophy. While philosophies and mission statements are sometimes discounted as unimportant, in reality they may determine whether or not you will find a good "fit" at the institution. For example, if you are interested in a broad liberal arts education, you might think twice about enrolling in a school that stresses business and engineering. Likewise, if engineering or computer technology are your areas, you may want to think again about the fit of a small liberal arts college.

Opening sections of the catalog frequently also list the governing officers and officials, describe the physical plant and facilities, recount a brief history of the school, and state its current accreditations (accredited institutions and programs are those that have met specific national standards). Accreditation is important because it assures you that a program is of an acceptable quality. Future employers and graduate school admissions officers pay special attention to the accreditation status of undergraduate schools.

Admissions Information. College catalogs serve many purposes, including student recruitment. So there is almost always admissions information in the catalog. This section will list the various categories of admissions and specify admissions procedures, application deadlines, and criteria for admissions decisions.

General Academic Regulations. General academic regulations include requirements, procedures, and policies that are applicable to all students regardless of individual majors or student classifications. Fully understanding and complying with these rules will help you progress through your academic years without running into roadblocks.

Students often distort or misinterpret academic regulations. To be fully and accurately informed, don't rely on second-hand, "grapevine" information. Become familiar with these rules directly from the catalog. If you don't understand something in the catalog, seek clarification from an official source. Your academic advisor or counselor may be able to connect you with such sources.

The regulations section outlines the institution's enrollment and registration procedures. It also explains the grading system, course credit options, grade point average calculation, and academic suspension system, and describes academic honors and graduation requirements as they apply to students throughout the school. It may also detail students' rights, including the confidentiality of student records and the right to appeal or petition for relief from certain academic regulations.

Financial Information. Your catalog may also outline the current costs of attending your institution: academic fee schedules, costs of various housing options, prices of meal plans, and schedule of fines, refund policies, and payment options. Government-assisted schools also include rules for resident and nonresident status and resulting fee differentials.

The high cost of a college education concerns most students, as it does most college administrators. Not only may cost have affected your choice of a school, but costs will probably continue to rise throughout your years in college. But the financial section may have good news for you: detailed information on financial aid, scholarships, loans, and work opportunities. Study this section for sources of financial help.

Academic Calendar. Most college catalogs include a current academic calendar, which states the beginning and ending dates of the academic terms as well as dates of holidays and other events within each term. Being familiar with the calendar in advance will help you make sound decisions. For example, if you are not doing well in a particular class, you may want to drop the course rather than receive a failing grade, but you must do so before the deadline for withdrawal. To facilitate general planning, some catalogs give the academic calendars for several years in advance.

Academic Program. By far the lengthiest part of most catalogs is the section on academic programs. This summarizes the various degrees offered, the majors within each department, and the requirements for studying in each discipline. The departmental outlines include most of the information that is unique to each department, supplementing any institution-wide rules and regulations. They also list any special admissions criteria for special programs, as well as the progression, curriculum, and degree requirements.

The academic program section also describes the individual courses offered at your institution. Basic information usually includes course number, course title, units of credit, prerequisites for taking the course, and a brief statement of the course content.

Remember, the catalog is only a *summary* of information. Individual department offices frequently offer more detailed information in the form of course descriptions, curriculum checklists, departmental advisement guidelines, and so on. Your academic advisor or counselor may also have such supplemental information.

If you are planning to transfer to another school, be sure you also have a catalog from that school. Consult both catalogs about any articulation agreements between the schools, which will state what courses are necessary for transfer and what courses will receive transferable credit at your new school.

EXERCISE 16.3 Scoping Out the Catalog

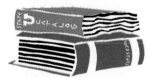

Bring your catalog to class. Form a small group with several other students who plan to follow a program or enroll in a major similar to your own. Do the following as a group.

1. From information in the catalog, answer the following questions about the program or major:
   a. What are the core requirements of the program?
   b. What prerequisites (if any) are there for the program?
   c. Is there a sequence that must be followed when taking specific courses? (For example, are there some courses that must be taken in order but are taught only in certain semesters?)
   d. What courses will each person in the group need or plan to take next semester?

2. Find at least one specific piece of information that might be useful or surprising to other members of the class. Prepare to report on that information.

YOUR ACADEMIC ADVISOR OR COUNSELOR

The idea of academic advising or counseling is certainly not new, but never before has it been regarded as so essential. There's good reason for this; with so many programs and so many choices, even experienced faculty and staff must check and double-check academic requirements and regulations to be certain students are making the right choices. Because so many students today are the first in their families to attend college, it is even more important that there be someone to advise them. In broader terms, if faculty and staff believe that college should help students develop holistically—that is, vocationally, emotionally, physically, spiritually, culturally, and socially as well as intellectually—the academic advisor can be the focal point for such development.

We already know that when a student has one person on campus who cares about his or her survival, that student stands a better chance of succeeding than the student who lacks a relationship with a significant other person. A mounting body of evidence has convinced colleges and universities that poor academic advising is one major reason students drop out of college. Thus academic advising has become one of the most important ingredients for student success. Although your "significant other" person may be an instructor, a staff member, an upperclass student, or a counselor, it might also be none other than your academic advisor.

What Is Academic Advising?

Academic advising is a dynamic process for obtaining the critical information you need to make the most important decisions about college, decisions affecting your academic major, career goals, elective courses, secondary fields of study, and co-curricular activities. Academic advising is also a one-to-one, highly personal, out-of-class form of learning. Academic advising includes periodic assistance in scheduling courses that you will take the following term and is inextricably related to the process of career planning and decision making. But beyond decision-making and scheduling considerations, it represents a relationship between two human beings who care about, understand, and respect each other and share a common goal: the student's education.

Some schools may practice a more holistic view of academic advising, in which the advisor serves as a personal counselor to whom you can turn for any sort of problem, especially if the problem is affecting your ability to successfully complete course work. Such problems might include a learning disability; a personal problem that causes stress, insomnia, or anxiety; perceived unfair treatment by a teacher; indecision about choice of major, career, or transfer to another school; an ethical or moral dilemma; inability to keep up with course work due to any number of reasons, including excessive employment hours; or poor grades that may lead to suspension.

Even if you have no serious problems, you may want to talk with your advisor for any number of reasons: to get advice on applying for a job, to get a reaction to a piece of writing or a project, to ask for the names of books in a given field that might be helpful to you, to share some good news about grades or job interviews, or to check on academic rules and regulations.

At most schools academic advising is less comprehensive, and you may need to ask about separate counseling services for nonacademic personal issues. At a minimum your academic advisor informs you about your program requirements and options and gives you approval to register for courses each

What Are You Looking for in Your Academic Advisor?

This graph from a recent study of students at Harvard shows that men and women tend to seek different qualities in advisors.

When asked about advising, men want an advisor who "knows the facts." Or "if he doesn't know the data, he knows where to get it or to send me to get it." Or one who "makes concrete and directive suggestions, which I'm then free to accept or reject."

Women more often want an advisor who "will take the time to get to know me personally." Or who "is a good listener and can read between the lines if I am hesitant to express a concern." Or who "shares my interests so that we will have something in common." The women's responses focus far more on a personal relationship.*

What do you plan to look for in your advisor? What can you do to ensure that you get the advisor who is best for you?

*Richard J. Light. The Harvard Assessment Seminars, First Report (Cambridge, Mass.: Harvard University Graduate School of Education and Kennedy School of Government, 1990).

What Students Want from Their Academic Advisor (percentage indicating "very important")

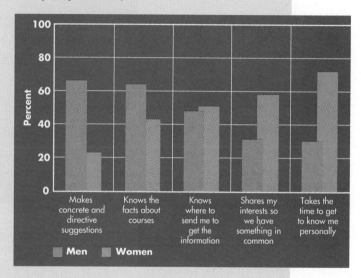

term. Ideally academic advisors also help you explore life goals and vocational goals, select academic programs, and choose and schedule courses.

Academic advising should be a process whereby you communicate regularly with someone you respect about a broad range of concerns. The process should be linked to career planning and may include personal counseling. It may also include an "early warning system" through which the college monitors your academic progress and sends frequent grade reports during your first term to your advisor. He or she then contacts you and refers you, as needed, to other counseling and support resources to assist you with academic difficulties. The purpose is not to criticize you but to help you cope with the academic problems you may be experiencing.

Academic advising may also include a process that monitors your class attendance during your first semester and alerts you if you miss too many classes. Later the process will include your advisor making sure that you have met all the requirements for graduation and certifying that you are eligible to receive your diploma.

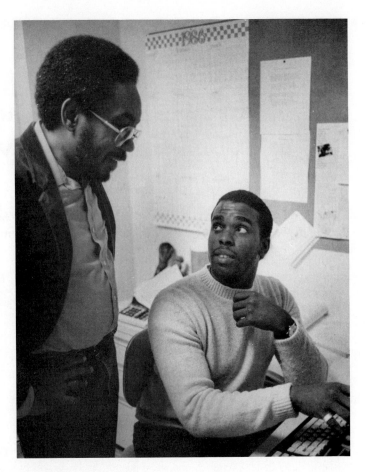

The best academic advisor is someone who really wants to get to know you and welcomes your questions and concerns. It these qualities seem to be missing, think about whether there is something you can do to improve communication. Or consider looking for an advisor with whom you feel more at home. (Stephen Goldblatt/photo courtesy of Swarthmore College)

EXERCISE 16.4 Academic Advising at Your School

Explore the academic advising or counseling process at your institution. To find out about it, you may have to contact your advisor, the advisement center, your department head, or another campus resource. Knowing how to locate resources is an important skill to develop in college!

Try to answer these questions and others you may have:

1. Who are the advisors?

_____ Teachers

_____ Counselors

_____ Professional advisors

_____ Other: _____

2. What services do they offer?

_____

_____

_____

_____

3. How does a student get assigned to a particular advisor? Does a student normally have the same advisor throughout college? How can a student go about arranging for a different advisor if necessary?

4. What other counseling and advising services can your academic advisor help you find when you need them?

5. Are there specific counselors for transfer purposes?

Who Are Academic Advisors?

At many colleges academic advisors are full-time faculty. At some schools they may be educators whose sole professional responsibility is advising. At other schools you'll find a combination of faculty and professional staff members as advisors.

In many community colleges academic advising is done by counselors in the college counseling/advising center. These counselors are trained in and responsible for assisting students with both academic and personal issues. If you haven't declared a major, you may be assigned to an advisor who specializes in dealing with undecided students. You may be attending an institution that, as a matter of policy, does not initially assign new students to advisors in their intended major field, but does so later on. Even if you are not assigned a faculty member from your special area of interest, your advisor is usually expected to be familiar with the requirements of your program. If your advisor is not familiar with them, there may be a center on campus where a staff advisor can give specific program information.

EXERCISE 16.5   Who's Your Academic Advisor?

Find out and record the name of your academic advisor, along with his or her office location, phone number, and normal advising hours. If you have not already done so, arrange to meet this person.

Name: _____

Office location: _____

Phone(s): _____

_____

Hours: _____

Where and When Is Academic Advising Conducted?

One of the many differences between high school and college is that most college faculty have private offices where they can meet with you during their posted office hours. At many institutions academic advising takes place in advisement centers. These centers may also include offices for personal counseling, career planning and placement, financial aid, and study skills.

Ideally academic advising is a process that involves more frequent interaction between you and your advisor. The nature and frequency of this relationship depend on how you and your advisor choose to pursue this opportunity. Like virtually everything in college, academic advising will be what you make of it.

Generally, at least once a term, students are notified to sign up for appointments with their advisors to discuss the selection and scheduling of courses for the next term. This advising period may last up to two weeks and is usually widely publicized on campus. It is very important that you be aware of these periods and schedule a conference to discuss your course selections for the coming term.

EXERCISE 16.6   Advising Process and Schedules

To prepare for your basic academic advising sessions, do the following:

1. Find out when the course selection and scheduling process for next term

   begins, and record the date here: _____

2. Record what you need to do to prepare for this process (include any important dates):

   _____

   _____

   _____

   _____

   _____

Don't forget to transfer the important dates to your calendar so you'll be prepared!

RELATING TO YOUR ADVISOR

Advising is likely to be much more successful for you if you take the relationship seriously and work hard to make it meaningful. Take responsibility for keeping your advisor informed of your progress or problems. At the very minimum make an appointment to meet at least once a term to discuss plans for the next term. Ask for advice on course prerequisites, interesting courses to take, good teachers to study under, or other options.

Discuss any major decisions—such as adding or dropping a course, changing your major, or transferring or withdrawing from school—*before* making them. You may also need to discuss personal problems with your advisor. If he or she can't help you with a certain problem, ask for referral to a professional on campus who can. Your advisor should be someone you can always turn to. Even if he or she doesn't know the answer immediately, the advisor should know who to call to get you the help you need. Will your advisor respect your request for confidentiality on such matters? That's something you will need to clarify.

Your advising sessions will be more productive if you are already familiar with your college catalog. Make up a list of questions before your appointment and also arrive with a tentative schedule of courses and alternate choices for the coming term. At many colleges your entire academic record will be stored in an online data base that your advisor can access on a personal computer during your advising sessions. At others the department office will have your academic records on file for use in the advising session.

EXERCISE 16.7   Questions to Ask Advisors

Read the following description of Frank, a first-year student:

Frank has had an average first term. He excelled in English Composition and Western History but was disappointed with his performance in biology and math. He was a good student in all subjects in high school, so he's somewhat baffled by his performance. He thinks it may be because his job keeps him up late at night, so he's not alert for his morning classes, which happen to be math and biology. Or it may be the way those classes are taught—lots of students, lots of lectures, little personal attention. Whatever it is, he's decided to switch his course-work focus from the biosciences to philosophy. He's not sure how to tell his family about this—they think he wants to work in science. He also wonders what kind of job he'll get if he eventually gets his B.A. in philosophy. One thing he does know is that the philosophy courses a friend of his is taking sound a lot more interesting than his science classes! Actually his friend's whole life sounds a lot more interesting. How does he have time to get involved in so many things when all Frank can manage to do is study, work, and make it to class?

1. Frank has an appointment with his academic advisor tomorrow. What questions would you suggest Frank ask?

   _____

   _____

   _____

   _____

   Compare your suggestions with those of other students in your class.

2. Now spend some time reviewing your school term so far. Jot down some of the issues you're experiencing, or questions you have, so you'll remember to speak with your advisor about them.

_____

_____

_____

_____

Is Your Advisor Right for You?

The key word here is *trust*. You will know you have the right academic advisor if you establish good rapport with this person. Do you feel comfortable with him or her? Does your academic advisor seem to take a personal interest in you? Does the advisor listen actively? Does the advisor provide enough time for you to accomplish what needs to be done? Does he or she either make an effort to get you the information you request or tell you where you can find it yourself?

If your advisor isn't right for you, you could discuss your lack of satisfaction with him or her as tactfully as possible. But since this may be awkward, a better approach might be to ask for another advisor. To find a better advisor, you might consider asking one of your instructors, perhaps one with whom you have developed a personal rapport or whom you respect. Get his or her agreement, or check with your departmental advising coordinators about other possibilities for advisors. Then make the change officially. *Never* stay in an advising relationship that isn't working for you.

Colleges and universities have made enormous strides since the mid-1970s in improving the condition of academic advising, and it is now being taken very seriously at many schools. A number of advisors are now being trained, evaluated, and rewarded. The process of personalizing academic advising will more than likely continue, and more and more students like yourself will have the opportunity to benefit from it. Be certain that you do.

EXERCISE 16.8 Preparing to Meet with Your Advisor

Think ahead to your next appointment with your advisor. What questions do
you have in each of the following areas? Record those questions here. (You may
be able to answer some of these questions yourself by consulting your catalog.)

1. Your major and potential career:

   _____

   _____

   _____

2. Alternate majors and potential careers:

   _____

   _____

   _____

3. Classes you need next term:

   _____

   _____

   _____

4. Proper sequencing of classes you need to take:

   _____

   _____

   _____

5. Difficulty level of classes you may be taking next term:

   _____

   _____

   _____

6. Good balance in the combination of class work loads and types of classes
   you have chosen:

   _____

   _____

   _____

7. Electives you might be interested in:

   _____

   _____

   _____

8. Schedule problems:

   _____

   _____

   _____

9. Teaching styles of specific instructors:

_____

_____

_____

10. General campus information:

_____

_____

_____

11. Information about scholarships, internships, cooperative education, or other opportunities:

_____

_____

_____

12. Other questions or issues including change of major (don't forget the notes you recorded for Exercise 16.7):

_____

_____

_____

   Throughout the rest of this term use this worksheet to record other questions for your advisor as you think of them. The night before your appointment, review the list for any additions or deletions. To make good use of your appointment time and not forget anything, take this list and your catalog with you. If you're considering transferring, also bring the catalog from the school to which you may want to transfer.

JOURNAL

What has your academic advising experience been like to date? Describe your satisfaction or your lack thereof with the academic advising you have received. Comment on the characteristics and personality of your academic advisor. Also describe what attempts you have made to develop a relationship with him or her and how successful they have been.

SUGGESTIONS FOR FURTHER READING

Your college catalog.

Your student handbook.

Current schedule of classes.

CHAPTER

17

Choosing a Major and Planning a Career

Linda B. Salane
Columbia College

*M**y career inventory results said I should go into the funeral business. I'm a marketing major. Does that mean I'll be selling to the dead!? My counselor said it all made sense because funeral parlors have to sell their services to the survivors. Still, it was enough to make me think of changing majors again. Maybe I should do a little more than think.*

For many years students have indicated that the primary reason they attend college is to be able to get a better job. And every year many graduates are disappointed with the job offers they receive.

That doesn't have to happen to you. If you make your decisions based on your personal priorities and on the realities of the job market, your decisions can lead to an array of exciting career fields. Not only will you understand the rationale underlying your choices, but you will also be in a position to change direction as your priorities change. Of course, you should also be well informed about the variety of courses and majors available to you on your campus.

MAJORS = CAREERS? NOT ALWAYS

For some students choosing a major is a simple decision, but most students who enter college straight out of high school (and even some who've worked a while) don't know which major to select or which career they may be best suited for. The following exercise will help you begin to clarify where you stand.

EXERCISE 17.1   Some Opening Questions

Write a brief answer to each of the following questions. Try to answer each question even though you may feel uncertain about it.

1. In general, what kind of work do you want to do after finishing your education?

   _____

   _____

2. What career fields or industries offer opportunities for this kind of work?

   _____

   _____

3. What role will college play in preparing you for this work?

   _____

   _____

4. What specific things do you plan to do to enhance your chances of getting a job when you graduate?

   _____

   _____

   _____

Biology…evolution… history…literature…? Start your search for your major with some wide-ranging thought about your major interests. (Joe Rubino/photo courtesy of Earlham College)

5. Do your career goals seem compatible with your other life goals and values?

   _____

   _____

6. Is it likely that you will need to transfer to another college in order to get the education you need for your career?

   _____

   _____

You've probably met people who tell you how much they love their jobs and even marvel that they're being paid to do something they enjoy. You've probably also met people who dislike what they do, count the days until Friday, and are always looking for another job. We might say that the latter group has a place to work while the former group has work that has a place in their total lives.

Career planning stresses the importance of knowing enough about yourself, your personal values system, and specific career fields so that you can consciously make the right decisions. To identify work that will be a vital part of your life, you need two kinds of information. First, you need information you can obtain from self-assessment: personality type, interests, values, aptitudes, skills, and goals. Second, you need information you can obtain through career research to determine which career fields will let you explore your interests, exercise your values, demonstrate your aptitudes, use your skills, and fulfill your personal goals.

Before you actively begin planning your career, you need to realize several things about majors and their effect on careers. First, the relationship of college majors to careers varies. Obviously, if you want to be a nurse, you must major in nursing. Engineers major in engineering. Pharmacists major in pharmacology. There's no other way to be certified as a nurse, engineer, or pharmacist. However, most career fields don't require a specific major, and people with specific majors don't have to use them in usual ways. For example, if you major in nursing, history, engineering, or English, you might still choose to become a bank manager, sales representative, career counselor, production manager, or any number of other things.

Second, in most cases a college major alone is not enough to land you a job. There is tremendous competition for good jobs, and you need experience and competencies related to your chosen field. Internships, part-time jobs, and co-curricular activities provide opportunities to gain experience and develop these competencies.

The most common question college students ask is, "What can I do with my major?" Career planning helps you focus on a more important question: "What do I *want* to do?" This question leads you to explore yourself and fields where you can achieve what you want.

As you attempt to determine what you want to do, the choice of an academic major will take on new meaning. You'll no longer be so concerned with what the prescribed route of certain majors allows you to do. Instead you'll use your career goals as a basis for academic decisions about your major, your minor, elective courses, internships, and co-curricular activities. Consider these goals when you select part-time and summer jobs. Don't confine yourself to a short list of jobs directly related to your major; think more broadly about your goals.

FACTORS IN YOUR CAREER PLANNING

You are a unique and complex individual, a maze of characteristics. You have developed and will continue to refine an image of who you are. Some people have a very definite self-image when they enter college, but most are still in the process of defining (or perhaps redefining) themselves. Often we see ourselves as puzzles. To begin understanding this puzzle, we need to consider each piece—interests, skills, aptitudes, personality characteristics, life goals, and work values—separately and then consider the impact each has on the others.

Interests

Interests develop from your past experiences and from assumptions you formed in previous environments. For example, you may be interested in writing for the college newspaper because you did it in high school and loved it or because you'd like to try something new. Throughout your life your interests will develop and change. Involvement in different courses or activities may lead you to drop old interests as you add new ones. It's not unusual for a student to enter Psychology 101 with a great interest in psychology and realize halfway through the course that psychology is not what he or she imagined or wants to pursue.

EXERCISE 17.2 What Are Your Interests?

How do you identify what you're interested in? Take standardized inventories or tests through the counseling services at your school. Also try the following:

1. Look through your college catalog for courses that sound interesting. Write down five or six of them. Note why each course interests you.

2. Make a list of all the classes, activities, and clubs you enjoyed in high school or since then. Ask yourself why you enjoyed these things.

3. Write down any activities outside class that you intend to pursue at college.

4. Go to your college bookstore and browse through the textbooks of courses that sound as if they would be interesting. See whether your interest has a basis in fact.

5. Read a national newspaper and identify four topics you would like to learn more about.

Bring your lists to class so that you can discuss these thoughts.

Skills

To claim something as a skill, you must have proof that you are indeed already good at it. You can't claim to be a good writer, for example, unless you really do write well. You measure your current level of skill by your past performance. At the same time, skills can be developed. You may be a poor writer now, but by using resources available to you at college and by practicing, you can become a better writer.

EXERCISE 17.3 What Are Your Current Skills?

Use the following list to help you determine your best skills. First, place a check mark next to the skills you presently have. Then identify and circle the five skills you are most confident about, those about which you could say to anyone, "I am good at this." Finally, place an X next to the skills you would like to develop in college.

_____ writing	_____ explaining	_____ being accurate
_____ reading	_____ socializing	_____ getting results
_____ conversing	_____ making a team effort	_____ being neat
_____ reporting information		_____ keeping records

_____ interviewing	_____ helping others	_____ asserting self
_____ being creative	_____ teaching	_____ taking risks
_____ making machines and mechanical things work	_____ entertaining	_____ negotiating
_____ applying technical knowledge	_____ speaking in public	_____ selling
_____ building things	_____ being sensitive	_____ winning
_____ repairing things	_____ learning	_____ being friendly
_____ operating tools	_____ analyzing	_____ motivating
_____ observing	_____ evaluating	_____ managing
_____ listening	_____ handling money	_____ directing others
_____ coming up with ideas	_____ planning	_____ adapting
_____ cooperating	_____ solving problems	_____ encouraging
_____ being tactful	_____ scheduling	_____ other: _____
	_____ following through	_____ other: _____

A. Identify four ways you could strengthen each skill you said you would like to develop in your academic and extracurricular activities at college.

B. Select two or three of your strongest skills. Suppose you were asked to prove you possessed these skills. How would you do this?

Aptitudes

Aptitudes are inherent strengths. They may be part of your biological heritage, or they may have developed through early learning. Aptitudes are the foundation for skills, so high aptitudes generally indicate the potential for higher skill levels. Remember that practice and the use of available resources can improve a skill. For example, if you have an aptitude for writing and couple that aptitude with practice, you'll probably become a better writer than someone who doesn't have a strong writing aptitude. We all have aptitudes we can build on. Build on *your* strengths.

EXERCISE 17.4   What Are Your Aptitudes?

Read the following aptitude areas. Place an X next to those you know you are weak in. Place a question mark (?) next to those you are not sure about. Place a check mark next to your strongest aptitudes. Are they in the same family as the skills you previously checked?

_____ 1. *Abstract reasoning.* People with strong aptitudes in abstract reasoning can interpret poetry, work out scientific problems in their heads, and solve logic problems.

_____ 2. *Verbal reasoning.* People with strong aptitudes in verbal reasoning can talk through problems easily or can understand the problems more easily when they hear them described than when they see them on paper.

_____ 3. *Spatial relations.* People with strong aptitudes in spatial relations are able to understand the physical relationships between two- and three-dimensional objects or designs.

_____ 4. *Language usage.* People with strong aptitudes in language usage are able to write and speak effectively.

_____ 5. *Mechanical ability.* People with strong mechanical ability are able to physically manipulate the parts of a machine to make it work.

_____ 6. *Clerical ability.* People with strong clerical ability are able to do detailed general office work efficiently and to organize records or accounts.

_____ 7. *Numerical ability.* People with strong numerical ability are able to solve arithmetic problems easily.

_____ 8. *Spelling.* People with strong aptitudes in spelling are able to understand and remember patterns and details.

Select two or three of your strongest aptitudes. Suppose you were asked to prove you possessed these aptitudes. How would you do this?

Personality

What makes you psychologically different from others around you? The personality you've developed through the years makes you *you,* and those characteristics can't be ignored when making career decisions. The quiet, orderly, calm, and detail-oriented person probably will make a different work choice than the aggressive, outgoing, and argumentative person. Many psychologists believe that working in an occupation consistent with your personality will make you feel more successful and satisfied.

EXERCISE 17.5 Describe Your Personality

What ten words would you use to describe yourself? Write them down:

1. _____   6. _____

2. _____   7. _____

3. _____   8. _____

4. _____   9. _____

5. _____   10. _____

Ask at least three people who know you well (your parents, your spouse, your brother or sister, a close friend) to write down ten words they would use to describe you. How do the lists compare?

Life Goals and Work Values

Each of us defines success and satisfaction in our own way, and one person's perception of them may be quite different from another's. Defining these concepts is complex and very personal. Two factors influence our conclusions about success and happiness: (1) knowing that we are achieving the life goals we've set for ourselves and (2) finding that we value what we're receiving from our work.

EXERCISE 17.6   What Are Your Life Goals?

The following list includes life goals some people set for themselves. This list can help you begin to think about the kinds of goals you may want to set. Place a check mark next to the goals you would like to achieve in your life. Next, review the goals you have checked and circle the five you want most. Finally, review your list of five goals and rank them by priority (1 for most important, 5 for least important).

_____ the love and admiration of friends

_____ good health

_____ lifetime financial security

_____ a lovely home

_____ international fame

_____ freedom within my work setting

_____ a good love relationship

_____ a satisfying religious faith

_____ recognition as the most attractive person in the world

_____ an understanding of the meaning of life

_____ success in my profession

_____ a personal contribution to the elimination of poverty and sickness

_____ a chance to direct the destiny of a nation

_____ freedom to do what I want

_____ a satisfying and fulfilling marriage

_____ a happy family relationship

_____ complete self-confidence

_____ other: _____

NOTE: Adapted from Human Potential Seminar by James D. McHolland, Evanston, Ill., 1975. Used by permission of the author.

EXERCISE 17.7 What Are Your Work Values?

The following list includes typical work values, reasons people say they like the work they do. It can help you begin to think about what you want to receive from your work. Read each definition and place a check mark next to the items you'd like to have as part of your ideal job. Next, review the items you've checked and circle the ten items you want most. Finally, review your list of ten items and rank them in order of importance (1 for most important, 10 for least important).

_____ *Help society.* Do something to contribute to the betterment of the world.

_____ *Help others.* Be involved in helping other people in a direct way, either individually or in a small group.

_____ *Have public contact.* Have a lot of day-to-day contact with people.

_____ *Work with others.* Have close working relationships with a group as a result of my work activities.

_____ *Compete.* Engage in activities that pit my abilities against those of others where there are clear win-and-lose outcomes.

_____ *Make decisions.* Have the power to decide courses of action.

_____ *Hold power and authority.* Control other people's work activities.

_____ *Influence people.* Be in a position to change the attitudes or opinions of other people.

_____ *Work alone.* Do projects by myself, without any significant amount of contact with others.

_____ *Seek knowledge.* Engage myself in the pursuit of knowledge, truth, and understanding.

_____ *Hold intellectual status.* Be regarded as a person of high intellectual prowess, an acknowledged "expert."

_____ *Create (general).* Create new ideas and programs, not following an established format.

_____ *Supervise.* Have a job in which I'm directly responsible for the work done by others.

_____ *Experience change and variety.* Have work responsibilities that frequently change in content and setting.

_____ *Be stable.* Have a work routine that is largely predictable.

_____ *Be secure.* Be assured of keeping my job and reaping a reasonable financial reward.

_____ *Live at a fast pace.* Work in a setting where there is a high pace of activity and work must be done rapidly.

_____ *Gain recognition.* Be recognized for the quality of my work.

_____ *Feel excitement.* Experience frequent excitement in the course of my work.

_____ *Find adventure.* Have work duties that involve frequent risk taking.

_____ *Profit materially.* Have a strong likelihood of accumulating large amounts of money or other material gain.

_____ *Be independent.* Determine the nature of my work myself; not have to do what others tell me to.

_____ *Be in the right location.* Find a place to live (town, geographical area) that allows me to do the things I enjoy most.

_____ *Control my own time.* Have work responsibilities that I can accomplish on my own schedule.

NOTE: List reprinted with permission, from Howard E. Figler, *PATH: A Career Workbook for Liberal Arts Students,* 3d. ed. (Cranston, R.I.: Carroll Press, 1993). Copyright © 1993 by Carroll Press.

If you had difficulty with the preceding exercise, you might want to talk with a career counselor in your career planning and placement center. Career counselors are trained to help you identify your strengths and prioritize them according to what is most important to you.

EXERCISE 17.8   A Personal Profile

Use the chart at the top of page 287 to summarize and compare your responses to Exercises 17.2 through 17.7. From each of those exercises, copy your main responses into the chart. Get together in a small group. Share your responses with others in the group. Together, brainstorm some ideas for careers for each person in the group.

WHAT ARE YOUR CAREER OPTIONS?

You might be surprised to learn that the federal government lists more than 31,000 career fields. How many can you name? If you're like most college students, your list begins to get sketchy beyond thirty-five or fifty occupations. Unless you've already worked in a field for several years, you probably don't have accurate information about typical on-the-job activities, necessary skills, occupational outlook, salary range, methods of entry, or related fields—even for your most likely occupational choice. Obviously you can't make a good choice if you don't know what your choices are.

Interests	Skills	Aptitudes	Personality	Goals	Values

Dr. John Holland, a psychologist at Johns Hopkins University, has developed a system to help you identify potential career choices. He separates people into six general categories based on differences in their interests, skills, values, and personality characteristics—in short, their preferred approaches to life. His categories include the following:*

► **Realistic.** These people describe themselves as concrete, down-to-earth, and practical—as doers. They exhibit competitive/assertive behavior and show interest in activities that require motor coordination, skill, and physical strength. They prefer situations involving "action solutions" rather than tasks involving verbal or interpersonal skills, and they like to take a concrete approach to problem solving rather than rely on abstract theory. They tend to be interested in scientific or mechanical areas rather than cultural and aesthetic fields.

► **Investigative.** These people describe themselves as analytical, rational, and logical—as problem solvers. They value intellectual stimulation and intellectual achievement and prefer to think rather than to act, to organize and understand rather than to persuade. They usually have a strong interest in physical, biological, or social sciences. They are not apt to be "people-oriented."

► **Artistic.** These people describe themselves as creative, innovative, and independent. They value self-expression and relations with others through artistic expression and are also emotionally expressive. They dislike structure, preferring tasks involving personal or physical skills. They resemble investigative people but are more interested in the cultural-aesthetic than the scientific.

*Adapted from John L. Holland, *Self-Directed Search Manual* (Psychological Assessment Resources: 1985). Copyright © 1985 by PAR, Inc. Reprinted with permission.

- **Social.** These people describe themselves as kind, caring, helpful, and understanding of others. They value helping and making a contribution. They satisfy their needs in one-to-one or small group interaction using strong verbal skills to teach, counsel, or advise. They are drawn to close interpersonal relationships and are less apt to engage in intellectual or extensive physical activity.

- **Enterprising.** These people describe themselves as assertive, risk-taking, and persuasive. They value prestige, power, and status and are more inclined than other types to pursue it. They use verbal skills to supervise, lead, direct, and persuade rather than to support or guide. They are interested in people and in achieving organizational goals.

- **Conventional.** These people describe themselves as neat, orderly, detail-oriented, and persistent. They value order, structure, prestige, and status and possess a high degree of self-control. They are not opposed to rules and regulations. They are skilled in organizing, planning, and scheduling and are interested in data and people.

EXERCISE 17.9   The Holland Categories

A. Look back over Holland's list of categories. Which category most accurately describes you? Write it here:

1. _____

Now look back over the other categories. Which of the remaining categories most nearly fit you? Write your second and third choices here:

2. _____

3. _____

In choosing several categories that seem to best describe you, don't let one or two factors keep you from making a choice. Choose the ones that contain the *most* true statements about you.

B. Identify three career fields that may be interesting to you. We'll come back to these in the next exercise.

1. _____

2. _____

3. _____

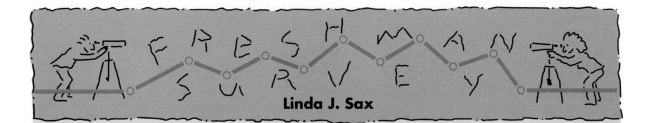

Linda J. Sax

Engineering and Computer Science

Freshman interest in engineering careers and majors fell sharply in the early 1970s, just after the first Apollo moon walk and the termination of funding for the American supersonic transport airplane project and other large government contracts. Potential engineering students saw televised coverage of unemployed engineers in Seattle, Long Beach, and St. Louis, cities where aerospace and defense contractors had large plants, and chose other fields and careers.

Interest in engineering careers rose again after 1975. This increase reflected a return of men into engineering as well as a growing (if still small) number of women. Later in the 1970s rising interest in technical careers such as engineering and computing was further stimulated by declines elsewhere in the economy; science and technology were the only "hot spots" in an otherwise slow job market.

In the last decade, however, student interest in engineering dropped surprisingly, about one-fourth, from a peak of 12 percent in 1982 to 7.7 percent in 1993. The proportion of freshmen planning careers as computer programmers fell even more.

Why the apparent declining interest in technical careers? Recent years have shown us that the market for jobs in engineering and computing is extremely sensitive to changes in the economy. Defense cuts and fewer government

Freshman Interest in Technology Careers, 1966–1993

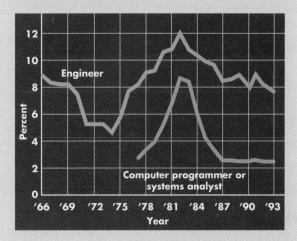

SOURCE: Higher Education Research Institute, UCLA

contracts have reduced the demand for new technical workers.

However, the growing trend in telecommunications and information systems, as well as the widening of international markets, may raise the need for engineers and computer programmers in the coming years. Can you think of other fields that are this responsive to changes in the economy?

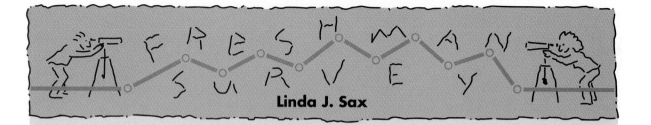

FRESHMAN SURVEY

Linda J. Sax

Changing Interest in Business and Health-Related Majors

Between 1966 and 1987 the proportion of first-year students interested in business careers doubled, as the first graph shows. Although interest in business careers has declined steadily since 1987, it is still the most popular college major and career choice. The percentage of first-year students planning to major in business increased from 14.3 percent in 1966 to 24.6 percent in 1987, and then dropped to 16.1 percent in 1993.

Women's interest in business careers has grown even more dramatically. Between 1966 and 1985 the proportion of women planning business careers increased sixfold. Indeed in some business specializations women now outnumber men. For several years more women than men have stated a preference for accounting majors and careers.

The second graph shows how sharply the declining interest in business in recent years contrasts with the rising interest in health-related majors. Today students are almost as likely to major in health-related fields (15.8 percent) as they are in business fields (16.1 percent). Why do you think the health professions have become so popular?

Freshman Interest in Business Careers, by Sex, 1966–1993

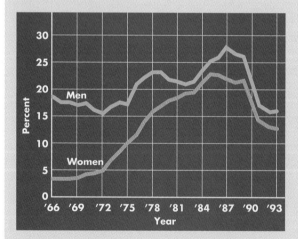

SOURCE: Higher Education Research Institute, UCLA

Freshman Interest in Business and Health-Related Majors, 1966–1993

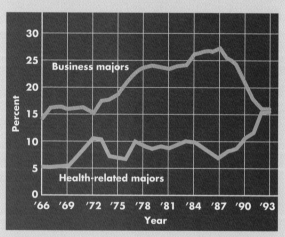

SOURCE: Higher Education Research Institute, UCLA

290   Chapter 17

Holland's system organizes career fields into the same six categories. Career fields are grouped according to what a particular career field requires of a person (skills and personality characteristics most commonly associated with success in those fields) and what rewards particular career fields provide for people (interests and values most commonly associated with satisfaction). As you read the following examples, see how your career interests match the category as described by Holland.

► **Realistic.** Agricultural engineer, barber, dairy farmer, electrical contractor, ferryboat captain, gem cutter, heavy equipment operator, industrial arts teacher, jeweler, navy officer, health and safety specialist, radio repairer, sheet metal worker, tailor, fitness director, package engineer, electronics technician, computer graphics technician, coach, PE teacher

► **Investigative.** Urban planner, chemical engineer, bacteriologist, cattle-breeding technician, ecologist, flight engineer, genealogist, handwriting analyst, laboratory technician, marine scientist, nuclear medical technologist, obstetrician, quality control technician, sanitation scientist, TV repairer, balloon pilot, computer programmer, robotics engineer, environmentalist, physician, college professor

► **Artistic.** Architect, film editor/director, actor, cartoonist, interior decorator, fashion model, furrier, graphic communications specialist, jewelry designer, journalist, medical illustrator, editor, orchestra leader, public relations specialist, sculptor, telecommunications coordinator, media specialist, librarian, reporter

► **Social.** Nurse, teacher, caterer, social worker, genetic counselor, home economist, job analyst, marriage counselor, parole officer, rehabilitation counselor, school superintendent, theater manager, production expediter, geriatric specialist, insurance claims specialist, minister, travel agent, guidance counselor, convention planner, career specialist

► **Enterprising.** Banker, city manager, employment interviewer, FBI agent, health administrator, industrial relations director, judge, labor arbitrator, personnel assistant, TV announcer, salary and wage administrator, insurance salesperson, sales engineer, lawyer, sales representative, marketing specialist, promoter

► **Conventional.** Accountant, statistician, census enumerator, data processor, hospital administrator, instrument assembler, insurance administrator, legal secretary, library assistant, office manager, reservation agent, information consultant, underwriter, auditor, personnel specialist, data base manager, abstractor/indexer

At first glance Holland's model may seem to be a simple method for matching people to career fields, but it was never meant for that purpose. Your career choices ultimately will involve a complex assessment of the factors that are most important to you. To display the relationship between career fields and the potential conflicts people face as they consider them, Holland's model is commonly presented in a hexagonal shape (see Figure 17.1). The closer the types, the closer the relationships among the career fields; the farther apart the types, the more conflict between the career fields.

Figure 17.1 Holland's Hexagonal Model of Career Fields

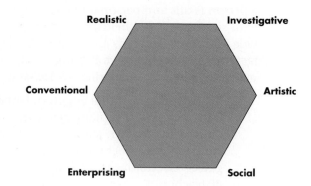

Realistic   Investigative

Conventional   Artistic

Enterprising   Social

EXERCISE 17.10 The Holland Hexagon

A. Go back to Exercise 17.9 and look at the three categories you selected as well as the three career fields. Based on the list of careers on page 291, how well do your career fields match the three categories you chose?

B. Now look at the Holland hexagon. See where your first, second, and third choices in Exercise 17.9 are located on the hexagon. Are they close together or far apart? If far apart, do you feel they reflect a conflict in your goals or interests? Write a brief statement about how the conflict has affected you so far. Discuss your categories and your written response with another member of the class.

Holland's model can help you address the problem of career choice in two ways. First, you can begin to identify many career fields that are consistent with what you know about yourself. Once you've identified potential fields, you can use the career library at your college to get more information about those fields. Find out the following information:

▶ Daily activities for specific jobs
▶ Interests and abilities required
▶ Preparation required for entry
▶ Working conditions
▶ Salary and benefits
▶ Employment outlook

Second, you can begin to identify the harmony or conflicts in your career choices. This will help you analyze the reasons for your career decisions and be more confident as you make choices.

College students often view the choice of a career as a monumental and irreversible decision. Some feel haunted by the choice as they decide on a college major. Others panic about it as they approach graduation and begin

Looking for an unusual major? Try bagpiping at Carnegie-Mellon University. Requirements include bagpipe instruction and music theory, composition and history, as well as a good set of lungs. Aerobic exercise may be recommended. (Ken Andreyo/ photo courtesy of Carnegie-Mellon University)

to look for a job. They falsely assume that "the decision" will make all the difference in their lives. In its broadest sense a career is the sum of the decisions you make over a lifetime. There is no "right occupation" just waiting to be discovered. Rather, there are many career choices you may find fulfilling and satisfying. The question to consider is, "What is the *best* choice for me *now?*"

EXERCISE 17.11 For Returning Students: Exploring New Fields

If you are a returning student who's chosen college as a path to a new career, the following exercise may help you sort out your options.

1. What interests have you developed from life and work that might be part of your future career planning?

   _____

   _____

   _____

2. What skills do you bring from life and work that might be assets in other careers?

   _____

   _____

   _____

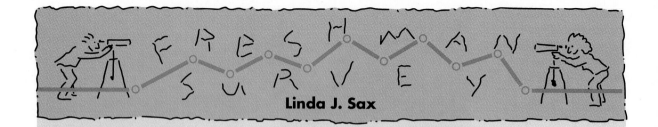

Linda J. Sax

Declining Majors in the Humanities

The humanities have declined in freshman popularity over the past two decades, with English and the fine arts especially hard hit. For example, between 1966 and 1993 the proportion of freshmen planning to major in English fell from 4.4 to 1.4 percent. (English actually dropped as low as 0.8 percent in 1982!)

Although many students indicate that they would prefer to major in literature, they also feel they need to study business to be competitive in the job market. However, some corporations prefer liberal arts majors to business students as management trainees, even though the former group may have comparatively little formal training in "business skills." You may be surprised to learn that in some organizations liberal arts majors actually have a better track record for performance and promotion than their peers who majored in business as undergraduates. For example, a twenty-year study of AT&T employees reveals that liberal arts majors advanced faster than other, nontechnical managers (that is, individuals who were not initially hired as engineers or researchers).

What advantages or disadvantages do you see in these fewer numbers for those who major in English and other liberal arts fields? Why do you think some corporations would prefer to hire liberal arts graduates over business majors?

3. What things do you most enjoy about your present or most recent work?

_____

_____

_____

4. What things do you least enjoy about your present or most recent work?

_____

_____

_____

5. Go through your college catalog and list any majors that interest you. At this point, don't worry too much about whether the subject seems unfamiliar or too difficult. List the majors below, along with the reasons they appeal to you. As much as possible, try to link the reasons to your comments in the first four items of this exercise.

Major: _____   Reasons: _____

_____

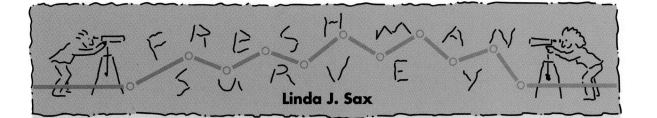

Linda J. Sax

Falling Interest in Science

Of all the traditional liberal arts fields, the sciences have shown the most severe decline in student popularity. Between 1966 and 1993 the proportion of first-year students planning to major in mathematics dropped by nearly 90 percent while interest in physical sciences majors (for example, chemistry and physics) fell by 40 percent.

Although there has been an overall decline in the proportion of freshmen pursuing science majors, the CIRP Freshmen Survey data indicate that men's interest in science has dropped by 50 percent since 1966, while women's interest in science has fallen by only 15 percent. How would you explain this difference?

Student interest in the biological sciences has fluctuated dramatically. Although interest in biological science majors reached a low of 3.7 percent in 1990, these majors have gained popularity in recent years. Why do you think there has been a sudden interest in the life sciences? What careers are biological science majors preparing for?

Freshman Interest in Science Majors, 1966–1993

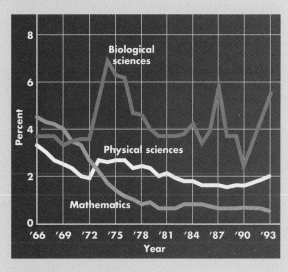

SOURCE: Higher Education Research Institute, UCLA

Major: _____   Reasons: _____

_____

Major: _____   Reasons: _____

_____

Major: _____   Reasons: _____

_____

6. Discuss your responses in class, with your academic advisor, and/or with a career counselor. Rethink your choices in light of these discussions.

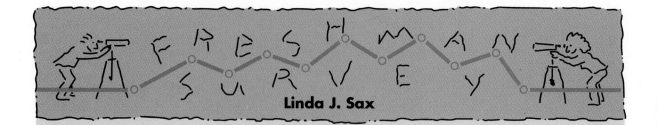

Linda J. Sax

A Teacher's Market

Talk has increased in recent years about the critical role of education in the nation's future, and students are once again thinking about teaching careers.

As the graph shows, teaching was an extremely popular career choice among young women in the late 1960s. But its popularity fell dramatically in the 1970s and the first part of the 1980s. Yet in recent years student interest in teaching careers has been rising. Why do you think freshman interest in teaching careers has been on the rise since 1985?

Although the numbers are up, current levels of interest in teaching are still far below those of the mid- to late-1960s—and well below the numbers required to meet future needs. Even though teaching is becoming a popular career choice again, we may not have enough new teachers to replace the many who will retire in the next ten to fifteen years. What effect do you think this may have on our educational system? What might be some of the attractions of a career in teaching?

Freshman Interest in Teaching Careers, by Sex, 1966–1993

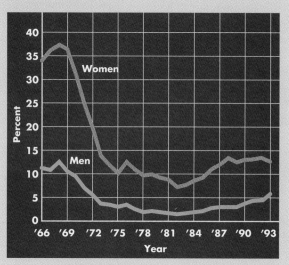

SOURCE: Higher Education Research Institute, UCLA

TIME FOR ACTION

In selecting a major, ask yourself these questions:

1. Am I interested in learning about the field?
2. Do I have the skills necessary for success?
3. Am I gaining skills, information, and perspectives that will be helpful in my career choices?

After choosing a major, begin to learn about other academic opportunities in your department. Talk with your advisor about minors, internships, independent study, study abroad, exchange programs, and other options that might broaden your academic experience.

As we said earlier, for some people there is a direct correlation between the major and the career; for others the choice of a major is best based on subject interest, not career considerations. If your major is not directly related to your career choices, plan to use work experience or campus activities to gain entry into your first job—many students are hired as bank management trainees or investment analysts based on their experience as treasurer of a student union committee rather than on their finance major.

Involvement in campus activities and part-time jobs are important in two ways. First, these experiences serve as the basis of a resume, which you will write to get your first job after college. Second, through these experiences you develop confidence in your career choice. It is better to discover that you hate inventory control *before* you graduate and accept a fabulous, high-paying job as an inventory control trainee.

Throughout this section you have done exercises aimed at gathering information about yourself and about the world of work and clarifying the most important issues involved in your choice of career and academic major. Here are a few other activities that may help:

- ► **Career exploration.** Once you've selected possible career fields, talk with people working in those fields to get a clear idea of what life is really like as a social worker or accountant or office manager. Read what people in this field read. Visit local professional association meetings.

- ► **Choice of major.** Talk with faculty members about the skills and areas of expertise you'll develop in studying the disciplines they're teaching. Ask if they're aware of careers or jobs in which the skills and knowledge they teach can be utilized.

- ► **Connection between major and career.** Ask employers if they look for graduates with certain majors or academic backgrounds for their entry-level positions.

- ► **Skill development.** Get involved in work experiences or campus activities that will allow you to develop skills and areas of expertise useful to your career plans. Find a summer job in that area, or volunteer as an intern. Keep a record of skills you have demonstrated.

By identifying and evaluating your interests and skills, obtaining career information, and assessing the role of goals and work values in your life, you turn career planning into an effective decision-making process. Career planning isn't a quick and easy way to find out what you want to do with your life, but it can point you to potentially satisfying jobs. Career planning *can* help you find your place in the world of work. Take advantage of it.

EXERCISE 17.12 Following Up on Careers

Look back over your answers to the previous exercises. Which career possibilities seem to recur and to utilize the personal attributes summarized in Exercise 17.8? Choose two or three such career ideas. Find the *Occupational Outlook Handbook, Career Book,* or some other career reference work in your library or campus career center. Read more about these careers.

JOURNAL

Look back at your answers to Exercise 17.1. Have your thoughts changed about them? How? If you are still undecided about your major or career, that's fine. You probably still have quite a while to work on answering these questions.

SUGGESTIONS FOR FURTHER READING

Bolles, Richard N. *What Color Is Your Parachute? A Practical Manual for Job Hunters and Career Changers.* Berkeley, Calif.: Ten Speed Press, 1994.

Carney, Clarke G., and Cinda Field Wells. *Discover the Career Within You,* 3rd ed. Pacific Grove, Calif.: Brooks/Cole, 1991.

Carter, Carol. *Majoring in the Rest of Your Life.* New York: Noonday Press, 1990.

Dictionary of Occupational Titles (DOT). Washington, D.C.: Bureau of Labor Statistics.

Directory of Directories. Detroit: Gale Research. Published annually.

Encyclopedia of Associations. Detroit: Gale Research. Published annually.

Felderstein, Ken. *Never Buy a Hat If Your Feet Are Cold: Taking Charge of Your Career and Your Life.* El Segundo, Calif.: Serif, 1990.

Holland, John. *The Self-Directed Search Professional Manual.* Gainesville, Fla.: Psychological Assessment Resources, 1985.

Jackson, Tom. *The Perfect Resume.* New York: Doubleday, 1990.

Lock, Robert D. *Taking Charge of Your Career Direction.* Pacific Grove, Calif.: Brooks/Cole, 1992.

Lucaino, Lani. "Finding a School That Fits." *MONEY Guide: Best College Buys* (September 1992): 18–19.

Occupational Outlook Handbook. Washington, D.C.: U.S. Government Publication Staff. Published annually.

Salzman, Marian, and Nancy Marx Better. *Wanted: Liberal Arts Graduates.* New York: Doubleday, 1987.

Simon, Ruth. "The State of the State Schools." *MONEY Guide: Best College Buys* (September 1992): 20–24.

Smith, Devon Coltrell, ed. *Great Careers: The Fourth of July Guide to Careers, Internships, and Volunteer Opportunities in the Non-Profit Sector.* Garrett Park, Md.: Garrett Park Press, 1990.

Stair, Lila B. *Careers in Business: Selecting and Planning Your Career Path.* Homewood, Ill.: Irwin, 1986.

U.S. Department of Education, Office of Educational Research and Improvement. "The Way We Are: The Community College as American Thermometer" (February 1992).

Whitaker, Urban G. *Career Success Workbook: Five Essential Steps to Career and Job Satisfaction.* San Francisco: The San Francisco Learning Center, 1992.

A Personal System of Values

Richard L. Morrill
University of Richmond

It amazes me to hear people talk about what's important to them. I mean, two of my friends think nothing of spending the night together three or four times a week. Someone else I know feels guilty if he misses church! I thought people here were going to feel more like I do.

Discussions about values often generate more heat than light because the word *values* means different things to different people. For some the word refers to specific positions a person holds on controversial moral issues such as capital punishment. For others it refers to whatever might be most important to a person, such as a good job, a fancy car, or the welfare of the family. For still others it refers to abstractions such as truth, justice, or success. In this chapter we offer a definition of values and explore ways to discover your values and apply them to the college experience.

DEFINING VALUES

Perhaps we can best define a *value* as an important attitude or belief. Let us include in the definition the idea that a value commits us to taking *action*, to doing something. We may not necessarily act in response to other feelings, but when we truly hold a value we act on it. For instance, we might watch a television program showing starving people and feel sympathy or regret but take no action whatsoever. If our feelings of sympathy cause us to raise funds to help those suffering, then those feelings qualify as values. Action does not have to be overtly physical. Action may involve thinking and talking continually about a problem, trying to interest others in it, reading about it, or sending letters to officials regarding it. The basic point is that when we truly hold a value, it leads us to *do* something.

Let us also define values as beliefs that we accept *by choice*, with a sense of responsibility and ownership. Much of what we think is simply what others have taught us. Many things we have learned from our parents and others close to us will come to count fully as our values, but only once we fully embrace them for ourselves. One must personally accept or reject something before it can become a value.

Finally let us make the idea of *affirmation* or *prizing* an essential part of values. We are proud of our values and the choices to which they lead. We also find ourselves ready to sacrifice for them and to establish our priorities around them. Our values draw forth our loyalties and commitment. Because they hold sway over us, our values can also be a source of self-condemnation when we fail to fully realize them in our daily lives. In other words a real aura of pressure or "oughtness" surrounds the values we have chosen.

In summary, then, *our values are those important attitudes or beliefs that we accept by choice, affirm with pride, and express in action.*

DISCOVERING VALUES

You probably already have at least a fair sense of what your values are. Yet one of your key tasks in college is to more consciously define your own approach to life and articulate your values. College is an opportunity to locate and test those values by analyzing their full implications, comparing them with the values of others, and giving voice to your beliefs.

No one is neutral, or without values, though values are held with varying degrees of clarity and commitment. Identifying your values is at once simple and complex. One way to start is by asking yourself directly what your most important values are. You began doing this in Chapter 17 in relation to a potential career. Let's continue in a broader vein.

EXERCISE 18.1 Prioritizing Your Values

Consider the following list of twenty-five values. Rank-order these values (1 for the most important value, 2 for the second-most important value, and so on down to 25 for the least important one). (*Note:* If you have difficulty with this part of the exercise, you may need practice at *values clarification.* The more often you reflect on your values and confirm or change their priorities, the easier this type of exercise will become.)

_____ 1. companionship

_____ 2. family life

_____ 3. security

_____ 4. being financially and materially successful

_____ 5. enjoying leisure time

_____ 6. work

_____ 7. learning and getting an education

_____ 8. appreciation of nature

_____ 9. competing and winning

_____ 10. loving others and being loved

_____ 11. a relationship with God

_____ 12. self-respect and pride

_____ 13. being productive and achieving

_____ 14. enjoying an intimate relationship

_____ 15. having solitude and private time to reflect

_____ 16. having a good time and being with others

_____ 17. laughter and a sense of humor

_____ 18. intelligence and a sense of curiosity

_____ 19. opening up to new experiences

_____ 20. risk taking and personal growth

_____ 21. being approved of and liked by others

_____ 22. being challenged and meeting challenges well

_____ 23. courage

_____ 24. compassion

_____ 25. being of service to others

Look at your top three choices on the list. What was the source for each of these values? We usually "learn" values from important people, peak events, or societal trends. List each value and try to indicate where you "learned" it.

NOTE: List used with permission from Gerald Corey and Marianne Schneider Corey, *I Never Knew I Had a Choice,* 4th ed. (Pacific Grove, Calif.: Brooks/Cole, 1990).

Value	Source
1. _____	_____
	_____
2. _____	_____
	_____
3. _____	_____
	_____

Review the values and their sources. Can you detect an overall pattern? If so, what does the pattern tell you about yourself? Were there any surprises?

EXERCISE 18.2 Evidence of Values

Another way to start discovering your values is by defining them in relation to some immediate evidence or circumstances. In the space below list fifteen items in your room (or apartment or house) that are important or that symbolize something important to you.

_____	_____	_____
_____	_____	_____
_____	_____	_____
_____	_____	_____
_____	_____	_____

Now cross out the five items that are least important—the ones you could most easily live without. Of the remaining ten, cross out the three that are least important. Of the remaining seven, cross out two more. Of the remaining five, cross out two more. Rank-order the final three items from most to least important.

What has this exercise told you about what you value?

Another way to begin discovering your values is by looking at some choices you have already made in response to life's demands and opportunities. For example, consider some of your reasons for deciding to attend this particular institution. Many students will say that they chose a certain college because of its academic reputation. How much do you value your school's reputation? And more precisely, what does the word *reputation* mean to you? Are you interested in the prestige that comes from enrolling in the college? Does this signify an interest in high achievement and in meeting demanding standards? Obviously a value such as prestige can run in several directions, one being social prestige, another reflecting commitment to intellectual distinction. Finding the values that stand behind your choices requires continual exploration of the implications of those choices.

Many students say they have chosen a college because it offers the best opportunity for a good job in the future. Is this true for you? The choice to

Choice shows value. What you choose to do with a few free minutes or hours of your time may say more about your values than what you spend long hours doing because you have to. (Photo courtesy of Earlham College)

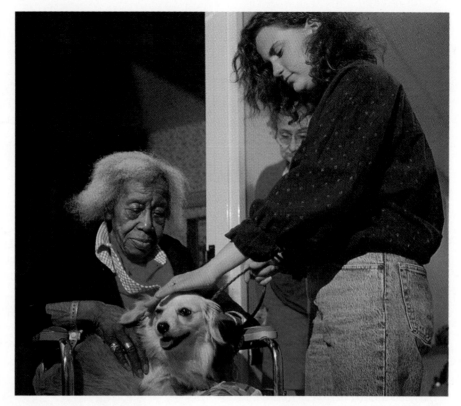

seek education in terms of its employment benefits suggests any number of possible values. Does this mean that economic security is one of your top values, or does it suggest that you are defining personal success or power in terms of wealth? And once again, what are the implications of the choice? How much are you willing to sacrifice to achieve the goals connected with this economic value? Does the achievement you are seeking bring fulfillment on a short- or long-term basis? How will your obligations to family and to society relate to this particular value?

EXERCISE 18.3   Why College?

List all the reasons you chose to attend college. Share your list in a small group, listening to the reasons others give. Attempt to arrive at a consensus about the five most important reasons for people in general to choose college. Then rank the top five, from most important to least important.

Share your final rankings with other groups in the class. How similar were the results of the groups? How different? How easy or hard was it to reach a consensus in your group? In other groups? What does the exercise tell you about the consistency or inconsistency of values among members of the class?

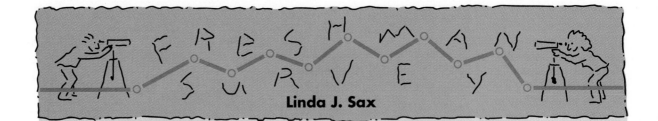

Linda J. Sax

What's Essential?

This graph shows dramatic shifts over the past two decades in the life goals of entering freshmen. Each year since 1967 the UCLA Freshman Survey has asked students to indicate the importance of "being very well-off financially" and "developing a meaningful philosophy of life." How would you interpret the results in the graph?

One striking aspect of these dramatic shifts in values during this period has been the changes in goals among first-year women. In 1967 first-year men were almost twice as likely as first-year women to identify "being very well-off financially" as an important life goal (54.2 percent for men, 30.0 percent for women). By 1993 the gap between men and women on this issue had narrowed from 24 to 5 percentage points (77.7 percent for men, 72.2 percent for women).

Changes in Freshman Life Goals, 1967–1993 (percentage indicating "essential" or "very important")

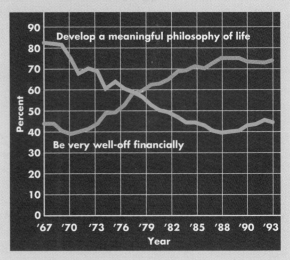

SOURCE: Higher Education Research Institute, UCLA

By asking questions about each of your supposed values, you can gain a fuller understanding of them and of the rest of your commitments. What are the reasons behind your choices? Are they made on the basis of your true values?

In exploring your values, you may also ask how you became committed to this value in the first place and how it relates to other values. Conflict in values is a frequent, sometimes difficult problem. How far are you willing to go in service to this value? What sacrifices do you accept in its name? How do the values you have chosen provide you with a meaning for your future? Few of us ever stop trying to give a sharper and clearer account of exactly what our values mean and what implications they have for ourselves and those around us.

The previous exercises present ways to begin identifying values. Of course this is not a one-time task—even seemingly strongly held values may change with time and experience. Thus you should not only develop a sense of your present values but also gain some sense of how they are evolving in a variety of areas: personal, moral, political, economic, social, religious, and intellectual. A major problem for most of us is sorting out how our own values resemble or contrast with those of our parents.

EXERCISE 18.4 Your Values and Your Parents' Values

The process by which we assimilate our parents' values into our own value systems involves three steps: (1) choosing (selecting freely from alternatives after thoughtful consideration of the consequences), (2) prizing (cherishing the value and affirming it publicly), and (3) acting (consistently displaying this value in behavior and decisions). List three values your parents have taught you are important. For each, document whether you have completed the three-step process to make their value yours.

Value	Choosing	Prizing	Acting
1. _____	_____	_____	_____
	_____	_____	_____
2. _____	_____	_____	_____
	_____	_____	_____
3. _____	_____	_____	_____
	_____	_____	_____

If you haven't completed the three steps, does it mean you have *not* chosen this value as your own? Explain your thoughts about this.

_____

_____

_____

_____

Let's turn our attention now to two special areas in which college is likely to affect your values: personal values and intellectual values.

COLLEGE CHALLENGES TO PERSONAL VALUES

Almost all students find that college life challenges their existing personal and moral values. The challenge typically comes through friendships and relationships with new people whose backgrounds, experiences, goals, and desires run counter to their own. This clash with diversity can be unsettling, threatening, exciting; it can also produce positive change.

Bye-Bye, Miss American Pie?

The American dream: The basic cultural pattern of the American middle class has been a generational investment in rising aspirations and economic mobility—parents sacrifice for their children so the next generation will live better. Parents hope that their children will equal or surpass them economically. Over the past forty years this upward mobility has been reflected in three unique symbols of the American experience:

► Purchasing a home

► Sending one's children to college

► Owning two cars and trading them in every four to five years

Today a growing number of students sense they may not be able to match the economic attainments of their parents. College, home, and even cars seem increasingly out of reach. Many students believe that the middle-class life

of the twenty-first century may require them to be wealthy, at least by their current understanding of the term. Most acknowledge that it will take two working parents to provide their children with the comforts that one working father once could provide.

Students differ from one another in everything from sleep and study habits to deep philosophical beliefs about the purposes of life. First-year students are often startled at the diversity of personal moralities to be found on any campus. For instance, some students have been taught at home or in church that it is wrong to drink alcohol. Yet they may find that friends whom they respect and care about see nothing wrong with drinking. Likewise students from more liberal backgrounds may be astonished to discover themselves forming friendships with classmates whose personal values are very conservative.

How do you react when you do not approve of some aspects of a friend's way of life? Do you try to change his or her behavior, pass judgments on the person, or withdraw from the relationship? Often part of the problem is that the friend demonstrates countless good qualities and values that make the conduct itself seem less significant. In the process your own values may begin to change under the influence of a new kind of relativism: "I don't choose to do that, but I'm not going to make any judgments against those

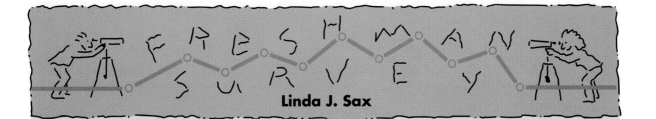

Linda J. Sax

Where Are You Politically?

Popular wisdom has it that students in the 1960s were very liberal and in recent years have become very conservative. Is it true? During the 1970s and 1980s students' political views shifted from liberal to moderate. However, trends for the 1990s indicate that college students are actually becoming more polarized in their political views.

In Fall 1993, 27.2 percent of entering freshmen identified their political views as "liberal" or "far left," marking the highest level of liberalism since 1977. At the same time, the proportion of students who identified their political views as "conservative" or "far right" reached an all-time high of 22.9 percent. How would you explain the apparent "polarization"?

Political Orientation of College Freshmen, 1970–1993

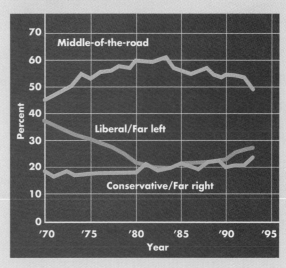

SOURCE: Higher Education Research Institute, UCLA

who do." A similar response pattern often develops regarding sexual involvements. People become friends with others whose behavior and values differ from their own, and the result is personal turmoil.

EXERCISE 18.5 Friends and Values

Consider several friends and think about their values. Pick one who really differs from you in some important value. In a small group discuss this difference in values. Explore how it's possible to be friends with someone so different.

You probably get along most easily with people who dress and act like you do. You expect to have a lot in common. At the same time, you may find that you learn a lot from friends whose backgrounds and values are very different from yours. (Photo by Hilary Smith)

In such cases one can always recommend tolerance, since tolerance for others is a central value in our society and one that often grows during college. Yet it is easy to think of cases in which tolerance becomes indulgence of another's destructive tendencies. It is one thing to accept a friend's responsible use of alcohol at a party, and quite another to fail to challenge a drunk who plans to drive you home. Sexual intimacy in an enduring relationship may be one thing; a never-ending series of one-night stands is quite another. Remember, the failure to challenge destructive conduct is no sign of friendship.

EXERCISE 18.6   Values in Conflict

Choose part A or B. Read the situation and discuss your responses in a small group. Describe any similar situations you've experienced. How did you respond to the situation? Were you successful? How did you define success?

A. You have become good friends with your roommate since the beginning of the term. You know he or she uses drugs once in a while, which usually results in some rowdy behavior you're not always comfortable with. He or she certainly doesn't use drugs every day, but you wonder if even occasional use is healthy. You've tried to discuss the topic with him or her and received very little response.

Last night, while under the influence of drugs, your roommate set fire to a number of flyers and posters on the hallway walls. Today your resident assistant (or house supervisor or landlord) wants an explanation and demands to know who is responsible. Your roommate doesn't seem willing to come forward.

Which of your values may come into play here? Will any of your values conflict with one another? How might your values conflict with those of your roommate? Your resident assistant, supervisor, or landlord? How would you resolve the situation?

In addition to the questions above, discuss how changing one part of the scenario might change your response. (For instance, what if your friend burned *your* posters on the door to *your* room?)

B. You get a ride to school fairly often with a person who happens to be in one of your classes. You haven't known this person long but do consider him or her a friend on campus. From your talk while you commute you know that he or she lives a somewhat wilder life than you do and at least occasionally takes drugs as part of an outside social scene.

Yesterday he or she was driving badly on the way to school and got into an argument with some other motorists at a stoplight. You had the feeling alcohol or some other drug was behind the problem.

It really is convenient to ride together. It saves you several hours a week in travel time. Also, you don't have a lot of friends on campus and would like to keep this friendship if you can. When you meet later in the day, you try to find out what was wrong that morning, but your friend denies that there was any problem.

In addition to the questions above, discuss how changing one part of the scenario might change your response. (For instance, what if you were driving and the person's behavior somehow interfered with your own safe driving?)

Are there better and worse ways to deal with these challenges to personal and moral values? The framework for an answer rests in an awareness of the nature of values themselves. As we saw earlier, true values must be freely chosen and cannot be accepted simply on the authority of another person. After all, the purpose of values is to give active meaning to our lives. Trying to make sense out of the complex circumstances of our own lives by using someone else's values simply doesn't work.

At the same time, it is appropriate to talk about values with those with whom we seem to be in conflict. What are the other person's true values (consciously identified, freely chosen, and actively expressed)? Do his or her current behaviors correspond to those values? Much can be learned on both sides.

Many people make the mistake of fleeing from the challenge of diversity and failing to confront conflicting value systems. The problem with this strategy is that at some time in their lives, often within a year or two, these people find themselves unable to cope with the next set of challenges to which they are exposed. They do not grow as persons because they do not prize their own values and their behaviors are not consistent with what they say they value. Although it's only a first step, you must work through challenges to your own personal values by finding answers that truly make sense to you and help you to move ahead with your life.

CHANGING INTELLECTUAL VALUES

Intellectual values such as clarity, accuracy, rigor, and excellence cluster around the central value of truth. One of the most striking transitions that occurs during the college years has to do with the way in which a person's notion of truth changes.

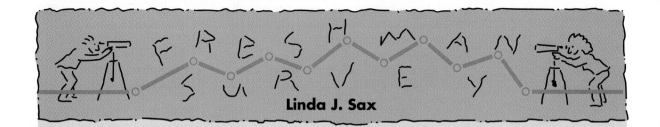

Linda J. Sax

Social and Political Issues

How have the personal values of first-year students changed in the past fifteen years?

What does the first graph suggest about student attitudes on some key political and social issues? Although it suggests a movement toward more liberal positions in recent years, entering freshmen have also become increasingly conservative on selected issues over the past fifteen years, as the second graph shows.

Do any of these percentages surprise you? In what respect? Do you think these numbers would hold for your campus? What is the mood on political issues on your campus? Among your friends?

Freshman Attitudes on Political and Social Issues, 1978 and 1993 (percentage who "agree" or "strongly agree")

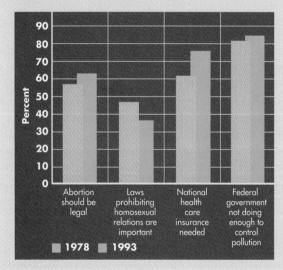

SOURCE: Higher Education Research Institute, UCLA

Freshman Attitudes on Crime-Related Issues, 1978 and 1993

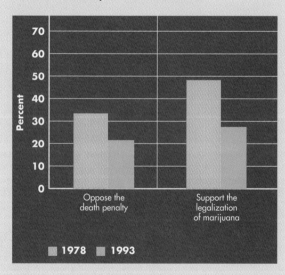

SOURCE: Higher Education Research Institute, UCLA

Many students enter college assuming the process of education is one in which unquestioned authorities "pour" truth into the students' open ears. Some students believe that every problem has a single right answer and that the instructor or the textbook will always be the source of truth. However, most college instructors don't believe this, and their views on truth often initially shock these students (see Chapter 2).

Academics tend to see "truth" in a much more contextual, flexible, and variable way. It's not that the teacher is cynical about the possibility of truth, but rather that the scholar's role is understood as involving an ongoing, open-ended search. He or she is seeking as many valid interpretations of the information as can be found. College instructors continually ask for reasons, for arguments, for the assumptions on which a given position is based, and for the evidence that confirms or discounts it.

Just as with personal and moral values, college-level education involves the assumption that as a student you will become a maker of your own meaning, on your own, with the ultimate responsibility for judgments of truth and falseness resting in your hands. The whole system of a university's intellectual values—openness, freedom of inquiry, tolerance, rigor, and excellence—is based on this approach, and there is no escaping it.

EXERCISE 18.7 Applying Your Values in College

While values are not always expressed directly and openly, they can be found in many places in your school's environment. Values surround you in the form of institutional mission statements, academic integrity policies, and behavior exhibited by you and the people around you. The variety of values expressed can often lead to conflict—within an individual, between individuals, or between an individual and the institution. From the following three topics, choose the one you're most interested in and work through the exercise.

A. *Institutional purpose.* Most institutions of higher education are based on a broad collection of values, beyond academic freedom and the search for truth (although these are vitally important). To learn more about your institution's guiding values, undertake a "document analysis." Obtain a copy of the institutional mission statement (it should be in your college catalog). As you read it, copy down phrases that seem to imply a value, identify the implied value, and then assess whether it concurs with a value you hold.

Phrase	Value(s) Implied	Fit with Your Values?
_____	_____	_____
_____	_____	_____
_____	_____	_____
_____	_____	_____
_____	_____	_____
_____	_____	_____
_____	_____	_____
_____	_____	_____

If you disagree with one or more values, what will the consequences be for you? How will you respond?

B. *Academic integrity.* Recall the section in Chapter 9 dealing with academic integrity, which described the intellectual values held in higher education—honesty, freedom of inquiry, openness, and excellence. Academic dishonesty sometimes occurs when these values conflict with those of individual students. What values might lead students to commit an academically dishonest act? How can this be avoided?

C. *Values and personal behavior.* Recall Chapter 5 on time management, which discussed prioritizing activities that are more important or less important to you. This is a way of expressing your values through actions. For the two values identified here, list a variety of actions that would express those values.

Achieving Excellence in College

1. *Reading one book each week not required for class but related to my major.*

2. _____

3. _____

4. _____

5. _____

Maintaining a Great Social Life

1. *Spending weekends out of town with friends.*

2. _____

3. _____

4. _____

5. _____

While achieving excellence and maintaining a social life may not seem like conflicting values, the actions that express the values may cause conflict. In other words acting on one value may prevent you from staying true to the other. Which of the actions you've listed in each column might conflict with one another? If you held these two values, how would you reconcile each of these conflicts?

RIGHT VALUES

We have stressed that the essential first step in developing a value system is for you to become your own maker of meaning whether in the sphere of personal, moral, or intellectual values. But it is only a first step; you must be aware not only of making meaning but also of making a meaning that can lead to a coherent and fulfilling life. As crucial as it is to develop your own values, it is equally important that you find the *right* values. Little is accomplished if you develop a genuine system of values that leads to egocentric, dishonest, cruel, and/or irresponsible conduct.

The question of what the right values are cannot be answered simply. There are no automatic criteria (though perhaps the "Golden Rule" will serve as well as any). Yet clearly all of us who have accepted life in a democratic society and membership in an academic community such as a college or university are committed to many significant values. To participate in democratic institutions is to honor such values as respect for others, tolerance,

The Right to Vote

No matter what their political preference, college students have a poor record of showing up to vote. Government data suggest that voting in presidential elections among 18- to 21-year-olds has dropped steadily since 1972, the first year persons under 21 were allowed to vote. Americans ages 18–24 have the lowest levels of voter turnout of any age group.

How would you explain this apparent lack of interest in voting?

equality, liberty, and fairness. Members of an academic community are usually passionate in their defense of academic freedom, the open search for truth, honesty, collegiality, civility, and tolerance for dissenting views.

Yet many issues relating to values are open for continuing and legitimate discussion and disagreement. For instance, to what extent should the college or university take it upon itself to ensure the success of each of its students? To what extent may it simply offer certain opportunities for learning and then let each student sink or swim?

Perhaps what college can do best with regard to values is teach a process for making value choices, for thinking seriously about values, just as a good education teaches us to think in other realms. That is, an education in values can teach us how to assess our values while leaving us to choose our own actual values. This might involve in part the posing of a series of overarching questions relating to values.

For example, are our values *consistent* with one another? Contradictions among values can be just as harmful and foolish as contradictions among ideas. Are our values sufficiently broad in *scope*—that is, do they provide us with a comprehensive outlook on life? We learn that our values may work very well within the small circle of our family but produce conflict with individuals from a different background. This presses us toward common ground, areas of agreement based on which we can overcome conflict. The pressure always to enlarge our circle of association, to move toward the universal sphere of the human family, beyond all divisions of race, sex, and the like—that is where we have to go to find our true and best selves.

Other tests can also measure the depth, the richness, and the adequacy of our values. We know that many of our choices fail to meet the test that *time* itself provides. Others fail to meet the test of *relative worth*. Life teaches us that transient satisfactions and pleasures leave us with little if they rob us of opportunities and accomplishments that may stay with us for a lifetime.

And so it goes. Life itself continually tests which of our values will create coherent, consistent, and enduring results, the greatest fulfillment of our potential. Just as we can be educated with regard to ways of thinking, so we can be educated with regard to our values and our choices. This too is what college is all about. The opportunity for growth is yours.

JOURNAL

This chapter suggests that any belief or behavior that is primarily a result of what someone else expects of us without our own active and free choice is not the expression of our own true values. It also suggests that for many students college is a time and an experience in which everyone's true values are tested. Describe your current system of "true values" (chosen, affirmed, and acted upon). In what ways has college already tested or changed those values?

SUGGESTIONS FOR FURTHER READING

Bellah, R., R. Madsen, W. M. Sullivan, A. Swidler, and S. M. Tipton. *Habits of the Heart.* Berkeley: University of California Press, 1985.

Chickering, A. *Education and Identity.* San Francisco: Jossey-Bass, 1969.

Corey, G., and M. S. Corey. *I Never Knew I Had a Choice,* 4th ed. Pacific Grove, Calif.: Brooks/Cole, 1990.

Kolak, Daniel, and Raymond Martin. *Wisdom Without Answers: A Guide to the Experience of Philosophy,* 2nd ed. Belmont, Calif.: Wadsworth, 1991.

Lewis, Hunter. *A Question of Values.* New York: Harper & Row, 1990.

Morrill, R. L. *Teaching Values in College.* San Francisco: Jossey-Bass, 1980.

Niebuhr, H. R. *Faith on Earth.* New Haven, Conn.: Yale University Press, 1989.

———. *The Responsible Self.* New York: Harper & Row, 1963.

Pojman, Louis P. *Ethics: Discovering Right and Wrong.* Belmont, Calif.: Wadsworth, 1990.

Rokeach, M. *The Nature of Human Values.* New York: Free Press, 1973.

Simon, S., L. Howe, and H. Kirschenbaum. *Values Clarification.* New York: Hart, 1972.

Racial and Ethnic Diversity on Campus

Joan A. Rasool
Westfield State College

I know "diversity" is in these days, but I'm not much into talking about it. I'm not even sure what it means. We had "diversity celebration days" in high school, but nobody took them very seriously. They seemed to separate us, not bring us together. I'm open to meeting other people but I don't want to force anything. Live and let live.

Ask almost any person in this country about his or her racial or ethnic background and you have the start of an interesting story:

My father is mostly Arab and part Kurdish. He always said that his strength and determination came from his Kurdish background. My mother's background is Scottish and English. She told me her mother's side of the family came over on the Mayflower. *My parents met when my dad was a graduate student and my mother was an undergraduate. She was studying economics and he agreed to tutor her. I came to this country when I was 4 years old and I'm still figuring out what it means to be an Arab American.*

—Baidah

My racial background is African-American. The other thing I would add is that I see my background as black and working class. Those two things go together for me; they are a part of my roots. How I grew up was kind of varied. On one hand I was born in California and on the other hand I was raised in Texas during segregation. Part of me grew up in a strongly segregated part of the South, and another part of me, as an adolescent, grew up in integrated California.

—Terrell

I'm American. I don't feel like I have a strong attachment to any particular group. My family is Italian, Polish, Irish, and French. On St. Patrick's Day I say I'm Irish. If I go to an Italian restaurant, I pretend I'm Italian! I call one grandmother "Bapshee" and that's about how bilingual I am. Maybe I'm not anything.

—Eric

I'm Filipino American, and like most Filipinos I am also Catholic. Family values are stressed in my home. Outsiders might say that my culture is very patriarchal, but I certainly grew up watching my parents share power equally. My mother was a very strong woman, and as I remember the final decisions were always hers. I am the youngest of six children and am very opinionated so no decision is ever easy in my household. In addition to family, education is heavily stressed. Attaining a college degree is a must—no, not a must, it just should happen—like breathing.

—Cristina

Neither the United States nor Canada are as they used to appear on television—homogeneously white and more or less middle class. They never were. But now more than ever our societies are multiracial and multicultural. A quick glance at official college calendars will give you a clue. All major holidays for members of the Buddhist, Baha'i, Christian, Hindu, Jewish, Muslim, and Sikh faiths may be listed!

You may also be aware of or have experienced the racial tensions on college campuses today. Racial harassment, the lack of greater numbers of students and faculty of color, and the need to pluralize the curriculum are some of the issues being discussed. These are serious issues that merit serious attention.

If you are like most students, you see college as the beginning of an exciting new stage in your life, a time when you can learn a lot about yourself and the world as well as prepare for the future. How can you be sure that

Figure 19.1 A Diversity Attitude Scale

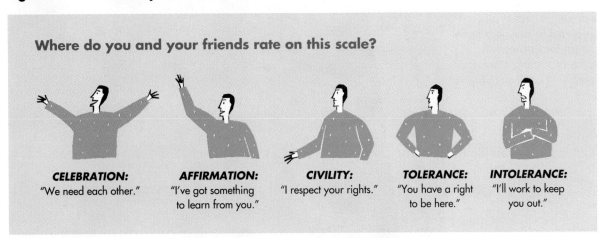

Where do you and your friends rate on this scale?

CELEBRATION: "We need each other."

AFFIRMATION: "I've got something to learn from you."

CIVILITY: "I respect your rights."

TOLERANCE: "You have a right to be here."

INTOLERANCE: "I'll work to keep you out."

you will feel comfortable here, that you can be yourself, and that you will have the opportunity to meet new people and have new experiences? What is your responsibility to help create a campus environment in which all students can pursue their goals? (See Figure 19.1.)

This chapter should increase your appreciation of your own and others' backgrounds. It will also show you how campus culture influences students' academic and personal lives and help you develop strategies for making the campus a more welcoming place for everyone.

RACE, ETHNIC GROUPS, AND CULTURE

The word *race* generally refers to a group of people who are distinct from other people in terms of certain very obvious inherited characteristics—skin color, hair color and degree of straightness, body build, proportions of facial and other body features. *Ethnic group* may refer to people of different races or to people of the same race who can be distinguished by language, national origin, religious tradition, and so on.

Culture refers to the material and nonmaterial products that people in a society create or acquire from other societies and pass on to future generations. Culture includes a society's intangible beliefs, values, norms, and language as well as tangible realities such as cellular telephones, futons, basketballs, and college yearbooks. Nonmaterial culture can't be touched, held, or transported, but it plays a major role in influencing how people define reality. Recall Cristina's statement about the high value her culture places on education. Many European-Americans believe children should learn how to be independent and self-sufficient at an early age. Many Hispanic-Americans place a high value on strong family ties.

You celebrate your background as easily as you breathe in air. From the moment you open your mouth and say "buenos dias," "good morning," or "magandang umaga," you affirm your cultural ties. The music you listen to, the food you eat, the clothes you wear, the holidays you celebrate, the "walk you walk" and the "talk you talk"—all make statements about the importance of culture.

Most colleges make an effort to help students feel welcome, respected, and supported in every way that the students themselves feel is important. (Photo courtesy of Earlham College)

EXERCISE 19.1   Sharing Your Background

In the beginning of this chapter, Baidah, Eric, Cristina, and Terrell start to tell "their stories." Now it's your turn. Write a two-part essay. In the first part describe the racial or ethnic groups to which you belong. Can you belong to more than one? Absolutely. Think of your own background. Be sure to include some of the beliefs, values, and norms in your cultural background. In what ways do you celebrate your background? What if you are like Eric and don't feel a strong attachment to any group? Write what you know about your family history and speculate on why your ethnic identity isn't very strong.

In the second part of your essay, discuss a time when you realized that your racial or ethnic background was not the same as someone else's. For example, young children imagine that their experiences are mirrored in the lives of others. If they are Jewish, everyone else must be too! If their family eats okra for breakfast, then all families do the same. Yet at some point they begin to realize that there are differences. When did you realize that you were African-American or Hispanic-American or European-American or Korean-American or biracial or whatever?

Share your essays with other members of the class. In what ways are your stories similar? In what ways are your stories different?

CULTURAL PLURALISM: REPLACING THE MELTING POT WITH VEGETABLE STEW

For years students were taught that the immigration of different people to the United States created a "melting pot"—as diverse groups migrated to this land, their culture and customs mixed into this American pot to create a new society. The reality of what happened, however, is more complex. Instead of "melting" into the "pot," most immigrants were asked to become more like what was already here—an Anglo-European soup. For example, in order to get ahead immigrants had to change their names to make them sound more Anglo-American; they had to make sure their children gave up their native language and learned English; and they had to do business the American way. Some groups could accomplish this more easily (for example, the Irish, French, and Germans), although not without experiencing some discrimination. Today members of these groups may be more likely to see themselves as Eric does—as "just American." It is important to note, however, that many European-Americans have retained strong ethnic ties. Equally important is the recognition that other non-European groups (for example, Africans, Japanese, and Chinese) found both laws and racial barriers impeding their integration into the culture at large.

As a result many sociologists and educators have concluded that American society is less like a melting pot and more like vegetable stew. While each group has its own unique characteristics and flavor, all the groups together create a common broth. The dominant culture has begun to acknowledge and affirm the diversity of cultures within its borders. After years of stressing commonalities, we are now focusing on our differences.

Cultural pluralism has replaced the melting pot theory. Under cultural pluralism each group is free to celebrate and practice its customs and traditions, and in return each group is expected to participate in the general mainstream culture and abide by its laws. "Unity in diversity" is the new rallying cry.

Whoever you are, in some ways you are part of the mainstream culture. In other ways, however, you probably feel that you are part of a smaller group, a microculture within society.

EXERCISE 19.2   Creating Common Ground

Examine the items in the following chart. For each item decide whether you would describe your preferences, habits, and customs as reflecting the mainstream or macroculture or a specific ethnic or microculture. Enter specific examples of your own preferences in the appropriate column (two examples are given). For a given item, you may enter examples under both Macroculture and Microculture, or you may leave one or the other blank. In filling out the chart, you may want to look back at the essay you wrote in Exercise 19.1.

Category	Macroculture	Microculture
Language		
Food	*hamburgers*	*sushi (Japanese)*
Music (for your peer group)		
Style of dress (for your peer group)		
Religion		
Holidays celebrated		

Category	Macroculture	Microculture
Heroes/role models	_____	_____
Key values	_____	_cooperation) (Native Amer)_
Lifestyle	_____	_____
Personal goals	_____	_____

Compare answers in a small group. Do most people in the group agree on what should be considered an example of the macroculture and what is an example of a microculture? Is there anyone who identifies completely with the macroculture? Is there anyone who feels completely outside it? What do you and others in your class regard as significant differences among you? In what areas do you share common ground?

Cultural pluralism doesn't mean groups must remain isolated. In fact, as you learn more about another ethnic group's heritage, there may be customs and traditions in which you would like to participate. Particular values stressed in one culture may better suit you. For example, you may prefer the punctuality emphasized in European-American cultures or the more "relaxed" time schedule of Arab-Americans. You may value the sense of duty and family obligation among Hispanic-Americans or admire the sense of individual control and independence offered in the Anglo culture. Or your preferences may be directed toward language, music, food, dress, dance, architecture, or religion. The possibilities are endless.

UNDERSTANDING THE PERSPECTIVES OF OTHERS

Remember the children's story of the Three Little Pigs? The big bad wolf "huffs and puffs" and blows down the houses of the first two little pigs. He finally meets his downfall when he attempts to climb down the third little pig's brick chimney only to find himself landing in a pot of boiling water. All this is refuted in the recent publication of *The True Story of the 3 Little Pigs! by A. Wolf:*

> *Everybody knows the story of the Three Little Pigs. Or at least they think they do. But I'll let you in on a little secret. Nobody knows the real story, because nobody has ever heard* my *side of the story…. I don't know how this whole Big Bad Wolf thing got started, but it's all wrong…. The real story is about a sneeze and a cup of sugar.*

The "real story," it turns out, is that Mr. A. Wolf had a cold the day he went to his neighbor's house to borrow a cup of sugar. Unfortunately he sneezed so hard that the house fell down killing his good neighbor—the pig. He was then *forced* to eat him because he couldn't let a good meal go to waste!

All these years and no one thought to ask the wolf for his side of the story! And yet that is just the point. If we are going to accept and affirm the differences of other groups, then each group needs to be ready to listen to the other. This is not to say that "the other group" is the villain, but that groups tend to look at one another's perspective or side of the story as misguided, wrong, or backward.

"That Corner in the Cafeteria"

When I think about my freshman year at a predominantly white university, these are the things I remember: "'Negro' students who graduate from your high school tend not to do well at this university; therefore, we encourage you to attend a summer precollege program," said a representative from the university. (I did.) "You'll do well here if you never take a math course," stated my advisor during the freshman orientation program. (I never did take a math course, and I paid for it!) Of the 300 students in Psychology 80, no one would sit next to me!

One day, by accident, I wandered into the commuter cafeteria, and there they were—black people! I was so glad to see them that I think I ran toward them. The group was composed primarily of upper-class students and two graduate students. "Hey, what's your aim in life?" hollered Jack, one of the graduate students, as I approached the group. I opened my mouth to respond, but I don't think anything coherent came out. Can you imagine how I felt when they told me that we were in a university of well over 20,000 students and that maybe, just maybe, there were a total of 50 black undergraduate

and graduate students? Later I found out that 15 out of the 50 black students were freshmen!

As the semester progressed, I spent a considerable amount of time in the cafeteria and became better adjusted to the university. That corner in the cafeteria was my home away from home. Those black students were my family and support system. They reprimanded me for cutting class and applauded me for my achievements. There were no black faculty, as far as I knew.

Interaction with white students was fairly minimal. They appeared not to know what to say to me, and vice versa. Communication with white faculty members was a little different. They had the information; therefore, I did talk to them. My grades were not that fantastic, though, and it wasn't until my junior year that I became a serious student.

SOURCE: Francine G. McNairy, vice president for academic affairs and provost, Millersville University of Pennsylvania. Reproduced, with permission, from *College Is Only the Beginning: A Student Guide to Higher Education*, 2nd ed., John N. Gardner and A. Jerome Jewler, eds. (Belmont, Calif.: Wadsworth, 1989).

EXERCISE 19.3   Hearing All Sides of a Story

This exercise involves forming caucus groups. A caucus group is defined as any group in which you feel you automatically belong. For example, you might form caucus groups under the following headings: commuters, learning-disabled students, Catholics, biracial students, gay and lesbian students, African-American women, men, nontraditional students, and so on. First generate a list of possible caucus groups, and then decide if there are enough potential members in the class to form a group of three or more members.

Join a caucus group. Meet in your group to discuss the following questions: How does your group experience campus life? What are the major academic, residential, or social concerns of your group? How well does your college meet the needs of your group?

A healthy diversity on campus depends on a general willingness to let social groups form in whatever patterns are helpful and constructive. It also depends on groups and individuals welcoming communication and exchange. (Photo by Hilary Smith)

As a caucus group, report on your discussion while other class members just listen. Afterwards the listeners may comment or ask questions on what has been said, but they should refrain from challenging the *perceptions* of the group they are listening to.

THE DIVERSITY OF CAMPUS CULTURE

How diverse is your campus? Are you aware of the diversity that does exist on your campus? In what ways does your school encourage all students to feel welcome? How easy is it for students to express their culture and to learn about their backgrounds or the backgrounds of others?

EXERCISE 19.4 **Getting the Diversity Facts on Your Campus**

Consider campus diversity in a broader context—among the student body, faculty, administrators, and staff; in the curriculum; in social and residential settings; and at the institutional level (that is, the overall policies and procedures followed by the college).

In a group with three or four other students in your class, investigate one of the areas in the following list. Use the questions under each heading to help guide your research. Your instructor may be able to offer suggestions on where to locate relevant materials or appropriate people to interview. Each group should report to the class their general findings in the various areas. Groups should focus on two questions: (1) How easy is it for students to express their culture and to learn about their backgrounds or the backgrounds of others on this campus? and (2) In what ways does our school try to make all students feel welcome?

A. Diversity in Numbers

1. In what ways are your student body, faculty, administrators, and staff diverse? What percentage of students, faculty, administrators, and staff come from different ethnic/racial groups?

2. What religious, linguistic, socioeconomic, gender, and geographic differences are there among students?

B. Diversity in the Curriculum

1. What are you learning about the contributions and concerns of people of color in any of your classes? Are you learning about different perspectives as a central focus of your courses, or are the views of "others" highlighted in special chapters or special sections of chapters? Give examples.

2. What courses or workshops are available if you want to increase your racial awareness and understanding?

C. Diversity in Social and Residential Settings

1. Who or what groups are reflected in the artwork, sculptures, and names of buildings on your campus?

2. Whose food preferences are served on a regular basis at the college dining facilities?

3. If your school has campus residences, does residential life staff schedule ongoing discussions on issues of diversity and tolerance? Who is in charge of these programs?

4. Do students from different ethnic groups have organizations and hold social events? Give some examples. How does school governance support a variety of diverse activities being brought to campus?

5. Where does cross-racial interaction exist on your campus? Is the atmosphere one of peaceful coexistence and/or resegregation? Where do students find opportunities to work, study, and socialize across racial/ethnic lines?

D. Institutional Commitment to Diversity

1. How does the mission statement of your school address cultural pluralism? (Your college mission statement may be printed in the college catalog.)

2. What policies and procedures does your school have with regard to the recruitment and retention of students of color? (Contact your admissions office for information.)

3. What policies and procedures does your school have with regard to the recruitment and hiring of faculty and staff of color? (Contact your affirmative action/equal opportunity office for information.)

4. Does your school administration feel responsible for educating students about diversity, or does it assume that students and faculty of color will do this?

The "New Majority"

Why are institutions of higher learning so concerned about diversity on their campuses? One reason has to do with population figures. In 1990, 48 million Americans (about one-fifth of the total population) were identified as "minorities." By the year 2020 they will make one-third of the population, and by the last quarter of the twenty-first century they will be the majority.*

As part of their mission, colleges and universities educate and train the nation's work force. College administrations realize that the "new majority" will be a major economic strength to the nation and will be responsible—through their taxes, Social Security payments, and other contributions—for helping to maintain *everyone's* standard of living.

The total U.S. population in 1990 was about 250 million according to the Bureau of the Census.† Here are some of the groups currently considered minorities in the United States, although in some areas of the country they are actually in the majority.

African-Americans

African-Americans make up about 12 percent (30 million) of the U.S. population. They come from diverse cultures and countries in Africa, the Caribbean, and Central and South America. Excluded from the mainstream white culture despite the end of slavery, they developed a system of historically black colleges and universities dating from the mid-nineteenth century. As of 1980 these schools still awarded nearly 70 percent of all bachelor's degrees received by African-Americans.

Alaskan Native/American Indians

About 2 million Americans identify themselves as (non-Hispanic) Eskimo, Aleut, and American Indian, from more than 300 tribes. Their heritage includes more than 120 separate languages.

Asian-Americans

Since discriminatory immigration laws ended in 1965, Asians have become one of our fastest-growing groups, expected to reach 10 million (4 percent of U.S. population) by the year 2000. The largest of the many groups are Chinese, Japanese, Korean, Asian Indian, Filipino, and Vietnamese. Asian-Americans have made major contributions to the economies of the American West and Hawaii.

Mexican-Americans

Hispanics made up 12 percent of the U.S. population in 1990. The fast-growing Hispanic group is Mexican-Americans (almost 13 million). Mexican-Americans have deep roots in the American Southwest from past centuries when that region belonged to Mexico and Spain. More than half of Mexican-Americans live in Texas and California.

Puerto Ricans and Cuban-Americans

Around 1990, Puerto Ricans living on the U.S. mainland numbered 2.3 million, and those living in Puerto Rico 3.3 million. All are U.S. citizens. There are more than a million Cuban-Americans, mainly in Florida.

Of course, many millions of individual "white" and minority Americans can claim a blended heritage of European, African, Asian, and Native American ancestors.

*Quality Education for Minorities Project, *Education That Works* (Cambridge: Massachusetts Institute of Technology, 1990).

†This and other figures below come from the U.S. Bureau of the Census.

RACISM ON COLLEGE CAMPUSES

Unfortunately incidences of racism and acts of prejudice are rising on college campuses. While some schools may not be experiencing overt racial conflict, tension may still exist; many students report having little contact with students from different racial or ethnic groups. Moreover a recent national survey, "Taking America's Pulse," conducted for the National Conference of Christians and Jews indicates that blacks, whites, Hispanics, and Asians hold many negative stereotypes about one another. The good news is that "nine out of 10 Americans nationwide claim they are willing to work with each of the races—even those they felt they had the least in common with—to advance race relations."*

In addition to being morally and personally repugnant, you should know that *racism is illegal*. Most colleges and universities have established policies against all forms of racism, anti-Semitism, and ethnic and cultural intolerance. These policies prohibit racist actions or omissions including verbal harassment or abuse that might deny "anyone his/her rights to equity, dignity, culture or religion." Anyone found in violation of such policies faces "corrective action including appropriate disciplinary action."

EXERCISE 19.5   Checking Your Understanding

How clear is your understanding of racism and prejudice? Check your knowledge by circling T (true) or F (false) for each of the following:

T	F	1. Positive stereotypes aren't harmful.
T	F	2. Prejudice is personal preference usually based on inaccurate or insufficient information.
T	F	3. Racism combines prejudice with power.
T	F	4. The problem of racism was solved years ago.
T	F	5. Racism hurts everyone.

(See page 326 for the answers.)

EXERCISE 19.6   Combatting Racism and Prejudice on Campus

What experiences have you had dealing with racism or prejudice on campus? Write briefly about the incident. Describe what happened and how you felt about it. Did you or anyone you know do anything about it? Did any administrator or faculty member do anything about it? Describe what was done. Do you think this was an effective way to deal with the incident? Explain.

*"Survey Finds Minorities Resent Whites and Each Other," *Jet,* 28 March 1994

If you have not experienced any problems like this, find out how your college would deal with acts of racism and prejudice. You may want to contact the college affirmative action/equal opportunity office for information. Find out what steps students would need to take if they wished to follow up on an incident.

Share your answers and information with other class members.

You don't have to wait for your school to take the lead in making your campus a more welcoming place. Everyone can work to create a community where diverse groups feel celebrated by "advocating for pluralism." For example, Cristina can stop laughing at her friends' racial jokes; Baidah can ask her English instructor to include some works by writers of color. Eric can work with Terrell to encourage greater diversity of representation on the student senate.

EXERCISE 19.7 Constructive Steps: Advocating for Pluralism

As a class come up with a list of steps that students could take at your school to "advocate for pluralism."

ANSWERS (to Exercise 19.5):
1. *False.* Stereotypes, even if positive, assume that all members of a group are the same.
2. *True.* Racism reflects attitudes and actions rooted in ignorance.
3. *True.* Racism occurs when individuals use their prejudice to deny others their civil rights.
4. *False.* Check current newspapers, periodicals, and television reports for the latest incidents of racism.
5. *True.* Everyone benefits when all individuals are allowed to reach their full potential. A victim of racism might just be the person who could find a cure for AIDS.

On Campus: No Racial Conflict—or Contact

Throughout my life most of my close friends have been black and Latino. I did not choose to change that when I came to college; yet I found myself in my senior year without one friend who was nonwhite. This occurred so swiftly and naturally that I did not know how to stop it.

When I first arrived at college, I moved into a dormitory with all white students. Although there were minority students in some of my courses, I rarely saw them outside of class. When I was looking for someone to eat with, study with, or play basketball with, it seemed that I had only white students to choose from. I look at the homogeneity of my social life now and realize that it does not reflect the person I am.

Never before did I have to consciously pursue diversity. I grew up in Brooklyn, N.Y., and attended public school there through junior high school, where I was one of only three white students. Because there were so few white students, integration was not an issue. I attended a Quaker high school that was not only numerically well integrated but also a successful, interacting community. Students seemed to choose their friends without thinking about race and certainly didn't feel separated from one another.

I assumed that I would continue to have a diverse group of friends.

At college there is no obvious tension between white and minority students, yet race still creates a barrier in personal relationships. While some students are able to cross the lines that separate white and minority students—for example, those who participate in highly integrated organizations like student government—most are not. Outside of classes the majority of students choose to associate with students who are just like them.

The natural pattern of campus life leads to racial separation. It takes more than an open mind to overcome racial boundaries, more than good intentions, more, even, than a genuine desire to surround yourself with a diverse group of friends.

Students cannot passively wait for chance meetings after class to take place because white and minority students do not socialize together.

Nowhere is this more apparent than at the fraternity parties that are the dominant social outlet; white and minority students attend separate parties. The patterns of social separation are not challenged, and race relations are only discussed when controversy arises.

I wrote an article about campus race relations for the college newspaper. I knew that if a student who wanted to lead a diverse life could not succeed, then something must be standing in the way of improving race relations.

The discussions I had with twenty of my schoolmates confirmed what I knew to be true after three years of college: Successful race relations, those that are meaningful and lasting, do not seem to happen naturally. Unfortunately forging positive race relations requires an effort that many students are unwilling or afraid to make.

The article gave me a way to meet minority students. In fact I spoke to more minority students in two days of interviews than I had in my previous three years of college. I enjoyed those conversations, but they troubled me as well because I saw what I had been missing in not hearing perspectives much different from my own. It was disheartening that the atmosphere on campus made me feel that I needed an excuse to speak with members of another race.

I thought about students, both white and minority, who did not have experiences like mine before coming to college.

If college was their first sustained interaction with people of other races, they would be less likely to find separation unusual or problematic, and less motivated to work for change.

I fear that college was probably more similar to the real world than my life until then had been. It is clear that I would have to actively pursue a lifestyle that I once took for granted. If we don't get to know one another at college, how would we in the outside world?

SOURCE: By Adam Cahill, Trinity College. Adapted, with permission, from *The Courant* (Hartford, Conn.), November 14, 1993.

JOURNAL

You may know a great deal about the contributions of Native Americans to U.S. history but know little about the role Asian-Americans have played. You may know a lot about African-American artists but little about classical music. Consider some specific activities that would further your knowledge and understanding. For example, you could plan to attend a lecture that challenges your present thinking, interview a fellow student about his or her experiences on campus, switch the dial on your radio, or make a meal!

Reflect on your thoughts and feelings about your racial and ethnic background and diversity issues on campus. Is there something that came up in one of the class discussions that you would like to comment on? Is there some idea that remains problematic for you?

SUGGESTIONS FOR FURTHER READING

Bell, D. *Faces at the Bottom of the Well: The Permanence of Racism.* New York: Basic Books, 1992.

Bennett, C. *Comprehensive Multicultural Education,* 2nd ed. Boston: Allyn & Bacon, 1990.

Carrion, A. M. *Puerto Rico: A Political and Cultural History.* New York: Norton, 1983.

DeVita, P. R., and J. D. Armstrong. *Distant Mirrors: American as a Foreign Culture.* Belmont, Calif.: Wadsworth, 1993.

Divoky, D. "The Model Minority Goes to School." *Phi Delta Kappan* (November 1988): 219–22.

Fisk, E. B. "The Undergraduate Hispanic Experience." *Change* (May/June 1988): 29–33.

Giovanni, N. "Campus Racism 101." *Essence* (August 1991): 71–72.

Halpern, J. M., and L. Nguyen-Hong-Nhiem, eds. *The Far East Comes Near: Autobiographical Accounts of Southeast Asian Students in America.* Amherst: University of Massachusetts Press, 1989.

Mathews, J. *Escalante: The Best Teacher in America.* New York: Holt, Rinehart & Winston, 1988.

Paley, V. G. *White Teacher.* Cambridge, Mass.: Harvard University Press, 1989.

Stalvey, L. M. *The Education of a WASP.* Madison: University of Wisconsin Press, 1989.

Tatum, B. D. "Teaching About Race, Learning About Racism: The Application of Racial Identity Development in the Classroom." *Harvard Educational Review* 62, no. 1 (1992): 1–24.

Wiley, E. "Institutional Concern About Implications of Black Male Crisis Questioned by Scholar." *Black Issues in Higher Education* 7, no. 9 (1990): 1, 8–9.

Zinn, H. *A People's History of the United States.* New York: Harper & Row, 1980.

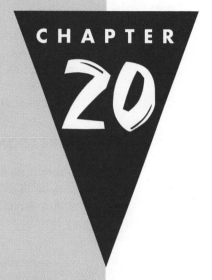

Getting Involved on Campus

Marie-Louise Ramsdale
City Year Southeast

Robert A. Friday
TransFormation

N̲o way I'm going to give up living for four years just because college is a lot of work. I need people. I need fun. I need to get involved in something outside books!

Looking back on college in a few years, you may well discover that you learned as much from activities outside the classroom as you did in your formal studies. This chapter encourages you to explore a broad range of *co-curricular* activities and suggests some ways to make the most of personal relationships that may develop.

TEN REASONS TO JOIN A CAMPUS ORGANIZATION

You might be wondering whether it's that important to get involved in co-curricular activities. You might be thinking that between your schoolwork and your social life there won't be any time left for anything else. Or you may simply wonder what's in it for you. If so, consider the following:

1. **You'll meet people.** Within your organization you will meet a diverse group of people who share a common interest that brings them together, people who will offer not only valuable information about campus life but friendship. Groups with political agendas such as the Young Republicans, Young Democrats, or NAACP can help you meet prominent political figures from outside campus. Sports clubs and other competitive or honorary societies can take you off campus to events or national meetings where you'll get to know like-minded students from other schools.

2. **You'll experiment and gain experience.** College is the perfect time to try something new. If you have always wanted to try sky-diving or ceramics, now's your chance. (And you can usually do so in college at a much lower cost through participation in a student organization.) Perhaps you've always wanted to act, but in high school you were afraid to try. College life encourages you to experiment and explore, so audition for that play. Even if you realize you're no Denzel Washington or Bridget Fonda, you might discover your hidden talent for stage managing. You'll never know if something you've always wanted to do is fun until you take that first step.

EXERCISE 20.1 Taking a Risk

Write down five activities you've always wanted to try. They may be sports, hobbies, recreational activities, or intellectual topics to explore. You will use these again in a later exercise.

1. _____

2. _____

3. _____

4. _____

5. _____

College may be your chance to experiment with things that few people get to try in "the real world." Your campus probably offers more groups, more facilities, and more special opportunities than you'll ever find in one place again. (©1992 Chuck Savage/photo courtesy of Beloit College)

3. **You'll improve your abilities.** There's nothing like giving an impromptu speech in the student senate on why smoking should (or should not) be banned on campus to improve your public speaking skills. Editing the literary magazine will give you insight into your own writing, and being responsible for planning a fund-raiser will do wonders for your organizational abilities.

4. **You'll get the most out of college.** There's more to life than working. While remembering the importance of academics, don't spend all your time studying in the library. Look at college as your own community and be active in it.

EXERCISE 20.2 Leaving Your Mark

By this time you've most likely found things you like and things you don't like about your institution. Your dissatisfactions can lead to involvement. If you could "leave your mark" by causing a change on your campus, what would it be? List two or three ideas here:

1. _____

2. _____

3. _____

Take one of your ideas and do some research on how you might proceed to advocate for change. Why does the present situation exist? What alternative would you propose? Why would your alternative work? Who has the power to make the change? What group would you need to join that might provide the influence and help you will need? Talk about this in a group.

5. **You'll feel at home faster.** There's nothing like serving barbeque at the homecoming cookout or planning the spring movie calendar to make you feel that you help make things "tick" at your school.

6. **You'll manage stress better.** If you're worried about a test or if you had a fight with your boy- or girlfriend, call a friend from the Running Club and take a few laps around the track. If you're not athletically inclined, go and throw paint on a canvas with some friends from the Art Club.

7. **You'll organize your time better.** Believe it or not, being busier helps you plan your day, your week, and your whole semester more efficiently. Knowing that you have responsibilities and must be somewhere at a specific time forces you to organize your life. If you know that you are going to go into the city to visit museums this weekend with people you met through the Art Club, then you also know you have to make the time to write the paper that's due on Monday morning before you leave for the weekend.

8. **You'll improve your resume.** Competitive employers and graduate schools are looking for the well-rounded individual, not the person with straight A's who remained in the library all through college. The skills you learn in clubs and organizations today can make you far more marketable as a graduate. If you're an economics major, think about getting involved in the accounting societies, but also investigate such related possibilities as running for treasurer of a campus group. If you want to go to law school, look into volunteer work with the court system through your school's office of community service programs.

EXERCISE 20.3   Helping Out Your Career

Write down a job you might have after graduation and the skills you'll need for it. In addition to primary skills like accounting, singing, or research, include secondary skills like managing meetings, doing promotion, and writing grants. Then write down some ideas about how you can get the experience you need.

Potential job after graduation: _____

Skills or Experience Needed	Campus Activity or Organization Where You Can Get It
1. _____ _____	_____ _____
2. _____ _____	_____ _____
3. _____ _____	_____ _____
4. _____ _____	_____ _____

9. **You'll meet organization advisors.** An unexpected bonus to members of many student groups (and one more reason to get involved) is the relationship they develop with the organization's advisor. The advisor, usually a faculty or staff member or interested person from the community, can lend support and advice not only to the organization and its officers but in many cases to the individual members as well. Club advisors are obviously interested in students or they wouldn't be involved with the organization, and if you need help or someone to turn to, the advisor of your club is a good person to start with.

10. **You'll make a difference.** Many people need your help, both within and outside your campus community. Tutor a child, serve food at a shelter, or organize your campus blood drive. Not only will you make a difference in someone else's life, but you'll be amazed by what you learn.

FINDING OUT ABOUT ORGANIZATIONS

Most colleges and universities have organizations for every type of interest imaginable, from racquetball to chess to foreign languages and literature. To find out what clubs are established at your school, ask your academic advisor or residence advisor or go to the student activities center, usually located in the student union, and ask for information about activities at your school. Many schools also have organizational interest fairs early each term when members of different groups are available in a central location to recruit new members. The campus newspaper and bulletin boards are also good sources of information.

Don't join any club because you are being pressured by one of the club members. If you are unsure about whether this club is really right for you after you have talked with some of the members, don't be afraid to say so. Of course you can always try one meeting to see if you like it; you don't have to sign up after you walk in the door if you find out that what you thought was the Astronomy Club is really the Astrology Club! Also, if more than one club seems interesting to you, go to several initial meetings. Attending a meeting doesn't bind you to the group for life, and going to several different meetings will provide a better perspective for choosing which clubs you actually want to join.

Here are some questions to think about in considering what organizations to join:

► **What are you already interested in?** If you have always been a "Francophile," then join the French Club. If you played football in high school and now want to play for fun and exercise, get involved with an intramural team.

► **What abilities or skills do you want to improve or learn?** You went to England last summer and ever since then have had a burning desire to row crew. You sang in the chorus in high school and think that joining the concert choir would be a great way to continue this activity, if only you could get up the nerve to audition. Get up the nerve!

► **How much time can you commit to this organization?** Does the organization meet once a week, every other week, or whenever the president decides to call a meeting? Does the meeting time fit into your schedule? What other club activities will you have to attend besides the regular meetings?

► **Does this club have dues, and if so, can you afford them?** If the dues are high, is there a payment plan or do they have to be paid at one time? Do you pay dues every year or just when you join?

► **What does this club require for membership?** Does it have an attendance policy that requires you to attend so many meetings in order to be able to participate in special club activities? Is there a certain pledge or initiation period before you can become an active or full member? Do you need to maintain a certain grade point average or take a special class in order to belong?

MAKING IT HAPPEN

Admittedly it can be an overwhelming challenge during your first few weeks at college to think about entering a room full of strangers for a meeting that you have seen advertised on a bulletin board. First, remember that there will be other students in the room in exactly the same situation as you, as nervous if not more so. Don't be afraid to sit down next to someone and introduce yourself. It might also be a good idea to take a friend with you to the meeting; in return you can attend a meeting that they are interested in. Introduce yourself to the club officers after the meeting and let them know about your interest. Leaders realize that new members are the future of their club, and they likely will be delighted to chat with you about their organization. If it hasn't already been mentioned, and you didn't want to ask during the meeting, this is an ideal time to ask about such things as dues, attendance policy, and other things you might want to know before joining.

How to Be a Great Club Member

Get involved in the clubs and groups that you decide to join. Make a personal commitment to attend meetings and to be dependable. If you say that you will write that article on the new dean of students by Thursday, stick to your deadline. It will be easier if you know your limits and don't volunteer for something you won't have time to do or don't know how to do. Being a good club member doesn't mean that you have to volunteer for everything.

If you budget your time wisely and pick a few groups you really want to get involved with, you will get a lot out of your participation as well as give a great deal back to your organization. On the other hand, if you overextend yourself you may find your grades falling and yourself resenting the time you spend with club activities you had previously enjoyed.

How to Serve While You Learn

Service learning is a recent trend in colleges and universities that helps students gain life skills and knowledge while making a difference in their communities.

Once you identify a community service project, perhaps in your area of career or skills interest, the opportunities for learning are endless. Students who volunteer at a local homeless shelter will often get the chance to learn about life on the streets from the residents and about the causes of homelessness from the program director. If you are majoring in health, you might volunteer at the local soup kitchen or food bank. As you prepare meals for people, you'll also receive a good education in nutrition. Future teachers may want to tutor at a local school; future structural engineers can help build or renovate low-income housing. It's a win-win situation: You help other people as you learn.

To get the most out of service learning, here are a few hints. Consistently ask yourself what you are learning, and challenge yourself to find out more. Good questions to ask yourself include the following: Why you are serving? Who are you serving? What are the benefits of service? Who are you serving with? What skills are you learning that can be applied elsewhere in your life? Look for links between your community service and your academic studies. Keep a journal of your service experiences.

How to get started? The community service center at your school should be able to link you with worthwhile organizations. Your local United Way is often another good source for volunteer placement referrals. Many campus organizations also are involved in community activities.

EXERCISE 20.4 Taking the Plunge

Get a list of campus clubs and organizations from the appropriate office on your campus. Using information from the previous exercises in this chapter, identify five organizations you might be interested in joining. Choose one, attend a meeting, and try to speak with an officer of the group. Obtain the following information:

Name of organization: _____

Purpose: _____

Meeting schedule: _____

_____

"They Didn't Know Me"

I was never that popular in high school—in fact, I hardly dated. Suddenly in college all these guys were asking me out. They didn't know me. About all they knew was that I looked Asian.

In fact my father's Caucasian. He met my mother in Japan when he was in the merchant marine. He had one day of leave in Japan. They met for one afternoon, standing in line at a shrine in Kyoto when she was still in high school. They wrote to each other for four years before he went back and proposed. With that kind of courtship you might think they didn't know each other all that well, but I'm sure they did because I've seen the stacks of letters. They got married and came back to the States. My brother and I were born here.

I like to think that if I'm an unusual person it's not just because of things like my hair or the shape of my eyes. But you would be surprised how many guys in college would see me once and act like they already knew everything about me.

My freshman roommate had another kind of problem. She's African-American, and in the first couple weeks she started dating someone who was also African-American. Then he kind of left her alone and started going out with whites. She might not have minded so much if there had been as many African-American men on campus as there were African-American women. But there weren't. She got pretty fed up with it—I guess lonely is the word.

My brother visited me one weekend in January, and we got to talking about this. He said his experience in college had been more like hers than like mine. Some women seemed to reject him simply because he looked Asian. At the same time, the Asian and Asian-American women were going out with whites. I was glad to hear him talk about this finally, but it also made me sad. My brother's a very sweet person, and I don't see why I should be accepted if he's not accepted also.

Dues: _____

Activities: _____

_____

_____

Membership requirements: _____

_____

Are you interested in joining? Write down your thoughts about it below. Your instructor may ask you to make a brief presentation in class about your experience at the meeting.

_____

_____

_____

_____

_____

Sketching or painting is one way to give yourself a little time to reflect in a quiet place. Writing is another. Just thinking is also fine. (Photo by Hilary Smith)

GETTING ALONG WITH YOURSELF AND OTHERS

One of the keys to successful involvement in college and the larger community is the ability to get along with others. Learning to accept others without losing faith in yourself doesn't always come naturally. This section begins with the most important lesson of all: getting to know yourself.

To know yourself, you need to look into your feelings and review your past. As you explore your history and compare your family, background, and values with those of others, you will improve your understanding of why you think what you think, say what you say, and do what you do.

EXERCISE 20.5   Finding a Place to Think

Locate several places on or near your campus or home where you can relax and spend some time alone. Make at least two appointments a week with yourself to visit one of these places.

Take your journal. Do not involve yourself in conversations with others. As you observe people, nature, events, or things, record the first thoughts that come to you. Ask yourself where these thoughts originate.

Before you leave your special place, list problems or concerns that have come to mind during the visit. Ask yourself what you need to know to solve these problems. Write down where and when you plan to find the information you need. Write something that expresses why this problem is important to you at this time in your life.

Once you start feeling comfortable with yourself, you can do a number of things to establish ties with others. The glue that holds any relationship together is honesty. When we are not honest with others, we force them to relate to a false image of ourselves. Until we can face up to ourselves truth-fully, listen to observations others make about ourselves, and honestly consider that some of what they say might be valid, our relationships with others will always be less than what they could be.

EXERCISE 20.6   How You See Yourself

A. Write a few words to describe yourself in each of the following areas:

1. Sense of humor: _____

_____

2. Important values: _____

_____

3. Friendships: _____

_____

4. Family relations: _____

_____

5. Handling conflicts with others: _____

_____

6. Interests: _____

_____

B. Based on your activities and relationships thus far in college, list a few words or phrases you think others might use in describing you:

Words or phrases family might use:

_____

_____

_____

Words or phrases instructors, staff, or other students might use:

_____

_____

_____

C. How do your answers to part A compare with your answers to part B? What aspects of yourself would you like to change? List some words and phrases you would like others to use in describing you by the time you finish college:

_____

_____

_____

"I Knew I Was Gay When I Was 13"

I knew I was gay when I was 13 years old. My friends were falling in love with members of the Fairview Little League team, and I was daydreaming about Mary Sue Cook. Still, I didn't even know what a homosexual was until the AIDS virus hit. Kids in my middle school had cheerfully announced that some disease was killing all the fags, and I had said, "Good riddance!" No one had told me there was a word to describe me. Fags got AIDS, so I spent the rest of that year pretending to have crushes on the Little League boys.

By the time I was 15 I knew a whole lot about fags. I learned that faggots were actually pieces of kindling used to start a fire and that the term was transferred to homosexuals when they were burned at the stake for moral crimes. I learned about the National Gay Hotline and about the sodomy laws that still exist in most states. The Good Samaritan Church started a youth group for gay teens. Up until that point the word lesbian had been "the L word," because I had never heard it spoken in a positive way. Now it is a definitive term for everything I have been through.

We were a fairly insecure lot in those days. We fought against traditional values by coloring our half-shaved heads and dressing in black clothing. We spent our time crouching in mall emergency exits listening to Depeche Mode or Dead or Alive. We exchanged antique jewelry and jotted down poetry about an unjust world. We hid our faces behind heavy eyeliner and burgundy bangs. We were America's gay youth, and we had already learned that hiding was the easiest way to survive.

When I went away to college I was still a loathsome "closet case." My roommate and I seemed to hit it off, and I was afraid that my "news" might scare her away. God knows I didn't want her thinking I was interested in her. That may seem like a strange thing to say, but you would be surprised at the way the "straight" world views a friendship with a homosexual. I had known Wendy for almost three months, but I knew that everything would change when she found out. She would treat me like a different person, and yet I would be the same. I did finally confide in her after months of isolation and insecurity, and she stood by me despite her own fears. She even admitted that she would have blindly hated me if I had told her when we met. I guess I was supposed to be glad that I had lied.

After that, it was relatively easy to come out to my friends. One of the girls across the hall from me clipped out articles from the student newspaper about National Coming Out Day. She told me I should go to the Gay/Lesbian Student Association meetings to meet other people. There were hundreds of gay and lesbian students at the University of South Carolina, and perhaps thirty of them were comfortable enough to show their faces at the Gay/Lesbian Student Association.

I just knew that there would be a line of gay-bashers waiting to see just who went to those meetings. I finally worked up the nerve to walk over to Harper College one evening but quickly retreated when I realized that there were classes being held that I would have to walk in front of to get to the stairs. I skulked back to my room to tell my roommate of my misadventure. I really thought she'd pour out the sympathy over my pitiful condition. Instead, she got up, put her shoes on, and told me that the two of us were going to march right back over there and go to that meeting.

I have come a long way from my 13-year-old fears of getting AIDS. The "coming out" process is more than finding loopholes in society where you might feel safe. It's not just asking society to accept you, but learning to accept yourself.

SOURCE: Jen Bacon, *Portfolio XI* (no. 1), Fall 1990 (a University of South Carolina student publication). Used with permission.

Want new friends? Develop your skills at communicating well with others. This chapter briefly suggests some techniques. Find out whether your campus offers workshops on assertiveness and other interpersonal tools. (Photo by Richard Tauber)

EIGHT KEYS TO SUCCESSFUL INTERPERSONAL COMMUNICATION

Here are eight concrete ways to improve how you get along with others.

1. Practice Self-Disclosure

Telling someone else about your experiences, feelings, and frustrations goes a long way toward making that person feel at ease with you. People feel comfortable with those who are willing to share personal information—it makes the other person feel trusted and valued and invites an honest exchange of feelings. Of course, you won't want to disclose your innermost thoughts to a complete stranger; that would only make both of you feel uncomfortable. But letting the other person know something about yourself, even if it's only to say, "I had a hard time with that new biology lab last term!" shows that you're willing to "let down your guard" and enter into a supportive, give-and-take relationship.

2. Show Mutual Respect

Just as you respect yourself, respect the rights of others to think differently from you. Trying to change someone is often not only futile but also disrespectful, because it sends a message that you're not satisfied with that person as he or she really is. If the views of someone you like bother you, have a frank discussion about your differences and explore ways to resolve them.

3. Find a Common Frame of Reference

When you find yourself part of a group and initially think you have little in common with the other participants, try to find some common frame of reference that will make you feel more at ease and that will allow you to engage the others in conversation. People who work at finding a common ground with others rather than concentrating on obvious differences become more effective communicators—and usually find that they're richer for the experience.

4. Listen Actively and Check the Meaning

Casually paying attention to what someone says is only the first level of listening. Most communication between two people is nonverbal. Facial expression, tone of voice, posture, and sense of physical, psychological, or emotional distance are all involved in active listening. Showing you're interested by asking questions is important, too. Get in the habit of making sure you understand what the other person is saying. Get used to asking, for instance, "When you say that, do you mean ... ?" In doing so you show respect and indicate you are actively listening.

5. Express Your Feelings Appropriately

There's a difference between saying, "You make me angry when you ..." and saying, "I feel angry when you ..." The first statement is an *accusatory* statement. It implies that one person is causing a feeling to occur in another person. The second statement is a *descriptive* statement. It describes a particular feeling that one person has in response to another person's actions. Using an accusatory statement is a good way to make the other person feel defensive and to shut down communication before it has even begun. Using a descriptive statement invites the other person to consider what you have said and respond to it, leading to a more constructive exchange.

6. Empathize

When you empathize, you "walk a mile in someone else's shoes" by placing yourself in the other person's situation and trying to see the world as they do. Empathy isn't sympathy (feeling sorry for someone); rather, it's taking the time to sit with others and trying to understand what happened and how it makes the person feel. Empathetic statements needn't express approval or disapproval, just understanding: "I can see how it must be frustrating to have worked so hard on that project and then feel the instructor didn't appreciate your efforts."

7. Acknowledge the Legitimacy of Another's Feelings

As you probably know, feelings are not always logical. Each of us experiences physiological cycles, mood swings, varying reactions to similar situations, and so on. Though another person's mental and emotional states may sometimes seem inexplicable, you must acknowledge the legitimacy of those feelings.

Few friends or family members forthrightly state their feelings unless they have known each other for a long time and have a history of good communication. As you seek to deepen meaningful relationships, indicate that you sense the other wants to talk, and ask what he or she is thinking or feeling. If the person seems reluctant to respond, try explaining your thoughts and feelings on the subject and then ask for feedback.

In our culture women tend to talk about feelings whereas men tend to keep feelings locked up inside. However, true intimacy can develop only when each partner learns to talk about the things that are important to the other.

8. Accept Conflict

Even in healthy relationships, conflict is bound to occur. When it does, it often indicates that one person sees a problem in the relationship and wishes to resolve it.

When conflict does occur, the important thing is to manage it constructively—and to fight fair.

The fair fighter avoids blaming the other person and concentrates on expressing feelings and needs in order to move toward accommodation. Recognizing differences, arguing, resolving, and making up are essential factors in effective communication. If you can conclude an argument with greater appreciation for each other, you can build a more positive relationship.

One important reminder: Never try to deal with important issues while racing to class or rushing to get the family off to work and school in the morning. Instead, say something like, "I would like to discuss how I feel when (whatever) … Can we find time in the next few days to discuss our feelings on this?" This allows both of you time to get ready. Remember, the objective is not to beat someone, but to arrive at a mutually satisfactory agreement.

EXERCISE 20.7 **Improving Relationships**

A. Think of a relationship with someone you respect or care about. In what ways might that relationship be improved? Review the eight keys to successful interpersonal communication and check below those you feel you should work on with that person.

_____ 1. Self-disclosure

_____ 2. Mutual respect

_____ 3. Common frame of reference

_____ 4. Listening actively and checking the meaning

_____ 5. Expressing feelings effectively

_____ 6. Empathizing

_____ 7. Acknowledging the feelings of others

_____ 8. Accepting conflict

Get together with a small group of students in your class who checked some of the same concerns. Talk about instances in which you've had to deal with this concern and felt you could have done better. Listen for useful advice.

Be supportive. As you participate in the group, try to put into practice the eight keys to good communication.

Here are two other exercises your groups might try.

B. *For listening actively:* Form a small group. Ask one member of the group to spend about 3 minutes describing a particular problem that has been bothering him or her. The problem could concern a relationship with a friend or family member, a difficult class or assignment, or any other life problem. Have the person describe the problem and how he or she *feels* about the problem. Now take turns having the other members of the group describe what they understood the person to have said. Did all those listening have the same understanding of the speaker's feelings and frustrations? Did they disagree about anything? Ask the speaker if the listeners' interpretations were accurate. Did the listeners fail to understand anything that the speaker tried to convey? What questions could the listeners have asked to ensure that they understood what the speaker was trying to say?

C. *For expressing feelings appropriately:* Think of a time when you were angry with another person. Write a paragraph describing the event using the phrase "He or she made me angry when ..." Write a second paragraph describing the event using the phrase "I felt angry when he or she ..."

Read your paragraphs to the group, and have others read theirs. Discuss the different reactions that you think would result from each approach.

Toward the end of the session, convene as a class and discuss the benefits of talking about relationships with others.

JOURNAL

To what extent have you already become involved in campus life? What organizations have you visited or joined, and what has been your experience so far? Write about a relationship you have now that is important to you. Did it result from your participation in college activities? What is your reaction to the comments in this chapter about developing honest relationships?

SUGGESTIONS FOR FURTHER READING

Crosby, John F. *Illusion and Disillusion: The Self in Love and Marriage,* 4th ed. Belmont, Calif.: Wadsworth, 1991.

Friday, Robert A. *Create Your Own College Success.* Belmont, Calif.: Wadsworth, 1988.

Fromm, Erich. *The Art of Loving.* New York: Harper & Row, 1956.

Hendrick, Clyde, and Susan Hendrick. *Liking, Loving, and Relating,* 2nd ed. Pacific Grove, Calif.: Brooks/Cole, 1992.

Patton, Bobby R., Kim Giffin, and Eleanor Nyquist Patton. *Decision-Making Group Interaction,* 3rd ed. New York: Harper & Row, 1989.

Managing Stress

Kevin W. King
Counseling Psychologist

*H*ey you! Yeah I said you! Watch where you're going. I mean, move and let me get by. I've gotta get to class, and I don't have time to hassle with you. What's the big rush?...What? Who are you tellin' to slow down, mister? I am not stressed out. Hey, I was up till four gettin' ready for class...so maybe I'm a little edgy today. So butt out, will ya?

Stress is natural. So, to the extent that stress is a sign of vitality, stress is good. Yet most of us never really learn how to cope effectively with stress-producing situations, and the result is that stress can overwhelm us, undermining our ability to perform. The primary way to manage stress is to modify it with something that enhances our feeling of control in the situation. For me relaxation is also very important in counteracting stress. It's impossible to be tense and relaxed at the same time, and relaxation is a skill that we can learn just like any other skill.

Did you realize you have actually *learned* to be tense in most stress-producing situations? Now you can learn how to identify the warning signs or symptoms of stress. And once you are aware of the warning signs, you can *choose* how you will react. That's what this chapter is all about.

WHAT HAPPENS WHEN YOU ARE TENSE

The signs of stress are easy to recognize and differ little from person to person. Basically your rate of breathing becomes more rapid and shallower; your heart rate begins to speed up; and the muscles in your shoulders and forehead, the back of your neck, and perhaps even across your chest begin to tighten. Probably your hands and perhaps your feet become cold and sweaty. There are likely to be disturbances in your gastrointestinal system, such as a "butterfly" stomach or diarrhea, vomiting, and frequent urination. Your mouth may become parched, your lips may dry out, and your hands and knees may begin to shake or tremble. Your voice may quiver or even go up an octave.

A number of psychological changes also occur when you are under stress. These changes are the result of your body and mind trying to "defend" you from some real or imagined threat. The threat could be from an actual situation, such as someone approaching you with a gun in hand. Or it could come from something that hasn't actually happened but that you are worried about, because the part of the brain that controls your defensive reactions doesn't do any thinking—it simply reacts. The stress you typically feel is just part of that defensive reaction. As a result you're more easily confused, your memory becomes blocked, and your thinking becomes less flexible and more critical. Along with these reactions your body's adrenal glands produce adrenalin and a group of hormones called corticoids. If the situation persists over a long time, you may also find it difficult to concentrate, and you may experience a general sense of fear or anxiety, insomnia, early waking, changes in eating habits, excessive worrying, fatigue, and an urge to run away.

EXERCISE 21.1 Your Signs of Stress

Recall your last troublesome experience. What signals from your mind or body (for example, worry, frightening thoughts, tense muscles, headache, stomach distress) let you know this was a distressing situation? How did you respond to those signals? What might you do next time to handle the situation more effectively?

The urges to stand and fight or to run away are two of the human body's basic responses to stress. But many times both urges must be suppressed because they would be inappropriate. For instance, a person taking an exam may want to bolt from the exam room, but it probably would not help the grade to do so, and it's pointless to fight with a piece of paper. So we often find we must cope with a situation in a way that allows us to stay and face it, and to do so using our potential and skills to the maximum. This is where learning to manage stress effectively can make a difference!

IDENTIFYING YOUR STRESS

Stress has many sources, but there are two prevailing theories as to its origin. The first is the life events theory, which attributes health risks and life span reduction to an accumulation of effects from events that have occurred in the previous twelve months of a person's life.

EXERCISE 21.2 The College Readjustment Rating Scale

The College Readjustment Rating Scale is an adaptation of Holmes and Rahe's Life Events Scale. It has been modified for college-age adults and should be considered as a rough indication of stress levels and possible health consequences.

In the College Readjustment Rating Scale each event, such as one's first term in college, is assigned a value that represents the amount of readjustment a person has to make in life as a result of change. In some studies people with serious illnesses have been found to have high scores on similar scales. Persons with scores of 300 and higher have a high health risk. Persons scoring between 150 and 300 points have about a 50-50 chance of serious health change within two years. Subjects scoring 150 and below have a 1 in 3 chance of serious health change.

To determine your stress score, circle the number of points corresponding to the events you have experienced in the past six months or are likely to experience in the next six months. Then add the circled numbers up.

Event	Points	Event	Points
Death of spouse	100	Sexual difficulties	45
Female unwed pregnancy	92	Serious argument with significant other	40
Death of parent	80	Academic probation	39
Male partner in unwed pregnancy	77	Change in major	37
Divorce	73	New love interest	36
Death of a close family member	70	Increased workload in college	31
Death of a close friend	65	Outstanding personal achievement	29
Divorce between parents	63	First term in college	28
Jail term	61	Serious conflict with instructor	27
Major personal injury or illness	60	Lower grades than expected	25
Flunk out of college	58	Change in colleges (transfer)	24
Marriage	55	Change in social activities	22
Fired from job	50	Change in sleeping habits	21
Loss of financial support for college (scholarship)	48	Change in eating habits	19
Failing grade in important or required course	47	Minor violations of the law (for example, traffic ticket)	15

If your score indicates potential health problems, it would be to your benefit to seriously review the "stress relief smorgasbord" that appears later in this chapter and select and implement some strategies to reduce your stress.

NOTE: Adapted with permission from T. H. Holmes and R. H. Rahe, "The Social Readjustment Scale," in Carol L. Otis and Roger Goldingay, *Campus Health Guide* (New York: CEEB, 1989).

If you find that your score on the preceding exercise is 150 or higher, it would be good preventive health care to think about why you experienced each of the scored events. In addition, you might consider what skills you need to learn either to repair the damage that these events caused or to prevent their recurrence. It would also be interesting to find out how the rest of the class scored on the scale. If there seems to be a need, the class might draw upon a resource person to help everyone develop better coping or learning skills. You might also find out that you already have experts within the class who might share with you how they have handled these or similar events.

The other major theory about the sources of stress attributes our general level of stress to an overload of personal hassles and a deficit of uplifts or reliefs. This theory encourages us to evaluate our immediate problems but, while doing so, to focus on what's good about our lives and to strive to notice positive events instead of taking them for granted. We are all going to experience reversals, whether it's because we don't get along with our roommate, can't register for the course or time slot we want, can't find a parking space, can't find the classroom, can't seem to handle the freedom of college, can't find the time to do all that we might, can't get into the "right" Greek or social organization, can't get our parents to "understand," can't find the money to do it all, and so on. What we can control is our *reaction* to these hassles. If we can adopt the attitude that we will do what we can do, seek help when appropriate, and not sweat the small stuff, we won't be as negatively affected by disappointments and hassles. It also helps to keep a mental tally of the positive things in our lives. The following exercise will help you to take positive stock of your life and to become more aware of the barriers to letting go of useless worries.

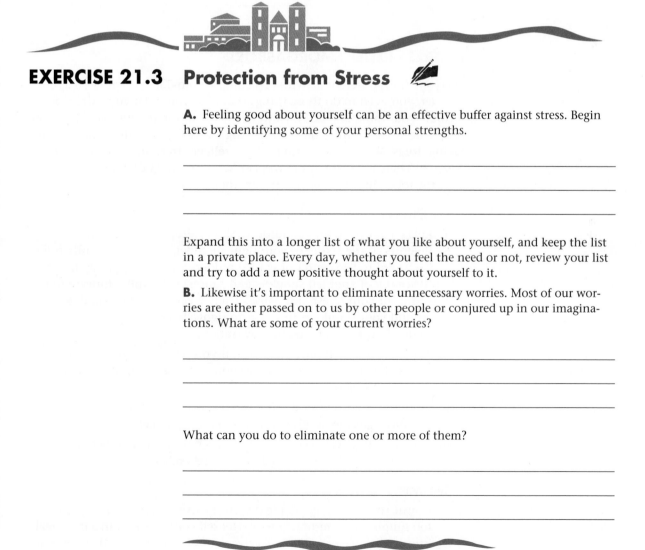

EXERCISE 21.3 Protection from Stress

A. Feeling good about yourself can be an effective buffer against stress. Begin here by identifying some of your personal strengths.

_____

_____

_____

Expand this into a longer list of what you like about yourself, and keep the list in a private place. Every day, whether you feel the need or not, review your list and try to add a new positive thought about yourself to it.

B. Likewise it's important to eliminate unnecessary worries. Most of our worries are either passed on to us by other people or conjured up in our imaginations. What are some of your current worries?

_____

_____

_____

What can you do to eliminate one or more of them?

_____

_____

_____

(Lynn Howlett Photography/ photo courtesy of Willamette University)

A STRESS RELIEF SMORGASBORD

Everyone finds different activities relaxing. To provide yourself with a sense of relief, you need to do those things that help you to let go of stress or invigorate your mind and body. However, many of the traditional things that people do with the intention of relieving stress—such as drinking alcohol, taking drugs, sleeping, or eating—don't relieve stress and may actually increase it! There are many other ways of handling stress that actually work. I offer the following as more effective methods.

Get Physical

1. **Relax your neck and shoulders.** Slowly drop your head forward, roll it gently to the center of your right shoulder, and pause; gently roll it backward to the center of your shoulders and pause; gently roll it to the center of your left shoulder and pause; gently roll it forward to the center of your chest and pause. Then reverse direction and go back around your shoulders from left to right. Remember that your goal is to slowly stretch muscles into relaxation.

2. **Take a stretch.** In any situation, if you pause to stretch your body you will feel it loosen up and become more relaxed, so stand up and reach for the sky!

3. **Get a massage.** Physical touch can feel wonderful when you are tense, and having someone else help you to relax can feel very supportive.

4. **Exercise.** Physical exercise strengthens both mind and body. Aerobic exercise is the most effective type for stress relief.

Get Mental

1. **Count to ten.** Many people discount this method because it sounds too simple. Your purpose is to master self-control and gain a more realistic perspective or outlook. To give yourself time to gain that new out-

Road Warrior

A student who commuted twenty-three miles to school was tailgated just before arriving on campus one day. The accident was minor, but unfortunately she had been sipping coffee at the time of the collision, and it splashed all over her dress. She was so embarrassed that she didn't go to class. Unfortunately that was a particularly important class, and her absence eventually cost her a full letter grade.

If you commute a long distance, carry a store of supplies. Leave your "survival" kit in your car if you drive, or in a locker at school if possible. Here are some things you should have in your kit. Talk with other students about other items that might be useful and add them to the list.

1. Emergency medical supplies
2. Flashlight
3. One dollar in change
4. Some pencils and paper
5. Jumper cables
6. Local bus schedule
7. Rag or towel
8. Spare set of clothes
9. _____
10. _____
11. _____
12. _____

look or to come up with a "better" way to handle the situation, count slowly while asking yourself, "How can I best handle this situation?"

2. **Control your thoughts.** The imagination can be *very* creative—it can veer off in frightening directions if allowed to do so. To gain control of negative thoughts or worries, imagine yelling "STOP!" as loudly as you can in your mind. You may have to repeat this process quite a few times until you master it, but gradually it will help you to shut out angry or frightening thoughts.

3. **Fantasize.** Give yourself a few moments to take a "minivacation." Remember the pleasure of an experience you enjoy, or listen to a child laugh, or just let your mind be creative. Make a list of some places or activities that make you feel relaxed and good about yourself. Next time you need to "get away," refer to the list, close your eyes, and take a minibreak.

4. **Congratulate yourself.** Give yourself pats on the back. No one knows how difficult a situation may have been for you to handle, or even how well you may have handled it, so tell yourself, "Good going."

5. **Ignore the problem.** This may sound strange at first, but many problems just don't need to be dealt with or can't be solved right now. Forget about the problem at hand and do something more important or something nice for yourself.

6. **Perform self-maintenance.** Stress is a daily issue, so the more you plan for its reduction, the more likely it will be reduced.

Get Spiritual

1. **Meditate.** All that meditation requires is slow breathing and concentration! Look at something in front of you or make a mental picture while you gradually breathe slower and slower, and feel the relief spread through your body and mind.

2. **Pray.** You don't need to go through life feeling alone. Prayer can be a great source of comfort and strength.

3. **Remember your purpose.** Sometimes it is very valuable to remind ourselves why we are in a particular situation. Even though it may be a difficult situation, you may need to remind yourself that you have to be there and to realize that the situation's importance outweighs its difficulty.

Use Mind and Body Together

1. **Take a break.** If possible, get up from what you are doing and walk away for a while. Don't let yourself think about the source of the problem until after a short walk.

2. **Get hug therapy.** We need at least four hugs a day to survive, eight hugs to feel okay, and twelve hugs to tackle the world. "Hugs" can come from many different sources and they can take many different forms. They can be bear hugs, smiles, compliments, or kind words or thoughts. If you have forgotten how to hug, ask a small child you know to teach you. Young children know that every time you give a hug, you get one back as a fringe benefit!

3. **Try progressive relaxation.** Perform a mental massage of each muscle in your body from your feet up to your head. Take the time to allow each muscle to relax and unwind. Imagine that the muscles that were all knotted and tense are now long, smooth, and relaxed.

4. **Laugh.** Nothing is so important that we must suffer self-damage. The ability to laugh at your own mistakes lightens your load and gives you the energy to return to a difficult task.

5. **Find a pet.** Countless studies have demonstrated that caring for, talking to, holding, and stroking pets can help to reduce stress.

Develop New Skills

1. **Learn something.** Sometimes your problem is that you lack information or skills in a certain area. The sooner you remedy your deficiency, the sooner your distress will end.

2. **Practice a hobby.** If you have one, use it; if you don't currently have one, then it's time that you did. The purpose of a hobby is to immerse yourself in an activity of your choice that provides you with a sense of accomplishment and pleasure.

EXERCISE 21.4   Adding to and Using the Stress Reduction List

A. Over your lifetime you've discovered some additional things that work to relieve stress for you. List them here:

_____

_____

_____

Expand your list by comparing notes with other students in the class.

B. Try at least one stress relief technique suggested in this section for two weeks. Give it a *good* try. To assist yourself in changing from a stress habit to a control habit, resolve in your mind that you deserve to be a more relaxed, confident person. Share your experience with someone.

The stress management habits that you are currently acquiring and practicing are likely to be the same ones that you will use for the rest of your life! Learning to handle stress in a healthy fashion is important not only to survive your first year and do well but to cope with the demands and opportunities of adulthood. A healthy adult is one who treats his or her body and

A Relaxation Process

Settle back and get comfortable. Take a few moments to allow yourself to listen to your thoughts and to your body. If your thoughts get in the way of relaxing, imagine a blackboard in your mind and visualize yourself writing down all of your thoughts on the blackboard. By doing this you can put those thoughts aside for a while and know that you will be able to retrieve them later.

Now that you are more ready to relax, begin by closing your eyes. Allow your breathing to become a little slower and a little deeper. As you continue breathing slowly and deeply, let your mind drift back into a tranquil, safe place that you have been in before. Try to recall everything that you could see, hear, and feel back there. Let those pleasant memories wash away any tension or discomfort.

To help yourself relax even further, take a brief journey through your body, allowing all of your muscles to become as comfortable and as relaxed as possible.

Let's begin that journey down at your feet. Begin by focusing on your feet up to your ankles, wiggling your feet or toes to help them to relax, then allowing that growing wave of relaxation to continue up into the muscles of the calves. As muscles relax, they stretch out and allow more blood to flow into them; therefore they gradually feel warmer and heavier. Continue the process on up into the muscles of the thighs; gradually your legs should feel more and more comfortable, more and more relaxed.

Then concentrate on all of the muscles up and down your spine, and feel the relaxation moving into your abdomen; as you do so you might also feel a pleasant sense of warmth moving out to every part of your body. Next focus on the muscles of the chest. Each time that you exhale, your chest muscles will relax just a little more. Let the feeling flow up into the muscles of the shoulders, washing away any tightness or tension, allowing the shoulder muscles to become loose and limp. And now the relaxation can seep out into the muscles of the arms and hands; gradually your arms and hands become heavy, limp, and warm.

Now move on to the muscles of the neck—front, sides, and back—imagining perhaps that your neck muscles are as floppy as a handful of rubber bands. And now relax the muscles of the face, letting the jaw, cheeks, and sides of the face hang loose and limp. Now relax the eyes and the nose, and now the forehead and the scalp. Let any wrinkles just melt away. And now, by taking a long, slow, deep breath, cleanse yourself of any remaining tension.

mind in a respectful manner. When you do that, you communicate to all other adults that you are handling yourself well and don't need them to "baby" you or to tell you how to live your life.

Sometimes our lives or problems are either too overwhelming or too complex to resolve by ourselves. If you find that to be the case, you might benefit from checking out the services provided by your college counseling center. Counseling centers often offer individual or group sessions on handling difficult times or situations in our lives, and the support and skills of a trained professional can help make the most difficult issues a lot more manageable.

EXERCISE 21.5 Your Social Support Network

Your social support network can be extremely helpful to you in difficult times, but many people aren't sure whom to count on for support or how to ask for it.

You first learned about getting support from your family. Think back to a time when you felt you really needed support. Was it when you were trying to accomplish something or when you felt discouraged or defeated? Whom did you ask for support? How did you ask? Did they respond in the way that you needed them to? Did you get the caring or comfort that you wanted?

Life's early lessons usually get reinforced over the years. Probably by now either you feel good about the level of support in your life or you don't.

Imagine you have a problem with a roommate that you want to discuss with someone else. Whom would you choose? Would you expect that discussion to leave you feeling the way you want to feel, or are you just used to feeling that you never get the support you need to feel good about yourself?

In different situations you may need different people for support. Are you still relying primarily on your family, or have you expanded your resources to get support from friends, professors, co-workers, and so on? Who is in your support network? Make a list of people you would support. Make a list of situations in which you sometimes need support. List the people who support you in them. Do you need to add someone to your network? Write yourself a note about how to get that person's support.

You may also want to consider the values that your current physical, emotional, and spiritual circumstances reflect. Are those values similar to or different from those of your family and friends? Are you acting in accordance with your values? Is this a source of stress? Remember, whatever you do to cope with stress, you will be coping either productively or counterproductively—it's your choice. Go forth and manage stress!

EXERCISE 21.6 A One-Week Checkup

To control stress, we need to heed its warning signs. Photocopy the chart on the next page and use it for one week to keep track of troublesome experiences and your *reactions* and *responses* to them. If at first you don't notice any reactions, pay attention to your general state during the day. Times when you feel suddenly fatigued, tense, angry, upset, frightened, and so on are stress points in your day.

| Event | Signals | | Your Response | What (If Anything) Would You Do Differently Next Time? |
	Physical	Emotional		

After the week is over, analyze the chart. Look for both positive and negative patterns. Based on this information, write down a plan for stress management:

I will _____

_____

I will _____

_____

I will not _____

_____

I will not _____

_____

JOURNAL

Which stress theory described in this section makes the most sense to you? Explore your reaction by recording some personal examples or experiences. Comment on some of your stress relief strategies. How effective are they for you?

SUGGESTIONS FOR FURTHER READING

Benson, H. *The Mind/Body Effect.* New York: Simon & Schuster, 1979.

Benson, H., and M. Z. Klipper. *The Relaxation Response.* New York: Morrow, 1976.

Brown, B. *Supermind.* New York: Harper & Row, 1980.

Butler, P. *Talking to Yourself.* New York: Stein & Day, 1981.

Clum, George A. *Coping with Panic: A Drug Free Approach to Dealing with Anxiety Attacks.* Pacific Grove, Calif.: Brooks/Cole, 1990.

Emmons, M. *The Inner Source.* San Luis Obispo, Calif.: Impact, 1978.

Glasser, W. *Positive Addiction.* New York: Harper & Row, 1979.

Green, E., and A. Green. *Beyond Biofeedback.* New York: Delta, 1977.

Hyatt, C., and L. Gottlieb. *When Smart People Fail.* New York: Simon & Schuster, 1987.

Kinser, N. S. *Stress and the American Woman.* New York: Ballantine Books, 1980.

Martin, R. A., and E. Y. Pollard. *Learning to Change.* New York: McGraw-Hill, 1980.

Otis, C. L., and R. Goldingay. *Campus Health Guide.* New York: College Entrance Examination Board, 1989.

Pelletier, K. *Mind as Healer/Mind as Slayer.* New York: Delta, 1977.

Pennebaker, James W. *Opening Up: The Healing Power of Confiding in Others.* New York: Morrow, 1990.

Powell, Trevor J. *Anxiety and Stress Management.* New York: Routledge, 1990.

Rice, Phillip L. *Stress and Health: Principles and Practice for Coping and Wellness,* 2nd ed. Pacific Grove, Calif.: Brooks/Cole, 1992.

Smith, Jonathan C. *Stress Scripting: A Guide to Stress Management.* New York: Praeger, 1991.

Sutherland, Valerie J., and Cary L. Cooper. *Understanding Stress.* New York: Chapman & Hall, 1990.

Vorst, J. *Necessary Losses.* New York: Fawcett, 1986.

Sexual Decisions

Lisa Ann Mohn
University of South Carolina

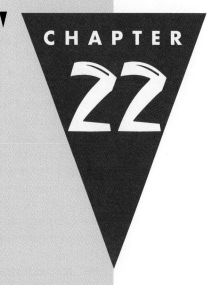

A *few of my friends are always bragging about who they were with last night. I'm not into that. Some women around here turn me on, but I just don't want a sexual relationship right now. I have enough to deal with. Down the road a little, if I find the right person, who knows?*

Because the goal of this book is to help you survive your first year in college, a chapter on sexual decision making seems almost a given. The main reason is that we know from numerous studies that about 75 percent of traditional-aged college students have engaged in sexual intercourse at least once. Another reason is that, depending on where you are from, what your family background is, what your school district's policies on sex education were, and so on, you may or may not have some critical information.

You may be wondering what our point of view will be. Are we urging you to fight "that urge"? Providing you some answers in case you find yourself in a compromising situation? Telling you that sex in college is inevitable, so learn all you can now? No. We will neither condone nor condemn your sexual decisions. But we will encourage you to know your options, to recognize that you have the right to choose what's comfortable for you, and to accept that, should you choose to have sex, you should also choose to protect yourself against unwanted pregnancy and sexually transmitted diseases.

SEXUAL DECISION MAKING

The first thing we need to say is that not all first-year students are sexually active, so if you're in this category you need not feel alone. However, college seems to be a time when recent high school graduates begin at least to think more seriously about sex. Perhaps this has to do with peer pressure or a sense of one's newfound independence, or maybe it's just hormones. Regardless of the reasons it can be quite helpful to explore your sexual values and to consider whether sex is right for you at this time.

While the "sexual revolution" of the 1960s and 1970s may have made premarital sex more socially acceptable, people have not necessarily become better equipped to deal with this sexual freedom. One sign of this is the alarming increase in the rate of sexually transmitted diseases (STDs) among college students. Another is the fact that unwanted pregnancies are not uncommon. More difficult to quantify is the degree to which young people may later regret impulsive decisions to have sex.

Why is it that otherwise intelligent people choose to take sexual risks? Well, sex isn't the only thing that college students take risks with. If you are 18 or so, you may feel you are invincible or immune from danger. Although you know certain risks exist, you may never have been sufficiently exposed to them personally to believe your own life could be touched. Or perhaps it's simply that sex and relationships are a confusing business. While there are many pressures to become sexually active, certainly many factors may discourage sexual activity as well. The following list compares these factors:

Encouragers	Discouragers
Hormones	Family values/expectations
Peer pressure	Religious values
Alcohol/other drugs	Sexually transmitted diseases
Curiosity	Fear of pregnancy
The media	Concern for reputation
An intimate relationship	Feeling of unreadiness
Sexual pleasure	Fear of being hurt or "used"

As you can see, there are powerful pressures on each side. Consequently some people get confused and frustrated and fail to make any decision. Or they may allow the encouragers to persuade them but not feel comfortable enough with that decision to take responsibility for their actions—the "If I don't think or talk about it, then I can pretend I'm not really doing it" syndrome. This irresponsibility or indecisiveness carries a risk: that sex will occur without the means to prevent pregnancy or STDs.

For your protection try to clarify your own values and then act in accordance with them. Those who do this usually wind up happier with their decisions. Take a moment now to reflect on whether you plan to be sexually active. Whatever you decide, think about how you will reinforce your resolve to abstain from sex or only practice safer sex and how you plan on communicating that decision to your partner.

EXERCISE 22.1 Personal Reflection on Sexuality

A. Ask yourself the following questions to prepare for part B: Have you taken time to sort out your own values about sexual activity? If you aren't willing to commit to a particular plan of action at this time, what keeps you from doing so? If you are sexually active, do your values take into account your own and your partner's health? If that's not a priority for you, what would it take to get you to a point where safer sex took priority over unsafe sex?

B. Write down some of your thoughts and intentions about sexuality. This should be for you alone to read. The act of writing may help you organize your thoughts. Committing your values to paper may also help you live by them when faced with tough decisions.

Birth Control

One sexuality issue that heterosexual students need to be concerned about is preventing an unwanted pregnancy.

What is the best method of contraception? Any method that you use correctly and consistently, each time you have intercourse. While one method may be more effective than another, if a couple does not prefer it, they will be less likely to use it consistently and correctly, and therefore it's not better for them. When choosing a method of birth control, consider all aspects of the method before you decide. Table 22.1 compares the major features of some common methods. Note the table's emphasis on whether each method protects against STDs. For most college students this is important in choosing one or more methods of birth control. Because of their importance in preventing disease, more information about condoms is included later in this chapter.

As the table indicates, all methods have advantages and disadvantages. Make sure that whatever method you choose, you feel comfortable using it. Consult your physician for the methods requiring a prescription and make sure to read all package inserts thoroughly, particularly for any products you buy over the counter.

Table 22.1 Methods of Contraception

ABSTINENCE (100%)*

What It Is

Choosing not to have intercourse.

Advantages

Only method that provides total protection against pregnancy and STDs.

Disadvantages

Does not allow for the benefits people look for from sexual intercourse.

Comments

Not an acceptable practice for many people.

NORPLANT (99.9%)

What It Is

Six matchstick-sized silicone rubber capsules, inserted into a woman's arm, that continually release a very low dose of progesterone.

Advantages

Highly effective. Works for up to five years. Allows for sexual spontaneity. Low dose of hormones make this medically safer than other hormonal methods.

Disadvantages

Removal may be difficult. Very expensive to obtain initially.

Comments

Users may have typical side effects of hormonal methods, causing them to discontinue during the first year. This makes it somewhat risky due to the high initial cost.

DEPO-PROVERA (99.7%)

What It Is

A progestin-only method, administered to women by injection, every three months.

Advantages

Highly effective. Allows for sexual spontaneity. Relatively low yearly cost.

Disadvantages

A variety of side effects typical of progestin-type contraceptives may be present and persist up to six to eight months after termination.

Comments

Method is easy and spontaneous, but users must remember to get their shots.

STERILIZATION (99.5%)

What It Is

Tubal ligation in women; vasectomy in men.

Advantages

Provides nearly permanent protection from future pregnancies.

Disadvantages

Not considered reversible and therefore not a good option for anyone wanting children at a later date.

Comments

While this is a common method for people over age 30, most college students would not choose it.

ORAL CONTRACEPTIVES (97–99%)

What They Are

Birth control pills.

Advantages

Highly effective. Allows for sexual spontaneity. Most women have lighter and shorter periods.

Disadvantages

Many minor side effects (nausea, weight gain), which cause a significant percentage of users to discontinue. Provides no protection against STDs.

Comments

Available by prescription only, after a gynecological exam.

INTRAUTERINE DEVICE (IUD) (98–99%)

What It Is

Device inserted into the uterus by a physician.

Advantages

Once inserted, may be left in for one to eight years, depending upon the type. Less expensive than other long-term methods.

Disadvantages

Increased risk of certain complications such as pelvic inflammatory disease and menstrual problems. Possible increased risk of contracting HIV, if exposed.

Comments

Women who have not had a child may have a difficult time finding a doctor willing to prescribe it.

CONDOM (88–98%)

What It Is

Rubber sheath that fits over the penis.

Advantages

Only birth control method that also provides good protection against STDs, including HIV. Actively involves male partner.

Disadvantages

Less spontaneous than some other methods because it must be put on right before intercourse. Belief of some men that it cuts down on pleasurable sensations.

Comments

Experts believe that most condom failure is due to misuse of condoms rather than breakage. Using condoms in conjunction with additional spermicide can increase effectiveness to near 100 percent.

DIAPHRAGM (80–95%)

What It Is

Dome-shaped rubber cap that is inserted into the vagina and covers the cervix.

Advantages

Safe method of birth control with virtually no side effects. May be inserted up to 2 hours prior to intercourse, making it somewhat spontaneous. May provide some protection against STDs.

Disadvantages

Wide variance of effectiveness based on consistent use, the fit of the diaphragm, and frequency of intercourse. Multiple acts of intercourse require use of additional spermicide.

Comments

Must be prescribed by a physician. Must always be used with a spermicidal jelly and left in for 6–8 hours after intercourse.

FEMALE CONDOM (80–95%)

What It Is

A polyurethane sheath that completely lines the vagina acting as a complete barrier. Two rings hold it in place, one inside and one outside the vagina.

Advantages

Highly safe medically. Does not require any spermicide. Theoretically provides excellent protection against STDs—almost perfectly leakproof and better than the male condom in this regard.

Disadvantages

Lower effectiveness rate than many other methods. Visible outer ring can be aesthetically displeasing.

Comments

While the research is not yet conclusive, this method seems to offer good STD protection that is controllable by the woman.

CONTRACEPTIVE SPONGE (80–90%)

What It Is

Small polyurethane sponge containing the spermicide Nonoxynol-9.

Advantages

Easy to obtain (over the counter) and use. Once inserted, effective for 24 hours with no additional spermicide needed.

Disadvantages

Frequent difficulty with removal. For women who have had a child, effectiveness is less than indicated here.

Comments

Must be left in for 6–8 hours after intercourse.

CERVICAL CAP (80–90%)

What It Is

Cup-shaped device that fits over the cervix.

Advantages

Similar to diaphragm, but may be worn longer—up to 48 hours.

Disadvantages

Not widely available due to lack of practitioners trained in fitting them.

Comments

Longer wearing time increases risk of vaginal infections.

SPERMICIDAL FOAMS, CREAMS, AND JELLIES (80–90%)

What They Are

Sperm-killing chemicals inserted into the vagina.

Advantages

Easy to purchase and use. Provide some protection against STDs, including HIV.

Disadvantages

Lower effectiveness than many methods. Can be messy. May increase likelihood of birth defects should pregnancy occur.

Comments

As with condoms, it is suspected that failure is due to misuse. However, spermicides seem to work better in combination with other methods (such as condoms).

NATURAL FAMILY PLANNING (80%)

What It Is

Periodic abstinence based on when ovulation is predicted.

Advantages

Requires no devices or chemicals.

Disadvantages

Requires a period of abstinence each month, when ovulation is expected. Also, requires diligent record-keeping.

Comments

For maximum effectiveness, consult a trained practitioner for guidance in using this method.

COITUS INTERRUPTUS (80%)

What It Is

Withdrawal.

Advantages

Requires no devices or chemicals. Can be used at any time, at no cost.

Disadvantages

Relies heavily on the man having enough control and knowing when ejaculation will occur to remove his penis from the vagina in time. Also may diminish pleasure for the couple.

Comments

Ejaculation must be far enough away from partner's genitals so that no semen can enter the vagina. Provides no protection against STDs.

*Percentages in parentheses refer to approximate effectiveness rates based on one year of using the method. Where two numbers are given, the lower percentage refers to the *typical* effectiveness, while the higher number refers to the *possible* effectiveness if used correctly and consistently.

Always discuss birth control with your partner so that you both feel comfortable with the option you have selected. For more information about a particular method, consult a pharmacist, a medical practitioner at your student health center, a local family planning clinic or Planned Parenthood affiliate, the local health department, or your private physician. The main thing is to get information somewhere and to resolve to protect yourself and your partner each and every time you choose to have sexual intercourse.

If you've already chosen a method, or have one in mind, the next exercise can help you decide whether it's truly the best method for you.

EXERCISE 22.2   Which Birth Control Method Is Best?

If you're choosing to be sexually active, it's time to choose a method of birth control. Both partners should be involved in this decision. Consider various factors to decide what's right for you, your partner, and your relationship. You can answer these questions on your own and then have your partner complete the exercise, with both of you keeping in mind a particular method you're considering. Or you can complete it together, discussing the issue as you go.

	Me	My Partner
1. Has a pregnancy ever occurred despite using this preferred method of birth control?	_____	_____
2. Will I have difficulty using this method?	_____	_____
3. If this method interrupts lovemaking, will I be less likely to use it?	_____	_____
4. Is there anything about my behavior or habits that could lead me to use this method incorrectly?	_____	_____
5. Am I at risk of being exposed to HIV or other STDs if I use this method?	_____	_____
6. Am I concerned about potential side effects associated with this method?	_____	_____
7. Does this method cost more than I can afford?	_____	_____
8. Would I really rather not use this method?	_____	_____

Sexually Transmitted Diseases (STDs)

The problem of STDs on college campuses has been receiving growing attention in recent years, as an epidemic number of students have become infected. The consequences of the most common STDs reach far beyond the embarrassment most students feel when diagnosed with a sexually related illness. The idea that "nice" young men and women don't catch these sorts

The most important thing you can do for yourself with regard to sexuality is simply to live consistently in keeping with your own values. Intimacy, belongingness, mutual acceptance, and support are all possible regardless of a person's sexual choices. (Photo courtesy of Earlham College)

of diseases is more dangerous and inaccurate than ever before. If you choose to be sexually active, particularly with more than one partner, exposure to an STD is a very real possibility.

This section will discuss the STDs students need to be most aware of. Chlamydia, herpes, and human papillomavirus are important because of their high rates and potential consequences. Gonorrhea is discussed briefly because it is so similar to and often accompanies chlamydia, although its rates are much higher in the general population than among college students. Hepatitis B can lead to serious illness and is on the rise, but a preventive vaccine is available. Naturally HIV/AIDS is a concern, not only because of its deadly consequences but also because of its increasing incidence among the college-age population.

In general STDs continue to increase faster than other illnesses on campuses today. Approximately 5–10 percent of visits to college health services nationally are for the diagnosis and treatment of STDs. For more information about any of these diseases, or others, contact your student health center, your local health department, or the National STD Hotline (1-800-227-8922).

Chlamydia. The most common STD in the United States is chlamydia. Over 4 million new cases are diagnosed each year. Chlamydia is particularly threatening to women because a large proportion of women who are infected do not show symptoms, allowing the disease to progress to pelvic inflammatory disease (PID), now thought to be the leading cause of infertility in women. When chlamydia does produce symptoms in women, the symptoms may include mild abdominal pain, change in vaginal discharge, and pain and burning with urination.

In men symptoms are typically pain and burning with urination, and sometimes a discharge from the penis. Occasionally the symptoms will be too mild to notice. Men who go without treatment may also become infertile, although this happens much more rarely than it does in women. In both sexes symptoms usually appear one to three weeks after exposure. Even if symptoms are not apparent, an individual infected with chlamydia is still contagious and may transmit the disease to subsequent sexual partners. If detected, chlamydia is completely treatable with antibiotics.

Gonorrhea. Gonorrhea is a bacterial infection that produces symptoms similar to chlamydia. While not quite as common as chlamydia, with approximately 2 million new cases nationwide per year, it still has a significant impact on the health of Americans. As with chlamydia, men will usually show symptoms, but women often do not. Gonorrhea is treatable with antibiotics, but in recent years new, more resistant strains of gonorrhea have made this process more difficult. Untreated gonorrhea, like chlamydia, can lead to more severe infections in men and women.

Herpes. Before AIDS came along, herpes was considered the worst STD one could get, because there is no cure. There are approximately 200,000 new cases nationwide per year, but it's estimated that 30 million people are infected with genital herpes, many of them asymptomatic (showing no symptoms). The characteristic blisters one gets on the genitals are very similar to the cold sores and fever blisters people get on their mouths, and in fact they are both caused by varieties of the herpes virus. (The strains of the virus are even interchangeable above and below the waist if transmitted through oral sex.)

Symptoms appear on the genitals two days to two weeks after exposure in the form of small blisters or lesions that erupt into painful sores. The first outbreak is usually the most severe, and about 50 percent of those infected will never have another outbreak. The other 50 percent are likely to have outbreaks several times a year, particularly when they are under stress or their immune system is being taxed.

Although there is no cure, the prescription drug Zovirax seems to reduce the length and severity of herpes outbreaks. People are most contagious to a partner after or right before lesions erupt, so it is important to abstain from any sexual contact at this time. It is difficult to determine exactly how contagious a person is at other times, but asymptomatic people can transmit the disease because the virus continues to live in the body. Some experts believe that most cases of herpes are transmitted this way.

Human Papillomavirus (HPV). While chlamydia may still be the most prevalent STD nationwide, HPV has become the leading STD affecting the health of college students. There has been a 600 percent increase of HPV in this population in the past twenty years, and some recent studies show that as many as 40–50 percent of sexually active college students may be infected.

HPV is the cause of venereal warts, which affect both men and women on their outer genitals and in the rectum of those who practice anal receptive intercourse, and it may even grow inside a man's urethra or a woman's vagina. A typical incubation period for venereal warts is one to three months, though symptoms may not appear for several months or years after exposure. Genital warts may be small, flat, pink growths, or they may be larger, with a cauliflowerlike appearance. In either case they are usually not painful.

Because HPV is a virus, there is no cure, but treatment is available in the form of burning, freezing, chemical destruction, and, in severe cases, laser surgery. Wart removal often takes multiple treatments, which can be painful but are less disruptive to a busy student's schedule. As with herpes the virus remains in the body and may cause recurrences and be transmitted to a partner over an indefinite period of time.

The major long-term health concern associated with HPV affects women. Certain strains of HPV don't cause the visible warts but invade the cervix and incorporate themselves into the DNA of the cells there. The subsequent cervical cell changes produce dysplasia, a precancerous condition that can lead to cervical cancer. In the past few years the correlation between cervical cancer and HPV has become very strong, and most experts believe HPV is responsible for the large majority of cases of cervical cancer in our country today. The incubation period for these changes can take many years. Fortunately, if women are screened regularly with Pap smears, precancerous changes can be detected and treated before they lead to cervical cancer.

Hepatitis B. There are about 300,000 new cases of hepatitis B nationwide each year, most of them in adolescents and young adults. Hepatitis B is transmitted through unprotected sex and through contact with infected blood, and it is 100 times more infectious than HIV. This means you have a much greater risk of contracting it if you are exposed.

People who are infected with hepatitis B can have varying symptoms. In fact, it's not at all uncommon to show no symptoms. When present, symptoms may include those similar to a stomach virus, in addition to yellowing of the skin and eyes. Occasionally people become very ill and are disabled for weeks or months. Most people will recover completely, but some remain carriers for life, able to transmit the virus to others. A small percentage of infected people go on to get chronic liver disease, which puts them at risk for cirrhosis and liver cancer.

There is no cure for hepatitis B, and no treatment other than rest and a healthy diet. What makes this STD unusual is that there is a vaccine available to prevent it. The series of three shots is recommended by the Centers for Disease Control and the American Academy of Pediatrics for all young adults. The major drawback to the vaccine is that it's very costly—up to $150 for the three shots—making it unlikely that many college students will invest in it.

HIV/AIDS. HIV/AIDS is very difficult to discuss briefly. We must assume that you have already been exposed to a good deal of information on this STD. The main thing we want to stress is that AIDS and the virus that causes it—HIV—continue to increase. During 1994, in the thirteenth year of the epidemic, the number of cases of AIDS had grown to almost 400,000, more than twice the number there were in 1990! The Centers for Disease Control estimate that there are at least 1–1½ million people infected with HIV. The routes of transmission for HIV are through blood, semen, vaginal fluids, and breast milk, or by being born to an HIV-infected mother.

While men who have sex with men and intravenous drug users still comprise the majority of AIDS cases to date, other groups have rapidly increasing rates of infection, including women, teens, heterosexuals, Hispanics, and African-Americans (who continue to be disproportionately represented among those with AIDS). Although we're discussing "risk groups" here, it's important to keep in mind that it's not who you are but what you do that puts you at risk for contracting HIV.

Living with AIDS

Most people only die once. I've already died twice. The first time was in the fall of 1981 when I surrendered to the fact that I was an alcoholic and pill-head. The second time was on a warm, sunny day in late April 1987, when my doctor said, "With these symptoms, I have to conclude that it's the AIDS virus."

Being dead can have its advantages. Sometimes I say to myself, "You're dead, you can do whatever you want. What are they going to do, shoot you?" You get to eat what you like. In fact, like the scene from Sleeper, *the doctors encourage you to eat steaks and ice cream. People don't castigate you when you sleep in. Planning for the future means drawing up a will. You don't save for retirement, you should live that long. I have a friend who went $27,000 into debt and then kicked the bucket. Now, he got the joke.*

Generally, though, being dead isn't much fun. Old friends often treat you like the proverbial hot potato, or like a time bomb. They pass you around, hoping you don't go off around them. Not that I blame them: We've all gone to too many funerals.

So you find yourself gravitating to the other HIVs. Then the game becomes more like musical chairs. Who's the next one out? When your friends start the fast slide, they are instantly old men, the

shadow-dead. Hair turns into fragile wisps, bodies gaunt down, eyes disappear into the recesses of emaciated faces. Then everyone knows, not much longer for this one.

Some are deserted by their families. More often, families kill with a kind of kindness. Well-intentioned, misguided, they nurse you through the last months, but they really want you to go out on their terms. I have a friend who was an invalid for his last six months while his ... family screened out all gay callers and "converted" him to Christ and prayer and away from the gay life.

Another unpleasant thing about being dead is that people objectify you, treat you like a thing rather than a person. This is, of course, what we do to dead things. Bad enough that the doctors and hospital medical staff treat you like a faulty piece of equipment to keep running and keep clean (although I've had indigent friends who were denied even that slim dignity in the final countdown). You begin to wonder how to justify all this expense and bother. Soon you hear subtle messages like, "Do you realize how much your decision to stay alive is costing us?"

Then there is all the shame that goes with being too sick to meet obligations, with losing your looks, with becoming helpless. Shame is an awesome

AIDS had not been a major problem on most college campuses as of the early 1990s. However, as more and more people become infected with HIV, college students are more likely to be exposed and to contract the virus. Because of the long incubation period suspected for AIDS, students may become infected with the virus while they are in college but not become sick until several years afterward.

Since other STDs are occurring at such a high rate, many students obviously are engaging in the behaviors that put them at risk for STDs, including HIV. In addition, having other STDs may actually predispose people to contract HIV more readily if they are exposed to the virus. Each person must try to evaluate his or her own risk of becoming infected and take precautions.

As with other STDs, abstinence, monogamy, and condoms (in that order) are the best ways to prevent the sexual spread of AIDS. Get as much information as you can through your student health service, your local health department, or the National AIDS Hotline (1-800-342-AIDS).

thing. My mother, who has otherwise been remarkable, cannot tell her friends that her son has this virus and is probably dying. She simply cannot do it.

Then there are all the lies. I lost a job because they found out why I was sick. I lost a job because I couldn't risk telling them I was sick. Better to leave with a question mark than with that trailing after you. Outside of the gay community I tell only a select few. I'll be [damned] if I'll surrender my personal power....

Gradually the gritty process of closing out a life begins. Can't make it into the office at nine? Go on disability. Can't keep your apartment up? Move in with Mom and Dad. Learn to like daytime television. Let's not even talk about a sex life. You end up disempowered, nudged to the edge of things by the busy, ignored, untouched, living in limbo....

Memorize this equation: silence = death. The mountains of medicine labor to bring forth a mouse. When you get an undeserved death sentence, you have the right to be angry. It is only the most belligerent and unpleasant among the sick who can hope to hope.

SOURCE: Adapted and reproduced, with permission, from *the Student Union* (a publication by students at Carnegie-Mellon University), 6, no. 3 (1990).

The Names Project has toured many American campuses. It is both an urgent appeal for everyone to face the reality of AIDS and a moving celebration of the lives of thousands of people—male, female, gay, straight—cut short by HIV. (Cassandra Ecker/photo courtesy of Illinois Media Company)

Preventing STDs

While the sexually transmitted diseases discussed here can be very serious and very scary, it's not all bad news. Good methods of protection are available, and you can choose what's right for you. The worst thing you can do is nothing. If you let concerns about sexual risks overwhelm you, they will. People who do not make conscious choices in advance are often caught making a decision that doesn't suit their values and may compromise their health.

Abstinence. The first choice you always have is to abstain from sex. Even if three-quarters of college students are having sex, that still leaves a solid one-quarter who are not. If you currently fall in this group, congratulations! It can be difficult to choose a behavior when you're in the minority, but you are surely reaping benefits.

Condoms

When selecting a condom, always consider the following:

1. **Use condoms made of latex rubber.** Latex serves as a barrier to the virus. "Lambskin" or "natural membrane" condoms are not good because of the pores in the material. Look for "latex" on the package.

2. **Use condoms with a spermicide to get more protection.** Spermicides have been shown in laboratory tests to kill viruses. Use the spermicide in the tip and outside the condom.

3. **Use a lubricant with a condom.** Check the list of ingredients on the back of the lubricant package to make sure the lubricant is water-based. Do not use petroleum-based jelly, cold cream, baby oil, or cooking shortening. These can weaken the condom and cause it to break.

SOURCE: Adapted from *Understanding AIDS: A Message from the Surgeon General.* HHA Publication No. (CDC) HHS-88-8404 (Washington, D.C.: Government Printing Office).

One thing that can make the decision to remain abstinent easier is realizing that abstinence doesn't have to mean a lack of intimacy, or even of sexual pleasure, for that matter. Abstinence (with a partner) encompasses a wide variety of behaviors from holding hands to more sexually intimate behaviors short of intercourse. These carry a lower risk of spreading disease, having an unwanted pregnancy, or possibly regretting sex than do vaginal or anal intercourse. Even if you've had intercourse in the past, you can return to a "secondary virginity" if you choose.

Monogamy. Another very safe behavior, in terms of disease prevention, is having sex exclusively with one partner who is uninfected. However, students find it difficult to practice this type of monogamy successfully for two reasons. The first is that having a long-term monogamous relationship is not always practical because college is a time when many people want to date and either aren't interested in becoming "serious" or just don't find the right person. And the "love of your life" this fall may not be the same next spring. The second reason is that it is hard to know for sure that your partner was not infected to begin with. Unless you're both virgins, you can't be certain, but your chances of remaining healthy are better the more limited the number of your prior sexual partners and the longer you progress in the relationship disease-free.

Condoms. Lastly there's the condom. In the 1990s the condom needs to be a "given" for those who are sexually active. Other than providing very good pregnancy protection, it can help to prevent the spread of STDs, including HIV/AIDS. The condom's effectiveness against disease holds true for anal, vaginal, and oral intercourse. The most current research indicates that

the rate of protection provided by condoms against STDs is similar to its rate of protection against pregnancy (90–99 percent). This was supported in 1993 when the National Centers for Disease Control endorsed condom use as a safe and effective method when used correctly and consistently.

Other methods of birth control, particularly those with spermicides containing Nonoxynol-9, may provide some extra protection against STDs, but no other method rivals the protection offered by condoms. Because STDs are epidemic on most college campuses, and because AIDS is a deadly disease, it becomes more and more important to use condoms.

To some degree, however, this is easier said than done. The condom has long had a reputation of being a less spontaneous method and of diminishing pleasurable sensations. It may take some discussion to convince your partner that using condoms is the right thing to do. Perhaps he or she will respond negatively to the suggestion. If this happens, here are some comments that may help you in your discussion:

Your partner: Condoms aren't spontaneous. They ruin the moment.

You: If you think they're not spontaneous, maybe we're not being creative enough. If you let me put it on you, I bet you won't notice that it's not spontaneous!

Your partner: Condoms aren't natural.

You: What's not natural is to be uptight during sex. If we know we're protected against unwanted pregnancy and disease, we'll both be more relaxed.

Your partner: It just doesn't feel as good with a condom. It's like taking a shower with a raincoat on.

You: I know it may not feel exactly the same, but I'm sure we can both work toward making it feel really *good*. Besides we can't have sex without one. Using a condom is going to feel a lot better than not having sex at all.

Your partner: I can't believe you carry condoms with you. Does this mean you'll "do it" with anyone?

You: Of course not! In fact I carry condoms because I think sex *is* special. I want to be responsible about it. Also I care about you, and if we decide to have sex, I want to make sure we're both protected.

Your partner: I won't have sex with a condom on.

You: Well, we can't have sex without one. There are other things we can do without having intercourse. Why don't we stick to "outercourse" until we can resolve our differences?

EXERCISE 22.3 What's Your Decision?

While you might know about the strategies to keep yourself from contracting a sexually transmitted disease, knowledge doesn't always translate into behavior. Use the following chart to brainstorm all the reasons you can think of that people *wouldn't* practice each of the prevention strategies: abstinence, monogamy, or condom use. In other words, think about the *barriers* to safer sex. Then go back over your list, and consider whether the barrier would apply to you (Yes, No, or Maybe). In this way you can better evaluate where you stand on the issue of safer sex and determine what areas you may need to work on to ensure that you protect yourself—always!

Barriers   **Does This Apply?**

_____   _____

_____   _____

_____   _____

_____   _____

_____   _____

_____   _____

_____   _____

_____   _____

SEXUAL ASSAULT

To this point our assumption has been that both partners were interested in having sex. An issue gaining much attention on college campuses lately, though, is nonconsensual sex. Sexual assault, which includes but is not limited to rape (forced intercourse), seems to be increasing on campus. At the

Rape Does Happen

I can remember a friend of mine talking about a party that she went to this summer. She was telling me about how she liked this guy and was flirting with him a little bit. She ended up having too much to drink and passed out in a friend's room. In the morning she woke up next to the guy she had been flirting with the night before. She thought that she was OK because she had all her clothes on, but when she was walking home she noticed that her underwear was in her pocket.

Every day I walk to school and in the past couple of weeks I have noticed stencils on the sidewalk—one saying "stop raping" and the other saying "sex – yes = rape." The sight of these are kind of eerie to me. Where are the rape victims on our campus? Do they have no one to turn to and therefore resort to making their concerns and hurts on the sidewalk?

This graffiti makes me think of the statistics that I hear floating around about 1 out of every 3 women getting sexually assaulted by the time they graduate from college. Sometimes I feel lucky because I got my one time over with already and the person did not get very far except for scaring me. But then I tell myself I am not that lucky—this could happen again at any time.

I was standing against a fraternity wall and someone that I knew pretty well came up to me and pushed his body against mine and started putting his hand up my shirt while trying to kiss me. I kept turning my head against the wall so he couldn't kiss me on the lips and I was trying to push him away by pushing on his shoulders. It was scary because he was bigger and stronger than I was. Even though I was pushing as hard as I could, he was stronger. After about a minute, which felt like an eternity, he got really embarrassed and backed off and said, "I'm sorry, I'm sorry, I know I shouldn't do that to you," and then he ran away.

That incident made me feel very uncomfortable and very scared. Uncomfortable because I felt a little guilty—like maybe it was my fault. I asked myself, "Why didn't I scream? What if someone else saw?" I was scared because something like that could happen to me and I was not strong enough to stop it. Also it scared me that this was someone that I knew. I had spent time alone with him in his room in the past and he had never touched me. I was confused about why all of a sudden, in the middle of this party, he would attack me. I became distrusting of him, but also of other men that I am not very close to.

It's very frightening to think about, but too often there comes a time when a woman's resistance to sexual advances is simply chalked up to her need for further seduction, for further convincing. Suddenly the female in question is no longer a feeling individual, she's just a woman, one of the ones who would eventually say "yes" anyway. At this point an act of what might have been sexual desire turns into a desire to control the situation and the woman. It is in these cases, when the someone is denied the right to say NO, that sexual assault occurs.

To understand even faintly what the experience of sexual assault is like, you must consider what it would be like to be robbed of something very personal. There are very few things that we can personally exert control over in this life, and when someone takes the control of your own body away from you, it is devastating. When something that you own is stolen, you will be justifiably upset and insecure. When your body is violated and control over your own person is taken from you, you can never regain the security of knowing that your self (physical, emotional, mental) is your own.

SOURCE: Reproduced, with permission, from Ingrid Bromberg, "Rape Does Happen at CMU," the Student Union (a publication by students at Carnegie-Mellon University), 6, no. 3 (1990).

least, victims are beginning to come forward in greater numbers, demanding that administrators take the issue more seriously. As a result more and more schools are developing sexual assault policies and procedures, designating specific personnel to deal with the issue, and providing more education for both men and women about how they can reduce their risk of becoming involved in a sexual assault.

Knowing a bit more about the profile of rape on campus may help reduce your risk. Anyone is at risk for being raped, but the majority of victims are women. By the time they graduate, an estimated 1 out of 4 college women will be the victim of attempted rape, and 1 out of 6 will be raped. Most women will be raped by someone they know, a date or acquaintance, and most do not report the crime. Alcohol is a factor in nearly three-quarters of the incidents. Whether raped by a date or a stranger, the victim can suffer long-term traumatic effects.

First-year students are at particular risk for being raped because they are in a new and unfamiliar environment, may not realize the risks, want to fit in, and may even appear to be easy targets. Knowledge is important, but there are also concrete actions you can take to avoid being raped or being accused of raping someone. These are presented here with the assumption that it is women who are being raped, and men who are doing the raping.

Women

1. Know what you want and do not want sexually, and when the issue comes up, communicate it loudly and clearly to a partner.

2. Go to parties or social gatherings with friends, and leave with them. Sexual assaults happen when people get isolated.

3. Avoid being alone with people you don't know very well, such as accepting a ride home with someone you just met or studying alone in your room with a classmate.

4. Trust your gut. If a situation feels uncomfortable in some way, don't take chances. Get out of it even if it means a few minutes of embarrassment.

5. Be alert to unconscious messages you may be sending. While it in no way justifies a man taking advantage of you, be aware that if you dress in a sexy manner, spend the evening drinking together, and then go back to his room, he may think you want something you are not necessarily interested in.

6. Be conscious of how much alcohol you drink, if any. It is easier to make decisions and communicate them when you are sober, and also easier to sense a dangerous situation.

Men

1. Realize that it is never okay to force yourself sexually on someone.

2. Don't assume you know what your date wants. She may want a different degree of intimacy than you do in the same situation. If you're not sure, ask.

3. If you're getting mixed messages, also ask. You have nothing to lose by stopping. If she really wants you, she'll let you know. And if she doesn't, then it's the right decision to stop.

4. Be aware of the effects of alcohol. It makes it more difficult to understand the communication you're receiving, and it is more likely to instigate violent behavior.

5. Remember that rape is legally, morally, and ethically wrong. If you have the slightest doubt about whether what you're doing is right, it's probably not.

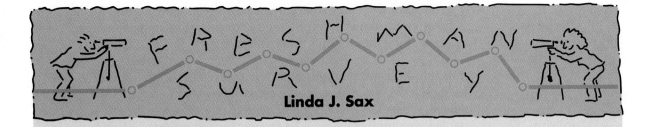

Linda J. Sax

"Date Rape" Unacceptable

As this graph shows, most students do *not* believe that a man is entitled to have sex with a woman just because he feels she has "led him on." Although women are more likely than men to oppose such nonconsensual sex, first-year males have become significantly more likely to oppose it in the six years since the question was first introduced on the CIRP Freshman Survey.

Attitudes on Date Rape, 1988–1993 (percent agreeing "somewhat" or "strongly" that "just because a man feels a woman has 'led him on' does not entitle him to have sex with her")

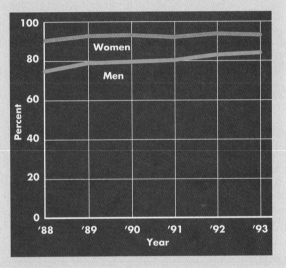

SOURCE: Higher Education Research Institute, UCLA

The following is a list of people or offices that may be available on or near your campus to deal with a sexual assault:

- ► Campus sexual assault coordinator
- ► Local rape crisis center
- ► Campus police department
- ► Counseling center
- ► Student health services
- ► Student affairs professionals
- ► Women's student services office
- ► Residence life staff
- ► Local hospital emergency rooms
- ► Campus chaplains

Regardless of whether a victim chooses to report the rape to the police or get a medical exam, it is very helpful to seek some type of counseling to begin working through this traumatic event.

Perhaps the most important thing to remember about sex is that when it happens in ignorance, in haste, or without regard for the other party involved, it may leave emotional scars that are difficult to erase. On the other hand, when individuals who have genuine feelings for each other can agree on the degree of intimacy and involvement, be knowledgeable and candid about all possible outcomes, take precautions to benefit both partners, and show respect for each other's needs and feelings, sex can be wonderful indeed.

JOURNAL

Reread the comments at the beginning of the chapter about our reasons for discussing sexuality and our promise to be open-minded. Rate us on how well we did. What specific information benefited you the most? How did your class react to the presentation of the material? What do you believe could have been omitted or told in a different way?

SUGGESTIONS FOR FURTHER READING

Boston Women's Health Collective. *The New Our Bodies, Our Selves*. New York: Simon & Schuster, 1984.

Hatcher, Robert, et al. *Sexual Etiquette 101*. Decatur, Ga.: Bridging the Gap Communications, 1993.

Lindquist, Scott. *Before He Takes You Out*. Marietta, Ga.: Vigal Publishers, 1989.

Parrot, Andrea. *Coping with Date Rape and Acquaintance Rape*. New York: Rosen, 1988.

Rathus, Spencer A., and S. Boughn. *AIDS—What Every Student Needs to Know*. Ft. Worth, Tex.: Harcourt Brace Jovanovich, 1993.

Alcohol, Other Drugs, and You

N. Peter Johnson with
University of South Carolina

Preston E. Johnson

I'm sick of hearing how bad it is to drink. You have to loosen up sometimes. So I have a couple of beers before I go to sleep. The way I see it, I'm old enough to make decisions on my own. So what if I drink a few beers every night? What's the big deal?

Writing a piece on alcohol and other drugs for students entering college is hardly an easy task. It's very tempting to come down hard on anyone who uses any form of drugs. For example, I could share with you my beliefs that alcohol is the most dangerous drug, that there is no such thing as "recreational use of drugs," and that even the caffeine in coffee can produce effects that will inhibit your chances for success in college and beyond.

If that's all I wrote, however, no matter how strongly I might believe it, you probably would think, "There's another guy preaching to me like he's my parent." I could hardly blame you. I gave considerable thought to this issue when my own son, Preston, began his college career at Emory University. I decided to write to Preston about my feelings on this subject. As an alcohol and drug educator I felt professionally obligated to let him know all I knew about alcohol and other drugs, yet the parent in me warned me not to overdo it.

When I was in high school, I was an athlete and followed my coaches' advice when they said, "Stay away from women, cigarettes, and booze." However, when I started college at the age of 16, the school I attended had few sports, and none in which I was any good. With no athletic niche for me, I immediately developed a profound interest in girls, cigarettes, and drinking. As a result of this change my freshman grades were so bad that I left college to join the Army. I don't recommend this course of action to anyone. I hope you will be more mature than I was.

After much thought, and reams of drafts that ended up in the trash, I think I finally began to make sense to myself as well as to my son. I began by telling him that, in spite of what we read in the newspapers, college students use drugs far less frequently than young people who do not attend college. Over the past ten years the number of college students using drugs other than alcohol has actually fallen. For instance, in spite of the image projected by "beach 'n' beer" movies, virtually no one takes sedatives such as Quaaludes. The only people you hear saying things like "Duh, like wow man, this is really heavy" either are truly dumb or are smoking marijuana, a topic we shall get to in due time.

However, college students are more prone to heavy alcohol usage than are their noncollege peers. Heavy drinking has been increasing on campus even as it declines among young people not in college. So college students use fewer drugs, but drink more alcohol. Male college students use more drugs and alcohol than female college students, with one exception: More college women than men are smokers.

EXERCISE 23.1   Alcohol and Drug Use on Your Campus

In a small group review the following list of questions, and add three or four of your own.

1. What percentage of students on this campus do you think are problem drinkers?

2. What percentage of students do you think use illegal drugs?

3. What drugs, excluding alcohol, are most popular on your campus?

4. What are the rules pertaining to alcohol and other drugs on your campus?

5. How many students have discipline problems due to alcohol and drug use?

6. What are the consequences of these discipline problems?

7. Why do students use alcohol and other drugs?

8. _____

9. _____

10. _____

11. _____

Now, using these questions, interview people from at least three of the following seven categories and note their answers. Each group member should report at least one interview.

First-year student   Dean of students or person in that office
Upperclass student   Health center staff person
Alcohol/drug educator   Discipline officer
Counseling center staff person

Discuss your findings. How are their answers similar? What would account for any differences in their answers? What did you learn that surprised you about alcohol and drug use on your campus?

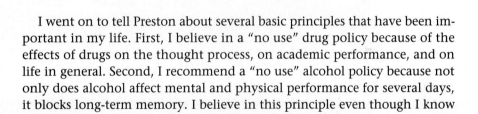

I went on to tell Preston about several basic principles that have been important in my life. First, I believe in a "no use" drug policy because of the effects of drugs on the thought process, on academic performance, and on life in general. Second, I recommend a "no use" alcohol policy because not only does alcohol affect mental and physical performance for several days, it blocks long-term memory. I believe in this principle even though I know that approximately 80 percent of college students drink alcoholic beverages at some time.

I refuse to minimize the consequences of using drugs and alcohol, and I detest the term *responsible drinking*. This phrase sounds suspiciously like something the beer industry coined in order to sell more beer. What it means is, "We know you're going to drink; therefore, we want you to drink responsibly." Perhaps the industry would like you to believe that drinking is inevitable for everyone, yet the truth is that 38 percent of American adults drink one or less drinks per year.

I don't support the term *recreational drug use* either, because there is no such thing. No one actually uses drugs recreationally. The word *recreation* derives from the Latin *recreatio,* meaning "to restore to health." Its use here implies that health is somehow related to drug use, when the exact opposite is true. In general, drug users are less healthy, physically and mentally, than the rest of us.

So, now that I've stated my opinions, let me pass on some further information about specific drugs to help you decide where you stand.

It Doesn't Quite Add Up: Beliefs Versus Behaviors of First-Year Students

In a recent survey of 500 first-year university students, only 1 percent felt they had a problem with alcohol, and only 0.2 percent felt they had a problem with other drugs.

But their answers to other questions suggested a striking lack of awareness of what constitutes a problem with alcohol and other drugs.

The survey asked about alcohol and other drug use, along with related problems that had occurred in the *previous six-month period*. The graphs show the results.

Thirteen percent of the students admitted to seven or more of the risk factor behaviors. Another 27 percent indicated four to six risk factors. Only 23 percent had no risk factors.

How would you explain the discrepancy between the students' beliefs and their behaviors?

Beliefs

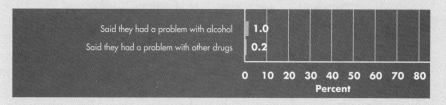

Behaviors

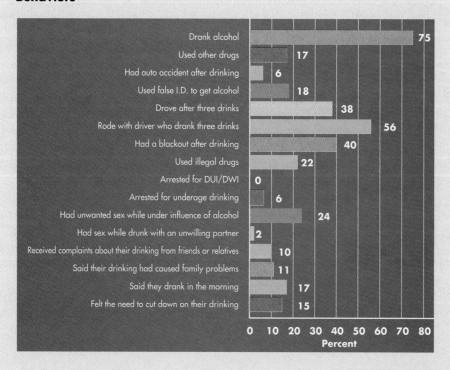

ALCOHOL

Alcohol consumption is the number-one cause of problems for college students. In fact drinking alcohol has become such an expected part of life on many campuses that some consider it to be "normal." Most of us forget or ignore its consequences until forcefully reminded by friends who suffer discipline problems, broken bones, head injuries, automobile accidents, sexual assaults including acquaintance rape, academic failure, near deaths, and death itself. Then in six months we ignore or forget again until still another tragedy strikes.

Many people can paraphrase the 1985 report (widely publicized by the alcohol industry) indicating that moderate drinking had positive health consequences. Fewer people know about other research since then showing that even moderate drinking can negatively affect the heart (enlarging and weakening the ventricles) and skeletal muscles.

Let's talk about alcoholism. Alcoholism is a disease in which a person consistently and continually causes harm to him- or herself or others as a result of drinking. Alcoholics are people who cannot resist drinking frequently or who cannot limit themselves when they do drink. In general terms the alcoholic drinks four or more days per week or has five or more drinks in a row. Six percent of adults in the United States are alcoholics—10 percent of all drinkers in this country.

You or a friend might say, "That definition doesn't apply to me. Everybody I know drinks that way." My answer is, "Birds of a feather flock together." Drinkers tend to hang out with drinkers, while nondrinkers tend to prefer the company of others like themselves.

But what if you drink? Even then, a little knowledge may lessen the damage you can inflict. For example, you should know that the alcohol in beer, wine coolers, wine, and distilled liquors is all the same alcohol. You can become intoxicated, or alcoholic, just as easily from drinking *any* alcoholic beverage.

You should also know that there are ways to reduce the quantity of alcohol you consume per hour. If you tend to gulp drinks, try alternating noncarbonated, nonalcoholic drinks with mixed drinks to keep the alcohol quantity down. Stay away from college drinking games, such as "quarters," "thumper," and "Indian," in which participants must consume large quantities of alcohol in short periods of time. Heavy drinkers frequently begin these games so that their drinking will appear normal. The games require that others become involved; try to be the student who is not enticed. And never drink on an empty stomach; the stomach rapidly absorbs alcohol, especially from carbonated beverages, when empty.

EXERCISE 23.2 Responses to Peer Pressure

Sometimes it's difficult to be the only one in the group not drinking. You may not receive *direct* pressure from others, but more often there is a subtle message that you should drink to "be like everyone else." Write potential responses to these remarks, made in situations in which you choose not to drink.

1. C'mon, you're not gonna be any fun if you don't loosen up and down a couple! _____

_____

2. Are you going to drink that? It's getting (cold/warm). _____

_____

3. Hey—alcohol is *healthy* for you! _____

_____

4. Man, you don't want to be sober all by yourself, do you? _____

_____

5. No, don't give _____ any—(he's/she's) not
   (your name)

drinking tonight! _____

_____

You should also know that the passage of time is the only thing that will sober you up after drinking. The enzymes in your liver process alcohol at a rate of about half a regular drink per hour. Cold showers, coffee, and exercise will not help at all. The joke is that coffee only makes for a more wide-awake drunk, but it really isn't funny.

Just as important is that rate of intoxication depends on age, body weight, gender, and tolerance levels. For example, women and older persons produce higher blood alcohol levels for the same amount of alcohol consumption, even if body weights are the same as those of younger men. Also, because of differences in body fat distribution, a stomach enzyme, and hormones, a woman weighing the same as a man may need only drink 45 percent of what the man drinks to reach the same level of intoxication.

If you play sports, be aware that moderate drinking results in loss of muscle coordination for at least 12–18 hours after consumption. The decreased muscle tone and other effects last for days, long after the alcohol is undetectable in the bloodstream. And since processing alcohol disrupts the liver from its normal process of making fuel for the body, muscles tend to tire faster. For 48 hours or longer you can also expect impaired reaction time, balance, and hand–eye coordination; distorted perception; reduced ability to make smooth, easy movements; decreased strength; increased fatigue; and a host of other problems. Alcohol impairs memory, too; isn't college tough enough as it is?

Drinking and driving is a special problem for college students. Were you aware that the highest automobile accident rates are for persons ages 18–24? This age group also ranks highest in binge drinking and per capita alcohol consumption. Almost 250,000 college students are arrested for driving under the influence (DUI) each year, and 75 percent of first-time DUI offenders will later be diagnosed as alcoholic. The likelihood of alcoholism for second-time DUI offenders is 90 percent. Driving a motor vehicle under the influence of alcohol also costs in many ways: jail time, legal fees (at least $500), and increased insurance costs (up to $1,000). The estimated lifetime cost in 1991 for DUI offenses is $10,000, even if no repeat occurrences take place.

Beer, Wine, or Liquor— Alcohol Is Alcohol

If you drink, know how much alcohol you are consuming. The absolute alcohol content varies according to the type of alcoholic beverage.

► Can of beer (2.3 percent alcohol)	12 oz × .023 =	.28 oz absolute alcohol
► Can of beer (5 percent alcohol)*	12 oz × .05 =	.60 oz absolute alcohol
► Wine cooler (5 percent alcohol)	6 oz × .05 =	.30 oz absolute alcohol
► Glass of wine (12 percent alcohol)	5 oz × .12 =	.60 oz absolute alcohol
► Glass of wine (15 percent alcohol)	5 oz × .15 =	.75 oz absolute alcohol
► MD 20/20 (20 percent alcohol)	6 oz × .20 =	1.20 oz absolute alcohol
► Liquor (80 proof/40 percent alcohol)	1 oz × .40 =	.40 oz absolute alcohol
► Liquor (100 proof/50 percent alcohol)	1 oz × .50 =	.50 oz absolute alcohol
► 151 rum (75.5 percent alcohol)	1 oz × .75 =	.75 oz absolute alcohol

*Alcohol content in some "light" beers is greater than in non-light beers.

Alcoholism should be a special concern for you if alcohol problems have occurred in your immediate family. If a parent, sibling, aunt, uncle, or grandparent has a problem, your likelihood increases. At the end of the chapter is a test that may help you determine whether you have a family problem with alcoholism. People who score above 3 on the test should be particularly careful about drinking or avoid it entirely.

MARIJUANA

I read recently that a custodian at a college campus was busted for possession of marijuana. Seems marijuana is everywhere and everyone is using it, doesn't it? Actually that's not so. Less than 20 percent of college students use marijuana, but about 5 percent of all college students develop pretty serious habits. That's disturbing, because marijuana is a strange drug. When I was in college, the authorities warned us about "killer weed," and since most of us

It Isn't Over Till It's Over

How long do the behavioral effects of marijuana last?

A group of scientists wanted to determine how long after smoking marijuana a person's judgment and performance might still be impaired. To do this, they trained ten experienced, licensed private pilots for 8 hours to perform a simple takeoff and landing procedure on a flight simulator. After this training each pilot smoked a cigarette containing THC, the principal active ingredient in marijuana. Each cigarette contained 19 milligrams of the drug, roughly the same amount a person is likely to smoke in a social setting. After smoking this drug, the pilots tried the landing task again.

The pilots' mean performance on the landing task showed impairment on all variables, including significant impairment in vertical and lateral deviation on approach to landing and distance off center from the runway.*

The pilots reported no awareness of impaired performance.

How long after they had smoked the drug would you guess that the pilots were tested?

a. 3 hours   **c.** 12 hours
b. 6 hours   **d.** 24 hours

(The answer may be found in the footnote on page 386.)

*Jerome A. Yasavage et al., "Carry-Over Effects of Marijuana Intoxification on Aircraft Pilot Performance: A Preliminary Report," *American Journal of Psychiatry* 142, no. 11: 1325–29.

knew it wasn't deadly—at least in the short term—we disregarded everything anyone told us. Actually marijuana has some pretty negative attributes. The ingredient most responsible for the "high" is delta-9-tetrahydrocannabinol, or THC, which is absorbed through the lungs and into the bloodstream immediately. If you detest tobacco smoking for what it does to the body, you should know that smoking marijuana has the same effect on the lungs. In fact it is even more cancer-causing than tobacco, though people generally smoke less of it. In addition, strains of marijuana available today contain higher levels of THC than ever before. For example, sinsemilla reportedly is as much as 15 times stronger than the marijuana of the 1960s and 1970s.

Once in the bloodstream, THC is absorbed by, stored in, and gradually released by fat cells. A single puff of marijuana has a half-life in the body of between three and seven days, depending on the potency and the smoker.

Effects of Marijuana

If you think marijuana isn't really that bad for you, perhaps you should consider the following list of potential adverse effects from chronic use.

- Chronically slowed reaction times
- Decreased tracking capability by the eyes
- Impaired hand–eye coordination
- Altered perception of time (for example, "slow motion" sensations)
- Impairment of depth perception
- Impairment of recent memory
- Increased suggestibility, suspiciousness, and fearfulness
- Apathy, loss of drive, unwillingness or inability to complete tasks, low frustration tolerance, unrealistic thinking, increased shyness, total involvement in the present at the expense of future goals
- Increased number of lung infections
- Increased likelihood of cancer (marijuana contains *ten times* more cancer-causing agents than found in cigarettes)
- Breast enlargement in males

After a period of chronic, heavy use, it can take as long as a month for THC to clear your system. One acquaintance of mine lost a job because marijuana showed up on a drug test even though he was not a user. Rather, for the previous year he had been regularly exposed to the second-hand smoke of a roommate and family members. He had stored up so much THC in his fat cells that it was as if he were smoking marijuana himself.

Recently a student with a very high grade point average asked me to help him stop smoking marijuana. He was about to graduate and was afraid he might be tested for drugs during his preemployment physical. He wanted to stop at least long enough to clear his system. He said he wasn't sure he could stop smoking that long, since it had been several years since he had gone without marijuana. We worked together, and after a month of abstinence, he commented that he could now think and remember much more clearly. The decrease in his thinking abilities had occurred so gradually that he was unaware of it. This can be a major problem for students who need to memorize quantities of information. Recent research shows that the measurable pharmacologic effects of marijuana can last for one full day, and the behavioral effects may last much longer.

COCAINE

Cocaine is a powerful chemical extracted from the leaves of the coca plant. People in the Andes Mountains use coca mixed with a little lime to avoid hunger pangs and to make work at high altitudes go easier. In concentrated form cocaine is a powerful stimulant; it overstimulates the pleasure centers of the brain. The user literally loses touch with even basic biological needs during a cocaine "high." Laboratory animals have been observed to self-

Effects of Cocaine

Cocaine use can lead to a staggering number of physical, mental, and emotional problems, both short- and long-term. Consider the following:

Adverse Effects from the Cocaine "High"

- Accelerated but unfocused thinking, disrupted concentration
- Misjudgment of timing and accuracy
- Misjudgment of physical and mental power
- Jumpiness
- Covered-up pain, increasing the possibility of injury
- Increased aggressiveness and sense of hostility toward others
- Extreme rises in body temperature (heat prostration)
- Heavy sweating, dehydration, and muscle cramping
- Rapid heart rate
- Heart irregularities and heart attack
- Stroke and seizures due to increased blood pressure
- Increased rate and depth of breathing (hyperventilation)
- Visual hallucinations ("coke lights")
- Restlessness and insomnia
- Shakes
- Convulsions
- Mental problems similar to schizophrenia (including hallucinations)
- Loss of appetite
- Cross-problems with alcohol including heavy drinking

Adverse Effects from the Postcocaine "Crash"

- Auto and other accidents from too much alcohol consumption while using cocaine
- Extreme hunger
- Decrease in energy
- Loss of motivation
- Inability to concentrate on specific tasks
- Depression ("coke blues")
- Suicidal thoughts and attempts

Adverse Effects from Chronic Cocaine Use

- Restlessness and inability to consistently study
- Continued insomnia and loss of sleep, leading to an increased use of cocaine and/or alcohol for sleep and other reasons
- Isolation from other people
- Irritability and fear
- Profound depression
- Seizures and convulsions
- Suicidal thoughts and actions
- Feeling that something is crawling under the skin ("coke bugs")
- Extreme hunger and self-induced vomiting in response to overeating

Causes of Death Related to Stimulants Including Cocaine

- Convulsions (seizures)
- Coma (loss of consciousness)
- Heart attack
- Stroke

ANSWER (to question in box on page 384): **d.** The pilots were tested one full day after smoking. At this time they were still clearly impaired in their ability to perform the flight simulation. Yet they were unaware of their impairment or of any continuing effect of the THC on performance, mood, or alertness.

administer cocaine until they die of thirst or starvation, ignoring their needs for food, water, and sex. Cocaine is one of the most addictive drugs known.

The street drug cocaine hydrochloride (what most people call cocaine) is sniffed into the nose. "Crack" is smokable cocaine from which the hydrochloride has been removed. Once the drug is in the bloodstream, both forms produce the same symptoms although the way the drug is delivered (smoked or snorted) causes differences in the immediate severity. Snorting cocaine causes runny noses, and in the long term it can "burn" a hole through the septum of the nose. Smoking crack causes respiratory problems and has destructive effects on the lungs and breathing tubes. Incidentally these same problems occur with methamphetamine, or "ice," its smokable form.

Cocaine produces an intense experience by enhancing certain chemical processes in the brain. For the cocaine user thoughts seem to come more quickly, each of the five senses seems heightened, physical energy seems unlimited, attitude becomes one of unwavering self-assurance, and fatigue and hunger disappear. It is easy to see why some students are attracted to this potent drug.

However, what goes up must come down—and in this case, rather quickly. A cocaine high starts in a few minutes, peaks in 15–20 minutes, and goes away in less than an hour. A crack high peaks within seconds and lasts about a minute. It is this speed of delivery that causes rapid addiction for many people. During the crash the user may feel tired and unmotivated. Mood may swing rapidly to depression and agitation, and the user may feel paranoid and restless and be unable to sleep.

CAFFEINE AND TOBACCO

Many students use lots of caffeine to stay awake while cramming for tests. A much better way to prepare, of course, is to study on a regular basis (see the chapters on developing sound study habits). But if you're in the habit of cramming, you should know that caffeine is often abused by students who would never consider using "real" drugs.

Because it is legal and readily available, many people assume caffeine poses no genuine health risks, but caffeine toxicity can produce serious ill effects. Doses equal to fifty cups of coffee can even kill you. If introduced today, many caffeine products would be restricted by the Food and Drug Administration as too potent for unregulated distribution and consumption.

I haven't said much about tobacco, the number-one killer drug, because few college students smoke. Because more women than men now smoke, the rate of lung cancer in women has surpassed that in men. The easiest time to break an addiction is before it starts. After that it takes courage and willpower, but in the long run it's worth it. I smoked for sixteen years and now regret every minute of it. Now that I've not smoked for another twenty years, I resent people who make me breathe their smoke. The number of reported cancers from passive inhalation continues to go up, and I don't want to be one of the victims.

The best defense against alcohol and drug abuse is information, and there's plenty of it available. You can start by contacting the alcohol and drug program on your campus. Hospitals are another excellent source of information. You can also call the National Clearinghouse on Alcohol and Drug Information at 1-800-729-6686. For cocaine information call 1-800-COCAINE.

College is a valuable time in the lives of each of us fortunate enough to reap its rewards. The more you remember the value of education, the less likely you are to take risks that could devalue that experience. This is why I hope you will think long and hard about what I have said in these few pages. I've tried not to preach to you, and I hope I have succeeded in presenting the facts as objectively as possible. As an alcohol and drug educator, I obviously have strong feelings about alcohol and drug use. As a human being so may you. All I ask is that you consider what I have written, discuss it with people you admire, and make a decision for yourself based on *your own* values, not on the prevailing attitudes of others.

EXERCISE 23.3   Campus Resources

Visit the places on your campus where resources and assistance related to alcohol and other drugs is available. You may find help in these places:

Health center   Counseling center
Student activities office   Drug/alcohol education office
Residence life office   Discipline office
Minister or chaplain's office

Note below the offices you visited, their phone numbers and hours, and the types of resources they offer to students.

Office: _____

Phone: _____ Hours: _____

Resources: _____

Office: _____

Phone: _____ Hours: _____

Resources: _____

Office: _____

Phone: _____ Hours: _____

Resources: _____

EXERCISE 23.4   Michigan Alcoholism Screening Test (MAST)

For each of the following items answer Y for yes or N for no.

_____ 1. Do you feel you are a normal drinker? ("Normal" means you drink less than or as much as most other people and you have not developed recurring trouble while drinking.)

_____ 2. Have you ever awakened the morning after some drinking the night before and found that you could not remember part of the evening?

_____ 3. Do either you, your parents, any other close relatives, your spouse, or any girlfriend or boyfriend ever worry or complain about your drinking?

_____ 4. Can you stop drinking without a struggle after one or two drinks?

_____ 5. Do you feel guilty about your drinking?

_____ 6. Do friends or relatives think you are a normal drinker?

_____ 7. Are you able to stop drinking when you want to?

_____ 8. Have you ever attended a meeting of Alcoholics Anonymous (AA)?

_____ 9. Have you been in physical fights when you have been drinking?

_____ 10. Has your drinking ever created problems between you and either your parents, another relative, your spouse, or any girlfriend or boyfriend?

_____ 11. Has any family member of yours ever gone to anyone for help about your drinking?

_____ 12. Have you ever lost friends because of your drinking?

_____ 13. Have you ever been in trouble at work or at school because of drinking?

_____ 14. Have you ever lost a job because of drinking?

_____ 15. Have you ever neglected your obligations, your schoolwork, your family, or your job for two or more days in a row because you were drinking?

_____ 16. Do you drink before noon fairly often?

_____ 17. Have you ever been told you have liver trouble or cirrhosis?

_____ 18. After heavy drinking, have you ever had severe shaking or heard voices or seen things that really weren't there?

_____ 19. Have you ever gone to anyone for help about your drinking?

_____ 20. Have you ever been in a hospital because of drinking?

_____ 21. Have you ever been a patient in a psychiatric hospital or in a psychiatric ward of a general hospital where drinking was part of the problem that resulted in hospitalization?

_____ 22. Have you ever gone to a psychiatric or mental health clinic or to any doctor, social worker, or clergy for help with any emotional problem where drinking was a part of the problem?

_____ 23. Have you ever been arrested for drunk driving, driving while intoxicated, or driving under the influence of alcoholic beverages or any other drug? (If yes, how many times? _____)

_____ 24. Have you ever been arrested or taken into custody, even for a few hours, because of other drunk behavior, whether due to alcohol or another drug? (If yes, how many times? _____)

Now compute your total score based on the point values listed here for each Y or N answer.

1. N2	5. Y1	9. Y1	13. Y2	17. Y2	21. Y2
2. Y2	6. N2	10. Y2	14. Y2	18. Y2	22. Y2
3. Y1	7. N2	11. Y2	15. Y2	19. Y5	23. Y2*
4. N2	8. Y5	12. Y2	16. Y1	20. Y5	24. Y2*

*Score 2 points for each time.

Compare your total score with the numbers listed below.

0–3 points = probable normal drinker

4 points = borderline score

5–9 points = 80 percent associated with alcoholism

10 or more = 100 percent associated with alcoholism

Regardless of your score, if you have some concerns about your drinking, assistance is available. Make an appointment to talk with someone on your campus who can help. This may be a counselor, alcohol/drug educator, campus physician, minister, or someone else with whom you feel comfortable. Take advantage of the assistance they can provide.

EXERCISE 23.5   Children of Alcoholics Screening Test

Place a Y for yes next to each question that you answer affirmatively.

_____ 1. Have you ever thought that one of your parents had a drinking problem?

_____ 2. Have you ever lost sleep because of a parent's drinking?

_____ 3. Did you ever encourage one of your parents to quit drinking?

_____ 4. Did you ever feel alone, scared, nervous, angry, or frustrated because a parent was not able to stop drinking?

_____ 5. Did you ever argue or fight with a parent when he or she was drinking?

_____ 6. Did you ever threaten to or actually run away from home because of a parent's drinking?

_____ 7. Has a parent ever yelled at or hit you or other family members when drinking?

_____ 8. Have you ever heard your parents fight when one of them was drunk?

_____ 9. Did you ever protect another family member from a parent who was drinking?

_____ 10. Did you ever feel like hiding or emptying a parent's bottle of liquor?

_____ 11. Do any of your thoughts revolve around a problem-drinking parent or do difficulties arise because of his or her drinking?

_____ 12. Did you ever wish that a parent would stop drinking?

_____ 13. Did you ever feel responsible for and guilty about a parent's drinking?

_____ 14. Did you ever fear that your parents would get divorced due to alcohol abuse?

_____ 15. Have you ever withdrawn from and avoided outside activities and friends because of embarrassment and shame over a parent's drinking problem?

_____ 16. Did you ever feel caught in the middle of an argument or fight between a problem-drinking parent and your other parent?

_____ 17. Did you ever feel that you made a parent drink alcohol?

_____ 18. Have you ever felt that a problem-drinking parent did not really love you?

_____ 19. Did you ever resent a parent's drinking?

_____ 20. Have you ever worried about a parent's health because of his or her alcohol use?

_____ 21. Have you ever been blamed for a parent's drinking?

_____ 22. Did you ever think your father was an alcoholic?

_____ 23. Did you ever think your mother was an alcoholic?

_____ 24. Did you ever wish your home could be more like the homes of your friends who did not have a parent with a drinking problem?

_____ 25. Did a parent ever make promises to you that he or she did not keep because of drinking?

_____ 26. Did you ever wish that you could talk to someone who could understand and help with the alcohol-related problems in your family?

_____ 27. Did you ever fight with your brothers and sisters about a parent's drinking?

_____ 28. Did you ever stay away from home to avoid the drinking parent or your other parent's reaction to the drinking?

_____ 29. Have you ever felt sick, cried, or had a "knot" in your stomach after worrying about a parent's drinking?

_____ 30. Did you ever take over any chores or duties at home that were usually done by a parent before he or she developed a drinking problem?

Now compute your score by assigning 1 point for each Y answer, and compare the total with the numbers listed below. (*Note:* This test is *not* nationally standardized.)

0–3 points = probably normal family

4–9 points = indication that a family member *does* have a drinking problem

10 or more points = severe dysfunction

Again, if you are concerned about family alcohol use and/or the effect it has had on you, visit with someone on your campus who is qualified to help.

JOURNAL

You probably found the author of this section very straightforward in saying what he believes. Be equally direct in discussing your views on alcohol and other drugs. In what respects do you agree? In what ways do you disagree? Try writing in response to specific new information you may have gathered from the reading. For instance, what do you make of the study of marijuana use by airplane pilots?

SUGGESTIONS FOR FURTHER READING

Cohen, S. "The Effects of Combined Alcohol/Drug Abuse on Human Behavior." Chapter 1 in *Treatment Research Monograph Series: Drug and Alcohol Abuse—Implications for Treatment.* Washington, D.C.: Department of Health and Human Services, Alcohol, Drug Abuse, and Mental Health Administration, 1981.

Gilbert, R. M. "Caffeine as a Drug of Abuse." In R. J. Gibbins et al., *Research Advances in Alcohol and Drug Problems,* Vol. 3. New York: Wiley, 1976.

Gold, M. S. *800-COCAINE.* New York: Bantam Books, 1984.

———. *Facts About Drugs and Alcohol.* New York: Bantam Books, 1986.

Griffin, T. M. *Paying the Price.* Center City, Minn.: Hazelden Foundation Press, 1985.

Johnson, Peter, ed. *Dictionary of Street Alcohol and Drug Terms,* 4th ed. Upland, PA.: Diane, 1993.

Johnston, L. D., P. M. O'Malley, and J. G. Bachman. *National Trends in Drug Use and Related Factors Among American High School Students and Young Adults, 1975–86.* Publication No. 87-1535. Washington, D.C.: Department of Health and Human Services, 1987.

Kaufman, D. W., L. Rosenberg, S. P. Helmrich, and S. Shapiro. "Alcoholic Beverages and Myocardial Infarction in Young Men." *American Journal of Epidemiology* 121 (1985): 548–54.

Kinney, J., and G. Leaton, eds. *Understanding Alcohol: A Handbook of Alcohol Information,* 3rd ed. St. Louis: Mosby, 1987.

Schwartz, R. H. "Marijuana: An Overview." *Pediatric Clinics of North America,* 34, no. 2: 305–17.

Strauss, R. H., ed. *Drugs and Performance in Sports.* Philadelphia: Saunders, 1987.

Whitfield, C. L., J. E. Davis, and L. R. Barker. "Alcoholism." Chapter 21 in *Principles of Ambulatory Medicine,* 2nd ed. L. R. Barker, J. R. Burton, and P. D. Zieve, eds. Baltimore: Williams and Wilkins, 1987.

▼▼▼▼▼▼▼▼▼▼▼▼▼▼▼▼▼▼▼▼▼▼▼▼▼▼▼▼▼▼▼▼▼▼▼

Glossary / Index

In addition to other terms discussed in the text, this glossary defines terms that you may need to know.

Bachelor's degree the formal name for a four-year college degree. Two major types are the Bachelor of Arts (B.A.) and Bachelor of Science (B.S.). 5

Back-up files, 237

Barzun, Jacques, 27

Biological clock, 78–79

Birth control, 361–64

Block scheduling, 77–78. *See also* **Time management**

Board plan a meal plan that you may have an opportunity to purchase while enrolled as a student, often less expensive than buying meals individually.

Body language, 201–2

Books, in library research, 160–62, 166. *See also* **Reading**

Brainstorming, 196

Bribery, 147

Bromburg, Ingrid, 373

Bulletin. *See* **Catalog**

Business majors/careers, 290, 294

Caffeine, 387

Cahill, Adam, 327

Calculators, 217

Calendar
   academic, 267
   personal, 63–66, 68–71

Campus Wide Information System (CWIS), 242

Career counseling/planning a variety of career-related services such as self-assessment and interest tests, job search workshops, decision-making workshops, and resume workshops, usually offered by counseling, student affairs, or placement offices. 10, 17, 286

Career planning and placement centers, 10, 17, 286

Careers
   aptitudes and, 282–83
   business, 290, 294
   co-curricular activities and, 332
   computer science, 289
   computers and, 229
   education, income, and, 12–14
   engineering, 223, 289
   health-related, 290
   interests and, 280–81
   life goals and, 284
   majors and, 13, 278–80, 297
   math/science, 220–23, 295
   minority students and, 19
   personality characteristics and, 283, 287–93
   planning for, 279–80
   skills and, 281–82
   teaching, 296
   work values and, 284–86

Carrel a study room or numbered desk and chair in the college library, sometimes assigned to individual faculty or students.

Catalog the official publication of the institution containing information about its regulations, requirements, and procedures, as well as opportunities for growth as a college student. It includes general information, admissions information, general academic regulations, general nonacademic information, financial aid and scholarship information, and academic programs. Catalogs usually include an academic calendar. In Canada the catalog is called a calendar.
   college, 264–67
   library collection, 160–62, 167, 228

Caucus group, 321

Cause and effect, 177

Categorizing, of ideas, 141

CD-ROM, 152

Cervical cap, 363

Champagne, David, 89

Chancellor title given to a high academic officer at some colleges and universities, usually the chief executive officer of a campus or a collection of campuses.

Chaplains, 17

Children of Alcoholics Screening Test, 390–91

Chinese students, 128

Chlamydia, 365–66

Citing, of sources, 144–47, 156

Class standing the standing of an individual student in relation to completion of a four-year undergraduate program, usually based on the number of courses or credits completed toward the degree. A freshman is working to complete the first one-fourth of college work. A sophomore is in the second fourth. A junior has passed the halfway point, and a senior has three-fourths of the requirements for graduation completed. This practice applies to students on the quarter and semester systems in four-year undergraduate programs. *See also* **Quarter system** and **Semester system**

Classes. *See* **Courses**

CLEP College Level Examination Program. A series of tests to demonstrate proficiency in various college subjects. Passing the test earns credit for certain college courses. CLEP subject exams cover individual courses, such as Introductory Psychology; CLEP general exams incorporate several courses, such as the one for social studies. Some colleges will accept CLEP subject exams, but not general exams. CLEP tests are usually administered through the college testing office. Information may be available from the admissions office and/or an advisor.

Clerical ability, 283

Clubs. *See* **Organizations, college**

Cocaine, 385–87

Co-curricular activities campus student activities provided by organizations, clubs, and so on, independent of a school's formal academic program. 10–11, 330
   discovering, 333–34
   success in, 334–35
   value of, 330–33

Coeducational including both men and women in an educational program. 6

Cognate courses apart from but related to a student's major and approved by his or her advisor. Such courses are required for graduation at many colleges. Cognates are junior- and senior-level courses. Colleges that don't require a cognate may require a minor. *See also* **Minor**

Coitus interruptus, 363

Cole, Johnetta, 41

Collaborative learning style, 84

College
   attendance rates, 4–5
   benefits of, 5, 14
   catalogs, 264–67
   as challenge to personal values, 305–9
   cost of, 266
   high school versus, 26–27, 46–47, 48, 60, 216
   keys to success in, 8–12
   reasons for attending, 2–3, 13
   reasons for choosing, 302–3
   support services, 9, 10–11, 17, 18, 375–76
   value of, 12–14

College Readjustment Rating Scale, 347–48

Commencement graduation. A ceremony in which colleges award degrees to graduating students. Some schools hold two or three commencements annually, but the largest ones are held in May or early June.

Common sense, 255–56, 261

Communication
   interpersonal, 337–38, 340–42
   with self, 337
   with sex partners, 364, 371–72
   with teachers, 9, 28, 132, 243

Community college a two-year college; may also be known as a junior college or technical school. These colleges most often award associate degrees; technical colleges may offer other types of degrees or certificates as well. 4–5, 271

Community service, 335

Commuter students students who live off campus and have to commute, or travel, to campus each day. Includes about 80 percent of all U.S. college students today.

handling of distractions by, 73

numbers of, 21

problems of, 7

services for, 17

survival kits for, 351

telephone directories for, 79–80

time management for, 75–79

Comparison and contrast, 176–77

Competitive learning style, 84, 85

Comprehensive examination some schools use this term to describe final exams, which are given during the last days of the term. The word *comprehensive* means that all material covered during the term may be included on the exam. Graduate students may also take comprehensive exams covering information learned in all courses to earn the master's or doctoral degree.

Computation skills quantitative, or mathematical, skills.

Computer science careers, 289

Computers

accessing, 234

accessing library resources with, 152, 162, 228, 239

approaches to, 231–33

E-mail, 238, 243–44

ethical and legal issues, 245–46

help with, 230, 232–33, 235

keyboarding, 234

preventing disasters, 236–37

rates of using, 230

software for, 238–40

Condoms, 362, 363, 370–72

Conflict, 342

Continuing education programs that enable the nontraditional college student to take classes without having to be admitted as a degree candidate. While continuing education students may take college courses for credit, some colleges have established noncredit learning programs under this name.

Contraception, 361–64

Contraceptive sponge, 363

Conventional personality type, 288, 291

Cooper, James Fenimore, 145–46

Cooperative education programs that provide an opportunity to work in academic major-related settings off campus in public and private agencies, as well as in business and industry, either by parallel scheduling (going to school part-time and working part-time) or by alternate scheduling (staying out of school for an academic term and working full-time).

Core courses/distribution requirements/basic requirements/general education a broad range of courses that a college may require mainly in the freshman and sophomore years, which introduce the student to a wide variety of subjects. *See also* **Prerequisite**

Corey, Gerald, 302

Corey, Marianne Schneider, 302

Counseling a wide variety of services to which students are entitled based on their payment of tuition. Most campuses provide confidential professional counseling and referral services in numerous different offices, including admissions, financial aid, residence halls, career planning, placement, veterans' affairs, study skills, academic advising, and counseling. 9, 375–76. *See also* **Academic advising**

Counseling centers, 17, 354

Course number different colleges number their courses in different ways. Undergraduate courses are often numbered at the 100 level through at least the 400 level. Graduate-level courses carry higher numbers. The 100-level courses are usually survey courses that introduce a subject and must be completed before you can take upper-level courses in that subject.

Courses. *See also* **Majors**

attendance and participation in, 10, 11, 26–27, 28, 269

block scheduling of, 77–78

computer literacy, 233

evaluations of, 9, 32

missing, 132

outlines or syllabi, 65

review, 10

withdrawing from, 150, 267

Crack cocaine, 387

Credit hour. *See* **Quarter hour**

Critical thinking careful observation of a problem or phenomenon followed by thoughtful, organized analysis resulting in a logical, reasoned response. 9, 248

common sense in, 255–56, 261

development of, 248–51, 261

experiences and, 256–57, 261

experts and, 258–59, 261

references and, 259–60, 261

Cuban-American students, 324

Cultural pluralism a concept of the integration of various cultures into a larger society that envisions continuing individual adherence to and general respect for separate cultural traditions. 318–20, 326

Culture, 317

Curriculum all courses required for a degree. Some colleges refer to all courses in the catalog as the curriculum, and many schools provide students with curriculum outlines or curriculum check-sheets in addition to the catalog. These check-sheets show what courses you must take and may indicate the order in which you must take them. That order is called "course sequencing."

Daily schedule, 9, 70–72

Database a computer application program for categorizing, storing, and manipulating large amounts of data. 239

Date rape, 373–75. *See* **Acquaintance rape**

Dates, college catalog and, 265, 267

Dean an upper-level college administrator who heads an academic department, college, or other program. A dean can grant exceptions to academic policy. Other types of deans are executives who may or may not work directly with students, although most work in student services. Some deans may have associate or assistant deans to help them.

Dean's list a list of students making high grades.

Deficiency lack of completion of a course that is required for entrance to a program or for graduation. Also, sometimes a low grade average that causes a school to prevent a student from continuing a course of study.

Degree audit, 264

Degree program the curriculum to earn a degree in a specific field.

Degrees. *See also* **Major**

offered, 267

requirements, 264, 265

Demonstrated financial need the eligibility for financial aid you are determined to have based on need; most commonly determined through the federal needs analysis system (the congressional methodology).

Department a college is often organized into academic departments. For example, a group of history faculty will develop a

Department (continued)
curriculum for students studying history. The history department will offer all history courses for every student at the school, including history majors.

Dependent learning style, 84

Depo-Provera, 362

Descriptive statement, 341

Desmond, David, 76

Diagram, for problem solving, 210

Diaphragm, 362–63

Directories, commuter telephone, 42

Dismissal at most schools dismissal means the same thing as suspension, and means you are ineligible to return to school for academic or disciplinary reasons. College catalogs explain the circumstances for dismissal. Dismissal or suspension usually is noted on your official record or transcript, and the requirements to reenter college will vary. *See also* **Leave of absence** and **Probation**

Dissertation an extended piece of writing (often book-length) that is required of a student seeking a doctoral degree or Ph.D. in most fields. Typically the dissertation must embody original research and takes several years to write. *See also* **Graduate student**

Distractions, handling, 73–74, 75

Diversity a reference to the growing variety of college student and faculty bodies, which include men, women, minorities, foreign students, and other groups that have been underrepresented on college campuses in the past.
attitude scale, 317
of campus culture, 322–23
cultural pluralism and, 318–20
personal values and, 305–7, 309

Doctoral degree the highest degree awarded by a university. Requires additional years of study beyond the bachelor's and/or master's degrees. Most professors have a Ph.D. (doctor of philosophy); other types, including the M.D. (medical doctor) and J.D. (doctor of jurisprudence), also require extensive study.

Dormitories. *See* **Residence hall**

Double-up schedule, 78

Downloading, 243

Drafting, 184. *See also* **Writing**

Drinking, 378, 381–83

Driving under the influence (DUI), 382

Drop most colleges allow students to drop (or quit) a course without penalty during specified periods of time. Dropping a course can be dangerous if you don't know the proper procedures, since you'll need to complete certain forms and obtain official signatures. If you're receiving financial aid, your status may change if you drop a course.

Drop-out students, 5, 268

Drugs, 378, 379
alcohol, 381–83
caffeine, 387
cocaine, 385–87
marijuana, 383–85
tobacco, 387

Drunk driving, 382

DUI/DWI police acronyms for driving under the influence of alcohol and driving while intoxicated.

Economy, student concerns about, 13

Editing, 184–86

Education, college
costs of, 266
liberal arts, 37–42, 294
necessity of, 5
value of, 12–14

Education revolution, 38

Einstein, Albert, 34

Electives an elective is a course you may select from an academic area of interest to you. The course will not apply toward your core, major, or minor/cognate requirements. Each college determines the number of electives you may take, and you may take them at any time.

E-mail electronic mail. Various systems by which computers are linked so that personal computers can be used to send and receive messages and information. 238, 243–44

Emergencies, 132

Emotion, in arguments, 250, 254

Empathy, 52–53, 341

Employment. *See also* **Careers**
college education and, 13–14
full-time course load and, 9
liberal arts education and, 41–42

Encyclopedias
general, 158–59
subject, 159–60

Engel, Elliot, 33–34

Engineering careers, 289

Enlightenment, 37

Entering students. *See* **First-year students**

Enterprising personality type, 288, 291

Essay tests
key task words and, 130, 135–38
planning for, 126
principles for taking, 133–35
studying for, 129–32

super recall columns and mind maps for, 130–32
time management on, 127, 133–34, 138–39

Ethnic groups, 317

Evaluation of courses. *See* **Validation of credits**

Examinations. *See* **Tests**

Exchange program an arrangement for attending another college or university for a specific time period at the same cost and for the same credits as at your own institution.

Exercise, 72, 350

Experience
critical thinking and, 256–57, 261
learning from, 55–56

Experts, critical thinking and, 258–59, 261

Explanation an argument that relies mainly on a careful process of reasoning and statements of facts, as opposed to emotional appeal. 179, 248–51, 254, 261

Extracurricular. *See* **Co-curricular**

Extroverted learning style, 85, 88, 89

Fabrication a form of academic misconduct that involves intentionally inventing information or results in the course of academic work. 147

Factual learning style, 83

Faculty the teachers at a college.

Fallacy any one of several erroneous patterns of thinking or arguing; for example, the fallacy called "hasty generalization" occurs when a person assumes that if one member of a group behaves badly, then all members of the group will also behave in that way.

Family emergencies, 132

Family life
effect of college education on, 14
of returning students, 11

Fantasizing, 351

FAQ in computing, a frequently asked question. 235

Feeling learning style, 85, 88, 89, 92

Feelings, expressing and acknowledging, 341–42

Fees charges that a student may have to pay in addition to tuition. Fees may be charged for housing, health care, labs, parking, and so on. Most college catalogs list fees and say when they are due. *See also* **Tuition**

Female condom, 363

Ficklen, Anne, 146

Fighting fair, 342

Fight-or-flight response, 346–47

Figler, Howard, 286

Files
for catalogs and academic documents, 264
computer, 237

Final exam a test administered at the end of most courses, usually written and often covering the entire content of the course.

Financial aid student scholarships, grants, and loans. Some forms of financial aid are gifts, but others are loans that must be repaid with interest. Some aid is offered only to new freshmen while other sources of financial aid are available to all students. To determine your eligibility for any aid, see your financial aid counselor. The application process for financial aid for a fall semester usually begins during the preceding January. 5

Financial aid and scholarship centers, 17

Financial information, 266

Fine arts the range of academic fields or disciplines including mainly the study of art, music, dance, and theater. 38, 155, 160

First-year students
alcohol, drugs, and, 380
journals of, 20
liberal arts and, 36, 40–41
problems of, 6–7, 46
rape and, 374
reading attention span of, 112, 114
reasons for attending college, 13
self-esteem of, 51
sex and, 360–61
values of, 304, 307, 310
word processing and, 240

Flaming, 243–44

Flashcards, 141

Flexibility, reading and, 122

Forgetting
note-taking and, 101–2
recitation and, 106–7

Forgetting curves, 101, 102

Frame of reference, 340–41

Fraternity. *See* Greeks

Freedom
academic, 30–31
new-found, dealing with, 47–48

Friendship, 10. *See also* **Peers**

Full-time student students enrolled for a specified number of hours, such as 12 semester hours or more. At most schools, part-time students receive the same benefits as full-time students. At others part-time students may receive limited benefits.

Gaffin, Adam, 152

Gender-balanced curriculum a curriculum that includes information about women equivalent to the quality and quantity of information about men.

Gender referencing attributing occupational, personality, or other characteristics to individuals of a specific gender. For example, taken by itself, the statement that "a nurse receives her training" seems to imply that nurses must be female.

General education requirements, 38–39

General encyclopedias, 158–59, 165–66

Genital warts, 366–67

Gift-assistance any type of financial aid that does not have to be repaid.

Glenwick, David, 76

Goals
grades and, 149
life, 284–86, 304
in math/science courses, 218
realistic, 12, 150
short- and long-term, 16–20

Gonorrhea, 365, 366

Grade point average (GPA) sometimes called the cumulative average, grade point ratio (GPR), or quality point average (QPA). Most colleges base grades on a four-point scale, with points assigned to each grade (A = 4, B = 3, C = 2, D = 1, F = 0). To compute your GPA for one term, you need only complete three simple mathematical steps: multiply, add, divide. *Multiply* the number of points representing the grade you receive for each course by the number of credit hours for the course. *Add* the points for all courses to determine the total number of points you've earned for the term. *Divide* the total points by the number of credit hours you attempted that term. The result will be your GPA. Some colleges complicate this with a three-point system or by using grades in addition to A through F. College catalogs explain the system at individual schools.

Grades or **grading system** most schools use the A–F system. A is the highest grade and F means failure. A–D are passing grades for which you will earn points and credits. If you transfer colleges, however, the D grades may not transfer. Most colleges require a minimum 2.0 GPA, or C average, for graduation; in addition, you might lose financial aid, housing, and other benefits when your GPA falls below a certain level.

Bad grades and low GPAs also may lead to dismissal or suspension. Some schools have pass/fail grades (P/F or S/U) and an incomplete grade (I), the latter representing work not completed during the term it was taken. 126
grading systems, 266
high school versus college, 26–27
minority students and, 18
overestimating importance of, 149
realistic goals for, 150
writing for, 185

Graduate student a person who has earned at least a bachelor's degree (B.A. or B.S.) and is enrolled in a program granting a master's degree (M.A. or M.S.), a Ph.D., or other graduate degree, for example, in law or medicine.

Graduation, 41

Graduation check, 264

Grants a type of financial assistance that does not have to be repaid.

Graphics software, 239

Grasha, Tony, 84

Grasha-Riechmann instrument, 84

Greeks fraternities or sororities whose names are based on Greek letters.

Griswold, A. Whitney, 37

Groups. *See also* **Organizations, college; study groups**
caucus, 321
writing in, 186

Guidance counselors, 97

GUIDE checklist, 194–99

Hartel, William, 12

Headings, subject, 162

Health. *See also* **Drugs; sex; stress**
college education and, 14
family emergencies, 132
importance of, 11

Health enrichment services, 17

Health-related majors/careers, 223, 290

Hepatitis, 365, 367

Herpes, 365, 366

High school, college versus, 26–27, 46–47, 48, 60, 216

Higher education any college courses you take or any degree you earn after completing high school (secondary education). Also called postsecondary education.

Hispanic-American students, 128, 324, 367

HIV/AIDS, 365, 367–69, 370–71

Hobbies, 353

Hogan, Craig, 89

Hogan/Champagne Personal Style Indicator, 97

Holistic development, 268

Holland, John, 287
Holland personality characteristics, 287–93
Holmes and Rahe's Life Events Scale, 348
Homosexual students, 339
Honesty, in relationships, 337–38
Honor codes, 143, 144
Honors most colleges recognize good grades in the form of academic honors. Dean's list is the most common award. Honors are also awarded at graduation to superior students, and the following Latin words are used: *cum laude* (with praise), *magna cum laude* (with great praise), and *summa cum laude* (with highest praise).
Hours credits. In general, if you enroll for 15 hours this term and pass all five of your 3-hour courses, you'll earn fifteen credits.
Housing centers, 17
Hug therapy, 352
Human papillomavirus (HPV), 366–67
Humanities the range of academic fields or disciplines including mainly the study of literature, foreign languages, history, philosophy, and religion. 38, 155, 160, 163, 294

Ideas
    main, 103–4, 106, 115–16, 196–97
    plagiarism and referencing of, 146–47, 156
Income, education, careers, and, 12–14
Incomplete. *See* Grades or Grading system
Independent learning style, 84, 85
Independent study a course in which you complete the requirements on your own time, under the direction of a professor, and outside a classroom setting.
Indexes. *See* Periodical indexes
Inductive reasoning, 208
Information age, 152, 164
Information superhighway, 152, 229, 235, 242
Information technology, 152, 229, 232. *See also* Computers
Institutional purpose, 266, 311
Instructor. *See* Professor
Intellectual values, changing, 309–12
Interests assessment, 280–81
Internet a worldwide system of telecommunication connections and procedures that lets computer users exchange messages and information via computer. 152, 229, 235, 242
Internship an arrangement that permits students to work and

receive college credit usually in their major. Internships are required for graduation in some fields, such as psychology, nursing, and medicine.
Interpersonal communication, 33–38, 340–42
Intrauterine device (IUD), 362
Introverted learning style, 85, 88, 89
Intuitive learning style, 85, 88, 89, 92
Intuitive teaching style, 93–94
Investigative learning style, 287, 291
Involvement, student. *See* **Co-curricular activities; organizations, college**

Jessel, George, 190
Jobs. *See* **Careers; employment**
Journals, 20, 163
Judging learning style, 85, 88
Jung, Carl, 85
Junior. *See* **Class standing**
Junior college. *See* **Community college**

Keyboarding, 234
Keyword searching, 162
Kolb Learning Style Inventory, 97

Labs
    computer, 233
    math, 219
Language usage aptitude, 283
Laughter, 353
Learning
    forgetting and, 101–2
    maximizing in lectures, 101–9
    process for, 174
    service, 39, 335
    stress relief and, 346
Learning styles, 9, 82–83
    classroom behavior and, 84–85
    developing other, 92
    formal assessment of, 84–90, 97
    informal assessment of, 83–84
    personality preferences as, 85–89
    study groups and, 90–91
    teaching styles and, 91–97
Leave of absence an arrangement that allows a student in good academic standing to leave the school for one or more terms, with the assurance that he or she will be readmitted later to continue studying.
Lecturer. *See* **Professor**
Lectures, 100–101
    maximizing learning from, 108–9
    note-taking after, 106–7
    note-taking during, 103–4
    preparing for, 102–3
Legal services, 17
Legitimacy of feelings, 341
Levinson, Daniel, 32

Liberal arts a curriculum of studies based on the Western concept of education as a balance of fine arts, humanities, and the natural and social sciences.
Liberal arts education
    curriculum for, 38–39
    defining, 37–38
    value of, 41–42, 294
Librarians
    dealing with, 197–98
    reference, 153
Library of Congress Subject Headings (LCSH) a set of reference volumes in the library that defines standard headings used in classifying books and articles by subject. 161
Library research
    books, 160–62, 167
    catalogs, 160–62, 167
    evaluating sources, 164
    general encyclopedias, 158–59, 165–66
    indexes, 162–64
    periodical indexes, 162–64, 168–69
    subject encyclopedias, 159–60, 166
    terminology, 169–71
    tips for, 156
    topic selection and clarification, 154–57
Life events theory of stress, 347–48
Life goals, 284–86, 304
Light, Richard, 269
Lipkin, Harry, 223
Listening, active, 104, 108–9, 341
Listserv a telecommunications function of computers that automatically distributes a message from one computer to several other computers.
Lying, 143, 144

Magazine indexes, 163, 168
Main ideas
    in lectures, 103–4, 106
    in oral presentations, 196–97
    in textbooks, 115–16
Major an undergraduate student's field of specialization in college.
    business, 290, 294
    careers and, 13, 278–80, 297
    computer science, 289
    computers and, 229
    engineering, 223, 289
    health-related, 291
    humanities, 294
    math/science, 220–24, 295
    selecting, 296–97
Mamet, David, 24, 25, 34
Marginalia, in reading assignments, 115–16
Marijuana, 383–85
Marking, of reading assignments, 115–20
Massages, 350

Pets, 353
Physical education centers, 17
Physical sciences. *See* **Natural sciences**
Physically challenged student services, 17
Placement office a campus office that helps students investigate and obtain employment after graduation.
Placement test a test that shows the level of a student's preparedness in entering a sequence of related courses at some specific level.
Plagiarism a form of academic misconduct that involves presenting another's ideas, words, or opinions as one's own. 144–47, 156
Planning
  for lectures, 102–3
  reading, 113–15
  for tests, 127
Poetry forgetting curve, 102
Political views, 306, 307, 310
Polya, G., 208–9
Portfolio building building a list or resume of skills, contacts, experiences, and credentials to present to potential employers.
Positive thinking, 49–50
Practicum like an internship, part of an academic course or program that gives a student practical experience related to some form of training. Usually shorter in duration and narrower in scope than an internship.
Prayer, 352
Précis (pronounced "pray-see") a written summary of a longer document. 123–24
Prejudice a preconceived judgment or opinion; for example, prejudgment of a person based solely on his or her ethnic or racial background. 325
PREP formula, 203–4
Preregistration a system (often computer-assisted) by which colleges try to simplify the process of signing up for courses. Preregistration usually occurs in the middle of the term prior to the one you're registering for. Preregistration gives students a greater chance of getting into the courses and sections they ask for.
Prerequisite a course or courses that must be completed as a condition for taking another course. Catalogs state prerequisites. A GPA or class standing may constitute a prerequisite for certain courses.
Presentation software, 239

Priorities, setting, 61–62
Private writing, 174–75, 181
Prizing, of values, 300
Probation a warning that you are not making satisfactory academic progress toward your degree or have violated certain standards of acceptable personal behavior. Probation is followed by suspension/dismissal unless the situation is corrected.
Problem-solving, 208
  four-step approach to, 208–9
  in math and science, 216–20
  strategies for, 210–15
Procrastination, 75, 112–13, 240
Professional degree a degree awarded for study in fields such as business, journalism, pharmacology, nursing, or one of the sciences where what you learn is directly linked to actual work in the career field.
Professor college teachers are ranked as teaching assistant, lecturer, instructor, or professor. Professor is the highest rank and includes three levels: assistant professor, associate professor, and (full) professor. When in doubt how to address a college teacher, say "professor." While many professors have earned a doctoral degree, this is not a rigid requirement for holding professorial rank.
Proficiency exam a test that measures whether a student has reached a certain level of knowledge. Such exams may allow you to exempt, with or without credit, certain lower-level courses. Math and foreign language departments often use proficiency exams.
Prose forgetting curve, 120
Public speaking
  anxiety and, 190, 191, 192
  audience analysis and, 193
  basics of, 191
  body language and, 201–2
  clarifying objectives in, 193
  handling mistakes, 204–5
  impromptu, 202–4
  organizing information for, 194–95
  practicing, 200–201
  visual aids in, 199–200
  voice and, 202
Public writing, 174, 179–86
Puerto Rican students, 324

Qualifiers, 139, 141
Quantitative studies the academic subjects that create systems for describing the physical world or human behavior in abstract or mathematical terms. They include

mathematics, statistics, and computer science.
Quarter hour a unit of credit given at colleges whose terms are called quarters, which last approximately ten weeks. *See also* **Semester hour**
Quarter system a college scheduling system of four terms, or quarters: fall, winter, spring, and summer. If you attend full-time and plan to finish in four years without attending summer school, you'll take courses for twelve quarters. *See also* **Semester system**

Race, 317
Racism discriminatory or differential treatment of individuals based on race. 325
Rahe, R. H., 348
Rape, 373–75
Reading
  assessing attention span, 113
  fifteen pages in less than an hour, 121
  flexibility, and different types, 122
  before lectures, 102–3
  marking assignments, 115–20
  planned approach to, 113–16, 121–22
  problems with, 112–13
  reviewing and reciting assignments, 121–22
  writing précis and, 123–24
Realistic personality type, 287, 291
Recall column, 104–5, 106, 116, 129
Recitation
  notes and, 106–7
  reading and, 121–22
  tests and, 127–28, 129
Record-keeping, 264
Reference any source of published information used in support of an argument.
Reference librarian, 153, 157–58
References, 259–60, 261
Referencing, of sources, 144–47, 156
Registrar the college administrator who maintains student transcripts and directs the registration process. When faculty submit final grades, the registrar posts them to your transcript and mails you a copy.
Registration the act of scheduling classes for each term. *See also* **Preregistration**
Regulations. *See* **Academic honesty**
Reinstatement or **Readmission** a return to college following suspension or a leave of absence; you must apply for reinstatement or readmission. In some cases, you'll be readmitted with no

restrictions. If your GPA is low, you may be readmitted on probation.

Residence hall   on-campus student housing provided by the school. Formerly called a dormitory.

Residency   state-supported colleges and universities charge a higher tuition to students who do not reside (maintain residence) year round in the same state and who are not considered legal residents of that state. If you live in the same state in which you attend college, you have residency in that state and are eligible for in-state tuition, provided you meet other specific requirements of your school.

Resident advisor or **Resident assistant (RA)**   an undergraduate or graduate student who lives in a residence hall and works with students to provide personal help and assistance; manage and facilitate small groups; facilitate social, recreational, and educational programs; provide information or act as a referral source to appropriate university or community offices and agencies; and interpret and enforce university rules and regulations.

Returning student   a student for whom several or many years have elapsed between his or her previous education and the start or continuation of a college program. Also called nontraditional student or adult student. 5

ROTC   Reserve Officers Training Corps. A curriculum in some high schools and colleges related to military training.

Sabbatical   a period of paid or semi-paid release time awarded every six or seven years to professors, who are expected, during this period (either one-half or one full year), to make a contribution to their continuing professional development.

Schedule of classes. *See* **Master schedule**

Scholarship   a financial award made for academic achievement.

Sections   different classes offered for a single course during the same term. For example, a large college might offer fifty sections of freshman English. Depending on the section you register for, you may have a different teacher, different textbook, and different meeting time than students in other sections of the same course.

Self-assessment. *See* **Assessment, student**

Self-help assistance   any type of financial aid for which you must do something in return—usually work or repayment.

Semester hour   the unit of credit you earn for course work that takes a semester to complete. Many college courses carry three credits, or semester hours.

Semester system   as opposed to the quarter system, a semester system consists of a fall semester, a spring semester, and (usually optional) summer school.

Seminar   a class containing fewer students than a lecture class (usually a small number), in which the teacher leads discussions and all students participate.

Senior. *See* **Class standing**

Service learning   a college program that recognizes and in some cases may give college credit for learning achieved through voluntary service to others. 39, 335

Sexism   discriminatory or differential treatment of individuals based on sex.

Sexual harassment   behaviors such as unwelcome sexual advances, requests for sexual favors, or demeaning sexist remarks that affect or become a condition of an individual's employment or educational status or that create an atmosphere interfering with an individual's academic or work performance.

Social sciences   the range of academic disciplines including mainly the scientific study of people and society, including such fields as sociology, psychology, and economics. 38, 155, 160, 163

Sophomore. *See* **Class standing**

Sorority. *See* **Greeks**

Special student   in most colleges this is a student who has not matriculated (has not been accepted into a degree program). A special student may have one degree, but may wish to continue his or her education by selecting courses without regard to a degree program. Military personnel are often admitted as special students. Special students may be exempted from certain prerequisites, but they don't receive financial aid or other benefits enjoyed by full-time students.

Spreadsheet a computer application program used mainly for budgeting, financial planning, and other tasks requiring calculations based on lists of numerical information. 238

Standardized tests, 19

Statistics, 197

STD sexually transmitted disease (AIDS, syphilis, gonorrhea, etc.). 360, 361
  chlamydia, 365–66
  gonorrhea, 365, 366
  hepatitis, 365, 367
  herpes, 365, 366
  HIV/AIDS, 365, 367–69, 370–71
  human papillomavirus (HPV), 366–67
  protection against, 362–63, 369–71
  risk factors for, 364–65

Sterilization, 362

Stress, 346
  assessing levels of, 347–48
  co-curricular activities and, 332
  management of, 11, 350–56
  mental relief of, 350–51
  mind/body relief of, 352–53
  physical relief of, 350
  relaxation and, 350, 353, 354
  returning students and, 10
  signs and symptoms of, 346–47
  skill development as relief of, 353
  sources of, 347–49
  spiritual relief of, 352

Stretching, 350

Structure, in writing, 181–83

Student union a campus building devoted to student co-curricular organizations, activities, stores, dining facilities, and various support services. Sometimes called the student center.

Students. *See also* **Individual types**
  expectations of, by teachers, 26
  fears and problems of, 6–7
  goals of, 16–20, 149–50, 218, 284–86, 304
  learning styles of, 9, 82–97
  obligations of, 28
  persistence factors of, 8–12
  self-disclosure of, 340
  self-knowledge of, 337
  self-management of, 150, 360–61
  support networks for, 10, 355
  support services for, 9, 10–11, 17–18, 375–76
  value of college for, 12–14

Study abroad a program that lets you attend a college or university in another country for a specific time, earning credit that will apply toward graduation requirements at your institution.

Study groups
  forming, 128–29
  importance of, 9, 225

learning styles and, 90–91
  writing in, 186

Studying
  assessing skills, 15
  throughout courses, 127–28
  for essay exams, 129–32
  for lectures, 102–3
  for multiple-choice tests, 139
  procrastination and, 75, 112–13
  reducing distractions, 73–74, 75

Styles. *See* **Learning styles; teaching styles**

Subject encyclopedias, 159–60, 166

Subject headings, 162

Subject periodical indexes, 163, 168–69

Success, keys to college, 8–12

Sundt, Melora, 148

Super recall columns, 130–32

Support networks, 10, 355

Support services. *See also* **Academic advising**
  counseling, 9, 375–76
  for minority students, 18
  for returning students, 10–11
  typical, 17

Survival kits, for commuters, 351

Suspension. *See* **Dismissal**

Syllabus one or more pages of class requirements that an instructor gives out on the first day of a course. The syllabus acts as a course outline, telling when you must complete assignments, readings, and so on. 65

Talking heads, 260

Task words, 130, 135–38

Teachers
  academic freedom and, 30–31
  bad, 32
  challenge of, 25
  choosing, 9, 31–32, 218
  communication with, 9, 28, 132, 243
  duties and tasks of, 27
  effective, characteristics, 29–30, 31, 33–34
  empathizing with, 52–53
  expectations of students by, 26
  high school versus college, 26–27, 46–47, 218
  interviewing, 31
  maximizing relationships with, 28, 29–30

Teaching styles
  assessing, 95–97
  clues to, 92–94
  exam preparation and, 94–97

Technical (tech) schools technical education systems established by many states that offer specialized two-year degrees and certificates. While these schools may be accredited, course work may be so technically oriented that it won't

transfer to a bachelor's degree program. If you plan to attend a tech school, be certain to ask about the "college parallel curriculum." *See also* **Associate degree**

Tehranian, Majid, 152

Telephone directories, commuter, 79–80

Tendering of information a form of academic misconduct that involves giving work or exam answers to another student to copy. 147

Tenure in higher education, the securement of a lifetime faculty position after a specified period of time and the meeting of specified requirements. Tenure is tantamount to a lifetime guarantee of employment that can be terminated in only a few select conditions. At most colleges and universities a high percentage of faculty are tenured.

Term assignment preview, 67–68

Test file, 149

Testimony, 197

Tests
  cheating on, 144, 145, 148
  essay, 129–38
  family emergencies and, 132
  matching, 142
  memory tips for, 140–41
  multiple-choice, 139–40
  preparing for, 126–28, 180–81
  standardized, 19
  teaching styles and, 94–97
  true-false, 140–42
  types of, 126

Textbooks. *See* **Reading**

THC, 384–85

Theories/opinions, 178

Thesis a relatively long paper, usually written as partial fulfillment of the requirements for a master's degree. Some schools require a thesis for the undergraduate degree.

Thinking. *See* **Critical thinking**

Thinking learning style, 85, 88, 89, 92

Thought control, 351

Time lag problems, 79

Time management, 60–61
  beating procrastination, 75, 112–13
  co-curricular activities and, 332, 334
  for commuters, 75–79
  daily plans, 70–72
  during essay tests, 127, 133–34, 138–39
  setting priorities, 61
  timetables and master plans, 62–64
  weekly assignment plans, 65–70

Timetables, 62–70

Tobacco, 378, 387

Tolerance, 306, 308

Transcript the official record of your college work and grades, which is maintained and updated each term by the registrar.

Transfer credit if you should transfer from one college or university to another, the number of courses the new college accepts and counts toward your degree are your transfer credits.

Transferring, 267

Transient student a student who receives permission from his or her college to take courses (usually in the summer) at a different college.

Transitions, 199

Treisman, Philip Uri, 128

Trueblood, Roy, 16

True-false tests, 140–42

Tuition the money you pay for your college courses. *See also* **Fees**

Twain, Mark, 145–46

Underemployment, 14, 42

Underlining
  in essay questions, 134
  of reading assignments, 115–20

Unemployment, 14, 42

Universities. *See* **Colleges**

Uploading, 243

Validation of credits procedure in which a school determines which credits from another school may be transferred. If you wish to transfer from one college to another, it is your responsibil-

ity to learn which courses and grades will transfer.

Values, 300
  college challenges to, 305–9
  defining, 300
  discovering, 300–305
  intellectual, changing, 309–12
  "right," 312–14
  sexual, 360–61
  stress and, 355
  work, 284–86

Values clarification a structured approach for understanding, choosing, and acting on a personal value system.

Venereal warts, 366–67

Verbal reasoning, 283

Visual aids, 199–200

Visual learning style, 84

Visualizing, of ideas, 141

Voting, 313

Walpole, Horace, 56

Weekly assignment plans, 65–70

Weiten, Wayne, 102

Wellness, 14

Whitehead, Alfred North, 34

Withdrawal a formal process of removing oneself officially from one or more courses within a certain time period while the course is still in progress. Failing to complete courses for which you have not submitted the required withdrawal forms may result in failing grades and academic suspension. Withdrawing usually permits a student to avoid a failing grade and request readmission to the same course later

on. 150, 267. *See also* **Reinstatement** and **Leave of absence**

Women students
  alcohol and, 374, 382
  business majors/careers and, 290
  health-related majors/careers and, 290
  as majority of college students, 6
  math, science, and, 223, 295
  rape and, 373–75
  teaching careers and, 296
  technical careers and, 289
  tobacco and, 378, 387

Word processing, 231, 233, 238, 240

Work. *See* **Careers; employment**

Work/study a federal student aid program based on need, which provides the opportunity for students to earn some of the aid for which they are eligible through employment, generally on campus.

Work values, 284–86

Writing
  to communicate, 181–86
  essay test answers, 133–34
  with friends, 186
  improving, 9
  plagiarism versus referencing in, 144–47, 156
  précis, 123–24
  private, 174–75, 181
  procedures of thought in, 176–79
  public, 174, 179–86
  as test preparation, 180–81
  on word processor, 233, 238, 240

Writing centers, 17

Wydro, Kenneth, 203

Zovirax, 366